THE WAR ON POVERTY IN MISSISSIPPI

THE WAR ON POVERTY IN
MISSISSIPPI

From Massive Resistance to New Conservatism

EMMA J. FOLWELL

University Press of Mississippi / Jackson

The University Press of Mississippi is the scholarly publishing agency of
the Mississippi Institutions of Higher Learning: Alcorn State University,
Delta State University, Jackson State University, Mississippi State University,
Mississippi University for Women, Mississippi Valley State University,
University of Mississippi, and University of Southern Mississippi.

www.upress.state.ms.us

The University Press of Mississippi is a member
of the Association of University Presses.

Copyright © 2020 by University Press of Mississippi
All rights reserved
Manufactured in the United States of America

First printing 2020

∞

Library of Congress Cataloging-in-Publication Data

Names: Folwell, Emma J., author.
Title: The war on poverty in Mississippi : from massive resistance to new
conservatism / Emma J. Folwell.
Description: Jackson : University Press of Mississippi, 2020. | Includes
bibliographical references and index.
Identifiers: LCCN 2019053564 (print) | LCCN 2019053565 (ebook) | ISBN
9781496827395 (hardcover) | ISBN 9781496827449 (trade paperback) | ISBN
9781496827401 (epub) | ISBN 9781496827418 (epub) | ISBN 9781496827425
(pdf) | ISBN 9781496827432 (pdf)
Subjects: LCSH: Poor—Mississippi. | Poverty—Political
aspects—Mississippi. | Poor African Americans—Mississippi. | African
Americans—Mississippi—Economic conditions—20th century.
Classification: LCC HC79.P6 F65 2020 (print) | LCC HC79.P6 (ebook) | DDC
362.5/5609762—dc23
LC record available at https://lccn.loc.gov/2019053564
LC ebook record available at https://lccn.loc.gov/2019053565

British Library Cataloging-in-Publication Data available

For Grandma.

CONTENTS

ACKNOWLEDGMENTS
- IX -

MAP OF MISSISSIPPI
- XI -

LIST OF ANTIPOVERTY PROGRAMS IN MISSISSIPPI
- XIII -

LIST OF ACRONYMS
- XV -

INTRODUCTION
- 3 -

Chapter One
FROM CIVIL RIGHTS TO ECONOMIC EMPOWERMENT
- 26 -

Chapter Two
MARJORIE BARONI, ADULT EDUCATION, AND THE MISSISSIPPI CATHOLIC CHURCH
- 50 -

Chapter Three
THE KU KLUX KLAN AND THE WAR ON POVERTY
- 72 -

Chapter Four
BLACK EMPOWERMENT IN JACKSON
- 99 -

Chapter Five
HELEN BASS WILLIAMS AND MISSISSIPPI ACTION FOR PROGRESS
- 127 -

Chapter Six
MISSISSIPPI REPUBLICANS AND THE POLITICS OF POVERTY
- 150 -

Chapter Seven
STAR, THE AFL-CIO, AND THE DIOCESE OF NATCHEZ-JACKSON
- 176 -

Chapter Eight
THE DEMISE OF THE WAR ON POVERTY
- 196 -

EPILOGUE
- 212 -

NOTES
- 222 -

BIBLIOGRAPHY
- 263 -

INDEX
- 285 -

ACKNOWLEDGMENTS

I have incurred many debts during the writing of this book. The archivists and librarians I have encountered on my research trips have been uniformly friendly, welcoming, and knowledgeable. I would like to extend my thanks to the staff at the Roosevelt Study Center in Middelburg, and to Allen Fisher and the reading room staff at the Lyndon Baines Johnson Presidential Library, as well as the staff at both the Richard M. Nixon Presidential Library and the Ronald Reagan Presidential Library. Also, the staff members at both the southeast NARA in Morrow, Georgia, and at the Department of Archives and History in Jackson, Mississippi, were immensely helpful. Mattie Abraham and the Special Collections staff of the Mitchell Memorial Library's Special Collections at Mississippi State University went out of their way to facilitate my research and provided me with an introduction to the kindness and generosity that has been my lasting impression of Mississippians.

Cindy Lawler and the staff of the McCain Library and Archives at the University of Southern Mississippi in Hattiesburg were so accommodating and generous with their time. The assistance and patience of Jennifer Ford and Leigh McWhite at the Archives and Special Collections in the J. D. Williams Library of the University of Mississippi in Oxford were instrumental in helping me navigate their collections. The support I received from Traci Drummond and all of the lovely staff at Georgia State University's archives were most appreciated by a very jet-lagged researcher. I would also like to extend my thanks to Mary Woodward and the Catholic Diocese of Jackson, Mississippi, for allowing me access to the papers of Bishop Joseph B. Brunini. The people I met on my travels across the South—from Georgia to Texas and many stops in between—were unfailingly kind, patient, and hospitable. There are so many people who, out of sheer good-heartedness, made my research easier and more productive—they gave me lifts, made dinners, pointed out interesting collections, and made great restaurant recommendations! Thank you to you all.

It would not have been possible to complete the research for this book without the financial support of the University of Leicester's Centre for

American Studies and Newman University's History Department. Grants from the Roosevelt Study Center and the Royal Historical Society, the Moody Grant from the Lyndon Baines Johnson Presidential Library, the John D. Lees Grant from the British Association of American Studies, and support from Newman University made it possible to undertake research trips to the US over the course of a number of years. I would like to express my gratitude to the University of Leicester, which provided me with an academic home over seven years of study, learning, and teaching. Andrew Johnstone encouraged what has become an enduring fascination with 1960s America when I was a final-year undergraduate, and at Oxford, Gareth Davies fostered my interest in the war on poverty. I would particularly like to thank George Lewis for being patient, supportive, and encouraging, and for providing insightful and invaluable critiques throughout my PhD and beyond.

My sincere thanks also go to the numerous colleagues, including anonymous reviewers, who have offered invaluable advice on this book in its various stages. Their feedback has often been challenging but always helpful and has greatly improved the book. Any remaining mistakes are mine alone. Vijay Shah and Lisa McMurtray at the University Press of Mississippi have been helpful and supportive with the final steps. My colleagues at Newman University have been a great source of support in the last few years. In particular Noelle Plack and Charlotte Lewandowski have been immensely encouraging—thank you.

Finally, the most significant debt I would like to acknowledge is to Alison and Robert Folwell. They have read more drafts and listened to me talk more about this project than anybody else. They are the most encouraging parents, the kindest and most hardworking people I've ever known, and the example to which I aspire. They have provided me with constant and unwavering support, love, and kindness. I owe them more than I could ever express.

Fig. 0.1. US Census Bureau Map of Mississippi, https://www2.census.gov/geo/maps/general_ref/stco_outline/cen2k_pgsz/stco_MS.pdf.

ANTIPOVERTY PROGRAMS IN MISSISSIPPI

Adams-Jefferson Improvement Corporation (Adams and Jefferson Counties)
Bolivar County Community Action Program (Bolivar County)
Central Mississippi Inc. (Attala, Carroll, Choctaw, Holmes, Montgomery, and Webster Counties)
Child Development Group of Mississippi (statewide)
Coahoma Opportunities Inc. (Coahoma County)
Community Services Association (Hinds County)
Delta Opportunities Corporation (eight Delta counties, Madison and Yazoo Counties)
Forrest-Stone Opportunity Inc. (Forrest and Stone Counties)
Harrison County Civic Action Committee (Harrison County)
Jackson County Civic Action Committee (Jackson County)
Lauderdale Economic Assistance Corporation (Lauderdale County)
LIFT Inc. (Lee, Monroe, and Pontotoc Counties)
Mid-State Opportunity Inc. (Grenada, Panola, Quitman, Tallahatchie, and Tunica Counties)
Mississippi Action for Progress (statewide)
Mound Bayou Community Hospital Association (Bolivar County)
Choctaw Community Action Agency (headquarters in Neshoba County)
Northwest Mississippi Development Association (DeSoto and Tate Counties)
Pearl River Valley Opportunity Inc. (Lamar, Marion, and Walthall Counties)
Prairie Opportunity Inc. (Clay, Noxubee, and Oktibbeha Counties)
Southwest Mississippi Opportunity Inc. (Amite, Pike, and Wilkinson Counties)
Strategic Training and Redevelopment (statewide)
Sunflower County Progress Inc. (Sunflower County)
United Community Action Committee (Benton County)
Yazoo Community Action Inc. (Yazoo County)

LIST OF ACRONYMS

AFL-CIO	American Federation of Labor and Congress of Industrial Organizations
CDGM	Child Development Group of Mississippi
CLS	Community Legal Services
CSA	Community Services Association
HEW	Department of Health, Education, and Welfare
KKK	Ku Klux Klan
MAP	Mississippi Action for Progress
NAACP	National Association for the Advancement of Colored People
NYC	Neighborhood Youth Corps
OEO	Office of Economic Opportunity
SMO	Southwest Mississippi Opportunity
SNCC	Student Nonviolent Coordinating Committee
STAR	Strategic Training and Redevelopment

THE WAR ON POVERTY IN MISSISSIPPI

INTRODUCTION

A "paper for pariotic [sic] citizens," distributed across rural Yalobusha County in the late 1960s—in the north of Mississippi, just outside of the fertile Delta region—declared that "the worst thing is to mix with the [n----rs] by teaching in [N----r] schools, and espailly [sic] those who are teaching in Head Start. Do you people want a [N----r] for a son in law or a daughter in law or even worse a [n----r] grandchild?" The vitriolic tirade continued, listing the names of the nine white women who, the paper claimed, were the worst of the worst. The paper appeared on the front lawns of these women's homes too. The "patriotic paper" was designed to stoke the fears of Yalobusha's white community that Head Start would bring integration and miscegenation into the county, and to warn other whites not to participate in race-mixing. The response of Yalobusha County's hate group to Head Start and its white teachers undermines the long-held notion that massive resistance ended in 1965. Neither the passage of civil rights legislation nor grassroots civil rights activism ended massive resistance—far from it. The passage of the Civil and Voting Rights Acts—the ultimate violation of states' rights in the eyes of white southern segregationists—instead marked the start of a new phase of white resistance to black advancement. Head Start, as another of the loathsome federal intrusions into the state that promoted integration, was an ideal target for this evolving white resistance.[1]

Far from perpetuating "race mixing," Head Start preschool classes in Yalobusha County in 1967 were attended mostly by African American children. Their teachers included the nine local white women targeted by the authors of the hate sheet. The women worked alongside African American colleagues, supervising three- and four-year-old children as they learned to read and to write. The children also learned to use indoor plumbing and received what was often the first medical checkup of their lives. Given the extent of poverty in the county, there were many poor white children in the county eligible for participation in Head Start. Most white parents, however, refused to send their children to integrated classes. While thirteen years had passed since the Supreme Court's *Brown v. Board* ruling to desegregate schools, three years since the Civil Rights Act, and two years since the Voting Rights Act was signed into law, the prospect of integrated classrooms was still an anathema to most white Mississippians. Such a refusal to allow preschool integration is perhaps unsurprising—after all, in 1967 fewer than 3 percent of the state's black children attended classes with white children. More startling was the response to the presence of the white women teaching in integrated Head Start centers.[2]

The education of young children in integrated Head Start classes was seen by many Mississippians as a direct threat to their way of life. The program and the wider war on poverty arrived in Mississippi in 1965 into what University of Mississippi history professor James W. Silver had described just a year earlier as a "closed society." In small communities across the state in the mid to late 1960s, war on poverty programs were met with a ferocious response. The federally funded war against poverty—the embodiment of 1960s liberalism—clashed explosively with Mississippi's closed society. The result, one Mississippian recalled, was "like all hell broke loose." From 1965 to 1973 both a war against poverty and a war against the war on poverty were waged in Mississippi. The war on poverty provided a powerful tool for black empowerment, drawing on the vitality of Mississippi's civil rights movement. At the same time, the fight against the war on poverty served as a template for white resistance and entrenchment, and as a way to undermine liberalism, marginalize black political power, and articulate a new conservatism. White Mississippians' resistance to social change, through the evolving resistance to the war on poverty, lay at the heart of the emerging new conservatism.[3]

This book explores both the war on poverty and the war against the war on poverty in Mississippi. It traces the attempts of white and black Mississippians to utilize antipoverty programs to address the desperate poverty in the state. The need for such programs in Mississippi was great. But these programs were about more than simply assisting poor Mississippians. The war on poverty and white opposition to it transformed Mississippi. The war on poverty was, at times, a powerful tool for black empowerment. But more often, antipoverty programs became a potent mechanism of white resistance to black advancement. Through the war on poverty, both black activism and white opposition to black empowerment evolved. White Mississippians used massive resistance as a template for resistance to black economic empowerment, forging antipoverty programs into tools to subvert the Great Society agenda and marginalize black political power.

Antipoverty programs gave black Mississippians a measure of economic power, undermining the economic power of segregationists. The varied white responses to the war on poverty illustrate the ways in which the massive resistance to black advancement evolved in the face of new challenges and exposes its connections to the new conservatism. Historians, including Kevin M. Kruse, Joseph Crespino, Matthew D. Lassiter, Michelle M. Nickerson, Lisa McGirr, Darren Dochuk, and Sean P. Cunningham, have provided compelling analyses of the rise of the new conservatism. This book traces a grassroots war against the war on poverty that laid the foundation for the fight against 1960s liberalism. This fight against the war on poverty served as a template for white resistance and entrenchment, and as a way to marginalize black political and economic power. Many white Mississippians forged this resistance into the political, economic, and social structures of the state, contributing to the development of the state's Republican Party and articulating a new conservatism.[4]

Racial discrimination pervaded Mississippi's antipoverty programs and crippled their operation. Mississippi was the location for some of the most intense racial struggles and sustained racial violence of the long civil rights movement. Both the movement and the war on poverty destabilized traditional race and class relationships and intensified growing class tensions, not only among African Americans, but also among other nonwhite minority groups. Historians, including Daniel M. Cobb and William S. Clayson, have shown how a multiracial constituency complicated the operation of many antipoverty programs. In Mississippi nonwhite minority groups included Chinese Americans and Native Americans. The state's Chinese immigrants had found an "economic niche" operating grocery stores in the Delta that catered to African American sharecroppers. Second and third generations were, however, increasingly likely to pursue economic opportunities outside Mississippi, meaning there was no involvement of Chinese Americans in the state's antipoverty programs. There was, however a significant poor population among the Mississippi Band of Choctaw Indians based in Neshoba, Leake, Kemper, and Newton Counties who benefited greatly from the creation of its own community action program. Federal funding combined with the Choctaws' relative isolation gave their program the ability to circumvent the South's white power structure. However, outside of the Choctaw reservation, Mississippi's war on poverty remained a biracial battleground.[5]

The poor of both races were losers in these battles. Racial discrimination served as a tool to exclude poor African Americans, and it worsened the omnipresent administrative failings of the war on poverty. This pervasive atmosphere undermined the work of dedicated antipoverty warriors, both black and white, who did not want their antipoverty programs to be used to entrench discrimination against poor African Americans. But the white resistance to black empowerment through the war on poverty relied on more than racial discrimination. This war against the war on poverty became a crucible in which racial hostility was forged into a powerful new conservatism. This white resistance did not take the form of the doomed "last-stands" or vitriolic racist rhetoric of the earlier massive resistance. Rather this evolving opposition adapted to racial change. It drew on tactics of the "classic" 1954–1965 massive resistance and combined it with a new language of opposition that utilized the grassroots legacy of Goldwater conservatism. White Mississippi—from the grassroots to the political elite—adopted new methods and mechanisms of resistance. Foremost among these was acceptance of integration in antipoverty programs. With this acceptance came the opportunity to regain control and direct the pace of racial change. It was a calculated maneuver, and one which by no means guaranteed success, but over the years, white Mississippians succeeded in forging many antipoverty programs into mechanisms of white control. And—perhaps even more significantly—the antipoverty programs deepened existing class divisions within local black communities and undermined the development of black leadership.

When the war on poverty arrived in the state, Mississippi was one of the most racially oppressive states in a nation that had just witnessed the passage of historic civil and voting rights legislation. In November 1964 President Lyndon B. Johnson secured 61.1 percent of the popular vote and carried forty-four states, winning a landslide victory in support of his liberal agenda. In Mississippi 87 percent of voters chose "Mr. Conservative," the Republican candidate Barry Goldwater. The legacy of an historic dependence on cotton agriculture, the 1890 constitution, which discouraged industrial development in the state, and a series of natural disasters combined to keep state's economy agricultural. The vast majority of Mississippians lived in small, rural communities. By contrast, the wider nation had been embracing industrialization wholeheartedly for decades. The resulting urbanization and suburbanization had transformed America's social, economic, and political landscape. Perhaps most significant of all: Mississippi was desperately poor and yet was part of one of the wealthiest nations in the world. Even among its fellow poor, rural Deep South states, Mississippi stands out.[6]

Poverty shaped—and continues to shape—Mississippi. The levels of poverty in Mississippi across the twentieth century were profound. In 1960, before Presidents Kennedy or Johnson attempted to institute programs to address poverty, 55 percent of the state's population lived below the poverty threshold. This was more than double the national poverty level, which stood at 22 percent. While both Mississippi and the nation's poverty levels fell over the course of the 1960s, Mississippi's poor population—as a proportion of the state's total population—remained the highest in the nation.[7] For the vast majority of these desperately poor Mississippians—both black and white—money was earned through farm labor, most often as sharecroppers on large plantations. Since the turn of the twentieth century, sharecropping determined the structure of Mississippi's economy and society. Emerging in the wake of the abolition of slavery and the failures of Reconstruction, sharecropping established a new relationship between laborers and plantation owners. Sharecroppers lived in plantation houses and worked the land—planting, tending, and harvesting crops, which the landowners sold. At the end of each year, the landowner paid the sharecropper a share of the money the crops made. The majority of this money, however, was used to pay off the "furnish"—the goods and produce sharecroppers had obtained from the plantation commissary to ensure their survival through the year. Often this furnish would exceed the amount paid to the sharecropper. Sharecropping trapped laborers in a cycle of debt and left them subject to the whims of the landowners, who had control of when and for how much to sell the crops, how much to pay the sharecroppers, and the cost of goods sold in the commissary. "The boss man would settle up with his 'hands' at the end of the year," Unita Blackwell recalled. "It wouldn't be much, a few hundred dollars for a whole season's work. If it wasn't as much as the sharecropper thought it should be, he really had no recourse."[8]

Life for sharecroppers was an endless struggle. Whatever gains had been made by African Americans in the post–Civil War reconstruction disappeared rapidly. As the decades of sharecropping went on, the situation worsened for black Mississippians. The black businesses that had been built during Reconstruction gradually disappeared, and by 1940 African Americans owned less farmland than they had in 1920. A civil rights activist and minister, John W. Perkins, born in 1930 in rural Lawrence County to a family of sharecroppers, recalls his early experiences of poverty clearly. "We lived in these plantation houses, and of course you could see the cracks, and in the wintertime when it would get cold, it would be this ice on the inside. These icicles would be on the inside of the house. It would always be five or six of us in the same bed. We slept at both the head and the foot, and I thought that's the way that everybody lived."[9]

Poor living conditions were not the only—or even the most serious—problem facing sharecroppers. Ensuring a family was fed was a constant struggle. "Syrup and biscuits for breakfast and even when we ran out of biscuits—and biscuits was pretty constant, but sometime we would run out of biscuit for a week, run out of flour for a week," John Perkins remembered. "And then we would have bread for breakfast, but actually biscuits and syrup and fatback, a piece of meat. We would eat a piece of meat with the skin on it, a fatback." Nutrition improved slightly later in the 1930s, when the New Deal's Federal Surplus Commodities Corporation began distributing surplus commodities. "Grits came to us with the commodities in about, along there with the Roosevelt thing in about '36, '37." Rev. Perkins remembered that was when "ground grits became a deal. Oh, the commodities made a—cheese, raisins, prunes, those dry foods that came from commodities was very important." The commodities came too late though, for Rev. Perkins's mother, who died from pellagra due to malnutrition when he was only seven months old.[10]

Sharecroppers' lives—not just their livelihoods—were controlled by the landowners. Minnie McFarland Weeks was born in 1926 in Clay County, in the northeast of Mississippi. In the 1960s, she was active in the civil rights movement in West Point, but in the 1930s she lived on her father's farm. He was not a sharecropper—he rented 150 acres and tended milk cows. Minnie Weeks saw vividly the difference between her family's experiences of poverty, and those of the neighboring sharecroppers. "One man," she recalled, "told my father he thought he was too much. . . . We was threatened because we had the little we did have. . . . But all around us, people sharecropped, and they only allow them to have fatback meat and meal to cook some cornbread. They wasn't allowed to have a garden. They wasn't allowed to raise chickens. They wasn't allowed to have a cow." The experiences of John Perkins in Lawrence County, south of Jackson, and Minnie McFarland Weeks in Clay County in the northeast of the state, illustrate the extent of rural poverty in Mississippi. There were local variations in the nature and severity of poverty, however. Poverty was less intense around Jackson, the state capital, and in the counties in the northeast of the state and on the Gulf Coast. Even there, poverty levels were significantly higher than the national average. But the most intense, devastating, and enduring levels of poverty were found in the Delta.[11]

Poverty in Mississippi remained widespread, and it affected the black and white population. In 1960, 42.3 percent of the state population was black, of whom 90 percent were poor. Thus the largest proportion of African Americans in the state was poor. Numerically, however, there were more white Mississippians in poverty than black Mississippians. In many ways white poverty echoed black poverty. There were many white Mississippians who endured the privations of sharecropping and economic hardship, living in plantation houses and struggling to feed their families. For black and white sharecroppers, the depression of the 1930s made their livelihood even more precarious. It was during the depression that activist Unita Blackwell, who would later become the first black woman elected mayor in Mississippi, first recalled recognizing white poverty. "I remember one time a white man and his wife and three or four pitiful-looking children walked up to our house," and the man asked Unita's grandmother for "leftover food." "It was strange to me," Blackwell recalled, "white people begging for food." The white man was "so ashamed." But it was the first time, Blackwell said, that she "knew that some white people were poor, too." "This helped me to understand white people when I was involved in the civil rights movement, that white people also suffer, and they *need* our help as much as we need theirs."[12]

By the late 1940s the social, economic, and even racial structures of Mississippi were altering. The system of racial violence was, according to historian Charles Payne, in decline in part because the cotton-based political and economic system from which it had grown was declining. In response to the economic and social changes within the state and within the framework of national and international developments, black activism picked up pace in the 1940s and 1950s among returning black soldiers and a small but growing black business class. Growth in National Association for the Advancement of Colored People (NAACP) membership led to the creation of a state conference of branches in 1946 to coordinate the branch efforts. These efforts were centered at first around the state capital, Jackson, and focused on what historian John Dittmer termed "modest voter registration efforts." In 1951 surgeon and businessman T. R. M. Howard founded a new organization to promote black advancement: the Regional Council of Negro Leadership, which included prominent businessmen and professionals, including World War II veterans Aaron Henry, Medgar Evers, and Amzie Moore. The World War II was an important factor both in framing black activism and in shaping the activism of returning veterans. While historian Neil McMillen, who has interviewed hundreds of black veterans, warns against drawing a simplistic connection between World War II and civil rights activism of the 1950s, he believes there is some relationship. The war did not lead directly to the overthrow of white control in Mississippi, McMillen argues, but it did touch "the lives of Mississippi's black service men and women in ways their white oppressors both feared and underestimated."[13]

This was certainly the case for Aaron Henry, Medgar Evers, and Amzie Moore, all of whom were incredibly important figures in the Mississippi rights movement, beginning in what Charles Payne termed the "socially invisible generation" of the 1940s and 1950s. All three would continue to play vital roles in the transformation of Mississippi in the 1960s, including the war on poverty. For Henry, Evers, and Moore, their wartime experiences were an important step in their developing activism. However, there is another, often overlooked, factor that was also significant in shaping the activism of this generation: their experiences of and responses to poverty. Poverty shaped both the nature and form of white supremacist violence and the personal philosophies of civil rights activists. Amzie Moore, for example, returned home from service intending to "put the poverty of his youth as far behind him as possible as quickly as possible." Moore's outlook on life was, he later remembered, "modified by having the living conditions of Delta Negroes shoved in his face."[14]

Medgar Evers, on the other hand, had grown up in poverty but in a hill county, where poverty was different from the poverty of the Delta. Selling insurance in the Delta in the summer of 1952, Evers saw the connection between black oppression and economic exploitation embodied by sharecropping. He was, Myrlie Evers later recalled, "like a student driven by horror to learn more." Aaron Henry's focus on inclusion was shaped during his junior year pharmacy apprenticeship, when he "became further convinced that . . . poverty is more common than race." Henry learned early on from this experience, biographer Minion K. C. Morrison suggests, that "if we focus on real human need instead of the false premises of race, it was entirely possible to alter the system of racial exclusion in the South."[15]

This rising activism brought about increased membership of the NAACP across the state. There was a fourfold increase in black voter registration— around twenty-five thousand registrants by the mid-1950s, out of a black adult population in Mississippi of nearly half a million. Levels of activism— like voting restrictions and white violence—were subject to intensely local variations. Oppression was, as ever, most intense in the Delta counties where, after the passage of the 1954 *Brown v. Board of Education* ruling, the White Citizens' Council was formed. In the Delta county of Leflore, where Emmett Till was murdered in 1955 and his white murderers acquitted, the brutal reality of life in Mississippi was put in full view of the nation. For many white Americans it was a horror that could not have been perpetrated in the land of freedom and opportunity. For many young black Americans, it was a moment of awakening—the spark that lit the fire of a generation of activism. For Anne Moody, who was less than a year older than Till and living in the southwest of the state, it sparked new fear. "Before Emmett Till's murder," she wrote, "I had known the fear of hunger, hell, and the Devil. But now there was a new fear known to me—the fear of being killed just because I was black. This was the worst of my fears. I knew once I got food, the fear of starving to death would leave. I also was told that if I were a good girl, I wouldn't have to fear the Devil or hell. But I didn't know what one had to do or not do as a Negro not to be killed. Probably just being a Negro period was enough, I thought."[16]

The fear Anne Moody felt permeated Mississippi in the late 1950s. As historian Françoise N. Hamlin phrased it, "the slaying of Emmett Till in 1955 and a string of killings that year and those following sustained considerable amounts of fear in all but a few brave souls." Despite the appointment of Medgar Evers as state NAACP secretary in 1954, membership of that organization went into a decline that the national NAACP feared was terminal by the late 1950s. The power of the newly formed White Citizens' Councils and the creation of the state-sponsored anti-integration watchdog, the Mississippi State Sovereignty Commission, in 1956 muted activism through terror, violence, and economic reprisals. Black Mississippians' powerful organizing tradition, however, ensured the survival of networks of activists. When a new wave of grassroots activism emerged in 1960, it built on the work of the previous generation and drew upon this organizing tradition. Student Nonviolent Coordinating Committee (SNCC) activist Bob Moses—who embodied this grassroots phase of Mississippi's activism—met with Amzie Moore on his first trip to Mississippi in 1960 and on his return to the state the following year, he stayed with NAACP branch leader C. C. Bryant.[17]

As James P. Marshall describes, veteran leaders, such as Moore, Bryant, Evers, and Vernon Dahmer, "not only provided an entry into local communities but also introduced many young people into the movement" who would go onto become leaders themselves. The model of SNCC—the Student Nonviolent Coordinating Committee—built a powerful and long-lasting grassroots movement that transformed activism in Mississippi. As Fannie Lou Hamer later recalled, SNCC made all the difference. SNCC "worked with the people. NAACP don't work with the people." The grassroots activists were often younger than the veteran generation; they were not wedded to the formal structures of the NAACP; and they were predominantly women. Both the veteran generation of the 1950s and the grassroots activists of the 1960s would shape Mississippi's civil rights movement and its war on poverty. But it was female grassroots activists, such as Fannie Lou Hamer and Unita Blackwell, who would take the lead in forging a new type of activism after 1965 by combining their grassroots work of the early 1960s with the federal funds of the war on poverty.[18]

Grand narratives of the civil rights movement tend to focus on Mississippi in the early 1960s for the dramatic events that captured national media attention at the time: the integration of the University of Mississippi in 1962, the assassination of Medgar Evers in 1963, and the events of Freedom Summer in 1964. But as historians in the last twenty-five years have illustrated, these were not the only events of importance occurring in Mississippi in those years. John Dittmer and Charles Payne blazed a trail not only for historians of Mississippi but for those of social activism everywhere with their grassroots studies of movement activism. A preponderance of local studies followed, exploring activism in communities in Clarksdale, in Claiborne County, and in Sunflower County, for example, and the lives of activists, including Medgar Evers, Aaron Henry, and Fannie Lou Hamer. Together these works have done much to uncover the contours and complexities of local and individual activism. Other scholars have focused on forms of activism. James F. Findlay Jr., Mark Newman, and Charles Marsh have explored the relationship between religion and religious organizations and their support for black activism. Carolyn Renée Dupont, Joseph T. Reiff, and Carter Dalton Lyon, meanwhile, have addressed the response of Mississippi's white religious groups to the activism of the early 1960s. There has been a rise in recent years in works exposing the nuances in white Mississippi's responses to the movement—incorporating everything from the violence of Mississippi's Ku Klux Klan and the massive resistance to school desegregation to the interracialism of the local women of "Wednesdays in Mississippi." Akinyele Omowale Umoja has exposed the role armed resistance played in the freedom movement in Mississippi, while the works of Lance Hill and Charles E. Cobb Jr. place this armed resistance in the context of the broader movement.[19]

These works have described the immense scope of the early 1960s. Voter registration and not direct action remained the focus of the activists under the Voter Education Project. The Council of Federated Organizations (COFO) was created in 1962, in part to direct federal funds. However, more significantly, COFO's creation reflected recognition among Mississippi activists that only together could the NAACP, the Congress of Racial Equality (CORE), SNCC, and the Southern Christian Leadership Conference succeed in challenging the white power structure. By 1963 the Mississippi movement was reaching its zenith—more active and organized than ever before. Much of this activism centered on Greenville, after a white man shot at three civil rights workers, nearly killing James Travis in February 1963. Other centers of activism included Clarksdale, at the top of the Delta, and the state capital, Jackson. Success was limited: the registration of voters was slow going (only 6.7 percent of Mississippi's African American population was registered to vote by 1964), and white power remained, mostly, intact. The survival of the movement under an onslaught of white violence and intimidation was truly remarkable. However, progress in Mississippi was slow even by the standards of the South—across the region as a whole, 40.8 percent of African Americans were registered. A new strategy was needed, one that capitalized on the growth of native Mississippi activists, that would bring national attention to the plight of black Mississippians, and that would involve white activists. That new strategy became Freedom Summer. It was a deceptively simply plan: bring northern college students, eager to address injustice, into Mississippi to spend a few weeks assisting with voter registration. The reality, of course, was anything but simple.[20]

White Mississippians viewed Freedom Summer as an invasion, an attack on their world. Newly elected governor Paul B. Johnson warned the "outside agitators" that they would not be tolerated. "We're not going to tolerate any group from the outside of Mississippi or from the inside of Mississippi to take the law in their own hands. We're going to see that the law is maintained, and maintained Mississippi style." Jackson's mayor Allen C. Thompson had prepared for Freedom Summer by expanding and heavily arming the Jackson police force, which was dubbed "Allen's Army." The state's white power structure—in all its diverse and uncoordinated brutality—did indeed make a potent attempt to maintain "Mississippi style" law. Klansmen and local police conspired to cover up the murder of civil rights workers Michael Schwerner, Andrew Goodman, and James Chaney. Activists—white and black, "outsider" and local—were arrested, terrorized, and attacked. Churches, homes, and businesses were firebombed. However, the scale and violence of the white opposition could not halt the activism. Freedom schools were established, giving poor black children access to better education, with curricula that incorporated black history and culture. Perhaps the most significant legacy of that summer was the creation of the Mississippi Freedom Democratic Party, bringing the attention of a nation onto the segregationist practices of the Mississippi Democrats. In terms of poverty, however, little improvement had been made. By the mid-1960s the median annual income of African Americans in the Delta was still only $465 and the per capita income across the state was $1,608, compared to a national average of $2,746. As Senator Robert Kennedy would discover during his visit to the state in 1967, hunger and malnutrition remained daily realities for black Mississippians in the Delta.[21]

Race had long shaped poverty. While the depression of the 1930s may have given rise to shared experiences of suffering, there were tangible differences between black and white poverty. The vast majority of poor whites maintained a strongly held belief in their racial supremacy. Poverty made their belief in their racial superiority more significant to their identity. During the depression white sharecroppers may have lived in houses as equally dilapidated as those of black sharecroppers, and they, too, suffered from constant hunger. But their race guaranteed them some privileges. JC Fairley, born to sharecroppers in Greene County, recalls the treatment of white sharecroppers was very different to that of black sharecroppers. "You might would hear of one every now and then complaining about how they were treated by the sharer. But as a whole everything was pretty well for the white sharecroppers. [They were] given their correct shares."[22]

Minister and civil rights activist Rev. Sammie Rash was born in 1942 in Sunflower County to a family of sharecroppers and spent many of his early years on the McGann plantation in Bolivar County in the Delta. He recalls playing with neighboring white children, especially the youngest son of the white family who lived opposite the Rash family. "We grew up together and, to be honest with you, we were real close. He was a white boy. We all came up together and we would play together." Like JC Fairley, Sammie Rash also recalled the difference in the roles of black and white sharecroppers. "Usually the whites that were on the plantation, they would more or less be in charge, supervising the other workers who were on the plantation." Rash's white childhood friend, though he would "come over to our house and sit up two or three hours during the day," would "never have to work in the field like we did." This, as historian Emilye Crosby has noted, is a significant difference in the white and black experiences of poverty. White children's work was generally less integral to family survival.[23]

Unita Blackwell was six years old when she started working in the cotton fields. "Every day except Sunday everybody would get up early and get dressed to go to the field," she recalled in her autobiography. "We wore our most ragged and patched clothes, which Big Mama [Blackwell's grandmother] had made from old flour sacks.... And nobody wore shoes." Sammie Rash clearly recalled his work "in the fields." "We had to take care of our crop. See that everything was taken care of before we could get into school.... We only had an opportunity to go to school probably from October until maybe May, or something like that; until it was time to chop cotton. It was kind of a difficult situation." The urgent need for African American children to take care of the crops affected their education. Schooling was dominated by the rhythms of the cotton culture. African American children went to school only during the summer, when the cotton crops were growing and did not need such intensive tending, and during winter. While the depression revealed to Unita Blackwell the existence of white poverty for the first time, the depression hit African Americans hardest. They were in the most desperate and precarious economic and social position. As historians such as J. Todd Moye, Clyde Woods, and James C. Cobb have shown, the government's response to the Depression and the economic disasters in the Delta "consolidated power in the hands of the white elites," entrenching the social and economic power of Delta planters to the further detriment of poor black Mississippians.[24]

For African Americans, sharecropping was a life not only of poverty, but one of terror. From plantation owners to storeowners to sharecroppers, white Mississippi terrorized its black population. More than poverty, Unita Blackwell recalls that life in the rural Mississippi was dominated by an "undercurrent of fear." "The power of white people was everywhere. They owned our house; they ran our school; they employed us. They paid us what they wanted to, when they wanted to." The mechanisms of white power—terror, violence, and economic control—were intertwined. Black sharecroppers who were not paid what they were owed by the plantation owners had no recourse. Those who spoke out were threatened or beaten, or both. Most then fled Mississippi in fear for their lives, often never to return to the state. Speaking out was only an excuse for violence, though. Often, much less was needed to prompt acts of white terror.[25]

For both poor white and poor black Mississippians, the 1930s and 1940s wrought dramatic changes to their way of life. The mechanization of cotton and increased use of chemicals on crops, alongside the decreasing value of cotton and New Deal policies paying plantation owners not to farm their land, transformed the southern rural economy. As Jason Sokol notes, four million of the fifteen million rural southerners left the Deep South in the 1940s. By 1960 the South's rural population had decreased to just seven million. Poor whites and blacks who had known nothing but sharecropping moved into the new urban and industrial areas. For African Americans, this migration was not only to seek new economic opportunities; it was an opportunity to escape the unceasing terror, tyranny, and violence of the Jim Crow South.[26]

However, migration was the pathway not only to new opportunities, but also to new economic challenges and new forms of racial oppression. In

Anne Moody's compelling autobiography, she described the poverty of her childhood years in rural Mississippi. Her stepfather, Raymond, eventually left Mississippi to travel to California to find work. "In Centreville there weren't any factories or sawmills that employed unskilled Negro men.... White businesses in town employed Negroes as janitors only, and there was never more than one janitor in any single business. The Negro man had a hard road to travel when looking for employment." But after a month in Los Angeles, Moody's stepfather decided to return to Mississippi. "Los Angeles is a big city," he wrote in a letter home, "but jobs are as hard to get out here as they are in Mississippi. And Negroes don't live as well out here as people at home think. I am coming home." Migration was a compelling option—African Americans were seeking to escape from a seemingly endless cycle of violence, oppression, and poverty. But it was not an easy option nor was it always a permanent or successful one.[27]

For those who stayed in Mississippi, white terror as well as poverty remained rife. Employment opportunities were thin on the ground and malnutrition or even starvation a terrifying possibility. When Minnie McFarland Weeks's brother was seventeen and driving his car into West Point to "get some medicine for his mama," dust blew in the face of some white men. They chased him down to "try to get to kill him," Weeks recalled, and followed him wherever he went. He left the state, not returning for decades, until he attended his father's funeral. "The white had all the authority," Weeks remembered. "The black didn't have no authority to do anything. If they said something was right, you don't say it's wrong. They say you didn't make but so-and-so, you can't say you made more." For Rev. John Perkins, an awakening to the economic power wielded by whites came early on. As a young man he worked for a white man—Mr. Lee—for a day, hauling hay. Perkins expected to make "about a dollar, a dollar and a half for that day's work because that was the going wages back in those days." Instead, at the end of the day, Lee gave him fifteen cents. "That was the beginning of my education," Perkins recalled. "That's when I really began to understand what was going on around me.... I really wanted to take that fifteen cent, and I really wanted to throw it on the ground and walk out of there and be through with it, really curse him, really ... but I couldn't. I realized if I had done that, my family would have been in trouble."[28]

African Americans' experience of poverty was shaped by white power. Whites' experiences of poverty were also shaped by their belief in their racial superiority. In part, this was expressed by their dominance on the plantations—white sharecroppers were "in charge" of black sharecroppers, as Rev. Sammie Rash recalled. When this dominance was challenged—when white superiority was challenged—the expression of power became violent. For some desperately poor white Mississippians, being better off, if only marginally, than black Mississippians was their only source of comfort and security. Instances of white men destroying the livelihoods of black farmers who were marginally more prosperous than they were fairly widespread. In some cases, this destruction was of livestock or homes. Sometimes, it went as far as murder. In her study of Claiborne County, for example, Emilye Crosby recounts the 1906 murder of Min Newsome, a "prosperous black farmer," by a white man, John Roan. The two men had played together as children. But as adults, Min Newsome was "successful enough to have a team of mules, a mare, a wagon and a surrey, and was working day and night to clear the 160 acres of swamp land he was purchasing." Roan killed Newsome, according to Newsome's family, "because he was jealous and believed the land Newsome was buying was 'too good for a black man to have.'"[29]

JC Fairley, who would later become president of the Hattiesburg chapter of the NAACP and involved in running his local antipoverty program, experienced a form of this violence and resentment from poor whites. Growing up in Covington County in the 1920s, Fairley's father was a sharecropper who managed to buy a piece of land to farm. "He had a horse he bought," Fairley later recalled. "This horse was the source of our living. It was back in the horse and buggy days. He had a nice buggy, and the horse did the farming. We rode the horse. The horse was everything to us and it was a nice horse. The white people in that community wanted to buy the horse. My father refused to sell the horse and so they poisoned the horse. In the raffle of poisoning the horse they also poisoned me." Fairley's father had bought feed from the local store, as they were running low. But Fairley ate the feed too—"we were so poor at that time I was eating about as much of the feed as the horse was." Fairley was sick but recovered; the horse died. He remembered "watching through the window [as] the horse died." The horse's death meant they could no longer farm, and they moved from the county. JC Fairley's father "told people and all, they just had sympathy with him. And they know somebody poisoned him, and at that time I believe someone told who was the man that put the poison in the sack. It wasn't nothing done. Back in that time black folks didn't have a chance of going up against a white man regardless of what he did."[30]

This poor white resentment of poor African Americans denotes the different form white power took in shaping race relations along socioeconomic lines. As historians of southern race relations have noted, white children grew up in close proximity to black people, sometimes "with considerable intimacy." A black nurse may have breastfed her white charge, for example. White merchants, Emilye Crosby notes, framed their recollections of interactions with black customers "in personal terms." These "personal affections," as Neil R. McMillen termed them were "a small but important part of a very complex story" of Mississippi race relations. However, it is important to note that these "affections" were, in the main, formed when white power was underpinned by economic control. Black nursemaids' livelihoods were held at the whim of a white employer; white shop-owners were at liberty to cut off credit or deny service to their customers. Such power meant that these "affections" were almost always accompanied by a paternalism that was based largely on perceived racial superiority but also on economic power that both bolstered and was bolstered by white power. Poor whites, lacking this economic superiority over African Americans and lacking any meaningful voice in government, employed a different form of white power. Poor whites invariably made the majority of white lynch mobs, for example. There was what historian Charles Payne describes as a "consistent relationship" between economic pressures facing whites and the number of lynchings. "When whites were feeling more economic pressure," Payne suggests, "they were more likely to turn to rope and faggot."[31]

It was into a maelstrom of intense poverty, grassroots civil rights activism, and threatened but still powerful white power structures that President Lyndon Johnson's war against poverty arrived. The war on poverty was created under the 1964 Economic Opportunity Act as a central part of President Johnson's Great Society. Federally funded antipoverty programs arrived in Mississippi at a time when Jim Crow was fatally weakened, though its white segregationist protectors remained fiercely defiant. The passage of the Civil Rights Act in July 1964 had been met with horror by many white Mississippians, at the same time as the activism of Freedom Summer gained momentum and drew national attention. State politicians—the segregated state Democratic Party—passed a series of resolutions denouncing the Civil Rights Act. The Economic Opportunity Act, passed a month later, compounded the fears of many southerners that this new war on poverty would use federal funds to force integration. The Great Society was, for many Mississippians, a "vicious" and dangerous "tool of integration." When the first antipoverty program began in Mississippi in the summer of 1965, most white Mississippians were reeling from the pace of racial change. But they remained determined to maintain segregation.

Mississippians quickly geared up to oppose the war on poverty in any way they could. For many, the first step in this fight was to write to their senators, Democrats John C. Stennis and James O. Eastland. The senators received thousands of letters in the late 1960s about the state's war on poverty programs. The overwhelming majority of them were critical. The programs were a waste of taxpayers' money, some wrote, or they were dangerous, or "socialist," an intrusion into the state of Mississippi. One such letter sent to Senator Stennis, written by a resident of Gulfport, Mississippi, who signed the letter as "Conservative," speaks to a number of these concerns. "Conservative" was "incensed" by reports of this program "teaching 'How to Integrate' and 'How to Behave when Integrated.'" One magazine article, "Conservative" reported to Stennis, actually "showed illustrations of Jewish Rabbis and Catholic Nuns with small Negro children.... I know for sure," Conservative continued, "that white southerners would not permit their pre-school age children to take any part in it ... [but] am astounded by the lies and misinformation which comes over the news media." Allegations of media bias and misinformation, or fake news, are clearly perennial. But "Conservative's" use of language, the tone and the threats speak to a specific time and place: the heart of the Deep South at the pinnacle of twentieth-century liberalism. In other words: Mississippi in the 1960s.[32]

Senator Stennis was the figurehead of white Mississippi's fight against the war on poverty. He became a lightning rod for these complaints, transmitting them to Washington, DC, and combining them with his senatorial power and influence. Stennis gave voice to the fear of many white Mississippians that federal war on poverty funds would provide poor blacks with the power to render their newly won rights meaningful, and thus challenge the state's white power structures. State politicians joined their constituents and Senators Stennis and Eastland in opposing the war on poverty. Mississippi's governor Paul Johnson believed that antipoverty programs would bring bloodshed and violence to the state. When Sargent Shriver, director of the Office of Economic Opportunity (OEO), announced that Mississippi's first antipoverty program would be operated by African Americans, the governor told him "you have funded my enemies." "Blood will flow all over the steps of the Mississippi State Capitol," he continued, "and it will be on the hands of OEO, not the state of Mississippi." While blood did not flow over the steps of the state capitol, Paul Johnson's predictions were, in part, realized. There was a vicious response to the war on poverty by many violent white supremacists who opposed federally funded integration. And there was an even more powerful, though less violent, response from white

Mississippians who employed a range of tactics to prevent federally funded black empowerment.[33]

This book joins the growing number of studies of the war on poverty in recent years. Scholars have taken up Allen J. Matusow's call for "an army of local historians" to recover the "lost fragments" of community action programs. Works include Crystal R. Sanders's study of Head Start in Mississippi, Susan Y. Ashmore's examination of the war on poverty in Alabama, William S. Clayson's in Texas, James L. Leloudis's and Robert R. Korstad's in North Carolina, Robert Bauman's in Los Angeles, and Thomas J. Kiffmeyer's study of Appalachian activists. These studies have begun to reconstruct the immensely rich and complex history of community action. Most have explicitly focused on the racial (and sometimes gendered) implications of the war on poverty. Together this "army" of historians has provided valuable new insights into community action and its connection with black activism in the later stages of the long civil rights movement.[34]

They have also illustrated that the history of the war on poverty—and community action in particular—is complex and messy and, in the words of Michael Woodsworth, it "evades master narratives." A common theme that has emerged in these studies is the politicization of the war on poverty across the nation. From New Orleans to Philadelphia and Brooklyn to San Francisco, the war on poverty entered into local communities and stimulated struggles for power, most often among groups on the left and especially within the left-of-center factions of the Democratic Party. Mississippi's war on poverty generated a number of power struggles, some of which echo the experiences of antipoverty programs across the nation. Chicago mayor Richard Daley's opposition to the role of the poor in community action programs and his desire to gain control of antipoverty funds, for example, mirror Mississippi governor Paul Johnson's attempts to assert his control over the war on poverty. The intent and outcomes of the efforts of politicians such as Mayor Daley and Governor Johnson were different, however. Mississippi's war on poverty did generate political conflict between left-leaning groups. However, the scale of the war against the war on poverty in Mississippi—and the race and class conflicts it engendered—provided a rallying point for conservatives and a significant opportunity for the development of the state Republican Party.[35]

By exploring this war against the war on poverty, this work also exposes the nuances in the white response to black activism. Massive resistance was powerful and enduring but it was not monolithic or unchanging, nor was it confined to the decade following the *Brown* ruling. Early studies of massive resistance limited their interpretations to the political maneuvers and social mobilization that arose in opposition to school integration after *Brown*. Numan V. Bartley's formative study articulates the complex and multifaceted white response to the Supreme Court's ruling in *Brown v. Board of Education* against which massive resistance emerged, tracing a neobourbon, elite-led movement to its climax after the Little Rock crisis in 1957. Neil R. McMillen, following with a study of White Citizens' Councils, traces white supremacists' subtler forms of intimidation, arguing that their demise was inevitable once it became apparent that some degree of desegregation was unavoidable. James W. Ely Jr. and Robbins L. Gates took massive resistance to refer only to the period of opposition to school desegregation in Virginia, while Francis M. Wilhoit focused on political facets of massive resistance, emphasizing the importance of the Southern Manifesto.[36]

As Charles Eagles noted, for nearly thirty years following the works of Bartley, McMillen, and Wilhoit, new studies of massive resistance were relatively few. Recently, however, there have been a number of studies which challenge the earlier interpretations of its origins, scope, and demise. Drawing on Jacquelyn Dowd Hall's conception of a long civil rights movement, massive resistance has been studied in the long duration from various perspectives: religion, gender, Cold War, community movements, and the institutions of white supremacy, as well as the more traditional studies of flashpoints of the civil rights movement and biographies of segregationists. These approaches have recast massive resistance not as a backlash but as an evolving social, economic, and political movement built from the grassroots over decades. As Elizabeth Gillespie McRae has illustrated, women were central to the construction of white supremacy and its maintenance and defense. As McRae phrases it, women were the "mass in massive resistance." In their works uncovering the depth and complexity of the white response to black advancement Jason Sokol, Glenn Feldman, Jason Morgan Ward, and Elizabeth Gillespie McRae have all clearly illustrated that massive resistance predated *Brown*. Arnold R. Hirsch and Michelle M. Nickerson have also challenged the characterization of massive resistance as southern by describing massive resistance that not only predated *Brown* but was located in Chicago and California. As Nickerson describes, "while the massive resistance of the early 1960s and antibusing demonstrations of the 1970s dominate most historical accounts of segregationist resistance ... California had been experimenting with integration and parents had been expressing their defiance of it for several years before the Warren Court handed down *Brown*." The earlier conception of a decade-long backlash to school desegregation led by political elites is clearly only one small facet of massive resistance.[37]

The works of Kevin M. Kruse, Chris Danielson, Frank Parker, Robert E. Luckett Jr., and Joseph Crespino have likewise extended the end date of massive resistance past its traditionally assumed demise in 1965. They illustrate the crucial connection between this post-1965 white resistance and the rise of the New Right. Kevin Kruse's study of the Sunbelt suburbs illustrates the ways in which massive resistance evolved into a more successful rhetorical stance based on the language of rights, freedoms, and individualism after 1965. Joseph Crespino looks beyond the failure of "symbolic last stands" by massive resisters in Mississippi to the success of "subtle and strategic accommodations" made by conservative white southerners. He shows that neither Mississippi nor the South were exceptional—while the country rejected the "ugly white racism" of the Citizens' Councils, they "implicitly and explicitly embraced the quiet protectionism that preserved the racial and class privilege of suburban America." Frank Parker and Chris Danielson describe the barriers whites erected to black political participation after 1965 by the white political leadership seeking to perpetuate its power. Robert Luckett describes an evolving resistance seen in the "practical segregationism" of Mississippi's attorney general, Joe T. Patterson.[38]

This study seeks to add to this increasingly nuanced understanding of segregationism. Massive resistance did not spring into existence in response to provocation or outside intervention. It was at times economic, social, violent, and political, and most often it was a combination of all of these. Mississippi often stood at the forefront of the evolving facets of white resistance to racial change, from the Mississippi Plan of 1875 and the adoption of the new state constitution in 1890 to the power of the White Citizens' Councils in the 1950s and 1960s and the rise of segregated, private Christian academies in the 1970s. A significant but often overlooked facet of this massive resistance is the wielding of economic power by white segregationists. Civil rights historians have illustrated the many instances of white segregationists robbing black Mississippians of their homes and livelihoods in retaliation for their activism. Tracing the white response to the war on poverty adds a new dimension to this relationship.[39]

Through their opposition to the war on poverty, white Mississippians forged powerful linkages between the racially based conservative opposition to social welfare from the New Deal to the rise New Right. These linkages were forged most visibly in Mississippi, but the patterns of white opposition to the war on poverty are evident across the South. White Mississippians utilized opposition to antipoverty programs to draw on a conservative ideology that opposed federal taxation and social welfare programs in race-neutral terms. Combining conservative rhetoric opposing the wastage of taxpayers' money with the massive resistance tactics (that evoked fears of radicalism and outside agitators) formed a powerful opposition to a number of antipoverty programs. This opposition linked the unquestionably—but rarely expressed—image of antipoverty programs as black, with the white middle-class, Protestant articulation of social welfare as un-American. Class was important in forging this opposition. The language opposing these programs appealed primarily to middle-class whites, indicating a similar constituency in the new conservatism of the Deep South to that of the Sunbelt suburbs. The white middle-class response to antipoverty programs—and particularly the attempts of Mississippi Republicans to manipulate this response to gain political credit—signifies a complexity to Deep South conservatism that has too often been overlooked.

Chapter 1 follows the white response to the state's first antipoverty program, the Child Development Group of Mississippi (CDGM). As a Head Start program run by black grassroots activists and white "outsiders," built on the Freedom Schools of Freedom Summer, CDGM faced fierce opposition from white Mississippi. While the program was a powerful force for black empowerment, the campaign against CDGM sparked the development of a new phase of white resistance to black advancement. This evolving white resistance represented the first step in what would become a systematic campaign to assert white control over federal antipoverty funds. Chapter 2 follows the work of Marjorie Baroni, a white Catholic activist in Natchez, and the statewide antipoverty program Strategic Training and Redevelopment. A program run by the Catholic Church, this integrated venture known as STAR achieved support from both white and black Mississippians through its focus on job-training and adult education. Chapter 3 traces the renewed wave of white supremacist violence that swept across the state in 1967, targeting antipoverty programs, placing this wave of Klan violence in the broader context of white supremacist violence.

Chapter 4 explores the role of African American activist Don Jackson—later known as Muhammad Kenyatta—in antipoverty efforts in the state capital. Don Jackson and his fellow activists, seeking black empowerment through the antipoverty program Community Services Association, clashed not only with the white segregationists who dominated the program, but also with black moderates and white civil rights activists who favored a more gradual approach. Chapter 5 follows the efforts of another female poverty warrior, Helen Bass Williams. Williams, a black woman, was the executive director of the statewide Head Start program, Mississippi Action for Progress, which in many counties replaced the defunded Child Development Group. While the program provided vital development opportunities for hundreds of poor children, Williams faced a concerted campaign against her by white moderates and the segregationist establishment.

Chapter 6 lays bare the crucial connections between white Mississippi's war against the war on poverty and the rise of the New Right. It examines the impact of Nixon's election on the war on poverty in Mississippi, illustrating how the Republican administration provided new opportunities for the nascent state Republican Party to gain ground through opposition to antipoverty programs across the state. Chapter 7 follows the challenges facing the statewide job training and adult education program STAR in this new political climate. Strategic Training and Redevelopment collapsed under the weight of the omnipresent racial discrimination that undermined the work of its supporters, the Catholic Church and the state AFL-CIO. The final chapter traces the decline of the war on poverty from 1972, as the regionalization President Nixon's OEO introduced facilitated Mississippi's white establishment in their increasingly successful attempts to stifle black empowerment through the war on poverty.

Together these chapters illustrate how Mississippi became a national model for resistance to social change through its evolving resistance to the war on poverty. This resistance lies at the heart of the emerging new conservatism. White Mississippi forged linkages between the racially based conservative opposition to social welfare from the New Deal to the rise New Right. These linkages were forged most visibly in Mississippi, but the patterns of white opposition to the war on poverty are evident across the South. Mississippi was the location for the most intense and sustained resistance to desegregation. It was the birthplace of White Citizens' Councils and home to the most powerful manifestation of state-sponsored white supremacy. The state thus was the nucleus for the violent and vocal massive resistance of the late 1950s and early 1960s. And it stood at the forefront of evolving mechanisms of white resistance to black advancement after 1965.

Mississippi has been variously characterized as a "closed society," the "most southern place on earth," or a microcosm of American society. The Mississippi that emerges from this exploration of the war on poverty is both distinctively southern and distinctively Mississippian. But while the evolving methods of white resistance to the war on poverty in Mississippi are unique and important, they are not exceptional. Mississippi's war on poverty does not stand apart from the struggles of hundreds of other antipoverty programs across the nation. But the devastatingly institutionalized racial segregation does throw into sharp relief the development of a new conservatism that drew on the sustained struggle to preserve the racial, class, and gender privileges of white Americans.[40]

- Chapter One -

FROM CIVIL RIGHTS TO ECONOMIC EMPOWERMENT

In his 1964 State of the Union address, President Johnson declared an "unconditional war on poverty." "It will not be a short or easy struggle," Johnson acknowledged. But, he vowed, "We shall not rest until that war is won." The war on poverty was to be the centerpiece of his Great Society, and Johnson threw his considerable political skill behind it. He made a quick decision for his choice of war on poverty architect, selecting Kennedy's brother-in-law and Peace Corps director Sargent Shriver. The president believed Shriver was ideal for the job. Shriver had the ability to "think unashamedly in the big" and his leadership of the Peace Corps had proven his ability to forge new initiatives into success. Shriver's appointment also ensured the war on poverty retained "a Kennedy imprimatur," which Johnson felt was vital to its success. While President Johnson was sure Shriver was the right man for the job, Shriver himself was less convinced. According to his biographer, Shriver wanted to stick with the Peace Corps, and he felt he did not know enough about poverty—particularly as Johnson wanted to announce his appointment quickly in order to retain the support of Congress and the public, who were still shocked by Kennedy's assassination. Johnson got his way, however, when Shriver reluctantly accepted the position. The announcement of Shriver's appointment as "Special Assistant to the President in the organization and the administration of the war on poverty program" was made less than one month after Johnson's January 8 State of the Union address.[1]

Shriver developed a task force to give shape and form to the idea Johnson had proposed. The task force also built on public and private local initiatives that had been developed to address poverty. Their proposals drew on the earlier antipoverty efforts of the Kennedy administration. Volunteers in Service to America was for example, a domestic version of the Peace Corps, a flagship program of Kennedy's New Frontier. Kennedy-era efforts such as Mobilization for Youth pioneered the model of community action adopted by Shriver's task force. Conceived in 1957 and funded in 1961, Mobilization for Youth served Manhattan's Lower East Side. It embodied the move from the "elite planning" model characteristic of earlier social programs to the "democratic participation" of low-income residents that would characterize community action programs. The demonstration projects of the Ford Foundation's Gray Area program likewise focused on community participation by fostering communication between stakeholders, including community activists, administrators, and city officials. As war on poverty planner Daniel Patrick Moynihan later noted, such programs, alongside Kennedy's Committee on Juvenile Delinquency, played a significant role in the genesis of the war on poverty. Together these pioneering programs of the early 1960s laid the groundwork for the community-centric nature of the war on poverty, which would become its most powerful, transformative, and enduring feature.[2]

Shriver's task force worked for months to develop programs designed to tackle poverty. The group consisted mostly of bureaucrats, economists, and sociologists, but also included those who had sought to enforce desegregation, such as Adam Yarmolinsky and labor activists, such as Jack Conway. The presence of perceived "radicals," such as Yarmolinsky and Conway, alarmed many politicians—particularly southern conservatives. They were concerned that antipoverty programs would combine the radicalism of Yarmolinsky and Conway with the new civil rights legislation. Their concerns were not unfounded: President Johnson had explicitly linked racism and poverty in his State of the Union address. It was these "radicals" who would shape some of the most controversial aspects of the proposed war on poverty, most notably the concept of community action. Privately, the president was not sold on all features of the proposed war on poverty, particularly community action. Although he initially misunderstood community action, it came to be a target of Johnson's "outright hostility" as it undermined the political power of Democratic mayors, angering his political allies.[3]

Whatever his private misgivings or misunderstandings, in public Johnson threw all of his political weight behind ensuring Congressional approval of the Economic Opportunity bill. "It's the only bill I gotta [sic] have this year—they can take the rest of them, I don't care," he told Texas Congressman Olin Teague in early August. When signing the act into law on August 20, 1964, Johnson spoke of his pride in the commitment the nation was making to "this historic course." His words were not hyperbolic; the Economic Opportunity Act did indeed set the nation on an historic course. Unlike President Franklin Roosevelt's attempts to fight poverty during the New Deal, the war on poverty addressed issues of racism and segregation alongside economic issues.

Coming just seven weeks after President Johnson had signed the Civil Rights Act, the Economic Opportunity Act had the potential to provide African Americans with economic equality.[4]

The Economic Opportunity Act created a new Office for Economic Opportunity (OEO) to coordinate the administration's antipoverty efforts, with Sargent Shriver at its helm. The new OEO was designed to both coordinate the antipoverty programs of other departments as well as to fund and operate its own programs. OEO began with a sense of energy and excitement. However, its challenging role—coordinating programs operated by other departments while developing and operating other antipoverty efforts—and the lack of experience of its staff meant the agency quickly ran into problems. On top of the confusion and inexperience inside OEO, the agency also faced a barrage of criticism from the left and right of the political spectrum from the moment of its inception. Established government departments responded to the creation of OEO with hostility. Social workers expressed their concern that the rhetoric of the war on poverty was raising unrealistic expectations. Community activists such as Saul Alinsky criticized OEO for not going far enough to empower the poor, while conservatives felt the antipoverty agency represented a dangerous overreach of federal power. Despite the confusion and criticism, Shriver's OEO moved quickly to implement the dizzying array of antipoverty efforts authorized by the Economic Opportunity Act.[5]

Title I of the Act established work-training and work-study programs, including Job Corps and Neighborhood Youth Corps. The Job Corps was modeled on the New Deal's Civilian Conservation Corps and provided education, vocational training, and work experience for poor sixteen to twenty-one year olds, "to prepare for the responsibilities of citizenship and to increase the employability of young men and women." There were a number of programs focused purely on education, such as adult basic education, designed to aid those over the age of eighteen "whose inability to read and write the English language constitutes a substantial impairment of their ability to get or retain employment." Title II of the Economic Opportunity Act created urban and rural community action programs. Title III focused on rural poverty, establishing programs to coordinate loans to rural families and assistance for migrant agricultural employees. Title IV provided assistance to small businesses, while Title V of the Act funded work experience opportunities. It was Title II's community action programs that would grow beyond their modest beginnings to stand at the heart of the administration's war on poverty. Over the first four years of the war on poverty, $3.5 billion funded over one thousand community action agencies spread across the nation. These community action programs provided black Americans with economic opportunity, as they were designed to bypass southern states' barriers to racial equality by circumventing local authorities.[6]

Community action programs embodied the crucial connection between federal antipoverty funds and the civil rights movement. The president made the connection between economic opportunity and equality clear in his June 1965 commencement address at Howard University. Here Johnson pronounced that "we seek not just equality as a right and a theory, but equality as a fact and equality as a result." Community action programs—new incorporated nonprofit entities—were designed to do just that by channeling funds directly to local communities in order to address poverty at the grassroots. The programs themselves were diverse: they could be unique projects tailor-made to address local poverty conditions or single-purpose programs based on an OEO template. This flexibility was an important factor in their early successes, but the most significant aspect of these programs was their mandate to achieve the "maximum feasible participation of the poor." This mandate definitively entwined the war on poverty with grassroots civil rights activism. It ensured the empowerment of "literally hundreds and thousands of people who had been out of it before," one war on poverty architect recalled. This maximum feasible participation requirement combined with the way program funding bypassed local power structures solidified the programs' revolutionary potential. This revolutionary potential made community action an attractive prospect to civil rights activists.[7]

Mississippi was home to the nation's earliest and most high-profile antipoverty efforts. But across the nation federal funds began to flow into local communities with transformative and often inflammatory consequences. The nature of community action programs—not only their potential to set poor, mostly powerless people against local and state political structures but also their diverse and locally developed design—meant that there was no common experience of community action. Intensely local battles were shaped by the nature of the program, the constituency of the poor community, and the broader political, economic, racial, and social context. For example, in Alabama civil rights activists, in their efforts to "remake their region," utilized federal antipoverty funds to find ways around the "intransigence of their state and local lawmakers." In North Carolina antipoverty efforts predated the war on poverty. Governor Terry Sanford created a fund in 1963 to tackle discrimination and economic deprivation, which later served as a "laboratory for Lyndon Johnson's Great Society," but retained a combination of private and federal funds that ensured its independence. In Texas antipoverty programs began a battleground between poor Mexican American and African American activists, conflict that was encouraged by the state's white political structure. Outside the South minority groups utilized the potential of antipoverty programs in different ways. In Los Angeles, for example, conflicts occurred between marginalized groups. In Appalachia activists seeking to address some of the most entrenched poverty in the nation were undermined by the local establishment who accused the Appalachian Volunteers of being communists.[8]

In Mississippi's community action programs, some of these features were evident. As in Alabama and North Carolina, Mississippi's poverty warriors faced an intensely racially hostile environment that hampered their activism. In common with community activists in Chicago, Illinois activists in Jackson, Mississippi, faced an intransigent and obstructive political structure. Black Head Start teachers in Mississippi were accused of being communists, as were the Appalachia Volunteers. However, Mississippi's war on poverty was also distinctive in a number of significant ways. As the site of the nation's earliest antipoverty program, Mississippi's war on poverty broke new ground and thus faced a particularly intense backlash. However, the early establishment of the program meant antipoverty activists had many more months in Mississippi than elsewhere in the nation to embed in networks of activism even as their opponents gained traction and funding began to diminish. The early start to Mississippi's antipoverty programs also meant the state received a high proportion of federal funds. Perhaps even more importantly, antipoverty programs connected quickly and successfully with the vibrant grassroots network of activism created in the early years of the 1960s, and which reached their zenith during Freedom Summer. There was one other distinctive feature of Mississippi's war on poverty: the nature of the opposition it generated. Just as poverty warriors tapped into the state's civil rights networks, the opponents of the war on poverty built on the structure of white supremacy that had been in place for generations. As these implacable and enduring structures of white power adapted to the challenge presented by the state's war on poverty, the evolving template of white resistance fed into the development of a new conservatism.

Head Start quickly became one of the most popular OEO template community action programs. The idea behind Head Start was a simple one: give poor prekindergarten children a "head start" to help them overcome the challenges they faced when they began school. Head Start programs offered basic literacy and numeracy lessons, and more importantly, they became the conduit for the provision of much-needed healthcare. It was a Head Start program that was the first, and most prominent and controversial, antipoverty program in Mississippi: the Child Development Group. In the poorest parts of Mississippi—which were indeed some of the poorest parts of the nation—the Child Development Group provided something even more basic than healthcare. Child Development Group centers provided poor children with the hot meal they would not receive at home and often their first experience of indoor plumbing. The impact on the children was profound, and CDGM proved equally transformative for its staff. The wages offered were considerably more than those paid for working in the fields or cleaning houses. One staff member previously earned three dollars per day for field work but was able to earn seventy-five dollars per week working for the Child Development Group. Significantly, these wages represented a step toward the dissolution of white economic power, as pay was not dependent on workers refraining from civil rights activism.[9]

The Child Development Group was initially funded in May 1965 with a $1.4 million OEO grant for a summer Head Start program. It quickly expanded to operate 121 centers across twenty-eight Mississippi counties, for over 12,000 poor African American preschool children. By July 1966 the CDGM employed 2,272 people, 98.9 percent of whom were local Mississippians. The program combined the potent activism of the Freedom Summer of 1964 with the federal funds of the war on poverty. Rosie Head, an assistant teacher with the Child Development Group, recalled that while children had been taught in Freedom Schools "even before we had the money," the federal funds provided the chance to expand. This expansion enabled activists to reach many more children and provide them with invaluable care and support. For many pupils, attending CDGM centers was the first time seeing an indoor toilet or taking a shower. "We taught them how to use a toilet, how to bathe themselves," Rosie Head recalled. "We taught them how to just share with other children, just everything. We taught them how to speak."[10]

The program faced innumerable challenges, though. It entered into a violent racial landscape with bleak economic conditions. Compounding these challenges were divisions within the movement in Mississippi. COFO, created to unite the "big four" civil right organizations, broke down in 1965, reflecting the deepening discord between activists. SNCC activists rejected involvement in projects funded by the federal government, seeing the war on poverty as an attempt to coopt the civil rights movement. The NAACP meanwhile was largely excluded from the operation of the Child Development Group, as it drew on grassroots activists—mostly women. It had been COFO that had empowered these activists who, unlike NAACP members, were mostly sharecroppers, farmers, and domestic workers. As COFO's remaining resources were funneled into the MFDP and SNCC diminished, grassroots activists like Fannie Lou Hamer and Unita Blackwell channeled their energies into antipoverty centers that embraced the "maximum feasible participation" mandate of community action programs.[11]

Staff encouraged parents to become involved in the program. A total of 1,006 people, virtually all of them poor, were accorded opportunities to make decisions directly affecting their own lives and the operation of CDGM centers. Willie Burns, a community organizer and CDGM employee in Holmes County believed that the group's impact on the community was as important as the work it was doing for poor children. "Now we in Holmes County have some idea of what is meant by self-respect and first-class citizenship," Burns believed, "because we are learning to do for ourselves." Federal antipoverty funds provided the opportunity, but it was the long tradition of community organizing in Mississippi that enabled CDGM to expand across the state so quickly. While some SNCC activists rejected the federally funded program, many embraced the opportunities CDGM provided. CDGM embodied the critical connection between the federal war on poverty and civil rights legislation. Using the organizing strategies of local activists along with funding and expertise from the federal antipoverty program, the Child Development Group made "tangible gains in the fight against poverty."[12]

However, the activists and poverty warriors of the Child Development Group faced formidable opponents. Just as black activists in the state were quick to recognize the potential of federal antipoverty funds, so Mississippi's white power structure was swift to see the threat the war on poverty posed to white supremacy. Mississippi's politicians were united in their disapproval of the Economic Opportunity Act. It was widely perceived as an unwelcome expansion of the federal government into the state, intent on enforcing integration. Local reporters portrayed antipoverty programs as a plot to "mongrelize" the nation. The Child Development Group was, according to one Mississippi newspaper, "one of the most subtle mediums for instilling the acceptance of racial integration and ultimate mongrelization ever perpetuated in this country." Soon after the Child Development Group secured its funding, segregationists sought to destroy the program. Politicians and reporters, landowners and Klansmen all worked to undermine the group, from the grassroots to the national level. Segregationist senator John C. Stennis, fresh from his fight against the civil rights bill, wielded his considerable political power in Washington to defund CDGM. Stennis's seniority in the Senate Appropriations Committee enabled him to pose a threat to Vietnam War funding and to secure an investigation of the Child Development Group independent of the Office of Economic Opportunity.[13]

In Mississippi Governor Paul B. Johnson took every opportunity to malign both OEO and CDGM, in correspondence with the president and Shriver, and in his public statements. Governor Johnson was proud of his history of opposition to federal intervention in his state. In 1962 as lieutenant governor, he stood beside Governor Ross Barnett to block the admission of James Meredith to the University of Mississippi. The following year he used this incident in his campaign to become governor with the slogan "Stand tall with Paul." Johnson avoided the starkly racist demagoguery of his predecessor, attempting to walk a line between the demands of the still powerful Citizens' Councils and those of the rapidly changing racial context. In his inaugural address, on January 21, 1964, he declared that "hate or prejudice or ignorance will not lead Mississippi while I sit on the governor's chair." He would not fight, he said, a "rearguard defense of yesterday." If he must fight, Governor Johnson declared that he would fight an "all-out assault for our share of tomorrow." Although he adopted more moderate policies than Barnett, Johnson remained trenchantly opposed to federally funded civil rights activism. In his part in fighting the war on poverty, Johnson did indeed seek to secure "our share of tomorrow" by preserving white supremacy in as many ways as he could without directly contravening the new civil rights legislation.[14]

The Child Development Group did not just face opposition from politicians such as Stennis and Johnson. In centers across the state, staff members were the targets of violent attacks. Shots were fired into the Head Start classrooms and crosses were burned outside CDGM's Mount Beulah office, at other centers, and at the homes of staff. Landowners evicted sharecroppers for enrolling their children in classes and refused to extend credit to participating black businesses. These measures weakened CDGM's ability to staff and operate its centers. Perhaps the most powerful opponent of the group was the Sovereignty Commission. The commission was a state-funded anti-integration watchdog, created by the Mississippi State Legislature in 1956, in the wake of the Southern Manifesto. Funded in part by the White Citizens' Councils, the commission was granted the power to "do and perform any and all acts deemed necessary and proper to protect the sovereignty of the state of Mississippi, and her sister states" from perceived "encroachment thereon by the Federal Government or any branch, department or agency thereof." The commission was staffed by a director, public relations officer, a few investigators, and clerical workers. Staff—and the state legislature to which they regularly reported—saw the commission as a mini-FBI. They wiretapped, bugged, and infiltrated civil rights organizations and antipoverty programs, acting as a secret police. The commission also provided funds to lobbying efforts in Washington to oppose the civil rights bill. Over the course of fifteen years of intense activity, the commission generated thousands of pages of reports that reveal its fanaticism to maintain white supremacy.[15]

The Sovereignty Commission's spy network infiltrated and threatened the Child Development Group, bringing their powerful opposition to bear on the organization. Commission investigators paid informants for information from inside CDGM's offices, using it to compile a dossier of information that ran into the hundreds of pages. Their reports alleged that staff members were corrupt, incompetent, and participated in civil rights activities on CDGM's time using federal resources. Seeking to undermine the credibility of the organization in the eyes of OEO officials and the public, commission investigators employed the familiar rhetoric of outside agitators and charges of communism, linking their opposition to the Child Development Group to wider national concerns. Commission director Erle Johnston Jr. journeyed to Washington, DC, to implore OEO staff to cease funding programs that he claimed had been "infiltrated by people on the FBI subversive list," but to no avail. Cries of communism failed to have any weight with OEO, a horrified Johnston reported to the commission's board.[16]

With the House Committee on Un-American Activities in decline and the Vietnam War increasingly unpopular, appealing to anticommunism was not finding a sympathetic ear within OEO. However, such accusations did find favor with the local press, who reported frequently on the "red influence" on OEO programs. Reporters made sensational claims that drew on their readers' fears of communism. In the *Commercial Appeal* Victor Riesel reported that the thousands of "tiny OEO headquarters" across the country "are loaded with literature and promoters of . . . the New Left, the independent Maoists, the Trotskyists, the pro-Peking Progressive Labor Party youth, and even Muscovite Communist party activists." Bob Howie, a regular cartoonist for White Citizens' Council paper *The Citizen* in the 1950s, depicted this "red influence" in one of his weekly cartoons for the *Jackson Daily News*. The cartoon, entitled "Poverty Hanky Panky," featured Howie's recurring character "Lefty" receiving Head Start funds from a federal official.[17]

Such imagery drew on the commission's unfounded allegations. Their reports were also used extensively by Stennis in his Senate statements. His

Fig. 1.1. Bob Howie, "Poverty Hanky Panky," *Jackson Daily News*, ca. August 1965. Credit: *Clarion-Ledger* (*Jackson Daily News*).

fellow senator James O. Eastland joined him, claiming that money for the Child Development Group could "funnel funds into the extreme leftist . . . beatnik groups." Commission reports provided a wealth of material for the local media to construct an image of Head Start as corrupt, a waste of tax dollars, and a source of funding of civil rights activism. As OEO Director Sargent Shriver noted, the impression created by these reports was "that something un-American has been going on here." Such impressions were picked up by local reporters, who echoed Stennis's calls for "responsible Mississippians" to run local programs. They frequently referred to the lack of judgment of administration bureaucrats and to the generous distribution of tax money. These reports drew on powerful Southern tenets opposing federal interference and concerns over the redistribution of wealth. But both the press and the Sovereignty Commission recognized that popular appeal within Mississippi was insufficient to fight the threat of the Child Development Group, which had gained powerful national support. So

CDGM's opponents took the opportunity to link Head Start to what they depicted as unsavory and threatening radicalism. In the wake of the 1965 Watts riot, local reporters seized on the new threat of Black Power. In one *Clarion Ledger* report, for example, CDGM was provocatively labeled as "an instrument of the black separatist movement."[18]

Evident in this white opposition to the war on poverty are the tactics of the earlier massive resistance. One of the most potent aspects of pre-1965 massive resistance had been politicians' and reporters' success in linking the overt racism of the Deep South with wider concerns. Both the Dixiecrat revolt and opponents of school integration drew on national concerns of the expanding power of the federal government, and anticommunism provided a rich vein of hysteria to exploit. These tactics were employed in the fight against the Child Development Group, and antipoverty programs across the Deep South. Alabama Congressman John Hall Buchanan Jr., for example, spoke of the "strange soldiers in the ranks of the battalions" of the war on poverty at the 1966 Economic Opportunity Amendment hearings. "It is no secret," Buchanan claimed, "that the Communist Party plans to infiltrate the poverty program's administrative groups." He went on to claim that antipoverty funds were already being used to support black militants in HARYOU-ACT in New York and Black Panthers in Lowndes County, Alabama. While Black Power had tangible links to rural Alabama, there was little evidence of this form of Black Power in Mississippi in 1965. Still, the tactic worked because the fear of Black Power resonated with a white population in Mississippi shaped by their perception of "outsiders" "invading" the state less than twelve months earlier.[19]

The perceived menace of Black Power was used by local media and the Sovereignty Commission to compound the threat posed by antipoverty programs. Segregationists seized on many white Mississippians' fears of black nationalism to articulate concerns about an outside alien force in a way that had national resonance. They depicted the battle against the Child Development Group as an extension of the fight against an intrusive federal government to preserve states' rights, of the fight against communism and against black nationalism. Entangling federal antipoverty funds with the threat of Black Power was a powerful tactic, and not one limited to Mississippi. In Houston, Texas, for example, the city's mayor manipulated widespread fears of riots by claiming the local community action program was "Black Power–infiltrated." In Alabama Governor George Wallace employed the specter of Black Power in his attacks on antipoverty programs in Lowndes and Wilcox counties.[20]

By 1966 the war on poverty was already faltering in the Deep South, though not only because of its connection with civil rights activists. The war on poverty was also facing economic and political challenges at the national level. The federal antipoverty efforts pitted liberals against conservatives, states' rights advocates against the federal government, state and city politicians against community activists, with all tensions feeding into broader racial, class, and gender conflicts. Other voices soon joined southern conservatives' in expressing concern about the nature of the war on poverty and about community action in particular. Throughout 1965 members of the House and Senate added their weight to the opposition of local politicians—notably mayors and governors—to community action programs. This opposition soon began to have an effect on the operation and funding of the war on poverty. Economic Advisor Walter Heller tried to persuade President Johnson to keep the Great Society growing at least modestly in 1966, despite the rising costs of the Vietnam War. "A billion or two . . . could spell the difference between progress and stagnation of the Great Society" and, Heller argued, could do a lot of good in strengthening the economic and political base for Vietnam. However, opposition to the bill from Republicans and southern Democrats was mounting. This opposition was compounded by the interdepartmental bickering that was resulting in internecine warfare in local communities.[21]

The war on poverty was facing increasingly bad publicity too. As a result the administration gave the 1966 antipoverty bill a low priority in its lobbying, and the bill's passage through Congress was delayed. By late 1966 the appropriations for the war on poverty had been cut, and new restrictions had been written into the community action budget. However Mississippi, once again, was the exception. While the community action budget was cut substantially, Head Start funding actually increased. The sheer magnitude of the program and the substantial degree of public interest in it—due in no small part to the attacks on the Child Development Group—meant Congress ring-fenced Head Start funds, setting them at $310 million. Mississippi received a disproportionately large share of these funds: $40.2 million OEO funds in 1967. This was only $6.9 million less than Texas (the state with the largest number of poor people in the country in 1966) and significantly more than Georgia's $31.4 million, Alabama's $18.4 million, and Tennessee's $21.4 million, each of which had greater numbers of poor people than Mississippi.[22]

Despite the weakening of the war on poverty across the nation, in Mississippi it was the segregationist campaign against the Child Development Group that was faltering. Although it drew on well-established tactics and powerful figures, segregationists did not succeed in destroying CDGM. Their campaign did, however, secure a temporary hiatus in the program's funding. In October 1966 OEO director Sargent Shriver buckled under intense political pressure from Mississippi senators Eastland and Stennis to cut off the group's funding in order to pursue evidence of alleged fiscal malfeasance. A national outcry followed his decision. A coalition of liberal, labor, and church groups took out a full-page ad in the *New York Times* emblazoned with the cry "Say It Isn't So, Sargent Shriver." Even Shriver's own staff publicly opposed this decision. Three hundred of them signed a petition asking him to reverse his decision. Civil rights activists begged Shriver to show that "maximum feasible participation is more than just a slogan." Shriver was appalled and hurt by the public outcry. He was deeply aggrieved at being in a position where he felt compelled to veto funding for a program he actually felt was striking a blow against Jim Crow. Head Start associate director Jules Sugarman recalled Shriver seeing the ad: "I'd never really seen him as moved and angry." Shriver, meanwhile, raged that his staff had told him there was no choice but to defund the Child Development Group, given the evidence of mismanagement in the program.[23]

Shriver overturned his decision two months later, partially restoring CDGM's funding. However, irrevocable damage was done to Shriver's (and OEO's) reputations, and to the Child Development Group. While some of the group's centers had continued to operate on a voluntary basis during the hiatus, others had no choice but to close their doors. Polly Greenberg, who worked in CDGM from its founding and wrote its "biased biography," recalled hearing a man comment, "I thought we poor peoples was doin' real good—I wonder what we done wrong why Mr. Shriver want to snuff this ray of sunshine from our lives?" In the turmoil of those two months without funds, CDGM lost staff and precious momentum. White Mississippi's campaign had irreversibly damaged the organization and robbed it of its ability to be an instrument for social change. Nonetheless, CDGM, remarkably, survived.[24] This survival was due in large part to the dedication of its staff and its spirit of volunteerism. But while the OEO did refund the program in January 1967, the grant renewal represented a massive reduction in the scope of the Child Development Group. CDGM's rejected August 1966 proposal had been for $20.2 million to serve 13,500 children in thirty-seven counties. The renewed grant of $4.9 million provided for centers in only fourteen of Mississippi's counties left many centers without funding. The grant also came with a host of new conditions that fundamentally altered the program. Despite this, the long-term legacy of the program was overwhelmingly positive. CDGM had a significant and constructive impact on Mississippi's preschool education system and its staff contributed to the continuation of Mississippi's powerful tradition of grassroots activism.[25]

This education and activism is not, however the most potent legacy of the Child Development Group. Even more powerful were the consequences of the failure of Mississippi's white establishment to eradicate the group. The failure transformed the landscape of white resistance to black advancement in Mississippi. White opposition to the war on poverty changed entirely. It became proactive rather than reactive, as white Mississippians from the political elite to the grassroots began to engage with antipoverty programs. Mississippi's war against the war on poverty began with the leaders of the campaign against the Child Development Group: Senator Stennis and Governor Johnson. They developed an ostensibly race-neutral language in their attempts to assert white control over the antipoverty funds flowing into the state. The refunding of the Child Development Group made it clear that OEO could not be relied upon to bend to their will, so Stennis and Johnson turned to Mississippi's "local responsible people." They urged these "responsible people" to create their own community action programs, or to sit on the board of their local programs. If Stennis and Johnson could not control the direction of federal funding in Washington, they could at least attempt to control the disbursement of the funds once they reached Mississippi.[26] Their inability to defeat the Child Development Group thus utterly changed Mississippi's war on poverty. There was another significant consequence: a decade of tried and trusted massive resistance tactics had failed. The mechanisms and rhetoric of massive resistance—notably the state Sovereignty Commission and language drawing on powerful fears of anticommunism—were potent weapons in the campaign against the Child Development Group. But their failure marked the death knoll of last-chance grandstands against racial change in Mississippi.

Segregationists had been honing social, political, and economic methods of bolstering white supremacy for decades when the 1954 *Brown* ruling ignited a new phase of mass opposition to school integration. The resistance to *Brown* took numerous forms. Initial outrage saw the creation of the White Citizens' Council in Indianola in the Mississippi Delta in July 1954 and the rejection of the Supreme Court ruling by the likes of Judge Tom P. Brady's *Black Monday*. Political opposition developed more slowly, reaching its peak in 1956 with the signing of the Southern Manifesto by 101 senators and congressmen, mostly from the Deep South. The Manifesto decried the Supreme Court's *Brown* ruling as an "unwarranted exercise of power by the Court, contrary to the

Constitution," which "is destroying the amicable relations between the white and Negro races . . . plant[ing] hatred and suspicion where there has been heretofore friendship and understanding." As civil rights activism gained paced, the acts of white segregationists became more desperate. A surge of white extremist violence resulted in the murders of hundreds of black activists, from leaders such as Medgar Evers to citizens simply attempting to register to vote. Segregationist politicians secured their reelection in highly publicized grandstands—in schoolroom doors and university offices.[27]

The passage of the 1964 Civil Rights Act and 1965 Voting Rights Act did little to dampen the anger and outrage of white segregationists. The passage of these acts did, however, alter the nature and form of their resistance. White segregationists were, by 1965, well versed in adapting their racist rhetoric to new challenges. The rise of the original Ku Klux Klan was the brutal response to emancipation and Reconstruction. The systems of sharecropping and Jim Crow produced new forms of legal, social, and economic separation and a reconstitution of slavery. When black activism swelled during and after World War II, a "consciously 'segregationist' countermovement emerged." It was a "carefully constructed political project" of which post-*Brown* massive resistance was one facet. The massive resistance campaign against the Supreme Court's *Brown* ruling ensured that only 0.2 percent of black schoolchildren in Mississippi went to school with white children by 1965.[28]

Massive resisters were thus well versed in adopting new forms of opposition: new rhetoric and mechanisms to undercut black advancement. They continued to do so, even in the face of the Civil Rights and Voting Rights Acts, which state politicians rejected and decried. For most black Mississippians registering to vote continued to be a dangerous and sometimes futile ordeal. Massive resistance was predicated on opposition to federal intervention; white segregationists did not just stop resisting that imposition because Johnson signed these laws. But antipoverty programs brought federally funded black empowerment directly into Mississippi in a way the Civil Rights Act and Voting Rights Act had not. It brought federal intervention directly into local communities, bypassing state white power structures. So the failure of the massive resistance campaign against the state's first war on poverty shook Mississippi's power structures. Stennis and Johnson had wielded their old weapons and failed. In response they developed a new language to call up the foot-soldiers of white segregationism to take up the fight against the war on poverty: the "local responsible people" who could, community by community, Head Start classroom by Head Start classroom, halt federally funded black empowerment. Massive resistance, never a stagnant phenomenon, began a new phase of opposition, evolving in response to the new challenges presented by the war on poverty.

Senator Stennis's and Governor Johnson's calls for local responsible people to establish antipoverty programs drew on a colorblind language that Senator Stennis had been using to oppose civil rights advances for years. Their calls were little more than a thinly veiled request for whites to enact a "defensive localism" that enabled whites to reestablish their control over African American advancement. The result was a mass white mobilization as application after application was filed to create antipoverty programs with white boards, staffed by white people. This mobilization was actually facilitated by OEO. Sargent Shriver himself approved the funding of this host of newly created white-controlled community action programs in order to appease Mississippi's powerful politicians in the wake of the debacle over the Child Development Group. By mid-1967, local officials and middle-class white businessmen populated the boards of community action programs across the state. These new, white-controlled programs sought to control the flow and direction of the state's antipoverty funds in order to undercut federally funded civil rights activism.[29]

The creation of these new antipoverty programs reshaped Mississippi's war on poverty. The state's antipoverty programs were no longer the reserve of civil rights activists intent on harnessing the power of the federal government to secure black economic opportunity. Poverty was big business in Mississippi. By 1967 the state had received over $40 million of OEO funds, 90 percent of which funded Head Start programs. Many Mississippians were determined that these funds—and the economic and political power that accompanied them—would not fall solely into the hands of black activists. Governor Paul Johnson moved quickly to create the state infrastructure for the war on poverty, including a state Office of Economic Opportunity. "They went around and told people, boards of supervisors, and city governments," African American poverty warrior Bennie Gooden recalled, "that if they didn't hurry up and get an organization going . . . the [n----rs] were going to get the money, and they were going to run it."[30]

Stennis and Johnson had failed in their campaign to eradicate the Child Development Group, but they had dealt it a devastating blow. The reduction in funds for the group meant that in many communities previously flourishing Head Start centers were left unable to pay to rent the classrooms, pay their teachers, or buy milk or food for the children. It was primarily in these communities that Stennis's call to action had most resonance. Many of these defunded Child Development Group counties, including Clarke,

Humphreys, Greene, Wayne, Neshoba, and Leflore, continued to operate their Head Start classes on a voluntary basis while desperately seeking funds. These five counties eventually received funding through a newly created group, Friends of the Children of Mississippi, which received an OEO grant (and continues to run Head Start in Mississippi today).[31] Other defunded counties received Head Start funds through Mississippi Action for Progress—the government-approved, biracial group created to replace the Child Development Group. Some centers though, were unable to secure funds through these organizations. In southwest Mississippi, for example, the defunded Child Development Group staff submitted their own application to OEO to re-fund their Head Start centers separately from CDGM.

In southwest Mississippi—and in counties across the state—local whites took up the fight against the war on poverty, responding to the dog-whistle call for "local responsible people" to act. Led by county boards of supervisors and local mayors, these responsible people submitted applications to OEO for funds to run their own antipoverty programs. OEO's policy was to fund only one community action agency per area, so community leaders knew that the sooner they acted in these local battles against the Child Development Group, the better. Members of the board of supervisors, local business leaders, and landowners in southwest Mississippi quickly submitted an application to OEO for their own antipoverty program. This program would serve the poor people of Amite, Pike, and Wilkinson Counties in southwest Mississippi, bordering Louisiana to the south and the Mississippi River on Wilkinson County's western border. Like most counties in Mississippi, Amite, Pike, and Wilkinson were in the 1960s overwhelmingly rural and poor. According to OEO's 1966 survey, the severity of poverty, the sufficiency of housing, and economic activity in Amite and Wilkinson Counties was worse than 90 percent of counties in America. All the residents of these counties lived in rural areas and the poverty rates were very high: 70.9 percent of Wilkinson County and 64.5 percent of Amite County lived below the poverty line. While not subject to the level of poverty of the Delta counties, poverty in the southwest of the state was nonetheless severe. Pike County, next to Amite, fared slightly better. With a poverty rate of 53.3 percent, Pike residents were not wholly reliant on farming for their income—there was some industry centered around the railroad. The antipoverty program Southwest Mississippi Opportunity was created by whites to assist the vast poor population of these counties. But its main function was to ensure that the former Child Development Group could not retain its foothold in the area.[32]

The existence of the Child Development Group in the area was, in itself, remarkable. White supremacy was violently maintained in these counties. In Amite and Wilkinson counties white landowners held the economic dominance that underpinned white power. African Americans' livelihoods and, all too often, their very lives depended on adherence to Jim Crow restrictions. In Pike County the presence of the railroad created jobs and union activism that meant, for some African Americans, employment that was not dependent on white landowners. In all three counties, however, white economic control was reinforced by a number of violent white extremist organizations. Multiple Klan factions, Americans for the Preservation of the White Race, and White Citizens' Councils had all been active in the area at varying times since the mid-1950s. There were also a number of civil rights groups active, groups which had weathered intense and sustained violence. NAACP, SNCC, and the Delta Ministry were all present in the area. The NAACP branches in southwest Mississippi actually withstood the repression of the 1950s better than many other branches in the state. In Walthall County, just to the north of Pike County, the local NAACP chapter was the first in the state to file a desegregation suit. However, despite determined voter registration drives spearheaded by the NAACP, SNCC, and later the Delta Ministry, these groups made little headway.[33]

That crucial connection of federal antipoverty funds and powerful grassroots networks had enabled the creation of Child Development Group centers in these counties. It was this organizing tradition that was enabling the centers to continue without funding, thanks to the generosity and efforts of the local black community. When the still-undefeated staff submitted their own application for funding, the local white community perceived a dangerous threat. In the midst of such widespread poverty, even a small OEO grant for African American activists to continue Head Start would affect the balance of power. It would provide the area's large African American population a level of protection from economic reprisals, and even more worrying for whites, it would empower the black community. As Noel A. Cazenave has illustrated, the war on poverty's community activism was a powerful force, contributing to "an expansion of more participatory democratic processes." At the local level this energy had the potential to disrupt the mechanisms of white control. Whites in these counties responded to this threat with a new form of opposition to black advancement: the war on poverty. Their application for OEO funding for Southwest Mississippi Opportunity (SMO) was successful. In October 1966 the group was granted $713,000 to fund an emergency food and medical services program, home service aid, and a Neighborhood Youth Corps. Unlike the African American Head Start operation in these counties, SMO was under white control. This was by no means accidental. Those involved in creating the program—an effort spearheaded by Maxie Sturgeon, a white publisher's representative—worked hard to ensure that the program would appear to adhere to all of OEO's guidelines regarding racial composition and representation, while in reality the board subverted OEO regulations in order to ensure white control of the federal funds.[34]

Sturgeon and his fellow applicants faced quite a challenge to secure this control. OEO's commitment to the "maximum feasible participation" of the poor was not always realized, but it did ensure that one-third of the board had to be elected members of the poor community. OEO also required that the board of a community action program reflect the racial composition of the area. Sturgeon's board did meet these requirements: the board consisted of thirty-six members, with twelve from each county. Eighteen members were black and eighteen white, in line with the racial composition across the three counties—51.4 percent of which was African American.[35] For OEO's officials assessing the application, the requirements were met. Indeed, on the face of it, the fact that Mississippi's white businessmen and community leaders were proposing to sit on a board that was 50 percent black was fairly remarkable, given the state's response to Freedom Summer just two years earlier. This biracial cooperation was not wholly a façade. Some white board members were genuinely committed to an integrated approach to addressing poverty.

Steve Reed, for example, volunteered to serve on the board of Southwest Mississippi Opportunity. He was a white leader of Wilkinson County board of supervisors, and OEO reports called him "forward-looking." While not a supporter of civil rights activism, he was not a hardline segregationist. In the early 1960s some boards of supervisors attempted to undermine civil rights activism by cutting off food distribution programs, action which had devastating consequences for poor blacks. Steve Reed was instrumental in ensuring that Wilkinson County's food distribution program was not cut off in response to black activism. There were also "moderate" black voices on the board, equally committed to testing biracialism. C. C. Bryant, for instance, was a civil rights activist, serving as president of the McComb branch of the NAACP since 1954. In the early 1960s Bryant hosted SNCC workers, including Bob Moses, in his home, for which his home and business was targeted by Klansmen. But unlike Bob Moses and SNCC, Bryant was committed to a gradualist approach to race relations. As such, he was willing to sit on the board of an antipoverty program dominated by white segregationists in order to attempt to provide a moderating influence.[36]

However, the good intent and goodwill of men such as C. C. Bryant and Steve Reed was not powerful enough to sway the board's white segregationists from their goal. Controlling the flow of federal antipoverty dollars into the three counties required control over the program's board. Neither white nor black moderates on the board could be guaranteed to ensure that control. That left one-third of the board to target: the poor community's representatives. It was with the target area representatives to the board, required by OEO to give a voice to the poor in the running of antipoverty programs, that white segregationists saw their opportunity to entrench white power. Two methods were employed to undermine the purpose of these representatives. This was done, first, through their election. The representatives were elected by the poor communities of these counties. However, most often their election was disputed by the very people they were intended to represent. These elections were disrupted, meaning that often the white leaders' preferred candidate was selected. Second, once elected to the board the poor representatives were excluded from decision making or were controlled by whites who wielded their economic power and threatened violent retribution.[37] Employment in an African American–operated Head Start program provided a measure of protection from economic reprisals, as job security did not depend on adhering to white control. However for many poor representatives on SMO's board, their livelihoods' lay in the hands of a white board member—or at least a member of the white community. Maxie Sturgeon and his fellow white community leaders thus used the creation of the antipoverty program to reassert white economic dominance, shaping the war on poverty program into a tool of a new form of white opposition to black advancement.

This evolving white resistance was successful: white control of the area's allotted federal funds was secure. With control of the money came control of the shape and nature of the antipoverty programs and of the level of integration they involved. But the creation and control of SMO had not solved the problem of the black Head Start program, the remnant of the Child Development Group still operating in the area. The activists running the program were as eager to ensure its survival and independence as SMO's board chair, Maxie Sturgeon, and executive director, Kathleen O'Fallon, were to see it under their control. The former group submitted its own application to OEO for its own grant, to be administered through Southwest Mississippi Opportunity. It was a shrewd move by the group, which they renamed the Child Development Council. The Head Start staff knew that under OEO regulations, having funded Southwest Mississippi Opportunity, the OEO would not provide funding to a separate community action agency. But applying for funds to run an existing network of centers, under an established community action agency, made it difficult for OEO to reject the council's application. And crucially, becoming a delegate of the establishment program would provide Child Development Council with a measure of independence. A delegate agency retained its own board, which was in control of program operation and staffing. Ultimate authority, however, would rest with the establishment program, Southwest Mississippi Opportunity.[38]

Unsurprisingly, Sturgeon and O'Fallon objected to the proposed delegate arrangement. They wanted to operate their own Head Start program, not be forced to cede partial control to what they termed "dangerous radicals." Giving the Child Development Council control over its employees and budget in a delegate arrangement would, Kathleen O'Fallon told OEO, ensure that the "radicalism" of the Child Development Group "infected" her program. However, in the tumultuous days following CDGM's defunding, OEO was eager to placate the outraged group staff and supporters. An OEO task force visited the area, interviewing staff members of SMO and the Child Development Council. This OEO task force concluded that the Child Development Council must retain power over Head Start employees. O'Fallon and Sturgeon were infuriated. They saw this recommendation as an attack on white control of the program. O'Fallon was horrified at OEO's failure to recognize and eliminate these "radicals." For help to prove how dangerous the Child Development Council really was, she turned to the state's anti-integration watchdog, the Sovereignty Commission.[39]

Commission head Erle Johnston was well versed in the kind of tactics that undermined black activism and destabilized antipoverty programs. He set to work immediately, dispatching investigator Leland Cole to the area. Johnston himself began in the extensive files the commission had collected on the Child Development Group. He found what he was looking for straight away: an October 1966 newspaper report that claimed twenty-two members of the Child Development Council's board had previously worked for the Child Development Group. Even if it were true, this would not be evidence of any wrongdoing—apart from in the minds of Johnston and O'Fallon, who viewed CDGM as "dangerous radicals." But, as Leland Cole reluctantly reported to Erle Johnston, there was no evidence to support the newspaper's claims. Only two members of the council's board had anything to do with the Child Development Group: A. Marks, a former CDGM center chair, and CDGM employee Loyce Duncan. Neither one was, in Cole's words, "troublemakers." Instead, Johnston instructed his investigator to target a black activist, Rev. Harry Bowie, who SMO director Kathleen O'Fallon had labeled "chief troublemaker." Bowie was an Episcopalian priest from New Jersey— one of the "outside agitators" the Sovereignty Commission so often blamed for racial unrest—who had arrived in Mississippi for Freedom Summer and became a Delta Ministry worker. Cole's investigation did not uncover any evidence of criminal activity, or of any wrongdoing, though he dug as hard as possible. Instead Cole filed a report on Bowie, which comprised gossip and malicious accusation as "witness statements." Based on these statements, he reported that "the whole CDGM is rotten and they are still holding on trying to get money from OEO. It is apparent, the way things are going in Pike, they may succeed, if something is not done to stop them. OEO," Cole concluded with no trace of irony, "is clearly guilty of intimidation."[40]

Erle Johnston sent Cole's report on Bowie and the "evidence" of the infiltration of the Child Development Council to Governor Paul Johnson, urging him to act. Johnston even included a statement he had drafted, including this allegation and the false charge that "at least 20 members of the Southwest Child Development area councils were CDGM personnel." Governor Johnson did act in response to the commission's "evidence." On November 1, 1966, the governor issued a statement announcing his veto of SMO's grant. His opposition was based on euphemistically phrased concerns that the delegate arrangement did not give SMO full "organizational control" over the Child Development Council. He also cited the commission's claims of infiltration by the Child Development Group. Just as in earlier phases of massive resistance, local and state mechanisms of white resistance worked in concert to undermine black advancement. Governor Johnson was attempting to force OEO to make white control of antipoverty funds in the southwest of Mississippi absolute. But the state mechanisms of white supremacy were inadequate to overturn OEO's determination to support genuine community participation in antipoverty programs. Less than three weeks after the governor's veto, OEO Director Sargent Shriver overrode it, formalizing the delegate relationship between SMO and the Child Development Council.[41]

Southwest Mississippi was left with a white-controlled community action program and a black-staffed Head Start which ultimately fell under white control. Federally funded black empowerment clashed with an evolving white resistance that employed methods of the earlier massive resistance, subverting the intent of the war on poverty in order to preserve white economic power. Community action programs had become a battleground— not just in southwest Mississippi—but across the state. White-controlled antipoverty programs were created in counties from Bolivar and Sunflower in the Delta to Lauderdale County and on the Gulf Coast. Just as in Southwest Mississippi Opportunity, the cost of maintaining white control was often a requirement that boards include "nonradical" African American members (often NAACP activists), thus submitting to a measure of integration. But for Sturgeon and O'Fallon and white community leaders across the state, this biracialism was a calculated concession that was worthwhile if it ensured the maintenance of white power.

The creation of these biracial antipoverty boards had another insidious, if perhaps unintended, consequence. The seating of these "nonradical" or "moderate" African Americans on community action boards—most often men of the veteran generation of NAACP activists—deepened the intraracial gender and class divisions within Mississippi's movement. While these veteran male activists worked to achieve black progress through biracial cooperation in board meetings, grassroots activists—most often the women who had been inspired by SNCC and COFO—remained struggling for funds for their Head Start centers and often kept classes running on a voluntary basis as white control of antipoverty funds tightened. The momentum of this grassroots activism was being eroded by divisions within the movement and increasingly by white segregationists targeting antipoverty programs.

When Stokely Carmichael left Greenwood jail in June 1966 he prefaced his famous call for Black Power with criticism of the failure of the federal government to support black economic and political advancement. "We begged the federal government," he said. "We've begged and begged. We've done nothing but beg. We've got to stop begging and take power." For African Americans in Mississippi living under the unimaginable oppressions of poverty, violence, and terror, the war on poverty represented that power. Funding for antipoverty programs was waning by 1966, undermining a war on poverty that had been underfunded to begin with. Internal class, gender, and ideological divisions within Mississippi's movement that had been deepening since Freedom Summer were making coordinated activism increasingly challenging. Nonetheless, community action programs represented an economic power that went some way to insulating black activists from economic retribution. They provided a way for Mississippi's grassroots activists to unite the powerful organizing tradition with federal funds and galvanize a black population that was, in the words of Fannie Lou Hamer, "sick and tired of being sick and tired." By the time of Carmichael's speech, black Mississippians had already begun seizing that opportunity for black power through the war on poverty. At the same time, however,

Mississippi's segregationists were once again blazing a trail of resistance for segregationists across the Deep South to follow, using the war on poverty to forge powerful new barriers to African American advancement.[42]

- Chapter Two -

MARJORIE BARONI, ADULT EDUCATION, AND THE MISSISSIPPI CATHOLIC CHURCH

Many white Mississippians participated in the war against the war on poverty, carrying out countless small acts of opposition. Most often, poor white parents refused to send their children to integrated Head Start classes or refused to attend integrated adult education classes, thus ensuring the centers violated OEO's requirement to serve poor of both races. Local politicians attempted to control antipoverty funds. White property owners refused to rent their buildings to community action agencies—most often when those agencies were run by African Americans. There were violent acts of opposition too. White supremacist groups targeted antipoverty centers with burning crosses and bullets. The media played an important role in opposing the war on poverty. In the local press most early reports adopted a cynical and dismissive tone in addressing early antipoverty programs. They were "nutty," the *Bolivar Commercial* reported, and would be "great for laughs if not for the fact taxpayers have to live with them and pay for them." Such cynicism turned into vitriol as the white battle against the Child Development Group gained pace. Instead of "great for laughs," the *Jackson Daily News* described antipoverty workers as a "flock of beatniks" and "gang of degenerates" who were "dipping into the taxpayers' pockets for government-subsidized civil rights agitation" to achieve a "subsidized revolution."[1]

While opposition was widespread, white Mississippi's response to the war on poverty was by no means monolithic. Even among opponents of the war on poverty, the intensity of their opposition and the methods employed varied. These variations resulted from the local nature of both white power and civil rights activism in the state. There were some white Mississippians who were willing to work on a biracial basis to alleviate the immense poverty.

Some, like SMO board member Steve Reed, were not supporters of civil rights but were aware that integration was unavoidable, and that the war on poverty was an opportunity not to be missed. Pragmatism was not the only driving factor for white supporters of the war on poverty, however. For some, involvement in antipoverty programs was a moral duty, impelled by their religious beliefs. For many Catholics faith was a motivating factor in their civil rights and antipoverty activism. The Delta Ministry, created by the National Council of Churches, drew ministers from across the country to dedicate their efforts to addressing the brutal poverty and discrimination of the Delta. Other religious poverty warriors contributed without the institutional backing of their churches. These activists were a small minority of white Mississippians, but their role was significant in the development of an integrated war on poverty.

White supporters of the civil rights movement were few in Mississippi, though white moderates had been present in the state in slowly increasing numbers since the late 1950s. In the main, state newspapers remained prosegregation into the late 1960s. One exception was Hodding Carter II's *Delta Democrat-Times*. Hodding Carter II was, according to his biographer, a "reconstructed racist" who did not fully support integration but did take a moderate stance on black voting rights. Hodding Carter II's writing in the *Democrat* reflected his belief in humanity dignity rather than outright support for black rights. Under the leadership of his son, Hodding Carter III, the newspaper moved from a moderate stance to one supportive of integration from the late 1960s. Many of Mississippi's white moderates were women. White supremacy was, in part, predicated on the idea of protecting "white southern womanhood" from the threat of black men, and women had played active and significant roles in the defense of white supremacy for decades. However, there was also a long tradition of Southern women who spoke out against racial violence during the decades of Jim Crow. In the wake of the violence at the University of Mississippi as James Meredith enrolled, a group of white women formed Mississippians for Public Education. The group—including Pat Derian, who would go on to play a significant role in the war on poverty—did not "necessarily support school integration," according to historian Charles C. Bolton. However, they "saw the inevitability of school desegregation" and sought to preserve the state's public education by avoiding massive white flight or violence. Likewise, it was middle-class white women who met with the integrated activists of the "Wednesdays in Mississippi" group during Freedom Summer and who began "taking the first steps towards integration."[2]

White women, from segregationists like Kathleen O'Fallon to supporters of civil rights, such as Catholic activist Marjorie Baroni, played a significant role in shaping Mississippi's war on poverty. Marjorie Baroni's activism was significant because of her whiteness, because of her Catholic faith, and because of her gender. She made immense contributions to two antipoverty programs and worked to support the local civil rights movement in her hometown of Natchez, the county seat of Adams County, on the Mississippi River. Baroni's faith, race, and gender all shaped her role in the war on poverty, and in turn, these factors illuminate important facets of antipoverty activism. As historians, such as Annelise Orleck, and social scientists, including Nancy A. Naples, have illustrated, the war on poverty provided significant opportunities for women. African American women, from New York to Las Vegas, organized at the grassroots and worked tirelessly to improve the quality of services in their neighborhoods. As Christina Greene has explained, these opportunities were not limited to black women. In her study of women's biracial activism in Durham, "most responded to the War on Poverty because of its focus on daily survival issues with which they had long struggled." Many of the studies exploring female antipoverty activism focus on the maternal aspect of this activism. For example, Orleck explores the role of black mothers, while Naples's work traces activist mothering. Laurie B. Green looks at women "saving babies in Memphis," and Adina Black illustrates "parent power" in the Bronx. This maternalism was an important feature of Mississippi's early war on poverty. The Child Development Group gave black women the opportunity to earn money and gain respect for their skills by fulfilling roles that they had been performing for years—caring, educating, and nurturing children.[3]

The war on poverty had significance for women beyond the "professionalizing" of maternalism, however. As Robert Bauman has shown, it created opportunities for women of both races as administrators, board members, and program directors. In Mississippi a number of women played prominent roles in antipoverty programs in addition to the grassroots activists and volunteer mothers running Head Start centers. Kathleen O'Fallon, a white woman, was executive director of Southwest Mississippi Opportunity. O'Fallon had a varied career before becoming director of SMO. She studied at Mississippi Delta State Teachers College and Louisiana State University, before working as a teacher and then an assistant principal at a segregated school in Crosby, Mississippi. In 1960 she was elected to the state legislature as a representative of Wilkinson County, a seat she won with the support of the local White Citizens' Council. Like many white Mississippians, she was committed to segregation. It is clear that her segregationist pedigree was likely more significant to her appointment as SMO executive director than her gender; as director of Southwest Mississippi Opportunity, O'Fallon coerced African Americans into cooperation with her regime, or failing that, excluded them from the program entirely. Nonetheless, as a female executive director of a program receiving over $700,000 per year in federal funding, O'Fallon had a powerful role in shaping her antipoverty program into a mechanism to preserve white supremacy.[4]

Moderate women also played important roles in administrating and coordinating antipoverty efforts. Pat Derian, one of the founders of Mississippians for Public Education, had a critical role in the state's war on poverty as an OEO consultant. For Derian the war on poverty was the first step on a long career dedicated to promoting human rights. She went on help found the Loyalist Democrats in 1968, a biracial alternative to the all-white Regular Democrats and the black Mississippi Freedom Democrats. In the 1970s she served as president of the Southern Regional Council, sat on the executive committee of the American Civil Liberties Union, and was later appointed by President Carter to serve as Coordinator for Human Rights and Humanitarian Affairs in the State Department.[5]

It was not only white women who were able to take advantage of the opportunities for leadership. Helen Bass Williams, an African American, was the executive direction of Mississippi Action for Progress, a statewide Head Start program. Williams's race and gender together exposed her to a sustained and often brutal campaign of opposition to her leadership. However, white female poverty warriors were not immune to opposition from the white community just because of their race. Marjorie Baroni was an activist. She wrote grants and petitions and worked as an assistant director of Adams Jefferson Improvement Corporation, a community action agency she helped create. Unlike O'Fallon, though, Baroni's activism was not predicated on maintaining white supremacy. On the contrary Marjorie Baroni dedicated her life to the pursuit of social justice and racial equality. As such, Baroni paid a price for her role in the war on poverty. As with Helen Bass Williams, Pat Derian, and Kathleen O'Fallon, Marjorie Baroni's role in the war on poverty had very little to do with motherhood. For these women, the war on poverty provided an access to the power that was mostly off-limits to women. The opportunity for women to direct antipoverty programs was particularly significant in Mississippi, a state with a limited range of professional employment opportunities for men and even fewer for women. Yet many women's leadership roles were subverted and undermined, most especially those of black women. The war on poverty remained, at its heart, a paternalistic construct that did little to challenge a society in which political, social, and economic structures were shaped to preserve white male power.[6]

Baroni, born Marjorie Rushing in August 1924 in Lincoln County, was the oldest of five children of a family of sharecroppers. Her childhood was marked by the poverty of sharecropping life. She and her family picked cotton and lived in a succession of rental homes and plantation shacks. Home life was tumultuous due to the family's precarious livelihood and her father's alcoholism. The family eventually settled in Natchez, and Marjorie attended Natchez High School but left before graduation to marry nineteen-year-old Louis Baroni, the son of an Italian sharecropping family, when she was seventeen years old. As her six children grew up, Marjorie Baroni gradually awakened to the injustice and discrimination that was ingrained in daily life in the Deep South. She later vividly recalled an example of how this awakening affected her life. Baroni loved the view over the Mississippi River from the high bluffs at Natchez. "At sunset there is a breadth of view, a beauty surely unmatched anywhere in the world," she recalled. "I used to go there whenever I wanted to refresh my spirit, whenever I wanted to get in touch with the unseen world." But that was Baroni's awakening to the sickness in Mississippi society: "I began to realize how many murdered bodies must have been thrown into the river." After that, Baroni recalled, "there were days and months and years that I couldn't go look at the Mississippi River because so many bodies were being found there." Marjorie was raised in the Baptist faith, but became interested in Catholicism and was baptized into the church when she was in her early twenties. She developed an enduring faith that provided the foundation for her commitment to addressing injustice, even when the costs of her activism mounted.[7]

Beginning in the 1950s, Baroni "stopped going out," because every entertainment in Natchez was segregated. She decided, she recalled, "If everybody couldn't go, then I wasn't going." She quit her job as a full-time editor of the woman's page of the *Natchez Democrat* in 1962 because she felt she could no longer work for a white-owned newspaper. She supported the local Freedom School in 1964, participated in efforts to integrate the local public library, and joined the Mississippi Council on Human Relations. When the war on poverty arrived in Mississippi, Baroni worked with Father Morrissey at the Holy Family Parish in the operation of the local STAR center (Strategic Training and Redevelopment, a statewide adult education and job training program), which operated out of the basement of the church. She was also the driving force behind the creation of the area's own community action

Fig. 2.1. Marjorie Baroni, Marge Baroni Papers, J. D. Williams Library, Archives and Special Collections, University of Mississippi, Oxford.

program, Adams Jefferson Improvement Corporation. Mamie Mazique, a black Catholic and NAACP secretary, believed Baroni's activism was hugely important. "She helped to open up a lot of avenues in the state of Mississippi," Mazique recalled, "but especially in these three counties here—Adams, Jefferson, and Claiborne. She worked with everybody. She helped to plan and put things together and wrote proposals and organized." Baroni's activism was not limited to her hometown—or even just the state. In 1969, for example, she served as consultant to a group of seventeen community action agencies meeting to discuss rural outreach in Wisconsin. She shared her experience of community action in Natchez, the local *Rhinelander Daily News* reported. Her experience of the war on poverty was one of collaboration to produce positive change. Baroni described "with compassion the killing of her friends in the south when the movement began. The purpose of the poverty program, she said, is to 'let people know that they have a right to be here.'"[8]

Baroni contributed to broader trends of Catholic activism on behalf of the poor and disfranchised. A voracious reader, Marjorie began corresponding with radical Catholic activist Dorothy Day in the late 1950s after reading Day's 1952 autobiography. This correspondence led to Baroni's contributions to the *Catholic Worker* newspaper, as well as to a lifelong friendship. When Day toured sights of Catholic activism in Mississippi in 1968, Baroni's home in Natchez was one of her stopping points. Day's own views on the war on poverty were somewhat conflicted. In her articles for the *Catholic Worker*, Dorothy Day urged Catholics to look around them and open their eyes to the reality of poverty. Day influenced a number of key actors in the war on poverty, including Michael Harrington and Sargent Shriver, whose Catholicism, biographer Scott Stossel argued, was "in some ways analogous to Day's: rooted in the ethics of the Christian Gospels; dedicated to working toward peace, social justice, and redemption of suffering *here on earth*." "The trouble is most people do not see the poverty," Day wrote in September 1964. "Sickness and destitution put some on the welfare rolls, and they are generally despised by the righteous tax payer. This is our attitude toward poverty when we do see it." While Day welcomed the war on poverty for helping to make poverty more visible, she also warned of the danger of unwieldy governmental bureaucracy. Catholics must not forget, Day cautioned, that there will always be those "left out of social-security programs, [or] whom social legislation does not reach."[9]

Individual Catholic activists and Catholic institutions across the country worked in the war on poverty. Nuns in Selma, Alabama, were already supporting local civil rights activism. This activism meant the nuns were ostracized by the wider white community in Selma; however, the movement contributed to the transformation of religious life. The war on poverty, historian Amy L. Koehlinger explained, was central to this transformation, functioning "as a kind of bridge between old and new elements of religious life for sisters." For Father Thomas Toonen, archbishop of Alabama and North Florida, antipoverty programs were "a practical means of spreading God's kingdom on earth." In Alabama, Michigan, Texas, Louisiana, Ohio, and New Mexico, Catholic institutions played central roles in supporting the development and administration of antipoverty programs. The Catholic Church was also an early and prominent contributor to interfaith efforts to support the war on poverty, notably the Inter-religious Committee against Poverty and Women in Community Service. While the interfaith committee was somewhat unwieldy due to its size, Women in Community Service successfully expanded upon the activism of Catholic women like Marjorie Baroni.[10]

Such activism was not without consequences, however, particularly in Natchez, which had been "the heart of the antebellum slave empire." It was, by the late 1960s, home to numerous white supremacist groups, including the White Knights of the Ku Klux Klan, Americans for the Preservation of the White Race, and the Mississippi Whitecaps. Baroni's activism had difficult consequences for herself and for her family. Marjorie's activism through antipoverty programs led to her family being smeared and threatened. In an "information sheet" written by the Mississippi White Caps, Marjorie and Louis Baroni were named as "local citizens who are working with Communist-backed integration movements," and their address was listed. "Marjorie," the Mississippi White Caps flyer continued, "are you one of the white women who patted Charles Evers on the back?"[11] Marjorie received threatening phone calls and threatening notes, and was followed as she went to work. When the family moved to a new house in Natchez, their new neighbors began a petition against them moving in. Louis Baroni, Marge's husband, recalled the ostracism of those years:

> *I was ostracized at the Armstrong plant, except for a couple or three people. Marge was spat on by my neighbor right down the street, and people just didn't know what to think because we were different—my wife was different, mainly. I wasn't involved as much as she was. But I was still ostracized because of what she did.*[12]

Even Louis Baroni's brothers and sisters stopped talking to him. The Baroni's house was shot into, and FBI agents moved into their street in order to protect them. "They [the FBI] called us one day," Louis recalled, "and said they wanted to come over and talk to us . . . they said, 'Well, we're over there to protect your property.'" When Louis asked whether they would protect their lives as well as their home, the FBI agents "didn't have much of a response for that." The agents did advise Louis to leave his car at home when he went to work, because it might be bombed. But Louis's car was not the one at the Armstrong plant who was targeted—Klansmen instead planted a bomb in the car of black activist Wharlest Jackson in February 1967.[13]

Baroni's faith was a significant driving factor in her activism. Her work on behalf of the poor and disfranchised derived from her belief in the significance of "the poor being always with us." She was also angry at the blatant contradiction between the inclusive teachings of Christianity and the racial discrimination of Natchez. "My friends used to tell me not to be so angry," Baroni said later. "But I was angry as hell, and very bitter, because the ordinary, simple acts of human kindness were forbidden." While she received support from some local priests, such as Father William Morrissey and Father William Danahy, and from black Catholics, such as Mamie Mazique, the majority of her fellow white churchgoers were active participants in her ostracism. At Sunday mass people would avert their heads from the family. "With the Host in their mouths . . . they keep their bitter looks," Baroni later recalled. Baroni's experience as a pioneering Catholic activist, antipoverty program founder, and board member is reflective of the experience of the wider church. Like Baroni, a number of Catholics saw involvement in the war on poverty as part of their religious duty. For parish priest Monsignor Roland T. Winel, diocesan involvement in antipoverty efforts was a moral imperative. Winel believed that in supporting the antipoverty program, the diocese "took on a responsibility which rightfully it should have assumed."[14]

The antipoverty program in question—in which Marjorie Baroni worked and of which Monsignor Winel was the executive director—was STAR: Strategic Training and Redevelopment. STAR was created in mid-1965 as a two-year "demonstration program," funded by the Department of Labor and OEO, with $1.6 million and $5.3 million grants respectively. It was sponsored by the Catholic Diocese of Natchez-Jackson, who provided a $500,000 contribution in kind, mostly through the use of facilities. A number of diocesan staff members were also involved in running the program, from the priest who served as executive director and the nuns who ran STAR centers to the Catholic laity who volunteered. The program was created to "systematically attack the causes and the effect of poverty" in Mississippi. "Not merely statewide" though, the program proposal avowed, this program would "have a direct, personal interest on the local level—the frontiers of poverty."[15]

The Diocese of Natchez-Jackson, which encompassed the whole state, was the only native religious institution in Mississippi to sponsor an antipoverty program. This support was in part a product of the Catholic Church's unusual position among Mississippi's white religious groups. The Catholic Church was Mississippi's third largest white denominational group, but it was a distant third. Communicants of Mississippi's two largest denominations, Southern Baptist and white Methodist, accounted for almost 60 percent of the white population of the state. The Catholic Church had a membership of 70,000, which was around 3.5 percent of the population. The institution's "outsider" (non-Protestant) status and its history of maintaining integrated churches and parochial schools set it apart from Mississippi's Protestant religious organizations. White Protestant churches remained, into the 1960s, bastions of white supremacy. The state's Catholic churches meanwhile were the only churches in Mississippi in which black and white priests and parishioners came close to practicing integration. This "integration" was, until the end of the 1960s, nominal. However, it did contribute to the Catholic Church's "outsider" status within the state which, from OEO's perspective on Mississippi's closed society, made it an attractive prospect to run an antipoverty program.[16]

In its funding application, the diocese declared itself the ideal institution to operate STAR. The diocese, the application stated, "consist[s] of dedicated persons *intimately* involved in the problems of poverty on the local level and armed with 'poverty fighting' tools." The diocese directed numerous humanitarian and educational efforts during its history and its "dedication in this state-wide effort is not easily matched." The application listed the special qualifications and capabilities of the diocese, which included its statewide organizational structure with "excellent facilities." Also listed were its "dedicated, professional, and experienced personnel" and "excellent rapport with state and local agencies." The diocesan organizational capabilities and record of fighting poverty was demonstrably strong. However, its history of support and engagement with black activism was less clear. Support for civil rights activism from the Mississippi Catholic Church in earlier phases of the black freedom struggle had been sporadic. The Mississippi Catholic Church "occupied an odd no-man's land," as mostly a white institution but "never . . . a 'whites-only' church." In the 1950s, activism was constrained by a number of factors, including the segregationist sentiments of parishioners. The intimidating tactics of violent white extremists also took its toll, as did the caution of the Bishop of Natchez-Jackson, Richard O. Gerow.[17]

Many white Catholics were part of the massive resistance to desegregation. But the church hierarchy also stood behind those priests, religious, and Catholic lay leaders who took to the streets for change. While Catholic churches practiced segregation, black and white priests did "enjoy a closer working relationship than ministers of different races in the Protestant denominations." With this tentative institutional support, individual activism among the laity and clergy slowly increased throughout the 1950s. It was given episcopal authority with the 1958 National Catholic Bishop's statement rejecting compulsory segregation as irreconcilable with Christian teaching. By the early 1960s, the diocese was involved in the small but significant biracial calls for moderation. Bishop Gerow, for example, was prepared to condemn lawlessness but not speak out against Jim Crow. He was "southern in many respects in his attitude toward African American people." But at the same time, he was "a man deeply committed to helping African American people in every way he could." His successor, Bishop Joseph B. Brunini, was a longtime opponent of racial segregation but his actions were likewise constrained. Even African American Catholics provided him with little encouragement to advance desegregation of parochial schools. Black converts to Catholicism were mostly middle class, and they largely held themselves aloof from the civil rights movement.[18]

For white Catholic activist Marge Baroni, the ongoing racial prejudice of nuns and priests was difficult to face. "Their thing was prudence," Baroni recalled. There was a "gap between the teaching and the practice of the church with reference to race," which was operating in line with this "racist, repressive society." Mississippi was, according to Baroni, "like a concentration camp. It was just that oppressive. We had all this beautiful land and all these crippled people." In the 1950s, Baroni recalled, "it was perfectly acceptable for white people to sit down and talk about how black people were mistreated, so long as one didn't do anything about it. You could read the Bible and you could study your religion, but you couldn't practice it." When civil rights workers James Chaney, Andrew Goodman, and Michael Schwerner went missing in June 1964, Martin Luther King appealed to numerous religious leaders in Mississippi. He hoped "to convince someone of the gravity of the moment and his certainty that the three men were dead." But no religious leaders wanted to listen, not even the liberal editor of the state's Catholic newsletter, Father Bernard Law. Bishop Gerow was equally unwilling to become involved in Freedom Summer. When out-of-state priests and seminarians attempted to participate in Freedom Summer, Bishop Gerow ordered them to stay away.[19]

Thus, diocesan involvement with STAR was, superficially at least, a marked change in the church's approach to race relations. It reflected Bishop Brunini's racial moderation and the institutionalization of formerly renegade activism on behalf of some members of the clergy and laity. The Second Vatican Council—which convened in 1962—was also significant in legitimizing an increasingly socially active dimension to the church. The war on poverty fit perfectly with the Second Vatican Council's emphasis on social justice. *Gaudium et spes*, one of the four constitutions resulting from the council, ordered that "to satisfy the demands of justice and equity, strenuous efforts must be made . . . to remove as quickly as possible the immense economic inequalities, which now exist and in many cases are growing and which are connected with individual and social discrimination." As Catholic historian Sandra Yocum Mize notes, Vatican II "seemed to open a floodgate of innovation in North American Catholic life." This innovation found expression in new approaches to social justice, new feminist theology, and "liberation theologies" among minority ethnic groups. The involvement with STAR then, was part of this "wider surge of ecumenism." Perhaps most significantly, though, it reflected the changes which involvement in the earlier phases of the civil rights movement had wrought on the Catholic Church. In Catholic churches across the South the balance between institutional segregation and individual activism was beginning to shift by the mid-1960s.[20]

For the Department of Labor, the choice of the diocese to sponsor a proposed statewide manpower training program was a pragmatic one. Of all the private organizations in Mississippi, only the church had the resources to take on the program. OEO's support for diocesan involvement was less disinterested in the racial dimension of its choice. While the infrastructure provided by the diocese was important, it also provided a viable alternative to state institutions that would prevent racial integration within STAR. The diocese offered at least the possibility of creating a racially integrated program. The support of the diocese may have provided much needed stability and infrastructure, but it did not endear the program to many white Mississippians. White opposition to the federal funding flowing through the diocese drew on a long history of religious animosity. The majority Protestant population had long considered the minority Catholics as "religious outsiders," while the Klan—in all its iterations—had targeted Catholics as un-American. This exposed STAR to renewed massive resistance rhetoric opposing outsiders. Congressman Thomas Abernethy received a number of complaints from his constituents about STAR's funding being overseen by the diocese, for example. Responding to such complaints, Congressman Abernethy grouped the Catholic diocese with the "bunch of left-wing carpetbagging" activists also funded by the Johnson administration. His words echoed earlier accusations of communism against southern Catholics to augment their outsider status.[21]

Other politicians received similar complaints. Writing to Senator Eastland, for example, the mother of a white Head Start employee in Gulfport went even further. L. B. Taylor blended rhetoric familiar from 1950s massive resistance with the menace of Black Power in equating the Catholic priest involved in that program with "black power thinkers" and "Communist-negro white haters." Mrs. Taylor included with her letter a cartoon from her local paper. The cartoon depicted "Reds in Cuba" ordering a black OEO employee in Nashville to "spread the word," to which the OEO worker responds, "I am!" Dislike of Catholics was widespread and it drew on a range of opposition from the violent and vitriolic anti-Catholic propaganda of the Klan to opposition to outsiders—whether northern, Catholic, or Jewish. Catholic priests who supported civil rights activism were routinely targeted by the Klan. Early on in Freedom Summer, for example, arsonists burned the auditorium of a Catholic church in Hattiesburg whose priest had complimented blacks for adopting nonviolent civil disobedience. Only eleven days later, arsonists targeted another Catholic church, this time a church in Clinton whose pastor taught a Bible class for African Americans. Such support for civil rights activism by Catholic priests was the exception rather than the rule. There was no coherent southern Catholic response to postwar civil rights activism. Most often, voicing opposition to the "outsiders" who threatened the racial status quo provided southern Catholics with an opportunity to overcome their own outsider status. It gave them some common ground with segregationist Protestants. However, as with the priests in Hattiesburg and Clinton and laity, such as Marjorie Baroni, individual Catholics were involved with movement activism. One of the most prominent of these Catholic activists was Father Nathaniel Machesky.[22]

Father Nathaniel of the St. Francis Mission was the "spearhead and heart of the movement" in Greenwood. The county seat of Leflore, Greenwood was the center of the Mississippi cotton trade and in many ways the heart of segregationism in the state. Father Nathaniel was active in the peaceful and highly successful attempts to destroy the segregated structures of the town. His activism made him the target of vitriolic abuse from local white supremacist organizations. Hate sheets distributed to houses of whites in the Delta town of Greenwood drew on the language of earlier massive resistance in their attacks on Father Nathaniel. These sheets claimed he and his "Negro . . . harem" were running the St. Francis Mission, which they termed a "cesspool . . . a hotbed of integration and agitation." Father Nathaniel also sat on STAR's board of directors and established "one of the most active" centers on church property. He was a driving force behind the diocesan involvement in STAR from the program's creation. Father Nathaniel's involvement with STAR did not attract the same level of vitriol as his involvement in the Greenwood boycott, but his was a masterly understatement when, recalling his involvement with STAR on his retirement in 1981, he commented "many people got very angry with me for letting the world know there were illiterates in Mississippi." Father Nathaniel was the most visible of a number of activist clergy and laity. Others include Kate Jordan also in Greenwood, Marjorie Baroni in Natchez, and Father Peter Quinn in Hattiesburg.[23]

This increased activism incensed much of the state's white Catholic laity. They responded with a rejection of this increasing social and particularly racial activism of their church. Father Quinn, for example recalled the response of some of his white parishioners to him eating Thanksgiving with African American members of his church. "Well, you don't have to be going to a black family," Quinn recalls being told. "That's an insult to me." Born in Ireland, Quinn arrived at his church in Mississippi fairly ignorant of the racial customs and history of the state, he remembers. When he used courtesy titles to address African Americans, one white parishioner told him not to. "Don't I owe respect to them just as much as I do to a white person?" Quinn queried. The response: "Well, yes, you do, but in Mississippi, we don't do that." Diocesan actions that reflected this move toward racial inclusivity were rejected. Diocesan policy, for example, was to twin churches. A church in a more affluent area of the state would adopt a poorer twin. But many churches refused to twin with Father Nathaniel's church in Greenwood. Some went even further. Father Maloney's parishioners, for example, received a petition from his parishioners asking him to disassociate from the St Francis Mission because of the ongoing activities to promote racial justice and racial peace in Greenwood. Such activism threatened the somewhat tenuous position many white Catholics had gained in their local communities by allying with white Protestants against racial change.[24]

OEO Director Sargent Shriver, himself a Catholic, was aware of the challenge STAR faced. Not only was STAR facing a hostile white establishment but the program was, by drawing on the support of the diocese, tied to the Catholic Church's "outsider" status. Shriver made every effort to make the program appeal to the white Protestant majority of the state. STAR was designed to transform 25,000 Mississippi families "from tax liabilities to self-sustaining citizens," Shriver told Mississippians. It would, Shriver declared, provide the training and education to enable poor Mississippians to move from welfare rolls and into jobs in the state's slowly developing industrial sector, saving taxpayers billions of dollars in direct welfare payments. Shriver's use of language here was significant. He emphasized the program's value in saving taxpayers billions of dollars and creating "self-sustaining" citizens. Shriver pitched the program using race-neutral language designed to evoke the white, Protestant, middle-class ideals at the heart of the American ideology regarding citizenship and responsibility. Shriver wanted to distance the program from association with the hugely unpopular, racially connoted concept of welfare. This perception dogged the war on poverty. Even those working in antipoverty programs were not always convinced that the programs were any more beneficial than welfare. Obie Clark, a black administrator in Lauderdale Economic Advancement Program, was skeptical about the value of many of the programs. "Well, in some areas like Head Start or jobs programs, I could make a list of ten programs, and I'd say half of them were beneficial," he recalled. "And the other half, to me, perpetuated the welfare mentality and kept people from progress."[25]

Shriver was attempting to pave the way for white Mississippi's acceptance of a program that was designed to address issues—the lack of educational and job opportunities—that disproportionately affected the state's African American population. STAR researchers conducted extensive studies which showed that "complete illiteracy or functional illiteracy exists on a wide scale throughout the state." In 1965 nearly two-fifths of Mississippi's adult population had less than eight years of education, a lack of education that was heavily racially skewed. The median education level of Mississippi white adults compared favorably with the rest of the nation, while the median educational level of adult African Americans was almost half that of whites. STAR's focus on job training addressed the mass unemployment that developed due to the mechanization of agriculture and the state's lack of industrial development. These issues affected Mississippi's African Americans to a greater extent than whites. As agricultural mechanization continued to reduce the need for black labor and the pressures from civil rights activism increased, white leaders did little to create jobs for African Americans and thereby slow northward migration.[26]

Despite Shriver's efforts, STAR was met initially with a cool reception from Mississippi's press, politicians, and public. However gradually, there was an acceptance of the program from a cross-section of Mississippians. This acceptance was impelled by the carefully constructed language used by Shriver to introduce the program. It also reflected the dire need for manpower training and adult education in the state. One reporter expressed the hope that the program could "cut out the boon-doggling, that is reminiscent of the New Deal days and see if the Great Society can't be more constructive." STAR's adult education program also meant the program avoided one of the most explosive racial issues that Head Start programs faced head on: the integration of children. Even Governor Johnson, in the midst of the vehement campaign against the Child Development Group, showed an acceptance of STAR. Johnson was politically compelled to uphold an outward facade of opposition to the "boon-doggle" programs of the Great Society, but STAR propelled him to show increasing behind-the-scenes support for OEO programs. It also produced better relations between the governor's staff and OEO. STAR helped forge positive relationships between community action programs and state officials. In December 1965, for example, the program's outgoing executive director James J. Hearn thanked the governor for his "insight" and support of the goals of the program.[27]

STAR exemplifies the contradictory nature of southern opposition to federal interference. On one hand, federal intervention has been loudly and repeated decried as an anathema to southerners' much-vaunted states' rights. On the other hand, federal intervention, largely in the form of funds, had been welcomed for the sake of Mississippi's economic progress. During the New Deal, for example, the federal government invested over $60 million in the work of the Civilian Conservation Corps in Mississippi. Flood protection in the Delta, new highway construction, and the spread of electricity made the lives of many Mississippians better. As a result Mississippians "appreciated their federal government and all but worshipped FDR." But the New Deal did little to threaten segregation. With the passage of the 1964 Civil Rights Act, and the maximum feasible participation clause tying the war on poverty closely to civil rights activism, federal intervention was once again abhorred by many Mississippians. Given that southerners historically benefitted from federal largesse, there is little doubt that their opposition to the war on poverty was rooted in the association between the effort and civil rights.[28]

Governor Johnson continued to decry federal intervention in his state publicly. He was, after all, elected in 1963 asking Mississippians to "stand tall with Paul," referring to his role blocking the enrollment of James Meredith. His governorship was thus built on the rejection of the federal government in state affairs. Yet STAR's promise to turn Mississippi's uneducated and unproductive population into trained industrial workers was a tempting prospect. While the program would have to operate on an integrated basis to keep its federal funding, its economic potential compelled Johnson's support and cooperation. The initial goodwill between OEO and Governor Johnson did not last, though. Shriver's decision to refund the Child Development Group in early 1966 caused huge problems between the governor's office and OEO. But OEO's failings to maintain a good working relationship also played a part. OEO deputy director Bernard Boutin wrote apologetically to Shriver in February 1966 to explain the breakdown. It was OEO's failure to "coordinate with and keep Governor Johnson's office informed [that] threatens to undermine good relations that have been building with him." Boutin continued, the governor "is giving increasing behind the scenes support to OEO program and negative reaction could be avoided by more care for his concerns and sensibilities."[29]

However, unlike many antipoverty programs, STAR continued to find favor at the local level. The program continued to generate a positive response from businessmen, industrialists, and to a certain extent the political establishment. Letters expressing thanks to Paul Busby, the program's job development specialist, came from various sources. Many of these echoed the praise of one hotel manager who, in August 1966, commended Busby for the "services rendered by the people trained by your program" and their "highly satisfactory personnel." The initial two years of STAR's operation were so successful that its grant was extended for an additional two years in 1967.[30] Public, media, and political support for the program grew too. The voices of liberal white Mississippians were still muted; however, they were slowly increasing in number and volume. And these liberal voices singled STAR out for praise. In 1967, for example, the *Delta Democrat Times*, Hodding Carter III's paper, asked its readers for their opinion of the war on poverty. The only responses that mentioned specific programs referred to STAR, applauding the "opportunity and encouragement the program provides." STAR continued under its new grant to train its enrollees to high standards. In 1969 the manager of Taylorsville Manufacturing Company thanked the organization for "training people to become capable workers for our company" and asking that they send more personnel. The successful relationship between STAR and the Solar Hardware Corporation, meanwhile, resulted in 100-percent retention of STAR-trained employees over a number of years.[31]

The dynamic of the business-program relationship between Mississippi's burgeoning industries and STAR was markedly different from the business-community relationship in earlier phases of movement activism. Then, businesses had led calls for moderation in order to protect their economic interests, but by the late 1960s calls for racial moderation were no longer the key to protecting business interests. Mississippi's businesses were becoming involved in reciprocal relationships with STAR, as the training program provided a steady flow of trained workers. Thus, the moderating influence of white businessmen, far from supporting black advancement, manifested as a benign paternalism that prevented any genuine black voice in community action programs. As STAR board members, moderate businessmen, removed any staff members, black or white, whose influence was seen as representing the interests of the poor over their own economic interests. The acceptance of STAR by both moderate businessmen and some Mississippi newspapers was due in part to the level of white participation in the program; 45 percent of STAR's employees and 13 percent of its trainees were white. This level of white involvement in and acceptance of the program was the result of a range of factors, not least of which was the severity of poverty across Mississippi.

More significantly, though, STAR was never perceived as black and radical—a perception that plagued Head Start.[32]

The program thus garnered praise even from mayors and boards of supervisors in the Klan-dominated areas in southwest Mississippi. John Nosser, mayor of Natchez, for example, wrote to the director of the Natchez center. "I want to congratulate you," Nosser wrote, "and members of your staff for rendering the community such excellent and very needed services and assure you of our full cooperation." The county's board of supervisors followed Nosser's praise with a list of commendations, noting in December 1966 that STAR "is and has been enthusiastically accepted in the city of Natchez and Adams County. The people who have commented to us have all been high in their praise for the way the program has been conducted," and the letter continued, "we certainly join in this opinion." This praise was not limited to Adams County. Support for STAR was voiced by white politicians and businessmen in Adams County in the southwest of the state (where Marjorie Baroni was working) and also in the Delta counties of Washington and Bolivar, in Lauderdale County in the east of Mississippi and Marshall County in the north, and in Harrison County on the Gulf Coast. In part this support can be explained because STAR avoided the explosive issue of integrating children's classes. Also, it lacked the public perception of a "black" program or one connected to Black Power. The program claimed the potential to transform tax "burdens" into taxpayers and bolster Mississippi's weak economy.[33]

This potential fed into the desire of the increasing number of white moderates, industrialists, and businessmen (and eventually the political establishment) to forge a future for Mississippi's economy that would, by necessity, be integrated. Preoccupied with vitriolic attacks on the Child Development Group, Mississippi's press—and to a certain extent its white population—accepted STAR. The vast sums of money brought into the state through the program helped too. According to STAR supporter and labor activist Claude Ramsay, these funds brought whites and blacks "to the conference table" where they could "discuss problems of mutual interest." STAR's early success was, in part, the result of the sponsorship of the Diocese of Natchez-Jackson. While STAR's association with the Catholic Church did bring with it some criticism, it also provided a stable infrastructure. In its first couple of years of operation, STAR combined the individual activism of white Catholics, such as Marjorie Baroni and Father Machesky, with federal antipoverty funds, under the protection of a slow but developing institutional diocesan acceptance of integration. This potent combination of religious, racial, and antipoverty activism was not only occurring in STAR. A number of religious leaders of both races became involved in antipoverty programs. It was, Claude Ramsay believed, the involvement of Catholics in the creation and operation of STAR that spurred Baptists, such as Owen Cooper, into involvement in antipoverty efforts. Baptists and Catholics were far from the only religious denomination involved in Mississippi's war on poverty. In Columbia, Mississippi, Methodist minister N. A. Dickson helped create Marion County's community action program. There was also significant cooperation between religious organizations through antipoverty programs. In Lauderdale County, for example, Catholic priests, the Jewish rabbi, and Baptist ministers were united in their support for the program. Together they elected one representative to the county's community action program. The activist Episcopalian reverend Duncan Gray would, they all agreed, uphold the views of the entire religious community.[34]

Perhaps the most successful example of interfaith religious activism came from the National Council of Church's Delta Ministry project. The National Council of Churches developed from the Federal Council of Churches, founded in 1908. By the mid-1960s it was composed of all the mainline churches with support from other Christian denominations, including the Catholic Church. The organization was committed to bringing about positive change in society and had been an early ally of the civil rights movement, supporting Martin Luther King from the early years of his activism. As King himself said in a 1957 speech, the Council "condemned segregation again and again." The National Council of Churches became even more closely tied to activism in Mississippi in 1963, after the assassination of Medgar Evers. In 1964 the council sent volunteers to Freedom Summer, to work with COFO, CORE, and SNCC. After that tumultuous summer, the growing concern of religious leaders resulted in the creation of a "long-range ministry" to continue addressing both desperate poverty and racial inequality in the Mississippi Delta. The Delta Ministry was formally created on September 1, 1964, as "one of the most critical forms of church renewal," an "ecumenical response to the civil rights struggle in Mississippi, through recognition that human need transcends simple questions of political equality."[35] With contacts in both the civil rights networks and the white community, the ministry stood at the nexus of the various forms of activity in Mississippi in the mid-1960s: grassroots activism, antipoverty efforts, and voter registration.

The ministry also stood at the heart of the divisions in Mississippi's movement. SNCC was calling for the end to integrated activism. The defeat of the Mississippi Freedom Democrats at the Democratic National Convention in 1964 by the all-white delegation was a blow to Mississippi activists, who became more disillusioned than ever with the establishment. Class divisions that had long made NAACP and SNCC uneasy bedfellows reemerged. Thus the Delta Ministry's incorporating white middle-class outsiders was not guaranteed automatic acceptance by the region's vibrant and complex network of activists. As James F. Findlay Jr. has explained, the ministry's work was aided by the strength of Art Thomas's leadership that shaped the ministry's character as one of a "servant" church. The acceptance of the ministry and its achievements in registering voters and aiding education and antipoverty efforts stemmed from the "experience of local people fused with the support of a suffering, servant church." In fact, as Mark Newman described, Delta Ministry was so concerned with providing a practical, servant ministry that met the needs of the poor that regular worship was never really established. This servant ethos ensured that the Delta Ministry became "a significant civil rights group in Mississippi."[36]

The ministry worked through centers in Greenville, Hattiesburg, McComb, and Cleveland, with an interdenominational, interracial staff of fourteen, including outsiders—mostly ministers, such as Rims Barber, Harry Bowie, and Art Thomas—and local Mississippians. While the Delta Ministry, unlike the Catholic Diocese, did not run any antipoverty programs directly, they were central to the creation of the Child Development Group and played a role in the group's fight for survival in 1966.[37] Although serving a very different purpose than the Catholic diocese, the Delta Ministry illustrates the driving role religious activists played in the creation of the war on poverty. The Delta Ministry's ethos ensured it was more successful in overcoming the class and racial divisions than the diocese, but the Delta Ministry offered less scope for female activists. The ministry played an important role in supporting antipoverty efforts, but remained distant from OEO as the Child Development Group was independent from the Delta Ministry. The Delta Ministry could thus remain an "outsider," putting pressure on the government for increased antipoverty efforts. The diocese, on the other hand, was intertwined with OEO. The Catholic Church, though labeled an outsider, was functionally more part of a system through which existing racial and gender discriminations were reinforced.

Mississippi was not the only location where the war on poverty and religion intersected. Nor was it the only place in which that relationship created controversy. Across the country the flow of federal funds into the hands of churches sponsoring antipoverty programs raised questions about violating the separation of church and state. Many Protestants criticized Catholic programs and many Catholics criticized Protestant programs. But that did not stop OEO publicly supporting the role of religious organizations in the war on poverty. Indeed, in a 1967 interview Sargent Shriver, himself a Catholic, placed denominational efforts on the front line of the battle against poverty. These efforts, he argued, demonstrated how the war on poverty is "a people's war—America's war, not the federal government's war." Skating over suggestions that this use of antipoverty funds violates the separation of church and state, Shriver argued that churches were vital to the war on poverty. Their preexisting involvement in local communities and their almost intraregulatory nature meant they were ideally placed foot soldiers, he claimed. The Catholics are not going to "get away with something," Shriver suggested, because the Protestants will be watching them, and *vice versa*.[38]

Catholics were not the only religious organizations to participate in the war on poverty. The majority of American Jews supported the war on poverty. Involvement in antipoverty programs was an affirmation of the Jewish belief that the eradication of poverty was a moral imperative. Southern Baptists were also particularly prominent in their involvement and support of the war on poverty. Southern Baptist Minister Bill Crook, for example, was appointed by President Johnson to direct the "domestic Peace Corps" program, Volunteers in Service to America. In 1967 Baptist evangelist Billy Graham visited Washington to speak before over one hundred congressmen and forty-five of the nation's leading businessmen. Graham, who was speaking as Republicans were attempting to curtail OEO funding dramatically, nevertheless announced that "antipoverty efforts [are] a major teaching of the Bible."[39]

Both Shriver's belief that denominational programs were intraregulatory and Graham's usage of scripture to support the programs reflect an idealistic and somewhat naïve interpretation of the reality of the war on poverty. Shriver's blithe and perhaps purposeful willingness to hand over millions of dollars of funding to a Catholic church in Mississippi shows a lack of awareness of the religious and racial realities of the state. In funding STAR through the Catholic Diocese, OEO underestimated the level of opposition to Catholic activism in Mississippi—from within the church and outside. OEO also overestimated the institutions' commitment to securing racial equality. Individual Catholic activists, such as Father Nathaniel and Marge Baroni, had blazed a trail of commitment to social justice and racial equality. For Baroni, her work in the war on poverty was a stepping stone to further political and social activism. After leaving Adams Jefferson Improvement Corporation,

Baroni worked for ten years as an aide to Charles Evers who was in 1969 elected as the mayor of Fayette—the first black man elected as the mayor of a Mississippi town since Reconstruction. Baroni's social justice activism and her ostracism by the local community both continued into the 1980s.[40] As an institution, however, the Catholic Church remained more conservative. The diocese was unwilling to be an instrument of racial change at the expense of its white parishioners who did not share Baroni's commitment to racial equality. This lukewarm commitment to pursuing social justice and racial goodwill was not powerful or deep enough to ensure that STAR challenged the institutionalized racism in Mississippi.

- Chapter Three -

THE KU KLUX KLAN AND THE WAR ON POVERTY

In Mississippi in the mid-1960s, white power remained deeply and seemingly irrevocably entrenched. However, white Mississippians responses to the war on poverty were varied and they altered over time. Marge Baroni and Father Nathaniel Machesky are but two examples of a small minority of white Mississippians who embraced the war on poverty and used it as a means to continue their work to improve society and address racial inequality. There were also a number of white moderates involved with antipoverty efforts; men and women were unhappy with integration but saw it as unavoidable. Once the initial backlash to the Child Development Group faded, both white supporters and white moderates played an important role in shaping the state's war on poverty into a mechanism of white authority within the new integrated reality. These moderates increasingly worked in concert with moderate African Americans, most often NAACP leaders rather than SNCC and CORE activists. Together, such alliances shaped the post–Child Development Group landscape of the war on poverty. White and black moderates, for example, forged a new statewide Head Start program, Mississippi Action for Progress, to replace the Child Development Group. The new program was deemed acceptable by the state's white power structure because, while its board of directors was integrated, the board's white moderates eschewed the kind of radicalism and genuine black participation that had characterized the Child Development Group.

However, these moderate alliances were not the only forces shaping the war on poverty. Equally significant were white extremists. White supremacists took particular exception to the war on poverty. They believed it embodied everything they opposed: a "socialist-communist" framework; federal intervention in the state; black empowerment; and perhaps most offensively of all, its reliance on white moderates willing to accept integration to gain access to federal funds. While united in their hatred of the war on poverty, however, white extremists were deeply fragmented. White supremacist groups flourished in 1960s Mississippi, but they rarely worked together. Among the most violent of the white extremists was the Ku Klux Klan. Mississippi was home to a number of Klan groups in the 1960s: the United Klans of America; the White Knights of the Ku Klux Klan, and the Original Knights of the Ku Klux Klan. While rhetorically united as "white Christians" against common enemies—African Americans, the federal government, white race-traitors—these groups were in competition for members and disagreed over tactics and targets, but they all responded to the war on poverty with a mixture of vitriol and violence. They targeted African Americans, particularly Child Development Group staff who were working to use the federal funds of the war on poverty to promote widespread empowerment of poor blacks. Increasingly, as white moderates became involved in antipoverty programs—particularly Mississippi Action for Progress—extremist groups also targeted them. White Mississippi Action for Progress workers were labeled traitors of the white race and stooges of a federal government conspiracy to create a socialist "Black Republic" in the South.[1]

White supremacist violence drew on a powerful tradition in Mississippi. This extremism was most visible through the two earlier incarnations of the Ku Klux Klan during Reconstruction and in the 1920s. However, these were merely the most visible peaks of white violence, embodied in the easily recognizable white robes of the Klan. White violence against African Americans, Jews, and Catholics, and against whites who breached the accepted racial norms was an enduring feature of life in Mississippi. The first Klan 'den' appeared in Carroll County, Mississippi in 1866, only months after the Klan had been founded by six Confederate veterans in Pulaski, Tennessee. Throughout 1867 Klan dens sprang up in counties across Mississippi. Garbed in white robes, the Klansmen perpetrated acts of brutal violence against emancipated African Americans. This racial violence was by no means new, however. As historian Michael Newton has explained, the Klan's tactics closely resembled the slave patrols of the antebellum South. Rather than enforcing slavery, though, the Klan's ten-year reign of violence during Reconstruction had particular economic and political functions. Poor whites feared economic competition with freedmen, and so they joined the Klan to subjugate African Americans anew. Klan violence was also "blatantly political," supporting the Democratic Party in order to "overturn 'carpetbag' rule." The first incarnation of the Klan faded away in the mid-1870s, as Reconstruction collapsed and the state began to construct new mechanisms to oppress African Americans. But the violence did not end. New terrorist groups took their place. In 1891, for example, a paramilitary group called the Whitecaps spread across southwest Mississippi to control black labor through nocturnal terror.[2]

Acts of violence and terror continued through the early decades of the twentieth century. However, it peaked once again following World War I as the Ku Klux Klan became a powerful force. This second incarnation of the Klan grew out of a tumultuous environment of anti-immigrant, anti-Catholic, and anticommunist fervor, as well as the glorification of the original Klan in the 1915 film *Birth of a Nation*. When the Klan became a national political force in the 1920s, fraternal lodges flourished in Mississippi. Though this new incarnation drew on the earlier Klan formation and rituals, the Reconstruction-era Klan had focused its violence on African Americans, scalawags, and carpetbaggers. The primary role of the 1920s Klan however, was the "defense of state and society against the menace of Roman Catholicism." In Mississippi, Klansmen also targeted Jews, nonwhite immigrants, and particularly African Americans. The second Klan reached its peak in Mississippi in 1923 and dominated Mississippi's delegation to the 1924 Democratic National Convention, while nationally its membership reached five million. Klan influence declined rapidly in the late 1920s, although acts of terrorism did continue through the Great Depression. Whether the perpetrators were garbed in Klan robes or not, however, violence remained unabated. While lynching statistics are notoriously unreliable, it is clear that at least five hundred lynchings occurred in Mississippi between 1882 and 1951.[3]

The third incarnation of the Klan, in the civil rights era, resembled its predecessors in the belief that it was defending the "ultimate values of . . . society from hideous attack." A Klansman's outlook, David M. Chalmers has explained, was "a paranoid feeling of persecution with himself as the central object of an apocalyptic conspiracy." Edward L. McDaniel helped organize the White Knights of the Ku Klux Klan and spent two years as Grand Dragon of Mississippi's United Klans of America before becoming an FBI informant. His professed understanding of the civil rights movement reflects the paranoid feeling Chalmers describes. "I honestly believe," McDaniel told an interviewer in 1977, "the communist conspiracy was behind all the trouble we had. . . . Take the late Martin Luther King. He was proved by the FBI that he belonged to many communist front organizations. Now, I'm not saying that this man was a communist per se. But he was being duped and used and didn't realize it, or he may have realized it, I don't know." This "apocalyptic conspiracy" was a common narrative in the Deep South. It drove both Klan membership and a widespread acceptance of the Klan by many white Mississippians. The exact date at which the Klan began again in Mississippi is unclear. The Ku Klux Klan had been conspicuously absent in Mississippi even as it gained strength in many Deep South states in the 1950s. However, historian Michael Newton has noted that acts of violence occurring in Mississippi in the 1950s were distinctly "Klan-like." Key leaders were already involved in acts of violence or out-of-state Klans before the 1960s. Future Mississippi Klan leader Samuel H. Bowers, for example, joined the Louisiana-based Original Knights of the KKK in Natchez around 1955. By the early 1960s, and most definitely after the integration of the University of Mississippi in 1962, the White Knights of the Ku Klux Klan (an offshoot of the Original Knights) was growing rapidly in the state.[4]

The White Knights were the most violent and widespread of Mississippi's Klan groups. By May 1964 they had established fifty-two Klaverns in thirty-four of Mississippi's eighty-two counties, with an estimated 10,000 Klansmen. From his headquarters in Laurel, Samuel Bowers, the Imperial Wizard of the White Knights, oversaw the construction of an elaborate constitution and an organized, highly secretive, and militant Klan. Bowers retained tight control of the activities of the White Knights, giving orders to his Klansmen to carry out "projects," ranging from cross burnings to "eliminations." Bowers did not hold a monopoly on the Klan, however. Other Klan groups quickly followed the Original Knights and the White Knights. The Alabama-based United Klans of America (UKA), led by Robert Shelton, began recruiting in Mississippi in May 1964, making Adams County a base from which to invade the state. All the Klan groups professed to be nonviolent, while perpetrating horrific acts of violence, brutality, and murder. They drew on similar quasi-Masonic rituals and placed great importance on secrecy. The White Knights "made such a fetish of secrecy" that its entire operation was "underground." A 1964 directive, for example, ordered Klansmen to "train yourself to see yourself as a skilled detective would see you," and cautioned "remember, the men who join you are going to be walking around with *your* life in *their* hands." A 1966 directive entitled "Secrecy" warned the White Knights that "secrecy is more than just not talking. True secrecy is a HARDENED MENTAL ATTITUDE by which an individual convinces HIMSELF that he is not a member and that there is no such organization." All of the Klan groups used front organizations "usually to give the impression that the Klan is a sporting club or civic organization," often employing terms such as "Christian," "Defense," or "Civic." Whatever their varied fronts, the white supremacist organizations in Mississippi became the most ferociously violent of all Klans between 1963 and 1968.[5]

The Klans were not the only groups created to preserve and promote white supremacy. Mississippi was teeming with violent and ostensibly nonviolent groups, from the Americans for the Preservation of the White Race (APWR)—on the Klan end of the violence spectrum—to the less violent but more influential White Citizens' Council. The White Citizens' Council was created in the wake of the Supreme Court's 1954 *Brown v. Board of Education* ruling. Meeting in Indianola, in Sunflower County, Robert Patterson and other avowed segregations joined to form an organization to resist the Court ruling. Drawing on the work of Judge Tom P. Brady in his condemnation of *Black Monday*, the White Citizens' Council developed a powerful network of state-supported groups with an influential membership that worked to preserve white supremacy, primarily through economic and political methods. As historian David Cunningham has shown, the presence of this network of segregationist resistance organizations meant the Klan's existence was "rendered redundant by a myriad of other, less overtly brutal, forms of repression." In other southern states such as North Carolina, which lacked the depth of support for segregation from local government and White Citizens' Councils, the Klan was much more widespread. While civil rights–era Klan membership in North Carolina accounted for 50 percent of all Klansmen, Mississippi Klansmen accounted for only 8 percent of the total number. This model, which Cunningham terms the "mediated competition model," also explains the geographical spread of the Klan within Mississippi. Where existing mechanisms of segregation were strong and competition for economic, political, and social power between the races was limited by the powerful oppression of the local black population, Klan groups were limited or not present at all. This is particularly evident in the Delta, marked by intense violence and home to a number of White Citizens' Councils, but not home to the Klan. The Klan dominated a large swath of Mississippi, however: from Wilkinson and Adams Counties spreading northeast to Lauderdale, Neshoba, and Kemper Counties.[6]

Although never as widespread as in North Carolina, the various Klan groups in Mississippi committed a greater number of brutal acts of violence and terror. They reached the peak of their influence, membership, and violence during Freedom Summer in 1964. In addition to the APWR and multiple competing Klan factions, less well known white supremacist organizations also sprung up in response to Freedom Summer. Among them was the Mississippi White Caps, a rejuvenated 1890s violent group, and the Association of Tenth Commandment Conservatives, a group created to expel the impending "invaders." Together these white supremacist organizations set Mississippi ablaze in the summer of 1964. Over the ten weeks of Freedom Summer, at least thirty-seven African American churches were burned and many more homes, six people were murdered, and there were thirty-five shootings. McComb, in Pike County in the southwest of the state, was home to particularly intense violence, reflecting the town's high concentration of violent white supremacist organizations, which was estimated at over one hundred Klansmen in two Klaverns. During 1964 there were eighteen bomb blasts targeting African American homes and churches. Civil rights workers were beaten and threatened with shotguns. Local law enforcement officials did little to counteract this violence. Although three Klansmen were arrested in connection with some of these bombings in October 1964 and found guilty, they were given only suspended sentences.[7]

Among the targets in McComb was Aylene Quinn, an African American activist and owner of a diner, called South of the Border. Aylene Quinn was part of the early generation of activists who became engaged in rights activism in the wake of the World War II. She joined the NAACP and registered to vote in the early 1950s. On moving to McComb and opening her café in 1953, Aylene Quinn remained committed to activism, despite the white terrorism that shaped life in southwest Mississippi. As Aylene Quinn later told an interviewer, "If you were a member of the NAACP you kept it kind of a secret. If you had any kind of a job or anything you couldn't let it be known." Despite the dangers she faced, Aylene Quinn was undaunted. She was one of the many women, most of whom are not documented in the historical record, whose unflinching courage in the face of such violence ensured the movement survived. When SNCC activist Bob Moses arrived in McComb in 1961, Quinn welcomed him and "transformed her little neighborhood café into a hub of movement activity." She was known to the SNCC activists who frequented her café as "Mama Quinn." Mendy Samstein, a SNCC field secretary in McComb at the time, said of Quinn: "She is kind and good to everyone. But more than that, she is a towering figure of strength. She can't be intimidated." Even as the intensity of the violence reached fever pitch during Freedom Summer, Aylene Quinn stood firmly behind the COFO activists.[8]

Quinn had long been the target of threats and harassment for serving civil rights activists. The local police raided her café twice, once fining her $150 for selling liquor in a dry county. Her white landlord threatened to evict her if she did not stop serving COFO activists. On September 20, 1964, Klansmen bombed her home. The event was described by SNCC activist Mendy Samstein, who was in McComb that night. "The first bombing comes at 10.30 pm. Most of the Negroes of McComb are in bed—but only some are sleeping. These days most Negro adults in McComb don't fall asleep until the wee hours of the morning. Then the blast. That sickening, anguishing sound that has been heard twelve previous times over the last three months—the sound that Negroes in McComb have come to know so well." The bomb blasted "all but one of the eight rooms of the house." Aylene Quinn was not at home that evening, though her children and her pregnant babysitter were, and they managed to escape with only minor injuries. Even this attempt on her life did not stop Aylene Quinn, however. When local police accused her of bombing her own home, Quinn traveled to Washington alongside two other female bombing victims to meet with President Johnson and members of Congress. Johnson's advisors did not want him to take the meeting; only a month before the presidential election they felt there was "no political benefit in meeting with these people." But Johnson did listen to Aylene Quinn's request to send federal troops to McComb. The president did not send troops in, but as historian John Dittmer explains, it is likely he threatened to do so—and the threat proved enough. A week later eleven Klansmen were arrested, "along with enough weapons, ammunition, and explosives to start a small war."[9]

The local police response to the bombing of Quinn's home—first the suggestion she herself had bombed the home in which her young children were sleeping and, later, swift action to round up those responsible under threat of federal intervention—illustrates the depth of Klan support among law enforcement in Pike County. This was not unique to southwest Mississippi. In the Klan-dominated counties of the state, from Wilkinson County on the Mississippi River to Kemper on the Alabama border, Klan influence extended into sheriff's offices and spread among highway patrolmen. Known Klansmen included a sheriff in Adams County and two deputy sheriffs in Copiah and Holmes Counties. Those suspected of Klan involvement included two sheriffs in Amite and Walthall Counties. In Pike County powerful businessman and Klansman J. Emmett Thornhill claimed in 1964 that there were 10,000 Klansmen in Mississippi, among them police officers. As one journalist noted, Klansmen probably included Thornhill's son who was a police officer in Pike County. Thornhill was, according to a Sovereignty Commission report, the "wheels behind the fellows that are doing the bombings" in McComb in 1964, including the bombing of Aylene Quinn's home. Commission investigators believed his son was indeed a member of the Klan and was "allegedly assisting his father." Those not affiliated with or sympathetic to the Klan lived in fear of reprisals as Klansmen took over the guidance of thought patterns in local communities. Campaigns of terror were unleashed against whites and blacks who dared to defy their regime. There was, as James W. Silver described, a "hyper-orthodox social order in which the individual had no option except to be loyal to the will of the white majority. And the white majority . . . subscribed to an inflexible philosophy which was not based on fact, logic, or reason."[10]

It was in Neshoba County that the Klan's influence permeated most deeply into local law enforcement. Justices of the peace, sheriff's officers, and highway patrolmen numbered among Mississippi's Klansmen. As Reverend Clay Lee, a Methodist minister in Philadelphia, recalled, "for all practical purposes, the Klan . . . controlled what was said and what was not said." The FBI described Neshoba's Klavern of White Knights as "one of the strongest Klan units ever gathered and one of the best disciplined groups." Agent Joseph Sullivan recalled that Neshoba Klansmen "owned the place. In spirit, everyone belonged to the Klan. . . . [T]here proved to be no difference between a real Klansman and someone who was not a member but whose friends and neighbors were. Even if they themselves had declined to join the Klavern, they identified totally with those who had." It was in Neshoba County that the most brutal and high-profile violence of Freedom Summer occurred. Here, civil rights activists James Chaney, Andrew Goodman, and Michael Schwerner were murdered by Klansmen, a number of whom were police officers. Their disappearance sparked a manhunt that made Mississippi the focus of federal, national, and international attention. When the bodies of the three men were discovered buried in an earthen dam in Neshoba County, the FBI attempted to unravel the web of Klansmen and police officers who caused and covered up their deaths.[11]

Women were instrumental in shaping massive resistance and maintaining white supremacy, as historian Elizabeth Gillespie McRae has described, through the "myth of the sanctity of the white woman" and in more pragmatic roles. In the second incarnation of the Klan, women "poured into the Klan movement" making the Women's Ku Klux Klan "one of the largest and most influential right-wing organizations" of the 1920s. However, in the 1960s, women's did not organize Klan groups en masse. The Klan of the 1960s was more often used as a means of sidelining women. FBI agents in Mississippi often found that "a lot of Klansmen used the Klan as an excuse to go off and screw some women and their wife wouldn't know where they were." Many Klaverns were often drinking clubs, a place giving "alienated working-class whites a rationale for abandoning their wives and families to spend their evenings carousing and ineffectually cursing blacks." The vast majority of these Klansmen were poor. As David M. Chalmers notes, "the Klan . . . drew its membership almost exclusively from that resentful portion of society that looked on physical resistance as the necessary and suitable expression of beleaguered white manhood." The Klan's construction of "white manhood" cast its members in the role of defending passive, pure white southern womanhood from the sexual threat of black men. There were a number of factors significant to this idea of "white manhood," including religion, sexuality, and nationality. Whiteness was, as David Cunningham describes, "simultaneously inclusive and exclusive," and Klans tied racial anxieties to other values, most often (a Protestant) God and patriotism. Networks—families, neighborhoods, workplaces, and clubs—were important factors in drawing individuals into the Klan, but socioeconomic status was significant too.[12]

It was competition for jobs and economic resources that was the "baseline condition" for racial antagonism. For native Mississippian and FBI agent William Dukes, who investigated Klan violence in the 1960s, Klansmen were people who have "never had anything particularly. As a general rule they're a kind of the hard scrabble group; they've had to work hard for everything; they never had anything. They see on every hand the black group getting more and more benefits and, in their terminology, 'getting more and more uppity.' They see themselves—it's an ego thing with them is what it amounts to. I think essentially they're lashing out as a result of it." Klan membership "clustered in working and lower-middle class sectors," with high-status individuals more likely to join White Citizens' Councils. Being a member of the Citizens' Council was politically and socially acceptable for white Mississippians of a certain socioeconomic status, where Klan affiliation was not. In 1956, for example, on NBC's *Meet the Press* show, Governor J. P. Coleman defended the Citizens' Council but disavowed any knowledge of the Klan. White Citizens' Council members were, "the pillars of the community," according to former Klansman Edward McDaniel, most likely to be bankers, landowners, and merchants. For example, Citizens' councilman Judge Tom Brady was, McDaniel averred, "sympathetic [to the Klan], but he wouldn't have joined." As Judge Brady told an Indianola audience in 1954, "none of you men look like Ku Kluxers to me. I wouldn't join a Ku Klux [Klan] . . . because they hid[e] their faces; because they [do] things you and I wouldn't approve of [but] I'm not going to find fault with anyone who did [join the Klan]." For Imperial Wizard Samuel Bowers, this division between the White Citizens' Council and the Klan groups was primarily economic. "Most of the Citizens' Council people regarded themselves as economically superior to most of the Klan people.... The economic class lines actually prevented any kind of normal rapport which should have occurred [between the two organizations]." Membership of one organization did not bar you from the others, however. McDaniel, for example, was a member of the Citizens' Council, the Klan, and the Americans for the Preservation of the White Race.[13]

The Klan was thus dominated by poor whites who felt their economic status was threatened by the newly empowered African Americans. The war on poverty—offering economic opportunity to the state's poor population—was a target of particular hated. Poor whites, whether members of the Klan or not, most often refused to send their children to integrated Head Start classes or attend integrated adult education centers themselves. African American NAACP activist Franzetta Sanders played a central role in developing Head Start centers on Mississippi's Gulf Coast. She later recalled her efforts to recruit poor whites. "So, we had to get out and canvass door-to-door, 'Bring your children. Let them come to Head Start....' We had to go to all neighborhoods. We went to white neighborhoods, and some of them, like I say, they were just as poor as we were. Some of them poorer and some of them looked a whole lot worse than we did, but, 'No. They're not going to go. Not my children. Don't come in my yard. I don't want you n's in my yard.' And blah, blah, the n word, whatever." Rather than joining Head Start, the white community responded with force. The local mayor told activists to "stop going into the neighborhoods," and the "police came out with the dogs." The mayor told Sanders, "This is not going to be anything but a babysitting program. Some more money they're giving lazy people." "We wanted whites working along with blacks," Sanders recalled, "and we could not get it." For many white Mississippians, the economic opportunity of the Great Society appeared to be created solely for African Americans and was thus another facet of the federal government's attempts to overturn their social order.[14]

The responses of white parents and politicians to the war on poverty were reflected in the Klan's hate literature, which stoked opposition to Great Society programs. "You know this 'New Deal' business by Franklin Roosevelt who started it, and then Kennedy with the 'New Frontier' and now the President of the United States with 'The Great Society,'" one Klan flyer read. "What great society? It appears to be a society of homosexuals, racketeers, socialists and Communists. We don't want any great society, we are damn well satisfied with the 'old time Americanism,' that's the only society you want." Other flyers were created solely to address the perceived "give-away" and "socialist" nature of the Great Society. A UKA flyer, for example, was written as if from a child's perspective, questioning his elders on why they had failed to see the dangers of the Great Society. Written around the image of a child, the flyer asked "When I get sick, whose doctor can I go to, my doctor or the government doctor? . . . if I work a little harder, or better, or get lucky, will I be able to keep more of what I earn than the other fellow who didn't work as hard, or as well, or get as lucky. When did you get this idea that government can take care of everybody? You know you can't get something for nothing; yet you pretend that people in Washington can give you things without first taking them away from you." The flyer ended, "Aren't you ashamed!!!"[15]

For the Mississippi Association for Constitutional Government, a front organization for the Klan, liberal-socialist elements were "working so hard to diss-arm [sic] our country, mongrelize our citizens and establish an international, atheistic, class-less socialistic, one-world government administered by the UNITED NATIONS." The Klan's hate-sheet, *A Delta Discussion*, often attacked the war on poverty directly. The *Delta Discussion* sheet was, it pronounced, "a means of informing you so as to keep you ever alert to the dangers to our freedom and way of life that confront us today. As you know, most other means of mass communication are dominated by the left wing 'liberal' establishment in this country—thus presenting only their side of the issues involved." Unlike the national news media, *A Delta Discussion* reminded its readers, it was "Written—Printed—Distributed by local Patriots." In reality, *A Delta Discussion* spread white supremacist venom and incited violence against African Americans and whites perceived as supporting civil rights activism. Most often, the sheets were filled with description of storeowners who had served African Americans, or white antipoverty workers who were "promoting integration," along with their full names and addresses. For the authors of *A Delta Discussion*, the war on poverty was a "federal pig trough" that enables "outsiders" and, worse still "LOCAL WHITES" to "teach the 'art' of integration." Head Start is, one *Discussion* sheet pronounced, a "federal fisco [sic] which is nothing but a prep school for integration."[16]

The UKA propaganda went even further in connecting the Great Society to "black power" and venereal disease. A 1967 UKA flyer offered an ironic flyer ostensibly supporting Julian Bond, the SNCC activist who had won election the previous year to the Georgia House of Representatives but had been initially denied his seat by the state representatives until the Supreme Court intervened. The UKA flyer included a cartoon image ostensibly showing Julian Bond, which drew on a number of offensive racial stereotypes. Bond was depicted with an afro and a hoop earring, holding an arrow and wearing an NAACP armband. The crude racial stereotyping is familiar Klan territory. However the captions surrounding the cartoon reveal much about the Klan's ideology. It is important that the violence and vitriolic language and offensive imagery so often employed by white supremacist organizations not mask the complexity of the myths created to justify their actions. The flyer urges "Black Brothers, Bleeding heart liberals, White Sluts" to "vote Julian Bond, your banana canidate [sic] for Democratic Presidential [sic] nomination." The Bond depicted was captioned saying "Ah is youse canidate [sic] for welfare, white women and black power! Right on! Right on . . . Cadillacs, ripple, VD and Welfare! Right on!" The caption fuses the core myths and fears on which white segregationists drew—miscegenation, the spread of venereal disease, interracial sex, the threat of Black Power, and liberal welfare policies that benefited African Americans. The fusion of Cadillacs—a common reference among white segregationists to denigrate the aspirations of the black middle class—with welfare lays the groundwork for the myth of the "Cadillac-driving Welfare Queen," which Ronald Reagan would employ to great effect less than a decade later.[17]

Some Klan literature went further still. According to the *Christian Conservative Communique*, the Great Society was part of an effort to bring Mississippi "more directly under federal control." In August 1965 the *Communique* declared that the "Government of the Southern states" would "change completely." "With the illiterate negro and white voters commanding a bloc *that will decide all future elections*, with effective splitting of the already registered whites into factions opposing each other, we see that the South is to vanish forever under the heel of negro socialist dictatorship. The black republic is born!" This republic was being created by "federal dictatorship . . . established by the high command of the communist party through 'liberal' socialist agitators and professional organized mobs." The war on poverty was a vital part of this conspiracy, the *Christian Conservative Communique* told Mississippians. "From the 'Lincoln Project' planned in 1956 by the communist party and carried from the Highlander Folk School to the present day 'Head Start program' and 'Poverty act of 1965' the communists have succeeded in accomplishing their goal of a black republic." The "Poverty act" was only the first stage in this process, however. "Soon to follow will be the big push by negro nationalist movements (Black Muslims, etc.) for the establishment of a federally-supported area for blacks. This is the death sentence for the South! This is the punishment for voting against the fuhrer (Lyndon Johnson) in 1964." The "results" of this were, according to the *Communique*, "already clearly coming into focus." They included, "the rise of a new class of southern politicians, a breed of demogogues [sic] coming to power on a wave of pie-in-the-sky promises of free state money for everyone," "increased taxes," and "the movement of industry and business from the unbearable demands of the welfare state." The final stage would be, the *Communique* declared, "the establishment of federal reservations of the southern states, then populated only by government bureaucrats and their negro dependents . . . the establishment of the dictatorship of the proletariat."[18]

By the time the war on poverty arrived in Mississippi the Klans were under intense scrutiny from the FBI and from the House Committee on Un-American Activities (HUAC). The HUAC investigation into the Klan publicized the identity of Klansmen and revealed multiple examples of the defrauding of Klan members by their superiors. Edward L. McDaniel, for example, who developed the White Knights in 1964 before defecting to the UKA, was accused by Sam Bowers and others of skimming Klan money. HUAC investigations were somewhat successful in recasting the Klan as un-American and perhaps more significantly so in their discovery of the failure of Klansmen to pay their taxes. The FBI's COINTELPRO infiltrations of the Klan also served to weaken the Klan groups; McDaniel was a prominent example of a senior Klansman turned informant. However, the FBI operation also had unintended consequences. It led to hardcore Klansmen's contribution to the neo-Nazism, Christian Identity, paramilitarization, and anti-federal-government rhetoric prevalent in the 1970s. The FBI and HUAC investigation were not accompanied by statewide investigation in Mississippi. Alabama's attorney general Richmond Flowers conducted an extensive investigation into the extent and political influence of the Klan. Meanwhile Mississippi's attorney general Joe Patterson linked the existence of the Klan to the presence of civil rights activists. However, there was, according to an FBI agent working in McComb in the mid-1960s, increasingly productive cooperation between state and federal law officers. There was also an increased willingness and ability at the federal level (and much later, at the local level) to prosecute racial murder.[19]

"It was just really a war," former FBI agent William F. Dukes recalled. "We moved in there with—oh, I think at one time we probably had seventy men. Now when I say 'men' these investigations are the best illustrations that I know really of the close cooperation between law enforcement agencies at all levels, particularly the state, the Highway Patrol, and the FBI." Some Mississippi businessmen and local politicians also acted to lessen the damage done by Klan violence to their economic prospects. In Laurel, a Klan stronghold in Jones County (and home to Imperial Wizard of the

White Knights Sam Bowers), newly elected mayor William Henry Bucklew launched a campaign in 1966 to end the Klan's reign of terror in his town. A die-hard segregationist—he had been director of George Wallace's 1964 presidential campaign in Maryland, North Carolina, and Virginia—Bucklew faced strong opposition in his public confrontation of the Klan. Though no prosecutions resulted, Bucklew did succeed in securing the public support of law enforcement officials, local businesses, and churches in his campaign to end Klan violence. The campaign temporarily decreased instances of Klan violence in Laurel.

However, the Klan mentality remained in Laurel and across the state. In 1966 no schools were integrated and white-collar jobs remained off limits to African Americans. Most African Americans in Jones County were too afraid to participate in the limited activism of the local NAACP chapter. Bucklew, determined to maintain segregation but unwilling for the local economy to suffer as a result of Klan violence, was happy to reap the benefits of the oppressive atmosphere the Klan projected. In doing so, he fostered the conditions and complacency, if not the complicity, that sustained the Klan so racial violence in Laurel could again flourish.[20] No such attempts to lessen the stranglehold of the Klan were made in the southwest of Mississippi. The lack of industry—the total absence of it in Amite and Wilkinson counties—meant there were very few businessmen with a vested interest in stabilizing race relations. There were some whites who were willing to make efforts towards biracial cooperation. However, their involvement was aimed at controlling and containing moves toward racial integration. It thus had no effect on ameliorating the pervasive and threatening atmosphere of racial violence in southwest Mississippi.

White extremist influence remained potent and widespread. In Hattiesburg, Forrest County, Klansmen targeted activist Vernon Dahmer. Like Aylene Quinn, Dahmer was economically independent, "a prosperous farmer and father of eight," and a member of the older generation of NAACP activists. He had been president of the Hattiesburg NAACP since the 1950s and, in the early 1960s, opened his home to SNCC activists. Hattiesburg was home to the largest Freedom Summer project in the state. Dahmer dedicated his life to voter registration: "if you don't vote, you don't count" was his creed. His activism brought him to the attention of local Klansmen. As Vernon's wife, Ellie Dahmer, recalled, "We got phone calls all through the night. Cars would pull out in the yard, run up in the driveway, and turn around. In fact, we slept in shifts. I usually slept the first part of the night and Vernon slept the last part of the night, so that we could watch and protect our home." By

1966, though, "things had eased up. We had begun to not get any calls, not nearly as many as we used to get." Vernon Dahmer had not eased up in his activism, however. While the 1965 Voting Rights Act had abolished poll tax on presidential and congressional elections, it remained for state and local elections. On January 9, 1966, Dahmer announced on the radio that he would pay the poll tax of registered black voters, if they could not afford it.[21]

That night eight Klansmen drove once again to the Dahmers' home and this time, they attacked. They firebombed the house in which Ellie and Vernon Dahmer and their young family slept, and fired shots into the house. To give his family time to escape, Vernon shot at the Klansmen from the burning house. Both he and his ten-year-old daughter Betty were badly burned. Vernon's daughter recovered, but Vernon himself did not—he died of smoke inhalation in hospital the following day. His murder shocked the local community and prompted a response that was unprecedented. Donations flooded in to support Ellie and her family, to help rebuild the house and store that had burned to the ground. Donations came not just from African Americans in Hattiesburg, but from some whites too, including the Hattiesburg Chamber of Commerce. Klan influence over the local community was waning. Some members of the local white community were less tolerant of these extreme acts of extralegal racial violence, and they expressed dismay at the murder of Vernon Dahmer rather than the disdain that had been the most common response to the disappearances of Chaney, Schwerner, and Goodman.[22]

The attack on Vernon Dahmer and his family was an example of Klan influence spreading across county lines and between extremist groups; it involved the White Knights and the Americans for the Preservation of the White Race in Jones and Forrest Counties. However, there remained friction between Mississippi's rival Klan factions: the United Klans of America, White Knights, and Original Knights of the Ku Klux Klan. These organizations were rife with suspicion and discord not least due to the extensive infiltration of their ranks by the FBI. Membership numbers were dwindling, serving to lessen their power and influence. By 1967 the United Klans' membership was down to five hundred from its 1964 peak of at least three thousand, while the White Knights had two hundred dues-paying members from a 1964 peak of at least two thousand Klansmen. The diminishing Klan influence and membership did lead to a decrease in the levels of racial violence. It did not, however, translate into a decrease in the powerful grip of white supremacists. Other white supremacist organizations remained active, including APWR and White Citizens' Councils, which may have siphoned members from

Klaverns but which also served to bolster a white society accepting of racial violence.[23]

Americans for the Preservation of the White Race had been active in southwest and central Mississippi since its creation in Natchez in 1963. Its activities included organizing "buy-ins," occasionally in collaboration with the Klan or White Citizens' Councils, to support white merchants suffering under NAACP boycotts. The efficacy of these buy-ins was questionable. Indeed, a Sovereignty Commission investigator looking into the impact of the NAACP boycott on Edwards in Hinds County found that not only did APWR and Klan buy-ins not increase the amount of money the merchants took, but they also discouraged the few African Americans who had been breaking the NAACP boycott from purchasing. The APWR, like some Klan groups, attempted to cultivate a nonviolent facade. Arsene Dick, the president of the APWR, for example, claimed that his group was "non-political, non-profit, and by all means non-violent." In the wake of the bombings in McComb in 1964, police chief George Guy told Sovereignty Commission investigator Virgil Downing that the local APWR group had been "very cooperative" and assisted him in enforcing the law "in every way." Although the Klan, he conceded in a masterful understatement, did contain some radical members who had taken the law into their own hands.[24]

In reality, the APWR contributed to an atmosphere permissive of violence, and its members were linked to brutal acts of racial violence, including murder. As Ellie Dahmer recalled, "The Klansmen could have never thrived had they not had an atmosphere to thrive in, had people not gone along with their thinking with their lowdown doings, they never would have been able to go on with it like they had." In fact, several of the twelve men accused of murdering Vernon Dahmer in January 1966 had links with the APWR. Clifford Wilson, one of the accused, had been president of the Jones County APWR. The Laurel APWR, meanwhile, held a dinner to raise money for the accused men as the trial began in February 1968. Proceeds from the ten-dollar-a-plate dinner would go to "defend our white Christian citizens being charged and persecuted under the so-called Civil Rights acts," averred Sybil Nix, the wife of one of the accused. The main attraction at the dinner was guest speaker Asa Carter, a Klan leader from Alabama. Asa Carter was a speechwriter for Alabama governor George Wallace and was responsible for penning Wallace's 1963 inaugural address in which he declared "segregation now... segregation tomorrow... segregation forever." Carter went on to have a strange career in his later years as an author under the pseudonym Forrest Carter. He wrote westerns, such as *The Rebel Outlaw: Josey Wales*, and later what he claimed to be a memoir of his Native American childhood called *The Education of Little Tree*. Forrest Carter's true identity was revealed by historian Dan T. Carter in 1991. In the 1950s and 1960s, though, he spent years spreading his violent segregationist rhetoric across the country. He organized vigilante groups in cities in the Midwest, he led a group of Klansmen responsible for castrating a black man in Alabama, and he had run Jimmy Swann's unsuccessful campaign for Mississippi governor in 1967. Even before the fundraiser, Carter had spoken out in defense of the APWR, including in a television broadcast in 1967 in which he said the group consisted of "good, solid, decent people."[25]

Alongside Klan groups and the APWR, the Citizens' Councils continued to play a role in maintaining white political and economic power into the late 1960s. The Councils were never as widespread in the hill counties of the southwest as they had been in the Delta. Here, various Klan groups had dominated. However, as the Klan declined in influence, White Citizens' Councils became, at the end of the 1960s, active in the area. Responding to the declining membership of the Klan groups, the Pike County Citizens' Council staged a successful membership drive in 1968. The councils continued to hold yearly meetings that attracted prominent segregationist speakers, who expounded remarkably static anticommunist and anti-federal-government rhetoric. However, the councils' publication, *The Citizen*, reflected the pragmatic changes to the groups' focus. Editorials addressed the more practical considerations of avoiding rather than preventing the inevitable school desegregation. Council-run segregation academies were highly successful in preventing school integration, even in the poverty-stricken Amite and Wilkinson counties where parents could ill afford the costs of private education. According to Charles C. Bolton, Amite County's school board had voted to increase the level of local school tax in 1965, because they believed "the majority of the citizens and taxpayers of this county and patrons of this school district object to this board executing an agreement of compliance with the Civil Rights Act of 1964." The creation of segregated academies meant the vast majority of white pupils fled state schools, thus leaving Head Start on the front line of opposition to integrated education.[26]

While the Klan's influence in Mississippi did decline after 1964, it did not fade entirely. Its social and political influence continued, as did instances of racial violence and even murder. The Klan supported arch-segregationist candidates like Jimmy Swann for governor in 1967 and continued to provide a bloc vote for Senator Eastland. The unit vote controlled by the

Klan in that election was only slightly smaller than the unit vote of African Americans in Mississippi. Investigators reported to the mayor of Jackson of Klan plans to "blow up a Negro" in order to create racial friction to benefit Swan's gubernatorial campaign. Klan violence was not just directed at African Americans, however. Attacks on "race traitors" or "white [n----rs]" had been a feature of racial violence in Mississippi for decades. As David Cunningham has explained, when whites "engineered integrationist efforts, a clear boundary emerged between hypocritical, morally bankrupt 'others' and authentically 'real' Americans." Klan violence was directed at these un-American white "others," most often those who were involved in civil rights activism. Whites who allowed African Americans to patronize their stores or restaurants were also targeted. In Hattiesburg, for example, HUAC investigators found evidence of at least five assaults carried out by Klansmen from the White Knights and the UKA against "white youths active in civil rights activities." In Vicksburg, in March 1965, two Klansmen trashed a café when they found that the white owner served African Americans. The Klansmen viciously assaulted the African American who had entered, and they smashed the café, before returning a few days later to throw two Molotov cocktails. Into the late 1960s these individual and community-sanctioned instances of white supremacist violence kept many white Mississippians "in line."[27]

In 1967 there was a resurgence of this white supremacist violence targeting whites. This time the targets were poverty warriors. The increasing number of integrated antipoverty programs in the state combined with the perceived threat of Black Power and the long hot summer of riots across the nation stoked a wave of intense Klan violence. As Reverend Duncan Gray recalled, "It was like all hell broke loose." As the largest antipoverty program in Mississippi, Mississippi Action for Progress was an obvious target. Mississippi Action for Progress was created in 1966 as the state-approved, biracial replacement for the Child Development Group of Mississippi. The organization, headed by moderates of both races, received three million dollars to operate Head Start centers across the state. It entered a fraught political and racial landscape, alienating many black Child Development Group workers who felt they had been betrayed by the creation of a new program when their funding had been reduced so dramatically. While MAP was reluctantly accepted by the white establishment, its integrated Head Start classes enraged white parents and white supremacist groups. White MAP employees thus encountered some of the most intense outbursts of this renewed wave of Klan violence.[28]

Much of the violence was directed at those antipoverty workers working in rural communities. However, board members also received their share of abuse. While board chair Owen Cooper did not recall receiving a great deal of abuse, many of his fellow board members did, he recalls. "I had some friends that received a tremendous amount of hate mail, and obscene calls, and things like that." Such attacks were not limited to MAP. Whites involved in other antipoverty programs were also targeted. For example, the white executive staff of Forrest-Stone Area Opportunities, a community action program based in Forrest County faced violence, harassment, and intimidation. Outside Mississippi, too, this resurgent violence was evident. In Alabama, when white banker and White Citizens' councilman Victor Poole agreed to serve as area director of an integrated poverty program, he "received a visit" from the Klan. In the Louisiana Delta both black and white antipoverty staff, particularly Head Start workers, faced sustained violent opposition. Head Start workers were targeted most frequently because the integration of young children was a particularly volatile issue. Many communities across the state had set about ensuring that the Freedom of Choice integration plans resulted in no public school desegregation. In some towns, most notably the state capital, segregated academies sprung up overnight, funded by White Citizens' Councils. Thus, Head Start, a federally funded program requiring the integration of its centers, became a focal point for extremist opposition.[29]

The counties of southwest Mississippi were the focus of much violence. Head Start centers were burned to the ground in Lincoln County's Pearlhaven and Bogue Chitto. The power of violent white supremacist organizations remained pervasive into the late 1960s in this area of the state. The county's white supremacist groups were the first to take up the fight to prevent poor African American children and poor white children attending the same Head Start classes. White Knights of the Ku Klux Klan and APWR counted among their members local elected officials and businessmen. Their influence even extended into the local churches. This influence both supported and necessitated the refusal by poor white parents to send their children to integrated Head Start classes. While such extremists were in the minority in the county, their power was undeniable. Milton Bryant, the regional supervisor for Mississippi Action for Progress, expressed to the board his deep concerns about the power wielded by these Klan groups. While these extremists were in the minority, he wrote, "It seems that the majority has felt that it is better not to confront them and face possible grave consequences." Some local whites were in sympathy with their aims, if not their methods. Many poor whites were simply unwilling to entertain the idea of integration. Others feared retribution from the Klan if they did enroll their children in Head Start. When one poor white child was enrolled at one of the county's all-black MAP centers, for example, the child and parents were soon "frightened away."[30]

When Gus Roessler, a former president of the Clarksdale White Citizens' Council, became executive officer of the local antipoverty program Coahoma Opportunities Inc., he was ostracized by the white community. In Hot Coffee, a small unincorporated community near Mount Olive in Covington County, there was an arson attack on the Head Start center. In Lauderdale County, New Hope Baptist Church, the site of a Head Start center, was torched, and the following night Klansmen shot into the house of a Head Start bus driver and set fire to another Head Start center. In Jackson the home of Head Start employee Jane Schutt was bombed. The Hinds County Head Start program was subject to further intimidation, including a burning cross, which was set at the site of its staff-training center at Mount Beulah in Edwards. In Washington County extensive threats were made against Head Start in Leland, including threats to shoot children and staff using the outdoor play area on the "white" side of the street. In Calhoun County white Head Start teachers received ultimatums from White Knights to "resign or be destroyed." White employee John Ott was targeted while he was involved in developing the program in November 1966. Two white men accosted him at his home and used "obscene language and harassing tactics in asking him where he is from and what he is doing." These same men later followed his children and harassed them at their school "with the same line of questioning."[31]

In Wayne County, two white men entered a Head Start center, searching for the white teacher. When the men found he was not at the center, they verbally threatened the absent white employee, before pulling a knife and threatening to kill African American Head Start teacher William D. Carter in front of thirteen Head Start children. The incident resulted in the temporary closure of the center. Initial outrage led Owen Cooper, the head of MAP's board, to insist that the Highway Patrol investigate the incident. And he called on local law enforcement to step up their protection of the center, asking the Commissioner for Public Safety to "provide necessary protection and give positive assurance that those who would violate the law, intimidate citizens, and threaten the lives of workers will be diligently sought out, apprehended, and prosecuted." The commissioner, Colonel T. B. Birdsong, provided a terse response to Cooper's request three days later. It was not the responsibility of the Highway Patrol, he reminded Cooper, to provide protection—they "are

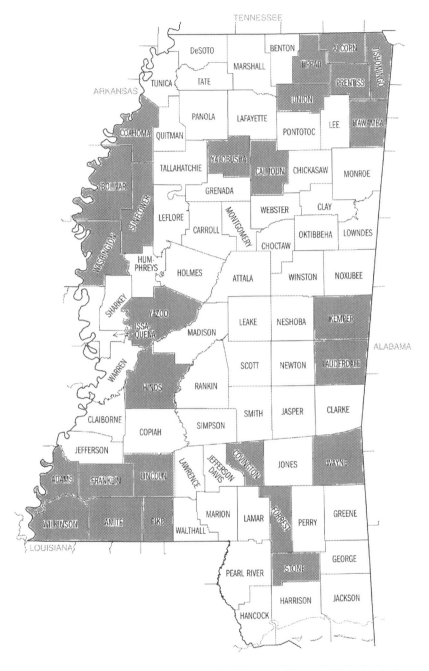

Fig. 3.1. Map of Mississippi showing counties in which antipoverty workers reported being targets of white supremacist violence in 1967.

not peace officers." The Highway Patrol would "continue in the future as we have in the past—to serve all of the people of the State of Mississippi toward and for the betterment of the State."[32]

Cooper backed down in the face of Birdsong's rebuke, adding that he was sure that "within the authority granted you that your organization will always seek to maintain law and order in the state." Not a very reassuring exchange for the people of Waynesboro or for Mississippi Action for Progress staff. Cooper's unwillingness to challenge the establishment and the prospect of the Highway Patrol continuing as they had in the past to maintain "law and order" did not bode well for the prospect of integrated Head Start centers or the suppression of white supremacist violence. State Sovereignty Commission director Erle Johnston, meanwhile, responded by urging local white leaders to suppress any further violence. If MAP were to break down, he warned local mayor Frank Ellis, then "outside irresponsibles" could arrive to take over the program's responsibilities. Johnston was practicing "practical segregation" by using the influence of the Sovereignty Commission to prevent further acts of white violence against Mississippi Action for Progress. He feared such violence would attract unwanted national attention, scrutiny that would threaten the mechanisms of white control being established in and through the program.[33]

Despite Johnston's efforts, however, the violence was so extensive that it did not escape OEO's notice. Widespread violence in OEO's southeast region in early 1967, particularly in Mississippi and Alabama, led to concerns being raised in the OEO in Washington. Sargent Shriver, always concerned about negative press, reacted angrily to a newspaper article by Rowland Evans and Robert Novak, which detailed the escalating Klan campaign. The article expressed outrage at violence directed not at "militant Negro civil rights organizations," such as SNCC, but at white moderates who were, according to the reporters, "sensibly and bravely trying to make biracialism work." Bertrand Harding, due to meet with deputy director of the FBI Cartha DeLoach and assistant attorney general for civil rights John Doar, was told by Shriver to "*please* get the FBI actually moving!" However, the FBI did little to address this violence. The limit of OEO involvement was to request the assistance of Governor Johnson and to acceptance of the offered assistance from Johnston's Sovereignty Commission in getting local police to work on these matters.[34]

The harassment of Mississippi Action for Progress staff, especially white staff, across the state persisted. As local tensions ratcheted up, so did the attacks. Jack Price, a white man who worked for MAP as a nutritionist, suffered from months of abuse. Beginning in early 1967 Price had endured threatening telephone calls, and Klansmen followed him as he traveled to MAP centers. Price was based in the northeast of Mississippi—including Union, Tippah, Alcorn, Prentiss, Itawamba, and Tishomingo Counties—away from the more intense and confrontational Delta and southwest regions of Mississippi. But there remained racial turmoil in this area, and MAP's white employees working in these counties were targets of Klan intimidation and violence. Racial tensions increased later that year when, on June 17, 1967, about twenty people marched into a grocery store in Corinth, Alcorn County. These activists were protesting after an alleged incident in which "a young Negro boy was beaten by the Chief of Police in a 'white' park." Three days later, Jack Price spent the evening in Corinth at the house of an African American friend, Robert Jones. Sitting in Jones's backyard, they noticed a police car drive by several times. Leaving at 11:00 p.m., Price drove south out of the city and was passed by several cars. But one car containing two white men, which had been following him since leaving Corinth, stayed behind him. Once the stretch of highway was deserted, the car pulled up beside him and cut out its lights. The driver pointed a pistol directly at Price and shouted, "Hey, [n----r] lover," before firing four shots, two of which hit the car, causing Price to drive off the road down a bluff. Price was shaken but not injured. Although Price was interviewed by Highway Patrol, the sheriff, and the FBI, no arrests were made.[35]

The executive director of Mississippi Action for Progress, OEO, the FBI, and the Sovereignty Commission were seemingly unable to stem this violence. In part, this was because the violence was not expanding in isolation. Such extremism could not be sustained without the complicity of the local white community. This complicity was born of the very real fear of Klan retribution and often sympathy for its goals, if not its methods. While many white Mississippians would no longer condone murder, opposition to integrated Head Start programs was widespread. In Wayne County, for example, the attempt of MAP staff members to recruit white children to the all-black Head Start centers was not acceptable to the local Klan group. Merely an expression of the "unhappiness" of the local Klan provided sufficient grounds for the president of the local school board to demand that staff stop the recruitment of white children or lose the lease for the center. This complicity ensured that Mississippi's white extremists felt secure in their immunity from prosecution. Rumors that the Klan was under the protection of Senator Eastland were widespread and widely believed. Local law enforcement rarely took action against the perpetrators of violence against Head Start centers. Meanwhile,

William Harold Cox, chief judge of the District Court for the Southern District of Mississippi, expressed many published doubts about presenting civil rights violations cases to the grand jury. So even if they were arrested, the perpetrators were unlikely to face a trial.[36]

Violence was not the only weapon at the disposal of white segregationists. They drew on a range of tactics honed in earlier phases of white resistance. Opposing the involvement of white women in the program, for example, white segregationists employed the gendered rhetoric of massive resistance. This language also drew on gendered opposition to the war on poverty. Such opposition was especially prevalent in opposition to Head Start, as a program dominated at the grassroots by women, including those employed and volunteering in local centers and participating Head Start mothers. In Tennessee, for example, white women involved in Head Start in Memphis were met with the harassment and paternalism that African Americans had been facing for years.[37]

While the involvement of white women in Head Start was not as widespread in Mississippi, some white women did work in antipoverty programs across the state. Their involvement both reflected the level of poverty among white Mississippians and drew on the legacy of white southern women activists. A small minority of white women in Mississippi had been working to undermine Jim Crow since the 1930s. In the 1960s some white women organized in order to manage the changes that were becoming inevitable. But the response of white segregationists to white women in Head Start was especially effective, as it drew on still-powerful fears of miscegenation. In Yalobusha County local whites distributed hate sheets attacking the white female Head Start staff. In a vitriolic tirade entitled "a paper for pariotic [sic] citizens," the author raised familiar fears of miscegeny, mixed with pious religiosity and patriotism. "The worst thing is to mix with the [n----rs] by teaching in [N----r] schools, and espailly [sic] those who are teaching in Head Start." The flyer went on to list the names and addresses of the local white women working for the program—familiar tactics that left these women vulnerable to attacks on their homes.[38]

The campaign of Yalobusha County's White Knights to undermine Mississippi Action for Progress was successful. It yielded the resignations of two white employees and the removal of seven white children from centers in the county. These methods of opposition were not limited to one Klan group. In Greenwood, Klan hate sheet *A Delta Discussion* named three white women faculty members of a white school in Itta Bena as Head Start teachers, questioning their readers, "Do you want them teaching your children next year?" Directing their vitriol at women and playing on fears of miscegeny, white extremists were successful in enlisting the outrage of local whites and directing that pressure onto whites involved in Mississippi Action for Progress.[39] The increasing statewide and nationwide racial tensions in 1966 and 1967 spurred this campaign. Tensions were heightened by the state's gubernatorial election and growing nationwide frictions that were particularly explosive in northern urban ghettoes. While violence remained the most widely used method of opposition to MAP by the end of 1967, it is difficult to ascertain the exact scope and nature of the violence. Some incidents were reported to the local law enforcement officers, and many more reported to the program's area supervisors and central office. However, many incidents of harassment went unreported, as the white targets were unwilling to provoke further attacks.

In July 1967 cities across the US exploded in riots. Mississippi did not experience such riots. The state lacked the kind of extensive urban environment that, with its complex and intractable problems and compact geography, provided ideal conditions for the rapid spread of violence. In Jackson, Mississippi's only city, the poverty and squalid housing was not compressed into a ghetto and confined to a few city blocks and high-rise tenements, but spread out in neighborhoods of single-level dwellings. Leadership was also lacking for African Americans in Jackson and across the state. The civil rights community was weakened by years of white supremacist attack and intimidation, and riddled with divisions, not least because of class tensions worsened by the presence of MAP and the demise of the Child Development Group. Whatever the contentions of the Sovereignty Commission, Black Power elements in Mississippi remained limited and lacking in power, and were unable to mount a sustained challenge against a white power structure that was still exercising tight control over Mississippian society.[40]

But the riots increased the pressure on President Johnson, from inside and outside his administration, to dismantle OEO. In August 1967 his special advisor Harry McPherson recommended folding community action programs into manpower training and the Neighborhood Youth Corps—under the control of the Department of Labor—and providing a "new tough mandate and a specific description of what [these programs] should be all about." Secretary of Labor Willard Wirtz was eager to take control of at least some aspects of the war on poverty. The president, supported by the National Advisory Council on Economic Opportunity, was unwilling to let OEO be "broken up by spin offs [or] transfers" as he feared it would look like a defeat. Congress did pass amendments to the Economic Opportunity

Act in the wake of the riots, however. While OEO was not "broken up," the amendments included a change introduced by Congresswomen Edith Green that undermined poor participation in antipoverty programs.[41]

While no riots occurred in Mississippi, the national riots had a powerful impact on both black and white Mississippians. In Sunflower County, where the African American Head Start program run by the Freedom Democrats and SNCC activists had been locked in a battle with the white establishment program, the race riots had the effect of making the black activists "more tractable."[42] White extremist violence had largely abated by the end of 1967. As the white community became practiced at securing white control over antipoverty programs across the state, they regained control over the extent and timing of integration. It thus became less necessary for white extremists to resort to violence. Antipoverty programs were becoming one of the mechanisms used by white Mississippians to control the nature of race relations and the pace of black advancement, obviating the need for Klan violence. This represented a softening of hardline segregationism, as white moderates were working in integrated programs and sitting on integrated boards. However it was a price many were willing to pay, especially after 1967 when the potential for Klan retribution for such involvement diminished. In return for this acceptance of integration, white Mississippians were gaining control over federal antipoverty dollars and, in the case of MAP, the chance to control—or avoid—the integration of black and white children in Head Start classes.

This shift toward practical segregationism reflected changes in Mississippi's racial and political climate. At the end of 1967 Mississippi's district court judges remained unwilling to prosecute civil rights cases. No state prosecutor would file murder charges against those accused of killing Chaney, Schwerner, and Goodman. However, the Department of Justice succeeded in trying the case against the murderers using federal charges to secure a guilty verdict in October 1967. By the time Vernon Dahmer's accused murderers were brought to their trials, Klansmen were no longer immune to prosecution at the state level. Forrest County prosecutors, the state attorney, and FBI worked together to bring the men to trial on both state and federal charges. Governor Johnson referred to the Klansmen who killed Dahmer as "vicious and morally bankrupt criminals." One Klansman, who had dropped his gun at the scene, pled guilty to arson and murder, while a jury convicted three others of those crimes.[43]

The verdicts marked the first time a Mississippi state court convicted white men for a civil rights killing. While their sentences were eventually commuted, the convictions were hugely significant. The verdicts, which were the subject of intense state and national attention, denoted the beginning of a change in the state. The governor, local law enforcement, local prosecutors, and judges were all more willing to condemn extralegal white violence than they had been even one year earlier. However the case against Imperial Wizard Sam Bowers, who ordered the attack on Dahmer, ended in a mistrial. Bowers had, by this point, already been found guilty of civil rights violations in connection with the murders of Chaney, Schwerner, and Goodman for which he served six years in federal prison. However, three further trials of Bowers also ended in mistrial due to juries deadlocked after jury tampering by Klan supporters. Despite the declining violence, Klan mentality clearly remained a potent force.[44]

- Chapter Four -

BLACK EMPOWERMENT IN JACKSON

Local battles over the control of community action programs intensified as the renewed white supremacist violence spread across the state. White extremists were sowing fear and spreading terror among white and black antipoverty activists. At the same time, some white moderates and savvy white segregationists saw the value of compromise, given the flood of antipoverty dollars into the state. Black activists were not willing to just hand over control of antipoverty efforts to local white leaders, however. Even as unlikely groups of Mississippians sat together on community action boards and worked together in community action programs, power struggles continued. The appearance of biracial cooperation was, most often, a veneer that barely covered pitched battles to control antipoverty programs—and thus gain control over the pace of black advancement. In the state capital, Jackson, the war on poverty became a site of renewed conflict between a thriving network of civil rights activists and the political and economic power structures that stood at the heart of white segregationism in Mississippi. Jackson's civil rights activists worked long and hard to combine their activism with the federal funds flowing into the county's community action program. Black activists such as Don Jackson wanted the antipoverty program to promote black empowerment through community action, not just through compromise and biracial cooperation. Members of the white segregationist establishment, meanwhile, sought control of the program in order to limit integration and to stifle genuine community engagement.

Jackson had stood at the heart of black political mobilization since the 1940s. It was home to the state's first NAACP office, opened by Medgar and Myrlie Evers in 1954. However the growth of activism was slow, due to the entrenched economic and political white power in the state capital. Medgar Evers kept Mississippi's NAACP alive, using the legal strategy favored by the NAACP to campaign for changes that served the city's middle-class black population. Evers also served as inspiration and guidance for a younger generation of activists who emerged in the late 1950s. Tougaloo College became a "rallying point" for this new generation. A private Christian college, Tougaloo was interracial but had mostly a black student population. By the late 1950s Tougaloo students had begun to organize, building the Jackson NAACP Youth Council. Inspired by the sit-in protests at Greensboro, the members of the Youth Council were the first to attempt direct-action protest in Jackson. On March 27, 1961, nine members of the NAACP Youth Council—the Tougaloo nine—staged a sit-in at Jackson's white-only public library. They were quickly arrested and later convicted for breach-of-peace, for which they were each fined $100 and given a thirty-day suspended sentence. African Americans who had gathered "quietly outside the courthouse" in support of the nine were "dispersed" by Jackson police using clubs and dogs.[1]

The library sit-in was a significant moment in Jackson's nascent movement. Though the sit-in was quickly squashed and supporters of the nine were brutally attacked, the protest brought national attention to the city and the courage showed by the nine inspired local activists. Dorie and Joyce Ladner, who went on to play significant roles in the Jackson movement, were expelled from Jackson State University for their attempts to arrange a prayer vigil in support of the arrested nine. As James Coleman recalled, the exceptional courage shown by the Tougaloo nine cannot be overstated. Coleman was a native Jacksonian, who studied at Tougaloo in the late 1950s before returning there in 1962 to work as an instructor and later teacher. "Having been reared in the Jackson area, knowing how law enforcement treated blacks, and knowing the viciousness and the hate and the brutality that took place with the police department and city officials, I mean, I still sort of shiver when I think of the fact that these nine kids put their lives on the line at a sit-in at the library."[2]

However the number of members of the Youth Council remained low. In the middle of 1961, Tougaloo sociology professor John Salter, originally from Arizona and newly arrived to Jackson, became the council's adult advisor. He recalled the great difficulty the council had in recruiting members. "Only about a dozen or so attended initially, but we began to pick up a few members here and there. The climate of fear was strong, though, among the youth and especially their parents, and out of that an apparent apathy had developed." It was not only the brutality of the Jackson police that stifled black activism, but also the economic power of the white community. James Coleman was not at that time active in the movement, solely due to fear of economic reprisals. "I was basically an observer, and I was one of those, and I wouldn't be afraid and ashamed to say it, I was one of those observers. . . . Maybe I'll put it this way, in hindsight: I was one of those who was really supportive on campus, and I was probably afraid because of the financial situation of my parents and the possibility of them losing their jobs. . . . It was not until I became a professional working, and then, that's when I was able to really make my decision and not worry about my parents losing their jobs. And of course, I started supporting then in the movement and the marches and those kinds of things."[3]

The survival of the Youth Council in the brutally repressive regime in Jackson was remarkable. Many other civil rights organizations simply failed to gain a foothold in the city. SNCC and CORE activists found the fortress of white power in the city too strong to breach. White power in the city was potent. Jackson was home not only to the state's political leadership, but also to the Sovereignty Commission, the Citizens' Council of Mississippi, and various Klan groups. It was from here that the state's political, social, and economic networks of white segregationism stemmed. White economic and political control was unassailable and the White Citizens' Councils' control of white society was absolute. The Jackson police were experienced in sowing fear among Jackson activists. Acts of police brutality were common. In 1961, for example, Jackson's mayor Allen C. Thompson, an unreconstructed segregationist, met the Freedom Riders with thinly veiled threats, despite the weight of national and international attention that followed them. The NAACP Youth Council remained the main source of activism in the city. They focused their efforts on economic boycotts and legal challenges to segregation. Activists staged protests on the city buses, boycotted the segregated annual state fair in October 1962, and instituted a longterm boycott of 150 white-owned stores.[4]

Given the extent of white legal brutality and economic power, gaining support for the boycott among Jackson's African American community was an immense challenge. Previous attempts at boycotts had failed because of lack of publicity and momentum. In 1962 support for the boycott among African Americans was at first limited. But members of the Youth Council were determined the 1962 boycott of Jackson's white businesses would be successful. They printed tens of thousands of pamphlets and sought support from the black community. In November 1962 the Youth Council sent a new plea, entitled "Start Putting Your Money on Strike." "Right now," the pamphlet read, "we want to remind people of the obvious: the coming up of the Christmas shopping season. And—we'd also like to remind people of what ought to be very obvious: the buying power—in the 150,000 resident Jackson area—of its 70,000 Negro citizens. We would like to remind Negro consumers that—as they fully well know—appeals to the 'nice, kind side' of most of these white businessmen are going to have absolutely no effect at all. On the other hand, speaking to them in the language that they know so well—money—will always produce a reaction. If you cut off the flow of nickels and dimes and dollars into their cash register boxes—they'll sit up mighty fast and take notice."[5]

As Christmas of 1962 approached, the boycott gained traction among the black community. But divisions began to appear within the movement. Younger activists wanted to hold mass protest marches to bring attention to the boycott and put pressure on Mayor Thompson to respond to their demands. But the NAACP—the main source of funding for Jackson's movement—did not endorse direct-action protest. Unlike in Greenwood and Natchez, where SNCC and CORE activists had made inroads, middle-class moderates dominated Jackson's movement. The NAACP accepted a few pickets but refused to support mass marches. Nonetheless, the pickets did produce arrests and a tirade from Mayor Thompson, all of which provided much needed publicity for the Jackson movement and growing support for the boycott. The boycott continued into 1963, as did white counter-maneuvers, most notably the attempts of Judge Harold Cox to ban picketing. While neither the mayor nor any white merchants responded to the NAACP demands, some white support came from the state's Methodists who, in early 1963, made a public statement, "Born of Conviction," condemning discrimination. A church visit campaign followed, as an integrated group of activists from Tougaloo attempted to attend Sunday services at Jackson's all-white Protestant and Catholic churches. The all-encompassing terror that had had a chokehold on Jackson was finally loosening, if only a little.[6]

In May 1963 Mayor Thompson finally responded to the demands of Jackson's activists. But he refused to speak with the NAACP activists and instead selected a group of conservative African Americans with whom he was willing to negotiate. Thompson offered only token concessions to NAACP demands. Younger activists, inspired by the Birmingham Campaign and angered by the mayor's token concessions, grew increasingly insistent in their calls for mass marches in support of the boycott. In response to the mayor's failure to address any of their demands, activists staged direct-action protest calculated to secure a response from Jackson's white community—a sit-in at a Woolworth's lunch counter. Almost immediately a white mob gathered and attacked the protestors with intense ferocity. John Salter, who arrived soon after the boycott began, recollected that the scene seemed "like a horrible nightmare." "It was all mass insanity, unlike anything I had ever experienced. It was chilling and unreal," Salter later wrote. He and other protestors were covered in ketchup, sugar, and mustard. Salter's back was spray-painted with the word "[n----r]," and a glass of water mixed with pepper thrown in his eyes, before he was struck with "several hard blows" to the head and back. Brutal as it was, the mob violence was extensively publicized and had an immediate impact. Mayor Thompson was, Salter recalled, "glad—very glad—to talk again." He agreed to concessions: taking down segregation signs, allowing blacks to use public facilities, such as parks and libraries, hiring African Americans to meaningful positions in city government, and setting up a biracial committee. These concession were, Salter said, "not much, perhaps, but by the standards of Mississippi and its rigidly segregated capital city, this was a beginning."[7]

However, only a few hours later, Mayor Thompson made a public announcement refuting claims he had conceded anything. Jackson's activists were appalled, though not surprised, by the betrayal. Worse still, the Jackson movement came under increasing internal strain. As direct-action continued after the Woolworth's sit-in, largely in the form of marches in support of the boycott, NAACP leaders were increasingly concerned about the direction of the movement. Younger activists meanwhile were pushing for more sustained mass protest. In June the NAACP broke the impasse. The organization decided to "alter strategy" in Jackson and to restructure the "strategy committee" to refocus on voter registration. As a result the Jackson NAACP came under the control of a conservative, black middle class. They were, Salter described, "well-dressed, affluent men and a few women. They were not the poverty-stricken people, living in the endless lines of shacks in the slum ghettos of Jackson who were still immobilized by fear of swift and certain economic reprisals if they became too close to the Jackson movement." Further blows followed. Judge Harold Cox passed an injunction preventing activists from protesting in Jackson. "There was no question in my mind," Salter recalled, "that the Jackson movement was almost dead." And then, less than one week later, Medgar Evers was assassinated.[8]

Medgar Evers had been, since the mid-1950s, an emblem of activism: "a living symbol of resistance . . . to Blacks across the state." Evers had been NAACP's field secretary, although "his style was more aggressive than was customary for the NAACP," according to historian Charles Payne. He chafed against the NAACP's refusal to endorse sit-ins, and according to Myrlie Evers, "Medgar had some difficult days trying to decide whether he should actually remain with the NAACP or not." Evers was also infuriated by the lack of cooperation and support Jackson's black middle class gave to civil rights activism. Despite the limitations placed on him by the NAACP, Evers played a significant role in developing youth leadership in Jackson and across the state. His dedication to boycotts, legal challenges, and improving opportunity for African Americans drove the Jackson—and broader Mississippi—movement. His assassination "sent shockwaves through Jackson," resonated across the state, and provoked national and international responses too. It left black Mississippi, and the broader civil rights movement, with an acute sense of loss. Martin Luther King spoke of Evers as a "pure patriot." President Kennedy invited the Evers family to the White House, giving Myrlie a signed copy of the draft civil rights bill assuring her that Medgar's death would "make the bill possible." Internationally Medgar Evers's assassination served to further tarnish America's global image.[9]

Back in Jackson, though, there remained a widespread reluctance among African Americans to join the movement. Tougaloo student Anne Moody, who had participated in the Woolworth's sit-in, and SNCC activist Dorie Ladner attempted to generate support among students at Jackson State University the day after Evers's death, but received little response. Myrlie Evers herself urged black Mississippians to take up the cause. At a mass meeting she told the gathered crowd, "I do not want his death to be in vain. That would be as big a blow as his death itself. I ask you for united action in this effort in memory of my husband. . . . Nothing can bring Medgar back, but the cause can live on." Despite the initial reluctance, five thousand mourners gathered at Evers's funeral on June 15, 1963, and marched in his memory, "the poor and unknown rubbing shoulders with noted dignitaries and celebrities." "The ripples of Medgar's death and the Jackson movement . . . were reaching out a long, long way," John Salter recalled. The impact of Evers's death, though, was complicated. It inspired many to join the movement, and it brought new pressures on the Jackson establishment and the Kennedy administration and Congress to act. But the Jackson movement remained divided, lacking in funds and its organization gutted by Evers's loss. African Americans attempting to protest in Jackson faced implacable white opposition. The mourners marching through Jackson after Evers's funeral were met with a brutal attack by Jackson's police. Evers's assassin, White Citizens' councilman Byron De La Beckwith, meanwhile, was quickly identified by police. Beckwith was tried twice, with both trials ending in mistrial. This was not just the result of white Mississippians' reluctance to convict a white man of killing a black man. It was also the result of concerted effort of state mechanisms of segregation. The Sovereignty Commission, for example, investigated potential jurors for the second trial and advised the defense team which jurors to accept and which to dismiss.[10]

The Jackson movement, already faltering due to internal divisions and NAACP restrictions, lost momentum in the wake of Evers's assassination. Youth Council activists who had been the driving force behind mass protest turned to other organizations, including SNCC and CORE. Activism continued, both through NAACP's legal strategy and direct-action protest. The creation of COFO's headquarters in Jackson brought together organizations that were expanding and uniting in preparation for Freedom Summer. But Jackson's white establishment was also preparing for the Freedom Summer "invasion." In anticipation of Freedom Summer, Mayor Thompson increased and armed the Jackson Police force, dubbed "Allen's Army." The centerpiece of this "army" was "Thompson's Tank," a newly acquired 13,000-pound armored battlewagon. The Mississippi movement, though, was more coordinated, organized, and invigorated than ever before. Freedom Summer launched a powerful assault on several fronts of white segregationism. The "social norms" of segregation were flagrantly challenged as integrated groups of activists traveled across the state. Black voters registered in vast numbers, refusing to give in to economic threats, terror, and violence. Freedom Schools provided education for young black children that reflected black history and culture, and rejected the pseudoscience that propped up Jim Crow segregation. Out of Freedom Summer came the Mississippi Freedom Democratic Party, to challenge the state's all-white Democratic Party. However, the events of Freedom Summer, the passage of the Civil Rights Act that summer, and the Voting Rights Act the following year did little to change the day to day realities of life for the state capital's poorest residents. Jackson's mayor remained committed to maintaining segregation. This commitment was reflected in the local segregationist press—including papers such as the *Jackson Daily News* and the *Clarion Ledger*—and the attitudes and actions of the Jackson police department.[11]

Activists continued to protest the segregation and discrimination. In June 1965 activists, encompassing MFDP, SNCC, and the National Council of Churches, staged a peaceful march to the capitol building in Jackson to protest against the Mississippi legislature. For these activists the state legislature was illegitimate because its members were elected while African Americans were denied the vote. But once again peaceful protest in Jackson was met with a brutal response. Jackson police arrested four hundred and fifty protestors, beating many of them, and holding them at a temporary site on the Jackson Fairgrounds. When SNCC activist John Lewis led another march the following day, two hundred more protestors were arrested and held for over two weeks. The activists were subjected to brutal and inhumane treatment. One SNCC activist, Hardy Frye, recalled of his arrest, "they backed us up, stopped us, put us in garbage trucks. John Lewis was with us. They hauled us off to a jail, and they gassed us. What they did was they put us in one of these county fairgrounds, and they backed Jeeps up to the thing, and they turned on the engines." Three white ministers in Mississippi with the National Council of Churches later reported to Congress on the treatment they witnessed in what they said they "could only describe as a concentration camp." They saw "systematic efforts to dehumanize, demoralize, and degrade these citizens which were being perpetrated by the police officials of the City of Jackson." Male prisoners were "forced to run a gauntlet—a double line of police swinging clubs and blackjacks"—while "female prisoners were subjected to constant lewd and suggestive remarks, including promises of release in return for sexual favors. Women asking for medical attention were subjected to physical examination in full view of staring policemen." "We are absolutely convinced, the ministers wrote, "that the primarily [sic] purpose of the Jackson concentration camp is not to serve as a place of incarceration, but rather as a place to break the spirit, the will, the health, and even the body of each individual who dared to assemble peaceable [sic] to seek a redress of grievances."[12]

As Mississippi's war on poverty was beginning, black activists in Jackson continued to face intense state-sanctioned brutality. Despite this, Jackson's activists remained committed to continuing their pursuit of "full freedom" through every avenue possible. The level of activism in Jackson left a legacy of activists—local whites and African Americans as well as out-of-state activists—who were well versed in utilizing their limited power to challenge the establishment. This long tradition of activism provided fertile ground for the development of community action. As the movement fragmented along well-established fracture lines, including class and strategy, a number of Mississippi's activists threw their energy and organizing experience into the war on poverty. Some were high profile: Fannie Lou Hamer played a central role in organizing Associated Communities of Sunflower County; Aaron Henry, in organizing and leading Mississippi Action for Progress; Amzie Moore, in the creation of Head Start in Bolivar County. COFO activist Lula Belle Johnson was an "indefatigable canvasser," and she was, as historian Charles Payne describes, "instrumental in bringing what would become the Head Start program to Leflore, over the objections of local politicians." John Salter became the director of training of an antipoverty program, though in North Carolina not Mississippi. There were many more veterans of Mississippi's movement—outsiders and native Mississippians, black and white—who continued their activism through the war on poverty. Many of them joined antipoverty efforts in the state capital. Freedom Summer activists John Harris and Jim Dann, for example, moved from the Delta to work in a Head Start program in Jackson. Dr. A. D. Beittel, the white president of Tougaloo College who had visited the Tougaloo nine in jail and joined the 1963 sit-in at Woolworth's, became part of a community group applying for OEO funding in Jackson in 1965.[13]

Don Jackson embodied this tradition of activism, honed in the furnace of Jackson's movement. Jackson was a Baptist minister from Chester, Philadelphia, who had spent time in activism in Pennsylvania and Atlanta before arriving in Jackson, Mississippi, in the mid-1960s. Don Jackson was active in the Mississippi Freedom Democratic Party and worked to promote voter registration. He also worked in the social services division of the Child Development Group of Mississippi and later in the community action program serving the state capital itself. Jackson was a frequent contributor to the Hinds County Freedom Democratic Party newsletter and statewide movement newsletters, urging unity among the black community. As an antipoverty warrior, Don Jackson worked with biracial groups, lobbied powerful community leaders and politicians, and fiercely defended the young African Americans with whom he worked. For activists such as Don Jackson, the war on poverty provided an opportunity to generate black power—to develop grassroots leadership and empower black communities. Don Jackson was part of a black community seeking genuine empowerment through community action, and he was committed to developing a new generation of black leadership.[14]

Activists in Jackson, while united in their determination to dismantle the structures of white segregationist power, remained divided about how to achieve their goals. They adopted federal antipoverty efforts as part of their efforts as soon as the war on poverty arrived in the state. A 1965 flyer calling on "citizens of Jackson" to "wake up" informed Jacksonians that "the federal government . . . has instituted specific programs for community action in the effort to eliminate poverty, to give educational opportunities to the culturally deprived, to give better job opportunities to those who have been discriminated against in the past." The flyer continued, "Let us take advantage of these opportunities as we continue our struggle for full freedom!" Freedom Democrats such as Don Jackson wanted to use community action to promote black empowerment. White liberals, mostly Freedom Summer activists who stayed on in Jackson, wanted to continue their efforts to promote civil rights. Moderates of both races got involved in antipoverty efforts in order to stop the white establishment dominating the program and to forge new forms of interracial cooperation. Activists thus had a range of reasons for joining Jackson's antipoverty efforts. However, they all agreed on the desperate need for these efforts. Indeed, the need to tackle poverty in Jackson and the surrounding Hinds County was great.[15]

The level of poverty in Hinds County, though still higher than the national average, was not as severe as in many areas of the state. In fact Hinds County fared significantly better than the rest of the state in terms of economic activity, employment conditions, and the extent of poverty. In Mississippi in 1966, 34 percent of families were poor while in Hinds County the poverty level was 20.2 percent.[16] But the number, if not the proportion, of poor people was higher in Hinds County. The county population was approximately 215,000 in 1966, with a racial composition of roughly 40 percent black and 60 percent white. Poverty was racially skewed in Hinds County, as in the rest of the state. In 1960 34 percent of the population of the county was black, of whom 67 percent were poor. Only 10 percent of the white population was poor, meaning there were over three times more poor African American families in the county than poor white families.[17] Life in Jackson for poor African Americans was different from life in other, more rural parts of the state. Whites still wielded considerable economic power, but employment came not on plantations but in domestic service. There was also the presence in Jackson of a black middle class, more established and larger than anywhere else in the state, which altered the tenor of race relations and the nature of civil rights protest. While the experiences of urban and rural life were undoubtedly different, discrimination, intimidation, and poverty remained constants. The unique position of Jackson as the state's only city shaped the war on poverty efforts. The nature of the connection between established networks of civil rights activists and the war on poverty ensured community action programs—created to be a uniquely flexible antipoverty effort—had wildly differing form and impact across the state and across the nation. The depth and endurance of white power in Jackson meant the white response to antipoverty activism was different than elsewhere in the state.

Out of the volatile mix of black and white activists and powerful segregationists, "concerned citizens"—activists, agitators, community leaders, the established black leadership, and those affiliated with the white power structure—all sought to gain control of federal antipoverty funds. Two viable groups emerged and attempted to establish antipoverty programs. One, an integrated group, was founded by members of the established black leadership, such as Rev. R. L. T. Smith, and liberal whites, including Rev. Donald Thompson and former president of Tougaloo College, Dr. Adam D.

Beittel. The other, a white group handpicked by Governor Johnson and led by attorneys Dan Shell and Shelby Rogers, both of whom were part of the segregationist establishment.[18] Shell was a partner in the law firm Satterfield, Shell, Williams, and Buford, which was involved in many lawsuits opposing the desegregation of schools and facilities in Jackson. A founding partner of that law firm, John C. Satterfield, had drafted legislation for White Citizens' Councils and was legal advisor to the Sovereignty Commission and the Coordinating Committee for Fundamental American Freedoms. In 1969 he was described by *Time* magazine as "the most prominent segregationist lawyer in the country." Shell himself was chair of the Legal Advisory Committee for the Jackson Citizens' Council and was one of the lawyers who represented Port Gibson's white merchants in their lawsuit against Mississippi Action for Progress and the NAACP. Shelby Rogers was a White Citizens' councilman and had been cochair of Paul B. Johnson's 1963 gubernatorial campaign.[19]

Equally powerful white men populated their group. They included political allies of or workers for Governor Johnson, White Citizens' councilors, mayors, and business leaders, such as the director of the Mississippi Power and Light Company. These men were committed to securing white control of the federal antipoverty funds. But they recognized the futility of creating a white-only organization in the wake of the 1964 Civil Rights Act. Thus Shell and Rogers's group decided to accept integration on the proviso that the African Americans they appointed would be under their control. Far from an accommodation to the post-1964 racial realities, Shell and Rogers were in fact drawing on the paternalism characteristic of earlier race relations. This paternalism was combined with economic intimidation—a fairly easy task, given the economic power wielded by the group. These tactics enabled Shell and Rogers to appoint African Americans from a list of people one activist described as being composed of those "acceptable to the white power people." These black members of the organization were figureheads, considered "safe" by the white establishment. The board was thus unable to carry the legitimate concerns of the poor black community because such actions would, according to one African American member, come at the cost of her livelihood. When a group brought some complaints to this board member, she told them "she was put on the board as a figure-head, and . . . she wasn't going to rock the boat by carrying the complaints to the right place because it might cost her her job." The domination of white segregationists also excluded white liberal and white moderate potential members.[20]

Dr. Beittel's group, on the other hand, was a loose coalition of black activists, established black leadership figures, and white liberals. Dr. Beittel, director of the Mississippi Program of the American Friends Service Committee, called together the group. Alongside Smith and Thompson, the group also included three members of the National Urban League: Kenneth Crooks, Jeweldean Jones, and James Johnson. But the group failed to achieve internal cohesion, and it did not receive full support from activists in the county. Most significantly, it was sidelined by the white establishment. Beittel's group appealed to Governor Johnson for support, but Johnson granted Shell and Rogers's group a charter on June 16, 1965. Johnson's decision was condemned by community leaders in Hinds County as a "murder of public trust," in response to the flagrantly white segregationist nature of Shell and Rogers's group.[21]

Having secured the support of the governor, Shell and Rogers wasted no time submitting an application for funding to OEO, which was quickly granted. The new program included a range of component projects, including neighborhood service centers, Neighborhood Youth Corps, Legal Services, family planning, an emergency food and medical program, and a sickle cell anemia screening program. This program was thus one of the most comprehensive antipoverty programs in the state. The new community action agency was named Community Services Association or CSA for short. The acronym CSA—familiar to all southerners—was no coincidence. "In Jackson, Mississippi," one OEO officer would later comment, "CSA stands for Confederate States of America; it also represents Community Services Association. Whether this relationship is purely accidental is subject to conjecture, but considering the general situation in the city and the county in which it is located, it is probably not." The use of the acronym CSA reflected the power of the white establishment in Jackson and signaled their intent to use that power to undermine black economic opportunity. The program's board, while ostensibly meeting OEO requirements regarding poor and minority representation, was in reality dominated by members of the white establishment. They wielded their economic and political power to suppress any opposition from poor representatives and activists. But this domination, while powerful, was not unchallenged.[22]

Since late 1965 community activists had been organizing to oppose the white domination of the program. A number of activists—both black and white, on the board of the program and working within CSA—were determined to challenge the white establishment's control. One of the loudest opposing voices was that of Ted Seaver, a white teacher from Vermont who first arrived in Mississippi during Freedom Summer. Seaver spend the weeks of Freedom Summer working to promote voter registration, but on his

Fig. 4.1. Ted Seaver and Jesse Montgomery in Jackson, 196-, Vermont in Mississippi Collection, Special Collections, University of Vermont Library, Burlington. Photography Credit: Tyler Resch.

return home, he felt that much work remained to be done in Mississippi. In particular he wanted to help in addressing the economic challenges facing the state's black population. He became director of Vermont in Mississippi, Inc., a project sponsored by the Vermont Civil Rights Union that raised money to support activism in Mississippi. In early 1965 Ted applied for a one-year leave of absence from his post teaching English at Montpelier High School. Instead of granting him leave, however, the Montpelier Board of School Commissioners dismissed him for "attitudes unbecoming a teacher." Despite this setback Ted and his wife Carol, an elementary teacher, were undeterred. They arrived in Jackson in June 1965 and immediately joined a number of community groups. Ted Seaver was active in the Mississippi Freedom Democratic Party and worked to publish evidence of police brutality against black people. The Seavers also oversaw the building of a new community center, named the Medgar Evers Community Guild. The guild offered a range of services, including housing the first daycare center in the area. It also served its purpose of empowering black community leadership: local black activist Reverend Jesse Montgomery (pictured with Seaver) gradually took over responsibility for the center. Under Montgomery's leadership, the guild continued to play a significance role in the local community. It provided valuable services and meeting spaces, facilitating the development of community organizations, including the Hinds County Community Council.[23]

The Hinds County Community Council became the focus of opposition to Community Services Association. The council was a biracial organization that included representatives from civil rights organizations and community leaders. They spent months monitoring the development of CSA's organizational structure. When it became clear that the OEO regional office had done little to address the white domination of the board of the new program, the council escalated its protest. Ted Seaver, along with Nancy Levin, legislative chair of the Mississippi League of Women Voters, wrote a pamphlet with the inflammatory title: "How to Perpetuate the Racist Power Structure in Mississippi Using Federal Funds . . . or the Atlanta Regional OEO in Action." The content of the pamphlet was as inflammatory as the title. It detailed the "influence of the White Citizens' Council" on the program and documented the persistent exclusion of liberal whites and the poor. Seaver and Levin heaped almost as much criticism on the regional OEO as on the white segregationists of the board. As these white racists took control of the program, the pamphlet begins, "hovering godlike over the fray has been the Atlanta Regional OEO, snug in their consensus minded Olympus, fearlessly ignoring the needs, wishes, ambitions, anger and frustration of the poor, cautiously avoiding contamination by the white liberals and moderates, always nudging towards control of the Community Action Board by the most racist members of the power structure." It was the first strike back by civil rights activists against white control of federal antipoverty funds. The pamphlet was distributed locally and sent to OEO's southeast regional director Frank K. Sloan.[24]

Despite their anger at the composition of CSA's board, Seaver and Levin noted that the Hinds County Community Council had attempted to work with the board at first. But the board and director of Community Services Association would not meet with them to discuss changes to the program, despite repeated requests. The complaints of the community council were largely disregarded by Sloan and his staff. Sloan merely told the community council members that they must cooperate with CSA. But the suggestion that they work with the new board and executive director, Colonel H. F. Frank, was unacceptable to the council. Frank was, they informed Sloan, the symbol of the white domination of CSA—the man responsible for excluding poor

Fig. 4.2. *Who Is Holding Up the Poverty Program Anyway?* Cartoon, Hinds County Freedom Democratic Party News 1, no. 11 (March 25, 1967), SCR ID # 6-65-0-4-1-1-1, Series 2515: Mississippi State Sovereignty Commission Records, 1994–2006, Mississippi Department of Archives and History, Jackson, http://mdah.state.ms.us/arrec/digital_archives/sovcom/result.php?image=/data/sov_commission/images/png/cd07/049825.png&otherstuff=6|65|0|4|1|1|1|49|10|.

blacks and local activists. Over the course of months in late 1965 and early 1966, Frank ignored requests from the council and poor community to hold community meetings. When he finally relented at the insistence of regional OEO and agreed to a meeting, Frank arbitrarily changed the meeting time and location without notifying the council. The time had to be changed at the last minute, he claimed, to ensure that the meeting would not be disrupted by the presence of "irresponsible people" who would ask "rowdy questions." Such an excuse did little to endear Frank to the local people, who wanted a say in the program, or to OEO. A cartoon of Frank, published in the *Hinds County Freedom Democratic Party News* illustrates the popular perception of Frank—an angry white man with a shotgun "guarding" the federal antipoverty funds from the county's poor people.[25]

Like so often during the earlier civil rights movement in Mississippi, it was national attention that finally brought about change. Mississippi came once again under the national spotlight in May 1967 when the Senate Subcommittee on Employment, Manpower and Poverty held hearings in Jackson. Senator Robert Kennedy, a member of the committee, toured the poverty-stricken communities of the Mississippi Delta as part of his visit.

Kennedy's trip garnered much media attention. Marian Wright Edelman, an attorney for the NAACP Legal Defense Fund (and the spokesperson, lawyer, and "backbone" for the Child Development Group) went with Kennedy. They visited a "dark and dank shack" in Cleveland, Mississippi—the home of Annie White. "It was very filthy and very poor," Edelman later recalled. "There was a child sitting on a dirt floor . . . filthy. And there was very little light there and he got down on his knees and he tried to talk to the child and get a response from the child. . . . And I remember watching him in near tears . . . I was moved by it."[26]

Senator Kennedy told his aide: "I've been to third-world countries, and I've never seen anything like this." He was both angered and motivated by what he witnessed in Cleveland. "There are children in the Mississippi Delta," he said,

whose bellies are swollen with hunger. . . . Many of them cannot go to school because they have no clothes or shoes. These conditions are not confined to rural Mississippi. They exist in dark tenements in Washington, D.C., within sight of the Capitol, in Harlem, in South Side Chicago, in Watts. There are children in each of these areas who have never been to school, never seen a doctor or a dentist. There are children who have never heard conversation in their homes, never read or even seen a book.[27]

Kennedy's visit prompted his renewed efforts to tackle poverty in the Senate. In Mississippi the media attention on the Delta led to accusations against the white establishment. The establishment was accused of perpetuating the deliberate starvation of poor African Americans— potentially even that genocide was being perpetrated. An intense political storm resulted, made worse by Governor Johnson's remark that "nobody is starving in Mississippi. All the Nigra women I see are so fat they shine." The Mississippi Republican Party, making use of any opportunity to gain political credit by undermining the Democrats, produced a pamphlet refuting the accusations. The accusations by visiting physicians and congressmen were, according to the Republican pamphlet, the "irresponsible accusations" of "bigoted elements." But it was the comment of CSA director Colonel Frank that incensed the poor citizens of Hinds County. Far from any effort to drive the poor from the county, Frank claimed there was "a sincere concern for the poor and conscientious efforts to come to their aid." In the midst of a media furor, in which pictures of starving Delta residents were published in national newspapers, Frank's comments were particularly galling.[28]

While Frank's comments horrified the poor residents of Hinds County, they forced the regional OEO to finally pay attention to the complaints of the community council. Despite the evidence provided in Seaver and Levin's pamphlet, the regional OEO had done little to check white segregationist control of the program. Now, however, with national attention and statewide outrage directed against the indifferent comments made by Mississippi's white power structure, OEO responded. In June 1967, one month after the furor sparked by the accusations of genocide, OEO finally demanded a restructuring of the board. Poor representatives, black activists, and some white liberals were democratically elected to the board. New appointees included two of the so-called "outside agitators" of Freedom Summer: Charles Horwitz and Ted Seaver. The success of the council in securing representation with CSA was, at last, a victory for the moderate activists. But it was, for the white establishment, an alarming development. Erle Johnston, now well practiced at using the power of the Sovereignty Commission to infiltrate community action programs, went into action. Investigators spend much of June 1967 meeting white CSA board members and spying on those members unwilling to talk. Commission investigators believed there was little to worry about from the white board members. "The majority of the board of directors are fine upstanding citizens," investigator Hopkins reported to Erle Johnston. One white board member assured the investigator of his motives. "Since they were going to have this program anyway," he was serving as a member "just as several other respectable citizens were doing, in order to operate the program as it should be operated." But Johnston remained concerned about the influence of Charles Horwitz and Ted Seaver.[29]

Horwitz, as a member of the Delta Ministry, raised once more the specter of the Child Development Group, which the Delta Ministry had supported. And Ted Seaver was a significant threat. Seaver was active in the Mississippi Freedom Democratic Party, authored articles in the Hinds County Freedom Democratic Party newsletter, and frequently published flyers advocating poor participation in CSA. Johnston had been keeping tabs on "outside agitator" Seaver since his arrival—particularly after the publicity surrounding Seaver's work to publish details of police brutality against black citizens. He was, according to Johnston, "number one troublemaker" and "chief burr under the saddle of most of the white segregationists and moderates of Jackson and Hinds County."[30]

In 1966 Johnston wrote an editorial in the *Scott County Times* documenting Seaver's record of activism, such as his involvement in the Greenville Air Force Base sit-in, support for the Child Development Group, opposition to STAR, and his connections to communists. Johnston hoped this litany of activism would undermine public support for Seaver and Vermont in Mississippi. Later that year, Johnston wrote to the chief deputy sheriff of Hinds County, alleging that Seaver was "quietly encouraging Negroes in Utica to boycott white merchants." When Seaver became a member of the Community Services Association board, the Sovereignty Commission expanded its spying activities to include the program. Investigators attended CSA meetings and made unsuccessful attempts to have Seaver removed from the board. On August 28, 1967, Johnston and his investigators "set in motion a plan to have Seaver removed as a member of the board." Johnston kept detailed records of Seaver and the other board members in their attempts to find the right person to lead the vote against him.[31] However, its attempted infiltration of CSA was unsuccessful. This failure did not deter Johnston from his witch-hunt, though. His December 1967 report on "attitudes in Mississippi" documents those he claimed were "communists among the civil rights activists," including Seaver's colleague and president of Vermont in Mississippi, Irving Adler.[32]

While the addition of white liberals such as Seaver and Horwitz challenged the dominance of white segregationists on the board, for many of the staff and participants of Community Services Association this was not enough. A number of the program's black staff saw little change in the program as a result of the addition of Seaver and Horwitz. Don Jackson, the black counselor of CSA's Neighborhood Youth Corps rejected the leadership of white "liberals," such as Ted Seaver, purporting to represent the African American community. Jackson also rejected the actions of those he accused of being "Uncle Toms," including established middle-class blacks of the board and the program's deputy director E. L. Lipscomb. Jackson's previous role in the social services section of the Child Development Group had brought him under the scrutiny of the Sovereignty Commission. Investigators claimed he turned in false expenses—a practice they alleged (without foundation) was "fairly widespread in the Child Development Group." Jackson also frequently contributed to the Hinds County Freedom Democratic newsletter and statewide movement newsletters. Such activism kept him on the radar of the Sovereignty Commission, whose investigators reported on his activities, his religion, his job status, and his family. Don Jackson was part of a black community seeking genuine empowerment and community action, which Neighborhood Youth Corps offered.[33]

The Neighborhood Youth Corps (NYC) was created under Title 1B of the 1964 Economic Opportunity Act as a work experience and training program for young people aged from fifteen up to their twenty-second birthday. The first NYC programs began in January 1965, administered by the Department of Labor and operated through community action agencies. The NYC was designed to break the cycle of poverty by preventing high school dropouts and providing work experience and training for the nation's poorest and most disadvantaged youths in cities and rural areas. The program provided trainees with paid work experience and "work readiness training." Such training included basic numeracy and literacy skills training, as well as imparting "self-respect and good habits as a worker," and meetings with a corps counselor. There were three NYC programs: an in-school program, an out-of-school program, and a summer program. The in-school program was the largest of the NYC programs: nationally 106,000 youths participated in 1966, earning $1.25 per hour for up to fifteen hours per week, with the number of enrollees increasing to 125,000 in 1967. However, given the number of youths eligible was estimated by the Department of Labor to be 1.2 million in 1966, the program, as with most in the war on poverty, was inadequate in scope and funds. The out-of-school program for those out of high school involved more hours—up to thirty-two per week—and more intensive counseling and "remedial education." The summer program lasted eight to ten weeks, designed to "enable the enrollee to earn the money that can make the difference between returning or not returning to school in the fall."[34]

Despite the lack of funds for NYC, early reports on its success were fairly positive. At the June 1967 Senate hearings on the war on poverty, the NYC was considered to have "functioned well toward accomplishing its goal of giving disadvantaged youths the means by which they can continue their education," although the committee noted that limited data was provided. More detailed reports later compiled by the Department of Labor, together with studies conducted by academics, showed considerable benefits for NYC enrollees, including reduced school dropout rates, reduced levels of juvenile delinquency, and "improved skills associated with successful job performance once the student leaves high school." A number of these studied found the NYC programs more beneficial for African Americans and particularly for African American women. Success in the programs, in terms of enrollee experience and outcome, was heavily dependent on two key relationships: the relationship between the enrollee and their workplace supervisor and between the enrollee and their corps counselor. As sociologist Palmer R. Anderson explained, when counselors viewed enrollees as clients and bought into the concept of a "culture of poverty," the impact on enrollees was problematic. On the other hand, some enrollees reported their relationship with corps counselors as among the most beneficial of their experiences, where the counselor became a key source of support. Likewise, some NYC enrollees reported their workplace supervisors as being "like a second mother." But where there was an uninformed or disinterested workplace supervisor, enrollees were more likely to become disengaged. In Jackson that enrollee-supervisor relationship became a method of re-entrenching white power and subverting the intent of the program and the wider war on poverty.[35]

By 1967 Community Services Associations' NYC program had fifty-eight trainees enrolled. As with STAR, the corps's work training emphasis provided additional appeal and distinguished the program from welfare connotations. Despite this distinction, poor whites remained reluctant to enroll in a program perceived as black leaving the corps predominantly African American. The lack of involvement of poor whites in the corps stands in contrast to the willingness of middle-class whites to become involved in CSA. Involvement in the program would bring poor whites into direct competition with poor blacks. Middle-class whites, on the other hand, were not threatening their socioeconomic status by sitting on community action boards. Far from it, in fact. Board membership on community action programs often gave white Mississippians opportunities to cement their social, economic, and political status. Poor whites, on the other hand, lacked these sources of power to dictate and control their relationships with African Americans. For many poor whites, participation in an antipoverty program was seen as a threat to their socioeconomic status. Involvement in an integrated program, where African American and white trainees would ostensibly be treated equally was still an unacceptable prospect for many white Mississippians in 1967. Worse still for these whites was the prospect of being under the supervision of black corps staff, such as corps counselor Don Jackson. The lack of white involvement in the corps was reflected across the CSA component programs (and in antipoverty programs across Mississippi). These class tensions had a powerful impact on the nature of antipoverty programs. In turn, antipoverty programs perpetuated historic patterns of class and race discrimination.[36]

Upon joining the NYC, the young enrollees were placed under the omnipresent racism perpetrated by the majority of corps staff, coworkers, and supervisors at job placements. One of the most blatant facets of this discrimination was the nature of job placements. For the majority black enrollees, their placements were in publicly owned and operated agencies such as the Game and Fish Commission, Naval Reserve, Mississippi National Guard Headquarters, Veterans Administration Center, and Inland

Revenue Office. The board refused to accept placement arrangements with private organizations such as the Poor People's Commission or the Delta Ministry when legislation was amended to allow partnership with private organizations. Placement in the acceptable, public agencies put the corps enrollees under existing mechanisms of segregation and discrimination. In these public agencies, very few African Americans were employed. Thus, the enrollees were given only menial chores and often faced racial abuse. At the Game and Fish Commission, for example, the trainees were subject to abuse and profane language from their supervisor. They were not, the trainees told Don Jackson, provided with any training. At the National Guard, trainees were used to sweep up and clean around the airplane hangar and did not receive their pay. When their supervisor went on a two-week trip, the trainees were left under the supervision of a man who had no idea what Neighborhood Youth Corps was or the purpose of the trainees' employment. In all placements except one, Don Jackson reported, the NYC "was providing free janitors and maids to various agencies and really not doing anything more."

This was not the empowerment that Don Jackson had sought for himself and the NYC enrollees he mentored. Jackson's boss, acting NYC director Stephen Canon, was unsympathetic in the face of Jackson's reports of the discrimination that many enrollees faced. When one black trainee working at the Game and Fish Commission complained of the corrosive working conditions and asked for a transfer to an alternate placement, Canon refused. The trainee was, according to Canon "acting like a savage." Don Jackson and some board members, including the Delta Ministry's Charles Horwitz, sought to address this situation. They proposed the program authorize placements in private organizations, such as the Poor People's Commission, National Sharecroppers Fund, Michael Schwerner Fund, Delta Ministry, and the Jackson Urban League, which regularly employed African Americans. The board steadfastly opposed such placements throughout 1966. But by mid-1967 the continued pressure from Don Jackson and the steadily escalating frustration of the enrollees finally gained a response. In July the board and program director reluctantly accepted placements through private organizations—a significant step forward for the corps and CSA.

But this success stood alongside other, more devastating problems with the Neighborhood Youth Corps and CSA. Alongside the destructive racism evident in the community action agency was a widespread mismanagement of the corps. Staff too often let down their trainees, not just by failing to find meaningful job placements, but also by failing to detect when vulnerable youths were in need of their assistance. The lack of care taken by some members of staff was hugely damaging to the trust that was essential to such an undertaking. It also proved detrimental to the self-respect that the program attempted to instill into poor youths. Together, the racism and staff failings undermined the intent of the creators of the Neighborhood Youth Corps. The administrative deficiencies of Community Services Association, meanwhile, destroyed the structural integrity of the program. Some members of the corps staff, led by Don Jackson, fought to improve the program. Jackson sought to protect his corps enrollees. He repeatedly raised their concerns with the corps director and CSA executive director Colonel Frank. In June 1967 he compiled a pamphlet of information on the failings of the program entitled "Neighborhood Youth Corps: A Broken Promise?" at the request of some board members, including Charles Horwitz and Ted Seaver. The pamphlet outlined the impact the racist actions of staff and job placement supervisors were having on the trainees. When little response was forthcoming, Jackson took his concerns before the August meeting of the board of directors.[37]

The board's response to Jackson's well-founded complaints was to terminate his employment. The reason for Jackson's dismissal was clear: he was challenging white control of the program and attempting to secure better treatment for the corps enrollees. The board was also concerned about the potential "radical" influence of Don Jackson, as he obviously, one commission investigator reported, "identifi[ed] with the Black Power movement." Speaking before a community meeting days later, Jackson told CSA staff, including—according to the commission investigator—"a number of civil rights workers," that Frank was closely related to General Walker who "helped incite the riot at Ole Miss when Meredith entered." Angry at the lack of response to his legitimate concerns, Jackson called Colonel Frank a "honky" and a "peckerwood." "This is the type of people running the program," Jackson told the meeting. Jackson responded angrily to what he saw as the board's attempts to defame his character through "lies and misleading statements" based on "spotty, incorrect, and often scurrilous evidence." For the black corps trainees, the firing of Don Jackson was a disaster. He had been looking out for their interests and had attempted to shield them from the effects of the white domination of the program. Jackson's firing was the catalyst for the enrollees' frustrations to become action.[38]

In late August thirty-three African American trainees of the NYC occupied Colonel Frank's office. In a peaceful sit-in protest, the trainees demanded that Don Jackson be rehired immediately. The group also demanded the resignation of Frank, whom they accused of being a "white racist," and E. L. Lipscomb and Rev. William Easterling, whom they labeled "Uncle Toms." They made other demands too, which were aimed at improving the working conditions for the trainees. The group asked for better jobs, a pay increase to the minimum wage of $1.40 per hour, and "an end to being coerced and called names like [N----r] by white supervisors."[39] Colonel Frank responded by calling the police, who immediately arrested the youths. The jailing of the group provoked a furious response from the black community. A flyer authored by the ad hoc Committee of Black Youth in Hinds County called for unity in opposing the actions of Frank. The flyer questioned, "How long will it be before we get together and stop these white racists by any means necessary???" For Don Jackson, Frank's actions were "the crowning disrespect for the law and for the rights of these Negro kids." These "kids," Jackson said, had taken the action they did,

> because they are tired of being disrespected, tired of being coerced, tired of being given "[n----r]-work" jobs and no training, tired of seeing the people who defended their rights being disrespected. In short, they're tired of being treated like [n----rs] and of what you showed total disrespect for the roles and the stated goals of the neighborhood youth corps.[40]

The corps enrollees were not just objecting to the discrimination they faced on the basis on their race. While the enrollees were mostly young men, a few young women were enrolled in the program. The combination of race and gender for black women ensured that it was incredibly difficult to escape poverty in a culture that discounted the value of women. The young women enrolled in the corps found themselves under attack on another front when they were targeted by a predatory staff member. The enrollees—both men and women—were thus opposing this gender discrimination in their protest. And on these grounds, their protest was slightly more successful. The accused staff member was investigated and dismissed by the board due to his conduct. But little response was forthcoming in response to the claims of racial discrimination.[41]

The black community in Hinds County was angry at the actions of those they accused of being "white racists" and "Uncle Toms" among CSA's board and staff. But further perceived betrayal came from the actions of white liberals. Liberals whom, according to the provocative flyer, "refused to lift one finger or loan us one dollar to help us get our children out of jail."

The actions of Ted Seaver came under particular criticism. Seaver's actions exemplified, for Don Jackson, the harm that white outsiders were doing to black activism. "Some of our leaders," Jackson wrote in an open letter in response to his dismissal "have had much more loyalty to themselves and to the white community than they do to us. The best example of that is of course Mr. Ted Seaver . . . the self-appointed spokesman for and moderator of Negro community in Hinds County."

Jackson rejected the notion that Seaver had come to Mississippi to develop local black leadership. Being from the north, Jackson contended, did not equate to a lack of racism. Seaver would have us believe, Jackson stated, that "white people [from the north] are different somehow." "I lived in the north from the time when I was a baby throughout most of my life," Jackson wrote. "I can bear witness that the difference is only a difference in method." Seaver had not helped to secure the release of the jailed youths, and according to Jackson, he had actually acted from self-interest. "Mr. Seaver was much more interested in negotiating with OEO and the Department of Labor officials than in getting the young people out of jail," Jackson wrote. "In fact on several occasions when we thought that there had been [bail money] raised through one of Mr. Seaver's contacts we found that these contacts back[ed] out after talking with Mr. Seaver." Jackson was not outright accusing Seaver of delaying the departure of the youths from jail. But he made clear that he "neither like[d] nor trust[ed] Mr Seaver." In fact, Jackson concluded, "I held him as much to blame as Mr. Frank, Mr. Lipscomb, and Mr. Eastland for the sorry state of affairs in CSA and NYC."[42]

Seaver's actions undermined the already strained coalition of white liberals and emerging black community leadership. The animosity between Seaver and Jackson over this incident fueled the rejection of white leadership by some black activists and antipoverty workers. Jackson and Seaver had been briefly united in opposition to the white segregationist leadership of CSA. But the racial and gender discrimination and class divisions in the antipoverty program weakened the coalition. Jackson's anger at Seaver even, according to Sovereignty Commission reports, resulted in a physical altercation between the two men. In a typically inflammatory style, the commission reported that "Don Jackson, with the aid of his friend Chuck Denson . . . beat Seaver to a pulp. Jackson also fired a gun at him as he was getting away." While this altercation was unlikely to have been as dramatic as painted by the commission, such internal strains in the program nonetheless ensured no cohesive response was forthcoming to challenge white control of the program. Frank later dropped the charges against the youths, but for Don

Jackson, it was simply too late. "We have seen the program that you said was going to help us. We have seen the program brutally misuse our youths, disrespected our young women and thrown us in jail," he said in his letter to Frank and the board. "Let me make it plain, the poverty program in Hinds County, Mississippi is just another plantation system with modernized slave masters and automated Uncle Toms."[43]

These events had a profound impact on Don Jackson. He had joined the fight against poverty in Mississippi—in both the Child Development Group and Community Services Association—as a means of securing black economic power. He had been frustrated in both programs by the power of the white establishment and, in the case of CSA, by what he saw as the collaboration of white and black moderates with this establishment. After he was fired from CSA in August 1967, he rejected interracial cooperation. His disgust in the failures of white leadership was reflective of the position of the Hinds County Freedom Democrats and more broadly of SNCC and Black Power activists across the country. Leaving the federally funded war on poverty behind him, Jackson enrolled at Tougaloo College and became active with the Tougaloo Group, a small alliance of Tougaloo students. Commission investigators kept tabs on him and were increasingly concerned about his influence—labeling him the "hub of all extremism in Jackson" and accusing him of dealing drugs. With the usual lack of concern for evidence, commission spies reported that Jackson's nickname on Tougaloo campus was "Pusher." What is clear however is that Jackson, far from dealing drugs, was providing a voice for the frustrations of many Tougaloo students. "At this time of crisis for the Black Community in our country," Jackson wrote in September 1967, "guns are as important as voting, decent jobs, good housing, better welfare and a better war on poverty. Defend yourself and your people." As an advisor to the Committee for Black Youth, Jackson reprinted Black Power material in newsletters that were circulated in Jackson and across the state. His articles included the Black Power slogans "burn, baby, burn," "Black Power is fire power," and "a dead man ain't got no civil rights." He urged his readers to study the diagram reprinted in the newsletter illustrating how to make a Molotov cocktail.[44]

Alongside these familiar Black Power rallying calls, Don Jackson also offered nuanced exploration of what Black Power could mean to the black community in Jackson. Shortly after leaving his post as youth counselor in CSA, he affirmed his belief in the central facet of Black Power as unity. In the *Hinds County Freedom Democratic Party* newsletter—in the page following the illustration of the Molotov cocktail—Jackson published an open letter to "white power in Hinds County." "I am writing to clear up the confusion about my former job with the Neighborhood Youth Corps," Jackson began. While the board of directors had asked him to keep working as a counselor for a thirty-day period, Jackson had refused. "The reason for this is very simple . . . I cannot and will not work for your so-called war on poverty as long as you insult the youth of Hinds County and their parents by refusing to meet with the Committee for Black Youth." "This," Jackson continued, "is just one more proof of the anti-Negro racism in this county which controls the poverty programs although 90% of the people in these programs are Black." "Let me make it plain," Jackson concluded, "*I will not sell out the youth and their parents for a few dollars.* I know that the time is approaching when other Black men and women will follow this example. The youth have led the way. I will not be alone in following them." Just as young activists had blazed a trail of direct-action protest earlier in the Jackson movement, in 1967 the young black participants in the Neighborhood Youth Corps were again leading the push for unity within Jackson's black community. In Jackson, Black Power was never really about separatism. It was about self-determinism, unity, and economic empowerment. It meant overcoming the class divisions that had long divided the black community of Hinds County. Activist John Salter believed that Black Power in Jackson was "grassroots power, that's really what all this is about. And if you're talking about separatism for the sake of separatism—that's where some of it began to go. . . . But I don't think it affected the grassroots that way."[45]

Don Jackson changed his name to Muhammad Kenyatta in early 1968. His name change did not denote a change in religion—he remained a Baptist minister. Rather, it reflected his admiration for black leaders: Elijah Muhammad, the leader of the Nation of Islam, and Kenyan President Jomo Kenyatta. He continued to work to alleviate the consequences of poverty and racism in Jackson through 1968, in the Southern Cooperative Development program, funded by the OEO and the Ford Foundation. The Sovereignty Commission, however, dedicated considerable time in their attempts to portray Kenyatta as a radical who was "spending a considerable amount of time . . . talking to groups of young colored males who he encounters on street corners . . . insighting [sic] them to hatred of the police department." Commission reports declared that Kenyatta was a "ring leader" in the "Black Panthers in the Jackson area" and was "hooked on marijuana to the point that he cannot do without it." His activism and name change, which Sovereignty Commission investigators noted with suspicion, brought him to the attention of FBI agents in Jackson, operating under the COINTELPRO black extremist operation. The FBI considered Kenyatta to be one of the "dangerous radicals" that agents were meant to be eradicating and targeted him. The three FBI agents wrote a letter to Kenyatta in April 1969, purporting to be from his fellow activists in the Tougaloo Group. The letter warned Kenyatta that, in light of his "unacceptable conduct," he must leave campus. Kenyatta believed the letter to be from his fellow activists in the Tougaloo Group. Disillusioned at his perceived exile, he left Mississippi immediately. It would not be until years later that the FBI's role in Kenyatta's persecution came to light. Returning to Philadelphia in 1969, Kenyatta continued to take an active role in improving the economic condition of black Americans. He was a founding member of the Philadelphia Black Economic Development Council and active in the Union of Black Clergy and Laymen. Kenyatta played a role in bringing the "Black Manifesto" of the National Black Economic Development Conference to national attention.[46]

At the 1969 Special General Convention of the Episcopal Church held in South Bend, Indiana, Kenyatta was among those who rushed the stage to pursue their agenda. The convention must, Kenyatta and Paul Washington (a black priest from Philadelphia) demanded, give attention to the Black Manifesto. This manifesto called for white religious institutions to give reparations for slavery. While the convention ultimately rejected this call, they did provide $200,000 for black economic development. Kenyatta's activism continued into the 1980s, during his time studying at Harvard Law School, when as president of the Black Law Students Association he was an active spokesman for boycott. After his graduation, community activism continued to shape his work—evident in his *Monthly Review* article entitled "Community Organizing, Client Involvement, and Poverty Law."[47] Kenyatta's determination to secure respect and economic security for his youth corps students—and his activism in Jackson, Mississippi— was ultimately frustrated. But his experiences with Community Services Association shaped his activism. His rejection of white leadership and calls for economic reparation speak to the frustrations and disappointments he faced as a Neighborhood Youth Corps counselor.

Kenyatta was one of hundreds of black activists turned poverty warriors across Mississippi and the rest of the Deep South who attempted to use the federal funds of the war on poverty to seek economic empowerment. The job security and better pay ensured Kenyatta could continue his activism. His role as NYC counselor gave him the opportunity to mentor young black men and women to seek, and expect, better education, pay, and opportunities. These activists, who used antipoverty programs to support the development of grassroots black leadership, embodied the call for Black Power. The failure of black community leaders and white liberals to challenge white establishment control of antipoverty programs disillusioned poverty warriors such as Kenyatta and his youth corps enrollees. Community Services Association had the potential to support black empowerment, to develop indigenous leadership, and to challenge the white power structure. But the program—and many antipoverty programs like it—failed to fulfill that potential. In part, this was due to the lack of unity among those challenging the white establishment. Perhaps more significant, though, was the adaptability of those white power structures in the face of the threat posed by antipoverty programs.

- Chapter Five -

HELEN BASS WILLIAMS AND MISSISSIPPI ACTION FOR PROGRESS

In June 1967 Helen Bass Williams, an African American woman, became the executive director of the state's largest Head Start program Mississippi Action for Progress. This was a momentous appointment, particularly given the violence that was sweeping across Mississippi. While Klansmen were shooting into Head Start centers and white women were targets of threats and smear campaigns for teaching in Head Start, it was remarkable that a black woman became executive director of a statewide, multimillion-dollar program. Many women found employment in antipoverty programs, from volunteers and teachers in Head Start centers to executive directors of community action programs. In antipoverty programs across the nation, women secured powerful positions. In Mississippi the war on poverty provided new opportunities as leaders and administrators for women such as Marjorie Baroni, Kathleen O'Fallon, and Patricia Derian. These women were white, however. For African American women opportunities were mostly limited to roles that centered on the care of children and drew on women's domestic experiences. Most of these roles were as teaching aides, cooks, and assistants in the Child Development Group. Helen Bass Williams, however, was a program leader. Perhaps most significantly, Williams was in a position of authority over a number of white staff, both men and women.[1]

Williams's appointment was controversial, within MAP's central office, among the members of its board of directors, and in wider Mississippi society. As with many of the decisions involving the creation and operation of MAP, Helen Bass Williams's involvement was not broadly popular, but it was politically astute. However, her role provoked a backlash. This backlash did not take a familiar form of white opposition to black advancement. Rather than subject Williams to a campaign of violence, threats, and intimidation, her white opponents harnessed the mechanisms of war on poverty itself to undermine her. Opposition to Williams's leadership came from a range of sources, but two white men in particular were involved in her removal from MAP. They were Owen Cooper, chairman of MAP's board of directors, and Erle Johnston Jr., the director of the Sovereignty Commission. These men were driven by very different ideologies. Johnston, an avowed segregationist, had spent his years at the commission investigating and infiltrating civil rights groups, smearing activists, and supporting White Citizens' Councils. Industrialist Owen Cooper, on the other hand, was a deeply religious man whose social conscience prompted his involvement in efforts to rebuild burned churches in the wake of Freedom Summer and to participate in the war on poverty. A conservative but pragmatic man, Owen Cooper became an unlikely but important tool in Johnston's attempts to reassert white control of Mississippi Action for Progress. The campaign against Williams had significant consequences. It slowed the pace of racial change and reshaped MAP as a mechanism of white authority. It also drove Helen Bass Williams from her position as executive director, from MAP, and ultimately from the state entirely.

Even before Williams's appointment as executive director, Mississippi Action for Progress was a controversial program. MAP was created as a result of the white campaign against the Child Development Group, which had seen its funding drastically reduced on the orders of OEO director Sargent Shriver. By late 1966 the reduction of CDGM's grant meant that many thousands of children no longer had Head Start classes to attend. There was thus an urgent need to create a statewide alternative to the Child Development Group. It would have to be a program that was integrated but which did not incite the ire of the state's white establishment. Governor Johnson demanded the program be placed under the auspices of his office, but the attention surrounding the Child Development Group's defunding had made Head Start in Mississippi a matter of national interest. With both the press and the administration awaiting Shriver's response, Shriver had more to consider than simply acquiescing to the demands of Mississippi politicians. He wanted to create a program that would still cater to poor black children but which would out of political necessity remain firmly if not directly under the control of the control of the white establishment. While this did little to pacify former Child Development Group staff and supporters, it did reassure Mississippi's white establishment. The new program was more than simply a way to neutralize the threat to OEO posed by angry segregationists, however. The creation of a new program was also a significant political opportunity for the Johnson administration. It had the potential to provide a base around which to rebuild a Mississippi Democratic Party that was not reliant on white segregationists but which included moderate whites and newly enfranchised African Americans.[2]

As the state Democratic Party continued to ignore African Americans, civil rights activists wanted to create an independent grassroots party what would demonstrate the "true nature of the voting population in Mississippi." The Mississippi Freedom Democratic Party (MFDP) was founded in the spring of 1964 to do just that. Their immediate goal was to challenge the regular state Democratic Party's all-white delegation at the national convention in Atlantic City in August 1964. In the early weeks of Freedom Summer, the MFDP gradually built its membership from the grassroots, culminating in a state convention in August attended by over two thousand black Mississippians. At the convention, sixty-eight activists were nominated to form the MFDP delegation that would challenge the regular Democrats at the Democratic National Convention. Among the delegation were grassroots activists who for years been the heart of the Mississippi movement, women and men, such as Fannie Lou Hamer, Unita Blackwell, Victoria Gray, Annie Devine, and E. W. Steptoe—many of whom would go onto play significant roles in the war on poverty. The MFDP delegation initially received support from a number of Democrats. Fannie Lou Hamer's testimony garnered the attention of a nation as she described the harrowing acts of violence perpetrated against her by Mississippi law enforcement officials. Hamer ended her testimony urging the national party to act. "If the Freedom Democratic Party is not seated now, I question America. Is this America, the land of the free and the home of the brave, where we have to sleep with our telephones off the hooks because our lives be threatened daily, because we want to live as decent human beings, in America?" Hamer's testimony was immensely powerful—as Walter Mondale later recalled, "You could not help but be moved."[3]

Not all of the Democrats shared Mondale's view, though. White southerners accused the Freedom Democrats of "having Communist ties" and threatened to walk out if they were seated. President Johnson had not yet arrived at the conference but was nonetheless keeping a close eye on events. He was ever mindful of the power of the white southern Democrats and did not want the convention to "blow up and embarrass him." Johnson tasked Hubert Humphrey to sort out the mess or, Johnson warned Humphrey, he would have "no future in the party." Hubert Humphrey, working with his Minnesotan protégée Walter Mondale, engineered a compromise. The regular Democrats would be seated, but the MFDP could have two at-large (nonvoting) delegates, Aaron Henry and Rev. Ed King. It was, Walter Mondale believed, "an honorable compromise," intended as a "symbolic gesture of support for the MFDP by the liberal Democratic leadership." Despite Mondale's optimistic recollection of the compromise, he did recognize that it was unlikely to work. "I was pretty sure the Freedom Democrats would find it inadequate and I thought it quite likely that the Mississippi regulars would walk out regardless."[4]

The MFDP delegation was indeed enraged. Not only to be rejected, but to be offered such a meaningless compromise and be told which members of their delegation should take the seats. Despite pressure on the MFDP from civil rights leaders, including Martin Luther King, to accept, they rejected the compromise. Returning the Mississippi, many Freedom Democrats were angry and disillusioned. This was another sell-out, Fannie Lou Hamer felt, as poor black Mississippians had too often experienced from middle-class groups, such as the "National Association for the Advancement of Certain People," as she often referred to the NAACP. However, despite the disillusionment and anger, the Freedom Democrats continued to be a potent force in bringing about change. Over the course of the following year, the MFDP challenged the seating of the five Mississippi congressmen, on the grounds that nearly half of the state's electorate had been prevented from participating in their election. They generated some support in Congress, though their attempts were ultimately blocked by powerful southern Democrats and the White House. Nonetheless, the pressure that the MFDP continued to apply did produce results. Mississippi's political establishment began—finally—to communicate with its African American constituents. The impact of the MFDP stretched beyond Mississippi. As a result of the MFDP's actions, the national Democratic Party indicated it would not accept discrimination in the selection of members of Congress or the conference delegation. The MFDP, as SNCC organizer Charles Cobb noted, laid the groundwork "that prepared the way for the Obama presidency." SNCC activist John Lewis believed that the ramifications of not seating the MFDP "permeated the political climate for years to come." It was a turning point, Lewis wrote, "for the country, for the civil rights movement."[5]

In the short term, however, the convention exposed and deepened major divisions within the Mississippi movement, and the broader civil rights movement. As Aaron Henry later recalled, "The attitudes presented that day [when the MFDP rejected the compromise] by the SNCC leaders represented the first concrete evidence of the ideological conflict between the more moderate NAACP leaders and the radical SNCC cadre.... This was the beginning of the division that would come to characterize two distinct factions in the Mississippi freedom movement. It was a painful time." SNCC activists in particular were "embittered" by the events in Atlantic City, particularly by the encouragement of middle-class SCLC and NAACP leaders to accept the compromise. SNCC activist John Lewis was devastated. When the compromise was offered, Lewis later recalled, one lesson many said they had learned was that "the 'white liberals' were not to be trusted." For Fannie Lou Hamer, Aaron Henry's advice that the MFDP accept the compromise was "among the first indications that the black middle class did not necessarily share her political goals." Bob Moses, who had held firmly to his belief that "an interracial democracy must be pursued interracially," abandoned that belief after Atlantic City. Some SNCC activists rejected interracialism altogether. Bob Moses concluded he could no longer "work within the system" and had, "within a year," changed his name and moved to Africa. Others turned their energy into the grassroots development of the Freedom Democrats and congressional challenge, or the expansion of Freedom Schools. In 1965 many MFDP members and delegates became the driving force behind the rapid expansion and early successes of the Child Development Group of Mississippi.[6]

For the regular Mississippi Democrats the offer to seat two MFDP delegates was a betrayal by the national party. All except three of the regular Democrats refused to take their seats at the convention, as they would not accept the compromise or sign the loyalty oath. They, along with 87 percent of Mississippi, supported Republican candidate Barry Goldwater in the 1964 presidential election. The three white segregationist regulars who remained loyal to Lyndon Johnson and kept their seats at the convention were Douglas Wynn, Fred Berger, and Judge C. R. Holladay. Johnson was grateful for their support, especially in the face of the magnitude white southerners' abandonment of the Democratic Party. Douglas Wynn in particular had additional ties to Johnson. He was married to the daughter of "one of the most powerful men in Texas," Edward Clark, a longtime friend of Johnson's and his attorney. Johnson was, in fact, godfather to Edward Clark's daughter Leila, Douglas Wynn's wife. Wynn stayed at the convention in part out of loyalty to Johnson and also because Senator Eastland "had called to urge the regulars to stay rather than let MFDP take the seats by default." Whatever Wynn's motivations, Johnson assured him in a phone call in the evening of August 25 that he was a "patriot" who "saved [his] state." For many Mississippians, however, Wynn, Berger, and Holladay were anything but patriots. Despite Governor Johnson's assurances that the three men would face "no recriminations from the executive department of the state of Mississippi," they suffered serious consequences for their loyalty to Johnson.[7]

In the days following his return home to Mississippi, Fred Berger received threats on his life from the Ku Klux Klan. Douglas Wynn, worried about Berger, called Johnson's special assistant Jack Valenti. Wynn "did not know who to turn to" in order to help Berger, as the local police were Klansmen—or in league with the Klan—Wynn told Valenti. President Johnson, concerned that Berger's loyalty to him was having such consequences, asked his incoming attorney general Nicholas Katzenbach to act. "I don't know what the procedure would be. I don't know whether any laws were violated or what, but the fellow, he was one of the three, you know, [from] Mississippi [that] didn't walk out," Johnson told Katzenbach. "And I don't want to get him involved in any way in politics, but I don't want somebody to get killed because . . . [they] exercised their right to stay in the convention." Douglas Wynn was targeted too by disgruntled Mississippians, who "just tried to bust his law practice and just damn near ruin him." When, in early 1966, OEO needed an "acceptable" alternative group to run Head Start in Mississippi, President Johnson saw an opportunity to build a new base for the Mississippi Democratic Party, one which began with loyalists such as Douglas Wynn but which also incorporated newly enfranchised African Americans. President Johnson's aide, Harry McPherson, worked closely with state organizations and businessmen and politicians to create a viable program that could achieve these political ends. To help him navigate the complexities of the state's murky political waters, Harry McPherson turned to Douglas Wynn.[8]

Wynn advised McPherson on the creation of a poverty program that he knew white Mississippi would accept. This was to be an interracial program; even Governor Johnson was now cognizant of the necessity for an integrated program. But Wynn was very clear on exactly what form that interracialism should take, and he warned McPherson to be careful about whom he allied with. In particular Wynn warned against any association with the Child Development Group or their supporters. He evoked a threatening specter: a coalition of the Delta Ministry, Child Development Group, and the Freedom Democrats. These groups were, Wynn told McPherson, working to undermine Mississippi in "every way possible." SNCC and the Freedom Democrats were trying to "defeat the moderate right-thinking people of Mississippi." McPherson took Wynn's warnings to heart. The board members McPherson recruited were all men, including white businessmen, such as industrialist Owen Cooper and plantation owner Oscar Carr Jr., and moderate whites, including Mississippi Young Democrats founder and *Delta Democrat Times* editor Hodding Carter III. These men were moderates—by Mississippi standards. Hodding Carter III, for example, was editor of the state's most "liberal" newspaper, *Delta Democrat Times*. The African Americans selected for new program included NAACP state president Aaron Henry, R. L. T. Smith, and Rev. Merrill W. Lindsey. Activists, undoubtedly, but men who, in Henry's case, wanted to accepted the Atlantic City compromise. These men shared a "predilection for conciliation" and gradualism, which led to Henry's estrangement from the Freedom Democrats, and a rejection of the Delta Ministry's move toward more radical challenges to racial inequality. The new MAP board was a recycling of loyalist Democrats, two of the members also members of Johnson's one-thousand-dollar-a-head President's Club. That is not to say that they were not genuine in their support of Head Start. As historian John Dittmer noted of the "coalition of Delta whites and old-line NAACP leaders," they were "genuinely committed" to keeping Head Start running. However, "they must have been aware that control over millions of dollars of Head Start funds would give them political patronage and power, enhancing their position as a credible alternative to the Freedom Democratic Party."[9]

For Reverend James McRee, former board president of the Child Development Group, the actions of Harry McPherson were appalling. "I was increasingly shocked and disgusted as I realized the extent of the political motivation and machination behind everything the government does, and all of it is dominated by a determination to keep power in the hands of certain white people and the black people they name. This is as true of the liberals as it is of the racists; none of them are about to relinquish power to the little people whose lives are at stake." The creation of Mississippi Action for Progress mirrored the compromise offered in Atlantic City, as Johnson's aide selected the "acceptable" black activists to participate. This time though, the MFDP had no voice. Their program, the Child Development Group, had already been cut from underneath them. Freedom Democrat Fannie Lou Hamer, who worked in a Head Start program in Sunflower County, responded scathingly to the involvement of Aaron Henry in the new program. It was, she said, nothing less than a sell-out by "a few middle-class bourgeoisie and some of the Uncle Toms who couldn't care less." The war on poverty was, in Hamer's view, "a war on us [poor people]." "Nothing in the world is so unjust as this poverty program in Mississippi," Hamer told an interviewer in 1966. "It's a disgrace and it's a shame before God for people to operate this kind of thing and call it a poverty program." The director of the Child Development Group, John Mudd, went even further than Hamer. He evoked the language of betrayal, drawing comparisons with post-Reconstruction-era plantations complete with a white leader and "head [n----r]." This anger was echoed in flyers which called on African Americans to demonstrate against Mississippi Action for Progress, in opposition to what was termed a "third era of slavery." As state AFL-CIO president Claude Ramsay recalled, "Aaron really took the wrath of a lot of people as a result of all of this. I mean that blacks, a lot of radical blacks, man they really went after old Doc with a passion on this one."[10]

MAP's creation deepened the intraracial class divisions within Mississippi's movement that had been exposed in Atlantic City. These divisions were not only evident among leaders. At the grassroots, staff and supporters of the Child Development Group directed their anger at local MAP staff and centers. In Wayne County, for example, former Child Development Group personnel threatened parents and staff. Parents sending their children to the new Mississippi Action for Progress centers were afraid for their children's safety. Mississippi Action for Progress teachers were, OEO consultant Patricia Derian reported, "given the idea that if they tried to walk the children from the center to their cars they could be hurt." CDGM supporters also threatened a boycott of local MAP Head Start centers. In Greenwood CDGM supporters disrupted the county advisory elections that would elect local people to boards to have a say in the running of their MAP centers. Local media seized upon the incidents, claiming that the Child Development Group was waging "tenacious guerrilla warfare against biracial moderates." However, despite the anger it generated, MAP's creation was still a remarkable achievement. The development of an integrated organization accepted by the white establishment and in command of millions of federal dollars was an incredible feat. And for thousands of poor children across the state, MAP's successful creation meant renewed funding for their local Head Start centers.[11]

By 1967 the state's war on poverty was firmly entrenched in communities across Mississippi. In Mound Bayou in Bolivar County the Tufts-Delta Health Center was not simply providing healthcare. The center addressed problems of malnutrition, inadequate housing, and unsafe water. On the reservations of the Mississippi Band of Choctaw Indians, across five counties in central Mississippi, the impact of the community action protest was enriching and empowering. In tens of less high profile, often single-county or single-purpose programs, black activism combined with war on poverty funds. In some places there was tentative cooperation between poverty warriors and the white establishment, such as in Coahoma Opportunities, Incorporated.

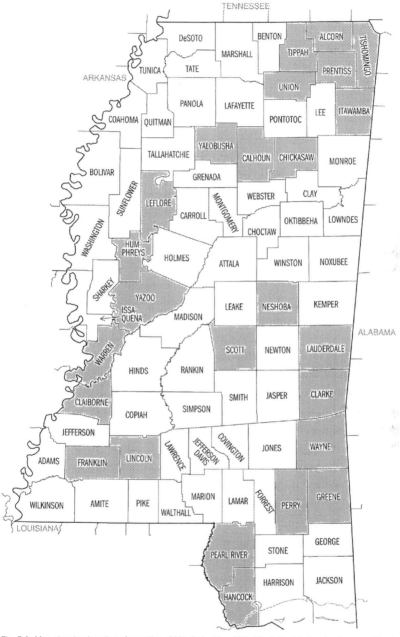

Fig. 5.1. Map showing location of counties of Mississippi in which Mississippi Action for Progress Head Start centers were located in 1966.

But the fight against the war on poverty was gaining traction too. White segregationists were becoming more proactive in their efforts to prevent federally funded black advancement. A coalition of civil rights activists in Jackson's Community Services Association fractured in the face of the power of the white establishment. White antipoverty workers came under a brutal campaign of Klan violence and intimidation. In the Delta, Head Start programs in Sunflower and Bolivar Counties became centers of renewed battles between civil rights activists and white segregationists. However, the Child Development Group, which had been subject to the most intense and sustained opposition from white Mississippi, went from strength to strength.[12]

Even during the three-month period operating without funds, CDGM kept open sixty centers for four thousand children on a voluntary basis. Still run mostly by African Americans, the Child Development Group continued to build on the legacy of Freedom Summer and achieved a level of success that Mississippi Action for Progress could not emulate. MAP, with a $3 million grant, had opened only five centers in two counties serving a hundred children in its first three months. The program—OEO founded, state sanctioned, and administration approved—was floundering. MAP faced the seemingly insurmountable challenges of operating a program with a biracial board, integrated staff, and integrated Head Start classes. Head Start under the Child Development Group was never wholly—or even mostly—about school preparation. It was about empowering and educating African American children about anything: from using a toilet to learning how to speak and write, and about black history. There was an equally significant health dimension to the early Head Start activities: children were given milk, often for the first time in their lives. Head Start medical staff pushed for the fluoridation of water, which was not widespread at the time. Head Start pupils received dental checks and medical attention. In 1965 Head Start employee Peter Stewart recalled, "Probably 60 percent of the children who were examined, enrolled in Head Start, suffered from malnutrition, anemia, internal parasites, most especially round worms, and tremendous oral cavity problems." Under Mississippi Action for Progress many—although by no means all—of these functions of Head Start were diminished, as the program narrowed its focus to school readiness. MAP centers, OEO consultant Pat Derian recalled, "tended to be a little more regimented.... [MAP] never had the spark that the Child Development Group did."[13]

From its inception Mississippi Action for Progress encountered problems among the biracial staff at its central office in Jackson and in centers throughout the state. Both black and white employees made accusations of discrimination, while personal antagonisms and rumor mongering fostered a destructive environment. White executive staff members were convinced of their own color blindness, perhaps buying into their own propaganda or equating opposition to the vociferous racism of Ross Barnett to a lack of prejudice. For many of MAP's black staff members, however, the racial discrimination was plain to see. One African American employee of Mississippi Action for Progress, Harold Jason, made a formal complaint in early 1967 that he was being blocked in his ambitions "because he is Negro." But his complaint was dismissed out of hand by MAP's white executive director, Walter Smith, who was, in fact, merely confused at such a claim. When he wrote to his former colleague John Ott for reassurance, Ott replied, "If the whites in the organization [MAP] could not be depended upon to be objective, then no white in the country could."[14]

Walter Smith—the husband of newspaper columnist Hazel Brannon Smith, famous for her attacks on White Citizens' Councils—was by no means an unreconstructed racist. His wife's newspaper, with its sympathetic stance on civil rights, had already cost him a previous job as a hospital administrator. However, his belief that all his staff shared an unimpeachable commitment to racial equality was, at best, naïve. When Smith was replaced as executive director by African American Helen Bass Williams in June 1967, however, things in MAP changed. Williams's appointment as executive director of the Mississippi's largest antipoverty program was a remarkable feat. As a woman and an African American, Williams was doubly vulnerable to the discrimination that beset the war on poverty's supporters, participants, and staff. To hold such a position in Mississippi was particularly impressive. The creation of MAP had marked a significant step forward for race relations in the state, despite attempts of some members of the white establishment to undermine the program from within.[15]

Williams's appointment was, in part, a product of this step forward, but her appointment was not simply a reflection of this progress. It was also the product of a divided board of directors whose members were seeking to achieve their own ends. Williams's tenure as executive director saw Mississippi Action for Progress make considerable strides toward genuine, rather than simply numeric, racial equality among the staff. Statistics showing equal numbers of African American and white staff members in MAP were lauded as signs of racial progress by the White House and national media. Indeed, any form of integration in Mississippi in 1965—particularly that sanctioned by the white establishment—was remarkable. Such statistics,

Fig. 5.2. Helen Bass Williams, pictured in 1968. Helen Bass Williams Personnel File, 1968–2012, Archives and Special Collections, Purdue University, Lafayette, Indiana.

however, failed to convey the true nature of integration in Mississippi Action for Progress. The attitudes of white and black staff hampered their ability to administer the program. Meanwhile, the actions and attitudes of some executive staff bolstered white control of Head Start while maintaining the appearance of interracial cooperation. Under Williams, Head Start classes fostered parent participation, and the rate of integration of centers increased. Although internal racial divisions and some external opposition continued to hamper the operation of Mississippi Action for Progress, by the summer of 1967 the program had gained significant ground. The program had reached twenty-five of Mississippi's eighty-two counties—as many as the Child Development Group had at its height. Williams's leadership meant the earlier unofficial understanding to avoid integrating centers was no longer in effect. In tens of integrated Head Start centers, children under five from low-income families were being prepared for school. MAP was beginning to function in spite of the many challenges of integration.[16] Such changes inevitably provoked opposition, and Williams's leadership style and administrative mismanagement caused many problems. Most destructive, however, was the sustained and intensive massive resistance campaign against Williams run by the Sovereignty Commission in collaboration with key MAP staff and board members.

Born in southern Illinois in 1916, Helen Bass Williams grew up in the tiny black mining community of Dewmaine and spent her twenties earning her degree and teaching. She also assisted her husband, who was the second black doctor in Southern Illinois, with his medical practice. After her husband's death in 1947 Williams attended the University of North Carolina on a full scholarship, receiving a master's degree in public health before working in the South Carolina Department of Health, Education, and Welfare. She moved to Mississippi in the early 1960s to take up a teaching position at Tougaloo College, where she became involved in civil rights activism. Williams was a "bridge leader" in the movement, forging crucial connections at the community level. Moving away from teaching, Williams worked briefly at the Child Development Group and as a consultant for the Office of Economic Opportunity before replacing Walter Smith as executive director of Mississippi Action for Progress in June 1967. A controversial appointment, Williams had extensive knowledge of education and Head Start but lacked administrative and managerial experience. She excelled at working with mixed-race groups and was committed to the belief that poor blacks could and would gain power in integrated groups if they persevered. Local white officials with whom Williams worked praised her as a "tireless, dedicated, and fair-minded person" who would "make an everlasting contribution toward tranquil relations" in Mississippi.[17]

During Williams's work in the health services division of the Child Development Group, her skill in dealing with the white establishment enabled her to secure funds for the group through the Mississippi Department of Public Health, which frequently "let federal money go" rather than accept integration. Williams's refusal to accept disrespectful treatment from the white health workers with whom she interacted gave poor blacks a "model of leadership" and affirmed "their dignity and self-worth." However, Williams rejected the separatism of CDGM and the Freedom Democrats. She was uncomfortable with the prejudice against the middle class that was "like a religious cult" during the summer of 1965. Williams saw Head Start as an opportunity for blacks to learn about running organizations and work with whites in what she called an "integrative approach." She remained committed to this approach, even in the face of violence, intimidation, and a prolonged campaign by the Sovereignty Commission to have her fired.[18]

The driving force behind the campaign against Williams was commission director Erle Johnston. He was uniquely skilled and positioned to target Williams. Johnston had worked as a newspaper editor before moving into public relations for a number of Mississippi politicians, beginning

Fig. 5.3. Erle E. Johnston sitting in his office, 196-, SCR ID # 8-17-0-52-1-1-1ph, Series 2515: Mississippi State Sovereignty Commission Records, 1994–2006, Mississippi Department of Archives and History, Jackson, http://www.mdah.ms.gov/arrec/digital_archives/sovcom/photo.php?display=item&oid=498.

with Senator Eastland's campaign in 1942. In 1960 Governor Ross Barnett appointed him director of public relations of the four-year-old state Sovereignty Commission. Three years later, Johnston was promoted to commission director. As director, Johnston continued to place considerable emphasis on the public relations function of the commission, lobbying successive governors, to no avail, to rename the group to reflect that aspect of their work that he considered most important. By 1967 the governor and other prominent leaders, including Mississippi's Economic Council, were pushing Mississippians to accept that a measure of integration was unavoidable. This left Johnston with the task not of selling Mississippi's beliefs to the rest of America, but selling integration to Mississippians. Clearly, Johnston had not become a prointegrationist overnight. Rather, he described himself as a "practical segregationist." Far from willing to accept full integration and equal rights for African Americans, Johnston recognized in the face of overwhelming national pressure and federal legislation that a continued commitment to maintaining absolute segregation was injurious to white Mississippi. A measure of acceptance, though resulting in token desegregation, would ensure whites remained in control of the process and of Mississippi's economic and political future.[19]

Johnston's limited acceptance of Head Start was based on the same philosophy. When discussing Head Start, he drew on the rhetoric of earlier massive resistance. Informing a rotary club meeting that if the federal government and the courts were going to force integration of the schools, Johnston said it would be better that "Negro children be taught the basics of hygiene, cleanliness, and concern for one another," all three of which he claimed were part of a Head Start curriculum. Johnston had realized that Head Start was unavoidable and remained committed to preventing a resurgence of the Child Development Group. Together with Governor Johnson's reluctant acceptance of Mississippi Action for Progress, this ensured Johnston's cooperation with the program's first executive director, Walter Smith. Despite being in sympathy with civil rights activism, Smith did not actively promote black community participation within MAP. Thus under his leadership, the program posed no threat to the white establishment. Indeed, Johnston believed that Smith's MAP could be held up as a model program, an example for OEO of what might replace programs functioning without the support of the state. Williams, an African American woman committed to developing meaningful grassroots involvement, threatened both white control of Mississippi Action for Progress and its model program status. Intent on removing her from the program, Johnston initiated a relentless campaign to secure Williams's dismissal.[20]

Williams's appointment prompted the first stirrings of unrest among some members of the Mississippi Action for Progress board. While the program was lauded nationally as a new era of interracial cooperation, its biracial board masked the determination of Mississippi's white establishment to maintain tight control over the program. An integrated board, staff, and centers were a necessary concession. But when Williams began to promote meaningful black community participation in the program, the board began to tighten its control of the program. The connection between two leaders of the state's largest antipoverty programs—Owen Cooper and Walter Smith—and commission director Erle Johnston was not unusual. Civil rights and antipoverty workers in Mississippi found it necessary to deal in some way with the commission. Charles Evers became a "valuable ally" of Erle Johnston in his efforts to "reduce the chances of racial agitation" in Claiborne County, for example. Often, cooperation was induced by the threats and smears of the Sovereignty Commission. Mississippi Council of Human Rights director Kenneth Dean and Erle Johnston quietly shared information in the late 1960s. "Erle Johnston called me one night at home," Ken Dean recalled.

I had met him a few weeks earlier and he had wanted to establish a working relationship. We agreed that we would try to work together to avoid any acts of violence. That's all. . . . I had been resistant to this because the Sovereignty Commission had been responsible for closing down the Council on Human Relations. . . . Here I was being invited to cooperate with a man and an agency who were purporting to have shifted from opposing blacks and defending segregation over to one of some kind of accommodation.[21]

The kind of "cooperation" described by Ken Dean was most often induced by the use of subtle—and in many cases overt—threats to smear or harass activists and their supporters. Owen Cooper had no involvement with the Sovereignty Commission until Williams was appointed executive director. Johnston responded to MAP employees with the usual combination of subtle intimidation and offers of help to weed out "agitators and revolutionaries" from MAP. Johnston met with Ike Sanford, MAP's public relations director, and recorded his version of the conversation in his files. Johnston recorded telling Sanford that he was "concerned that the revolutionists, the militants, and SNCC workers were getting a toe hold in the organization and we felt that if this trend continues, MAP would be in the same position as the old CDGM." Johnston's memo to file continued:

We told Mr. Sanford that if MAP would furnish us with a personnel list, we would check it thoroughly to see if any of these persons were already in MAP jobs. We told him we would report back to him if we found such people and recommend that they be released. We, also, told him we could find this information anyway but if MAP would cooperate, we will cooperate with MAP. If we get the information from other sources, we told him, we would probably turn it over to other people.[22]

Sanford conveyed the warning implicit in Johnston's message to Owen Cooper. MAP was being requested to cooperate with the Sovereignty Commission, or face the commission's lack of cooperation, which would involve turning information on suspect MAP employees to "other people." Owen Cooper telephoned Johnston three days later. Johnston's notes record the unlikely conclusion that "Mr. Cooper wanted to cooperate with the Sovereignty Commission in weeding out the agitators, revolutionaries etc. who might have infiltrated into MAP jobs," rather than the more likely scenario of Cooper's reluctant cooperation in the face of commission threats. "I was delighted," Johnston ended his note to file, "because this is the first time that Mr. Cooper has expressed any interest in the Sovereignty Commission and the services it could render. If the recommendations we make in the future can help clean out some of the undesirable in MAP, this contact with Mr. Cooper will certainly be worthwhile."[23]

Contact with the Sovereignty Commission by the mid-1960s was clearly a necessity, if only to monitor what the commission knew and who they were threatening. Indeed, Ken Dean urged Helen Bass Williams to cultivate a relationship with Johnston but cautioned her to keep such a connection private. The commission had made changes to its approach and tactics by the mid-1960s. By no means accepting of civil rights activism, or even of integration, the role of the organization had nonetheless evolved. No longer funding White Citizens' Councils, the Commission was employing what Johnston termed "racial troubleshooting" in order to blunt the extremism of the APWR and various Klan groups. The commission continued in its attempts to undermine civil rights activism, particularly implicating whites such as Ken Dean and Owen Cooper in order to foment distrust and division within the movement and within antipoverty organizations.[24]

The connection between Owen Cooper and Erle Johnston was not one aimed at reducing "racial agitation." A devout Baptist, Cooper was motivated to become involved in the program by his Christian duty to aid those less fortunate. And Cooper was not alone in this: Hodding Carter III recalled the religious motivation for many members of the board, "for whom conscience suddenly became larger than being the toast of the country club." Cooper was, Carter believed, "impelled, I mean a very conservative past, by his Christian conscience. . . . Owen truly was a Christian."[25] Cooper's involvement with MAP came at a moment when his conscience was awakened to matters he had previously "not even been conscious of the existence of." In a 1972 interview Cooper recalled that it was with his role with MAP that he came to understand that "the real help comes when you reach out and treat a person and try to help him as a peer, as an equal—equal at least in the sight of God—maybe not an economic equal, maybe not an educational equal, but an equal in the sight of God that you really begin to get yourself involved."[26]

He also became a member of the Committee of Concern, an interfaith coalition formed in the wake of Freedom Summer that condemned the violence and raised money to rebuild burned churches. Cooper served for ten years as chair of the board of Mississippi Action for Progress, as well as founding an organization called Mississippi Industrial and Special Services, into which he and other prominent businessmen combined their own money with grants from the federal government to build low-cost housing for the poor. Cooper, like the other "men of goodwill" with conservative backgrounds, was responding to his perceived Christian duty as well as to a pragmatic realization that Mississippi's economy would only suffer if the state continued to cling to segregation.[27]

These powerful and rich men—members of Mississippi Industrial and Special Services and of community action boards across the state—often genuinely wanted to alleviate the terrible conditions of Mississippi's poor people. They contributed greatly to their local communities. Cooper was awarded OEO's urban service award in 1968, recognizing not just his involvement in OEO but his services to his community, particularly to the poor in urban areas of Mississippi. Pat Derian recalled, on her appointment by OEO as a consultant and watchdog for OEO, "I went there thinking that I was going to be dealing with a bunch of closet racists and what I found was that wasn't true." However, neither their pragmatism nor religious convictions led Cooper or other white board members to cede any more control than was necessary to satisfy OEO guidelines. Cooper, according to Sovereignty Commission records, sent reports on Mississippi Action for Progress board meetings through his employee at the Mississippi Chemical Corporation, Jo G. Prichard. This material was a useful source of inside information for Johnston. In return Johnston provided Cooper with "information" obtained by his investigators on Williams and other MAP staff Johnston deemed as suspicious.[28]

Under Cooper, Mississippi Action for Progress enriched the lives of thousands of poor children. But his part in undermining Williams limited the extent of genuine grassroots participation that she had fostered, halted progress toward racial parity in the staff, and firmly established white control of the program in order to preserve the racial status quo. The board worked to ensure that federal funds went to segregated centers and allowed county advisory boards to operate with little accountability for their discriminatory activities. Their actions were redolent of the paternalism characteristic of earlier southern race relations. Such paternalism characterized the response of the white establishment to minority antipoverty programs from Alabama to Tennessee to Texas. Neither was Cooper the only board member or employee looking to secure Williams's removal. The pervasive distrust, resentment, and anger among staff provided the commission with numerous potential informants. MAP consultant Bruce Nicholas, for example, made a series of accusations against the executive director, at least partially in response to his personal grievance with Williams. According to Nicholas, Williams was responsible for "creating an atmosphere of distrust and anxiety throughout the . . . organization." She encouraged staff to report on their colleagues, Nicholas claimed, monitored telephone conversations, and read the mail of department heads.[29]

Fig. 5.4. Owen Cooper, 1960, Erle E. Johnston Jr., Papers, McCain Library and Archives, University of Southern Mississippi, Hattiesburg. Courtesy the Bob Hand Family.

Angry at Williams because she accused him of having an affair with "some woman," Nicholas no doubt exaggerated when he claimed Williams destroyed the interracial harmony that existed prior to her arrival. Not even the most optimistic observers could claim, as Nicholas did, that in 1967 native white Mississippians worked without incident under Negro supervision and employees, or that both black and white worked harmoniously together on the basis of equality. Williams's attempts to move toward racial parity in the central office did heighten tensions between black and white employees. She awakened the worst fears of the white establishment—that Mississippi Action for Progress would become controlled by African Americans and "degenerate to the level of the old Child Development Group." Such efforts led to increasingly unlikely accusations being leveled at Williams by MAP staff, board members, and the Sovereignty Commission. She was accused of firing white employees while doubling the central office payroll by hiring a number of consultants and advisors to patronize her friends.[30]

These "friends" became her "spy network" inside Mississippi Action for Progress, commission reports claimed, in order to build a "civil rights empire" out of the organization. Trawling through their extensive records, mostly containing press clippings and dubious reports based on hearsay and malice, commission investigators Tom Scarborough and Leland Cole compiled new reports on Helen Bass Williams's alleged spies, finding nothing more to accuse them of than lapsed SNCC membership and an arrest for breach of peace during a sit-in at Walgreens in 1962. White county advisory board members were quick to add their accusations to those of the central office staff. In Yazoo County, Williams had angered the MAP county advisory committee with her leadership style and actions. Williams had been developing parent participation in the county's Head Start centers, actions resulting in a stronger program built on a grassroots network of supporters, many of whom were black. For the white establishment that dominated Yazoo's Head Start program, a program strengthened by genuine community participation threatened its control.[31]

The Yazoo county advisory committee for Mississippi Action for Progress was headed by Herman DeCell. He was a state senator and public relations director for the Sovereignty Commission. DeCell was thus, unsurprisingly, a prominent and powerful voice in the campaign against Helen Bass Williams. He added weight to the information gleaned from Cooper and to the commission's unsubstantiated accusations. In January 1968 DeCell formalized his opposition to Williams, making an official complaint to the Mississippi Action for Progress board of directors. DeCell referenced Williams's "vulgar and obscene language completely unbefitting a woman," her lies, and "intra-MAP spies reminiscent of King Louis XV and his court." The Sovereignty Commission made tenuous reports on Williams's corruption and attacked her character. But Erle Johnston largely overlooked the very real problems caused by her divisive leadership and often-corrosive micromanagement. Instead, drawing on unsubstantiated allegations of Herman DeCell, the commission compiled a report comprehensively attacking Williams's character. In the report entitled "Evidence (or indication) of Race and Black Power tactics used by Mrs. Helen Bass Williams," investigators attacked Williams's leadership, conduct, and morality.[32]

The report made wild and unfounded accusations, claiming Williams was "preoccupied with SEX" (their capitalization). Stereotypes of black women as lascivious date back to slavery. Whites imposed on blacks an image of beastlike sexuality to justify both the rape of black women and the lynching of black men. Such stereotypes permeated the language of massive resistance. Accusations of immorality, particularly related to sex, were a powerful tactic of massive resistance, although such accusations were usually directed at men. Williams, as an African American and a woman, was thus doubly vulnerable to such attacks directed at her conduct and morality. Continuing over three pages, the report claimed, "All conversation with her included something to do with race," that she "cried on cue" and used profane, vulgar, and coarse language. Such accusations, depicting Williams as an unprofessional, emotionally charged agitator drew on racialized and sexualized stereotypes. The report continued with further spurious claims, accusing Williams of making derisive comments about board members to staff and forcing integration through a policy insisting same-sex personnel traveling together occupy one double hotel room.[33]

By early 1968 the Sovereignty Commissions' crude harassment campaign combined with her own ill health was beginning to take a serious toll on Williams. But while there may have been flaws in her leadership style, Williams remained dedicated to Head Start and to biracialism. She pursued this goal in the face of the commission crusade, betrayal by her staff, and the violent and intimidating actions of some white Mississippians. Like many employed in antipoverty programs in Mississippi, Williams worked under the constant threat of violence and harassment. While working for the Child Development Group, Williams was accosted by four white men who spat in her mouth and made her swallow—an incident she later recalled with feelings of debasement and terror. During her time as an OEO consultant in Sunflower County in 1967, Williams received death threats.[34]

As executive director of Mississippi Action for Progress, Williams was subject not only to attacks directed at her but also to the consequences of the persecution of her staff. Not long before her death in 1991, Williams recalled an incident that was characteristic of the indignities and injustices that MAP workers endured. An African American employee, having obtained a mortgage in order to purchase a house in a neighborhood that was "just turning," went to take possession of his new house. He found every surface in the house—walls, windows, and floors—had been covered in human excrement by the former owners, making the house totally unfit for habitation and almost impossible to clean. The police refused to help, telling him the owners had gone out of state. His bank also refused to help. Left with no home for his family and faced with a job he could not do, he killed himself.[35]

By January 1968 Erle Johnston and his investigators had set the stage for Williams's departure. Under pressure from Erle Johnston, Owen Cooper and the board stripped Helen Bass Williams of power and rescinded many of her policies and decisions. Cooper, Johnston reported, had been advised "firmly but gently that unless Mrs. Williams is dismissed and changes are made within thirty days, we will give our complete information with a suggested speech to Senator John Stennis." But while the commission was instrumental in destabilizing and undermining Williams, its role in her departure was kept quiet. Whereas the commission had loudly and publicly attacked the

Child Development Group, Johnston's opposition to Williams and the state-sanctioned Mississippi Action for Progress remained undercover. The commission's tracks were "well covered," Johnston assured newly elected governor John Bell Williams. Johnston ensured that his actions manipulating Owen Cooper and undermining Helen Bass Williams were kept from public notice but also made sure that the commission's role came to the attention of the incoming governor. The pressure orchestrated by the commission and applied by the board, together with the very real disruption Williams's management had wrought, ensured that Williams was systematically deprived of her authority. An executive committee of the board took over some of her responsibilities and rescinded many of her policies and decisions, firing a number of employees to whom the commission objected, including leaders of her alleged spy network, Ted Lawler and Calvin Williams. "It is possible," Johnston wrote in a note to file, "that the Chairman of the Board of Directors and a few others have done all in their power to bring about changes to their policies and procedures; however, MAP has degenerated almost to the level of the old CDGM."[36]

Johnston's unlikely assessment of the situation within MAP is a reflection of his decreased ability to manipulate the situation. During a March 4 meeting, when Williams was absent for surgery, Cooper called on the board for "unity and dedication." It was, Cooper was reported as saying, "time to stop infighting and dissension." Williams would remain in her position. However, by June, with her power and authority diminished and her decisions and actions questioned at every turn, Williams was demoted to deputy administrator in charge of program and training. Cooper described the demotion as a move to relieve her of the "burdensome and emotionally straining duties," which he described as being in the best interests of Williams's physical health. Helen Bass Williams resigned on August 31, 1968. In her memo to staff on her resignation, Williams remained dedicated to the "integrative approach." She spoke of the honest confrontation she felt Mississippi Action for Progress was producing between the races, which, she believed, would bring "honest solutions . . . to alleviate poverty in Mississippi."[37] Immediately leaving Mississippi, Williams moved to Indiana to become the first African American professor at Purdue University. Despite the suffering she endured and stress of her daily battles in Mississippi, Williams maintained her commitment to activism and improving the lives of the disadvantaged in her new role. She pioneered many of Purdue's diversity efforts, including creating the Black Cultural Center, and continued to support those in need—helping students pay for rent and tuition, sometimes at the expense of her entire paycheck.

Williams's house was a "headquarters for students who wanted to participate in the civil rights movement," and to many students it was even more than that—it was a home. "She always had a big pot of spaghetti on the stove for students who would come and speak to her about the movement and making the campus committed to civil rights," colleague Leon Trachtman recalled.[38]

In 1976 Williams was awarded Purdue University's Helen B. Schleman Gold Medallion Award for her contributions and concern for female students. "Mrs. Williams has given unstintingly of her time and effort to help people with troubles," Dean Robert L. Ringel said. "The troubles may have been malnutrition and disease . . . racial discrimination . . . educational or emotional. But whatever the troubles, Mrs. Williams had a commitment to help." In 1995, four years after her death, Purdue University created an annual scholarship in her name for African American students.[39] Despite her shortcomings as an administrator and leader, MAP under Williams expanded parent participation in centers across the state and at least began to move toward creating an integrated program. The commission's campaign drew on the racial and gender discrimination she faced on a daily basis from board members, colleagues, and county advisory boards. It illustrates the success of the evolving white resistance to black empowerment, particularly the use of a gendered language of opposition and the limitations of white accommodation to MAP's biracialism.

Owen Cooper's role in Erle Johnston's campaign against Williams, despite his racial moderation and Christian commitment to aiding the poor, denotes a development in the impact of white moderates and businessmen in the late 1960s. White moderates had played a vital role in securing a middle ground between white segregationists and civil rights activists in earlier phases of the movement.[40] In MAP, however, even the relatively benign motivations of white businessmen had a detrimental impact by limiting meaningful progress toward integration. Under threat or pressure from the Sovereignty Commission, white moderates—often unwillingly and sometimes unknowingly—became part of a system that perpetuated the work of the commission. The role of the commission was also evolving in response to the racial realities of Mississippi in 1968. No longer orchestrating supremacist violence, the commission was now focusing on character assassination. This development reflected a limited acceptance of racial integration. However this acceptance was a mask under which the Sovereignty Commission assisted white community leaders in forging Mississippi Action for Progress into a mechanism of white control.

- Chapter Six -

MISSISSIPPI REPUBLICANS AND THE POLITICS OF POVERTY

By 1968 increasing criticism directed at the OEO and community action was taking its toll on both President Johnson and the war on poverty. In the wake of long hot summers of riots, a reluctant Johnson was forced to reconsider his support for OEO. Once Johnson had confirmed his withdrawal from the presidential race on March 31, he began serious consideration of transferring or delegating Head Start to the department of Health, Education, and Welfare in order to protect its funding—concerned, no doubt about the future of OEO after his presidency ended. In his final budget address Johnson requested a two-year extension of OEO and a $2.18 billion appropriation for the fiscal year 1969 but with little hope of seeing his request secured. Republican presidential nominee Richard Nixon, focusing on promises of an "honorable end to the war in Vietnam," was notably quiet on the OEO during his campaign. His running mate Spiro Agnew was more vocal. Agnew stressed his desire to end the "waste and boondoggling," particularly through community action programs. Even Democratic presidential nominee Vice President Hubert Humphrey, who had been one of the biggest supporters of OEO, would not take the political risk of public support for the agency. Although he did praise individual, less controversial programs including Head Start and Upward Bound.[1]

Once Nixon won the election, the question seemed to be not if OEO would be dismantled, only when and how. In early 1969, in Mississippi and across the nation, opponents of the war on poverty waited expectantly for Nixon to "methodically defang the OEO." However, the circling vultures, whether press or political, Republican or Democratic, were disappointed. Southern reporters had been eagerly awaiting a much-delayed General Accounting Office report, which many hoped would lambast OEO for mismanagement. When it finally arrived however, the report merely provided a rather dull critique. Worse still was Nixon's failure to "defang" the OEO. The new president appeared undecided over the fate of the agency. In a draft of an August 1969 speech by Nixon, OEO was referred to as one of the "fundamental commitments of this Administration," though tellingly this was cut from the final version of the speech. Further complicating the fate of OEO, Nixon delayed the appointment of a new agency director, and he appointed Daniel Patrick Moynihan as his Counselor for Urban Affairs.[2]

Moynihan had served in the Kennedy and Johnson administrations and was one of the architects of the war on poverty. However, after leaving his role as Assistant Secretary for Labor in Johnson's administration in 1965, Moynihan became a vocal critic of the war on poverty. He was already a controversial figure after the publication of his 1965 report "The Negro Family: A Case for National Action," in which he claimed a "culture of poverty" was the result of the breakdown of the black family as African American women usurped the male provider role. In 1970 Moynihan courted further controversy in his book *Maximum Feasible Misunderstanding*, which was fiercely critical of the war on poverty. He coined the phrase "maximum feasible misunderstanding," a play on the controversial requirement of community action programs to achieve the "maximum feasible participation" of the poor in their planning and operation. Moynihan attacked community action programs, claiming they were "not understood and not explained." Moynihan believed that community action programs resulted in needless "social losses," which were compounded in new layers of bureaucracy that created more problems than they solved. Moynihan's claims laid the foundation for decades of neoconservative critiques of the war on poverty, notably in the work of Nathan Glazer. As Nixon's Counselor for Urban Affairs, Moynihan promised the president that he would, "personally undertake to see that all political activity by CAP [community action programs] is stopped."[3]

On top of Moynihan's appointment, the eventual choice of up-and-coming Republican Donald Rumsfeld as director of OEO signaled the fate of the war on poverty. It was "politically impossible" for Nixon to dismantle the war on poverty in 1969, but he wanted a "politically reliable operative" as OEO director to rein in the programs. Rumsfeld, whom Nixon characterized as a "ruthless little bastard," accepted his post on the condition that Nixon would not defund OEO from underneath him. Rumsfeld, who not only held the position of OEO director but also that of presidential adviser, oversaw fundamental changes within OEO. His appointment was the most visible of a number of staff changes Nixon demanded. The president placed "strong emphasis," chief of staff H. R. Haldeman reminded key staff, "on the need to change the local and regional personnel leadership of the community action program quickly and extensively."[4]

No longer an innovator of new antipoverty efforts, OEO became an incubator based on the ideas outlined by Moynihan in *Maximum Feasible Misunderstanding*. Instead of abolishing the OEO outright, Nixon reluctantly requested a two-year extension of OEO, while overseeing a slow dismantling of the agency through decentralization of power. Nixon began the process of moving programs out of OEO: among others delegating Job Corps to the Department of Labor and Head Start to HEW. The delegation of Head Start was, in particular, problematic for OEO. The presence of this popular program had been important in seeing OEO through some difficult times in Congress. But the decision to delegate, rather than transfer the programs outright, was encouraging. It was, indeed, far better than many OEO staff had feared, as it left OEO with certain fiscal and policy controls.[5]

Privately, though, President Nixon made it clear that the delegation was meant to ensure tighter control over Head Start. In a personally written, confidential memo to HEW Secretary Robert Finch, Nixon told him that Head Start had been transferred for "house-cleaning, not house-keeping purposes." Materially, this delegation was a significant decision too: together the two programs took seven hundred employees and $560 million out of OEO. Secretary of Labor George P. Schultz closed three-fifths of the existing Job Corps centers immediately on the program's transfer into Labor—a move vigorously opposed by OEO. Nixon did not plan to take the political risk of publicly destroying the war on poverty at this stage in his presidency, but he was responding to the concerns of the Republican legislative leadership. Moving Job Corps would, he assured them, "bring about a significant reorganization and a budget cut" to address the "boondoggle" program.[6]

However, Nixon did not just want the delegation of these two programs. Writing to all cabinet members less than a month after taking office, Nixon emphasized the significance of the reorganization that was taking place. "The restructuring of the Office of Economic Opportunity is already underway and other organizational changes will soon follow," he wrote. "I want to make it absolutely clear that the real purpose of restructuring and reorganization is to achieve financial economies as well as better administration." These economies would come, Nixon clarified, through restructuring but more significantly through a paring down of the program. "Our objective," he concluded, "is to eliminate duplication. . . . If we do our job properly there will be much less to coordinate."[7]

Nixon's meetings with his advisers reflect the importance they all placed on being seen to take action and "be different" from Johnson. Haldeman's notes reflect the importance Nixon placed on the appearance of change within OEO, because "the country is sick of it." Nixon was "in a hurry to change the name of OEO" early in his first term. John Ehrlichman, Nixon's assistant on domestic affairs, solicited ideas from a number of sources, creating a working group who listed over forty suggestions. These suggestions included "The Poverty Office," "Office of Career Development," "Agency for National Development," and "New Horizons Agency." A number of Nixon's advisors were eager to change the name of the agency: Moynihan suggested the "Agency for Citizen Action," while the president's speechwriter Lee Huebner liked the "Division of Domestic Development"—or 3-D for short.[8]

Huebner, who cofounded the Republican public policy organization the Ripon Society in 1962, was well aware of the need to separate Nixon from what he saw as the destructive centralization of Johnson's Great Society. This centralization was, Huebner wrote in 1966, "burdensome and inefficient," as well as "rich in statistics of progress but devoid of the satisfactions of meaningful public action." But while it was vital to sell Nixon's difference from Johnson, Huebner was not convinced renaming OEO was the right path. "I still think," he wrote to James Keogh, the head of Nixon's speechwriting team, "it would be easier to sell the concept that 'Nixon reformed OEO or the Job Corps and made them work'—than to sell the notion: 'Nixon abolished them and replaced them with something new—as is evidenced by their new names.' That's just not persuasive to my mind." It was not just Huebner who was unconvinced that rebranding would convince the public that the OEO would work under Nixon. Chair of the Federal Reserve, Arthur F. Burns, thought a name change was inadvisable. "It is not clear to me," Burns wrote to Nixon in March 1969, "that it is desirable to change the name of OEO. As long as the Community Action Program remains the mainstay of OEO, this organization is likely to be troublesome to you." After some consideration Nixon eventually dismissed the idea of changing the agency's name. The president decided it was important to retain the Office of Economic Opportunity title in order to ensure that Democratic politicians continued to share in the misfortunes of the agency's bad press.[9]

The fact the agency's name remained unchanged did not lessen the effects of the structural changes Nixon made. In Mississippi these changes had serious implications. Under HEW Secretary Robert Finch, for example, Head Start programs no longer had the protection of OEO against Mississippi Governor John Bell Williams's racially motivated vetoes. Secretary Finch was no friend of Deep South governors: he was a leading member of the "desegregation compliance faction," and HEW had a liberal reputation that persisted into the 1970s. But OEO's position as an agency somewhat outside the control of the administration had provided some protection against racial discrimination—protection that the Department of Health, Education, and Welfare could never ensure. Staff in the departments of Labor and HEW had a vested interest in cooperating with the local political establishment. Far from protecting and supporting those advocates of social change, these departments had their own entrenched racially discriminatory patterns that were often imposed on programs directly or through their connections with local Republicans. Though the war on poverty was not facing immediate termination, its future under the new Nixon administration seemed exceedingly bleak.[10]

Beyond the war on poverty, Nixon's electoral victory in 1968 had immense significance—it was a watershed political moment. Explanations of the political transformation of the South—from solidly Democrat to solidly Republican—have long centered on Nixon's "southern strategy." The southern strategy thesis, drawing on the work of Republican strategist Kevin P. Phillips in *The Emerging Republican Majority*, depicts Republican successes in the South as the result of a top-down strategy that began with Nixon's coded racial appeals in 1968. From the ostensibly race-neutral promises by Nixon to restore law and order to Reagan's attacks on welfare queens, the southern strategy thesis suggests that Republicans crafted rhetoric that would capture white voters who had been alienated by the victories of the civil rights movement. This interpretation builds into the notion of the "southernization of America," as the politics of southern resistance to desegregation moved northward and broadened into opposition to busing and then "ultimately the welfare state itself, which was depicted as benefiting primarily people of color."[11]

The southern strategy thus draws direct links between whites "massively resisting" to politics of the modern Republican Party. While there are clear linkages, the development of modern conservatism and its relationship with the Republican Party are far more complex than the southern strategy thesis depicts. Mississippi and the South more broadly transformed between 1950 and 1980. As Joseph Crespino has described, political power shifted "from the rural black belt to the modern, industrially oriented urban and suburban business class." Tracing a direct line from the politics of massive resistance to the politics of the Republican Party fails to appreciate the extent of these economic and political changes. Joseph E. Lowndes explains, "Backlash . . . masks what was a long-term process whereby various groups in different places and times attempted to link racism, anti-government populism, and economic conservatism into a discourse and institutional strategy through linguistic appeals, party-building, social movement organizing, and the exercise of state power." Indeed, where the "backlash" to the civil rights movement was strongest—in Deep South states such as Mississippi—the Democratic Party continued to hold sway at the local level into the 1980s.[12]

The southern strategy thesis also misreads the origins of southern support for the Republican Party and misinterprets the intent and impact of Nixon's rhetoric in 1968. While the white backlash did contribute to modern conservatism, the rise of the Republican Party in the South predates the 1960s. Southern support for the Republican Party came earliest and most strongly from the upper and urban South in 1950s. Historians, including Kevin M. Kruse, Matthew D. Lassiter, and Sean P. Cunningham, have demonstrated that the suburban Sunbelt was central to this political transformation. Matthew Lassiter explains that attributing the conservative shift in American politics to the top-down Southern strategy to exploit the white backlash to the civil rights movement "misses the longer term convergence of southern and national politics around the ethos of middle-class entitlement." The real power of Nixon's rhetoric in 1968 was not just that it captured the support of die-hard segregationists of the rural Black Belt, but that it also appealed to those in the Sunbelt suburbs. Nixon's rhetoric "bridge[d] the gap between the moderate, color-blind conservatives of the white, suburban middle class," and white segregationists of the rural Black Belt and thus, as Sean Cunningham explains, "helped lay the groundwork for a much more viable strategy for long-term Republican growth across the region."[13]

Historians of the Sunbelt together offer a more complex and dynamic view of the rise of conservatism and its connection to the modern Republican Party. Moving from a limited focus on electoral politics and public actors, these historians have shown how "a grassroots constituency emerged, which backed local and national candidates, created new circles in which to socialize, and developed a cultural component necessary to sustain the political apparatus." Historians of conservatism have shown how the rise of the modern conservative movement lay beyond the politics of race in the Deep South and long before the backlash of the 1960s. Kim Phillips-Fein, for example, has illustrated that to appreciate the scope and depth of the new conservatism, historians must look beyond cultural issues—and before the 1960s—to economic issues and business conservatives' response to the New Deal. Lisa McGirr and Michelle M. Nickerson have compellingly argued that in the postwar era women "shaped the conservative ascendancy with concerns, ideas, and issues that were drawn from the fabric of their everyday lives." Darren Dochuk and Steven P. Miller illustrate the significance of evangelical religion in the construction of the conservative Sunbelt. Historians of conservatism also point to the importance of anticommunism in fusing the conservatism of the South and West. Joseph Crespino's study of South Carolina Senator Strom Thurmond, for example, illustrates how with his focus on anticommunism, Thurmond "helped destabilize a Southern conservative order previously animated by race and forge a new synthesis that married South and West in the politics of national security."[14]

Particular attention has been given to the role of suburbia in the creation of a national conservatism. Matthew Lassiter emphasizes the importance of class in the rise of Sunbelt conservatism. For Lassiter the growth of southern Republicanism owed more to middle-class "corporate economics" than "working-class politics of racial backlash." Lassiter shows how a "color-blind defense of consumer rights and residential privileges" succeeded where "overtly racialized tactics of southern strategy had failed." Kevin M. Kruse, while also focusing on the suburbs, pays more attention to the role of race. Kruse traces the white flight to Atlanta's suburbs. More than simply a physical relocation, this white flight was a political revolution in which white southern conservatives abandoned their "traditional, populist, and starkly racist demagoguery" for a "'new conservatism' predicated on the language of rights, freedoms, and individualism."[15]

Underlying these facets of modern conservatism, some significant common factors emerge. As Lisa McGirr describes, the modern American right grew out of "the context of the Cold War; postwar demographic transformation; the dynamics of economic, cultural, and political change; and their cumulative impact on the values and beliefs of ordinary people." The conservatism that took shape in the 1970s was multifaceted, with deep roots. It was not linked to a particular place, though it had an especially transformative and powerful effect in shaping the Sunbelt suburbs. The conservative transformation encompassed the power of the religious right, absorbed and adapted to the consequences of the Warren Court rulings (on desegregation, school prayer, and abortion), drew on the white backlash and the rise of middle-class white suburbia, capitalized on the failures of Great Society liberalism, and transformed the Republican Party. This conservatism drew equally on economic, cultural, and social changes. This conception of conservatism does not rely on notions of an exceptional South, but rather allows for contributions made by distinctly southern conservatism that shaped an emerging national conservatism.[16]

Many of these features of conservatism can be seen at the grassroots in Mississippi in the 1960s and 1970s. As Joseph Crespino has described, the emerging conservative counterrevolution contributed to and stemmed from a transformation of Mississippi. This encompassed altered state demographics, voting districts, a briefly integrated public school system followed by the rise of private white academies, and the reshaping of white Mississippians theological worldview. Most of all the monumental cultural, political, and economic shifts were underpinned by the shift in power from the rural Black Belt to an urbanized and suburbanized business class. There are also features of conservatism evident in Mississippi that historians who focus exclusively on the Sunbelt suburbs do not fully encompass. With little urbanization and suburbanization, Republicanism in Mississippi developed differently from that of the Sunbelt suburbs. Chris Danielson suggests that much of the new scholarship on conservatism that focuses on "class and other nonracial issues is generally not applicable to Mississippi," because "race was the major factor behind the New Right shift of Mississippi's white electorate to the Republican Party." Danielson notes that Mississippi was and is a heavily "rural Sunbelt state," thus the suburban Sunbelt descriptions of conservatism encompass only an area around Jackson, not the vast majority of the state. In order to capture the conservative votes of both the Jackson suburbs and the "populist-leaning rural whites," Republicans could not just rely on the economic conservatism that attracted middle-class suburbanites.[17]

In Mississippi then Republicans articulated a "conservative colorblindness" deploying a language that was utilized in the white suburbs but that was not an invention of those white suburbanites. This language, as Crespino has shown, had "always been a part of segregationist politics in a Deep South state such as Mississippi." Republicanism in Mississippi drew less on a shared suburban environment than on a basic conservative cultural, racial, and religious foundation. The level of "ideological cohesion" between the segregationist Democratic politicians and new Republicans was greater in Mississippi than any other state as the overtly racial features of the old Mississippi politics were absorbed into a broader economic and social conservatism. The conservatism of Mississippians definitely owed much to segregationist politics. However, Black Belt conservatism was not purely based on racist demagoguery. Even here, where the most explicit racialized language endured the longest, there was a morass of often contradictory impulses underpinning conservatism. At its heart—as in the Sunbelt suburbs—stood a desire to maintain the privileges of white supremacy, whether that was experienced primarily through economic and class status, gender, or an explicitly racialized form. Central to understanding Mississippi conservatism therefore is the post-1965 development of white resistance. As historians, including George Lewis and Kevin M. Kruse, have illustrated, massive resistance contributed important and enduring strands to national conservatism. Lewis describes how, far from fading away after 1965, those southern resisters who were "sufficiently subtle in their approach," or had "chosen to encode any overtly racist appeals in such a way as to make them palatable to a broader, nonsectional audience," continued their work and merged "almost imperceptibly into a steadily evolving national climate of conservatism."[18]

To describe massive resistance as "another southern failure" that ended in 1965 follows a top-down approach that flattens massive resistance and inaccurately depicts it as monolithic. As Kevin M. Kruse notes, massive resistance was "never as immobile or as monolithic as its practitioners and chroniclers would have us believe." Segregationists were innovative, flexible, and imaginative in the ways they recast their defense of white supremacy. Such flexibility is not always reflected in studies of massive resistance, but it is not surprising, given the generations of white supremacists who had been perpetuating white power in equally innovative ways for decades. Racial segregation was never a fixed entity but a fluid relationship. Chris Danielson, Joseph Crespino, and Robert E. Luckett Jr. have demonstrated the range of forms of an evolving massive resistance in Mississippi after 1965. For Crespino, whites perpetrated a series of "subtle and strategic accommodations" to secure the maintenance of white privilege and power. Danielson has illustrated how Mississippi's opposition to integration became more sophisticated and legalistic and was expressed through a variety of vote-dilution mechanisms. Exploring the conservative response to the war on poverty in Mississippi and its relationship with the emerging Republican Party uncovers another facet of the evolution of massive resistance after 1965.[19]

The response of Mississippi's white conservatives and state Republican politicians to the war on poverty also illuminates a crucial connection between this evolving massive resistance and the state's ideological contributions to the emerging national conservatism. Antipoverty programs were sites of common experience between Black Belt and suburban modernity, where the ostensibly colorblind meritocratic rhetoric was forged from an evolution of the language and ideology of massive resistance. As Lassiter has shown, most middle-class whites of the 1970s believed their wealthy and prosperous suburban lifestyles were solely the result of meritocratic individualism, "rather than the unconstitutional product of structural racism." These whites rejected visible sources of government intervention, like the war on poverty, on the same ostensibly race-neutral grounds: the belief that the government did not owe individuals anything—that everyone could get ahead in the land of opportunity if only they worked hard enough. The grassroots conservative response to the war on poverty in Mississippi in the 1960s was based on the same ideology of meritocratic individualism, drawing in middle-class suburbanites with appeals to "responsible citizens" to reject runaway federal welfare spending. The opposition was couched in language that appealed to suburbanites and poor rural whites, by drawing on Protestant work-ethic, race-neutral references to the threat of communism, and the rejection of Great Society socialism. Women's groups in particular made significant contributions to the language of the emerging national conservatism in their fight against the war on poverty. That language was predicated on rights and individualism, entwined with potent racialized fears about welfare, and had much in common with the language of Sunbelt suburbanites, language that was later utilized in the coded racist appeals of politicians including Presidents Ronald Reagan and George H. W. Bush, and Mississippi governor Kirk Fordice.[20]

As Donald T. Critchlow notes, the "conservative ascendency" was twofold: the rise of a grassroots conservatism in the postwar era as the New Deal coalition collapsed, and the capture of the Republican Party by these grassroots conservatives. In Mississippi it was incredibly challenging for the nascent Republican Party to attract voters away from their generations-long commitment to the Democratic Party. The fear that a two-party system would split the white vote bolstered white voters' loyalty to the Democratic Party, even as the national Democratic Party moved further away from the conservatism of most white Mississippians. Into the 1960s southerners continued to vote paradoxically, voting for Democratic gubernatorial and senate candidates who railed against Democratic presidential candidates and policies, at the same time as voting for Democratic presidential candidates. In the urban and suburban South the 1952 election had established the Republicans as the "respectable party of the urban and suburban affluent whites in the South's large and small cities and a visible threat in presidential elections in the South." While pockets of middle-class white support for Eisenhower emerged in Mississippi, this trend was minimal. Into the mid-1960s the state Republican Party had a limited base of support.[21]

Republican Party chair Wirt Yerger and executive secretary W. T. Wilkins had been working since the 1950s to reestablish their party since their victory over the black-and-tan Republican Party. Their efforts were boosted in 1964, when 87 percent of Mississippi voters supported Republican presidential candidate Barry Goldwater. The state party brought in seventeen times its fundraising quota that year. However, the party did not have a nominee for governor or a serious nominee for the Senate until 1966. They remained ideologically divided, reflecting the conservative/moderate split in the national party. Moderates such as Gil Carmichael sought to steer clear of the segregationist rhetoric of the state Democratic Party. Moderate Republicans—moderate in relative terms, in the context of Mississippi politics—were looking to build a biracial party based on economic development and growth. A stronger, ultraconservative faction of the party spearheaded by Wirt Yerger was determined to follow the path set by Barry Goldwater and continue to "hunt where the ducks are." But out-segregationing the state Democrats was not a simple proposition. Although the Regular Democrats were asked to give up seats to the Freedom Democrats at the 1964 National Convention, they remained committed to segregation. Even when the Loyalist Democrats were seated in 1968, many Democratic politicians maintained their commitment to segregation.[22]

The Republican responses to the war on poverty reflected the ideological divisions with the party. For ultraconservatives like Wirt Yerger the war on poverty, as a concrete manifestation of Great Society liberalism present in communities across the state, was an ideal way for Mississippi Republicans to capture disillusioned conservative voters. State Republicans' ideological similarity to the Mississippi Democrats made them almost indistinguishable to voters, thus opposing the war on poverty was an opportunity to stand apart. Many southern Democrats, in the style of George Wallace, "expressed open disdain for welfare" but were "typical New Deal Southerners," who "welcomed federal monies for public works and welfare." As political scientist Charles Noble suggests, the Great Society was targeted by conservatives because, unlike the New Deal, the Great Society had "blurred the distinction between the 'deserving' and the 'undeserving poor'" and confirmed "most conservatives' fears about the ever-expanding regulatory reach of a bloated welfare state." Or as Michael Kazin phrased it, Republicans harnessed mass resentments to provide a home for "white refugees from the liberal crack up." Ultraconservative Mississippi Republicans were foot soldiers in the battle against the war on poverty. They sought to vilify the antipoverty programs by depicting them as un-American, an approach that was utilized by Republicans across the nation and which "helped conservatives connect with average (mainly white) voters." At the same time, moderate Republicans, such as Gil Carmichael, were willing to join the war on poverty and work in biracial coalitions running antipoverty programs.[23]

State Republicans observed how federal antipoverty funds flowing into Mississippi had, as one party member described it, drawn "liberals out of their holes," thus providing an opportunity for state Republicans to reinforce their conservative credentials—an opportunity to "out conservative" the Mississippi Democrats. With Democratic control of the state's infrastructure all but impenetrable, only at the grassroots could Republicans begin to build their strength. The war on poverty was not simply a way to capture disaffected white conservatives, however. There was also substantial money involved— money that was not under the control of the powerful state Democratic Party. The patronage potential of antipoverty programs meant Republicans—both moderates and the ultraconservatives who were opposed to biracialism and welfare—were willing to take up positions on the boards of community action programs. These businessmen and professionals sitting on community action boards tapped into this patronage potential, establishing a Republican voice in the use of federal antipoverty funds across the state.[24]

In Lauderdale County, Republicans played a significant role in creating and shaping the local antipoverty program, Lauderdale Economic Advancement Program. There was considerable need for an antipoverty program in Lauderdale County: 25.6 percent of the county population was poor in 1966, compared to a national average of 15.1 percent. Republican Gil Carmichael—who would later make unsuccessful runs for the Senate and for governor, and go onto serve in the George H. W. Bush administration— was heavily involved in facilitating the creation of the program. Carmichael worked alongside the African American board chairman, Charles L. Young Sr., in developing this program. This interracial cooperation was remarkable, given the "underlying hostility" in the county. As Young recalled, "Lauderdale County had more churches burned during the movement than any other county in the country."[25]

Unsurprisingly then, attempts to develop an antipoverty program were stymied by months of fractious debate. As community action programs provided access to a significant amount of federal funds, the construction of community action boards was often fiercely contested. Lauderdale County was no exception. Local labor groups came into conflict with African American groups over the number of board representatives each group would be assigned and the method of selection of these representatives. Carmichael and Young waded into the conflict. They eventually found a middle ground on which to build an integrated program to serve the community. After hours spent "bogged down in cautious and microscopic discussions," their perseverance paid off. The planning and application process was drawn out, but OEO finally granted the program $134,950 on June 21, 1967, to run a neighborhood service center, a housing program, and a family planning program. Carmichael, one of the more moderate of the Mississippi Republicans, and Young, a successful businessman who would later be elected to the Mississippi House of Representatives as a Democrat, were both motivated by concern about the economic prospects of their county and their state.[26]

Gil Carmichael withdrew from the program not long after its formation in order to focus on his business and his political ambitions. Republican influence in Lauderdale Economic Action Program remained, however. As ultraconservatives became more powerful with the state Republican Party, more and more Republican candidates chose to attack local community action programs in ostensibly race-neutral terms that reignited many white Mississippians basest racist fears of miscegenation and the rise of violent black power. In Lauderdale County, Republican influence remained in the form of the board's vice-chairman, Henry Damon. Damon was a civil engineer and lifelong Republican activist who ran unsuccessfully for political office on numerous occasions. He kept a close watch on the program for years and exerted influence that was not as benign as that of Carmichael. By 1970 the program was still looked upon with "some disfavor by the white community," although, according to an OEO inspector, it "enjoy[ed] an acceptable degree of support from the white power structure that is considered quite high for the state." Damon, however, felt "obliged" due to his "close ties with the Mississippi Republican Party" to inform the Republican administration of a "structural defect" in the program. Damon asked the Republican director of OEO, Don Rumsfeld, to launch a "low profile inquiry" into the board's African American poor representatives in order to "remove influences which are not necessarily helpful."[27]

Damon's attempt to use his Republican credentials to undermine the African American voice in the running of Lauderdale Economic Advancement Program was repeated in community action programs across the state. It proved to be a fairly successful tactic, appealing to those in the white community who viewed antipoverty programs with disfavor. At the same time, moderates, like Gil Carmichael, and those without ultraconservative ideological commitments and with a more pragmatic approach, such as Clarke Reed (who replaced Yerger as state chairman in 1966), continued to contribute to the war on poverty, not fight against it. Gil Carmichael's role reflected a vision of moderate, biracial Republicanism. For the more pragmatic and ideologically flexible Reed, involvement in the war on poverty was a patronage opportunity to be exploited. Given Mississippi's struggling economy, the small amounts of state funding for public welfare, and extensive poverty, a seat on the board of directors of even a small antipoverty program proved beneficial to the nascent state Republican Party, not least as a way to prevent antipoverty programs being used to build support for the Democratic Party among newly enfranchised blacks. But the positioning of these middle-class Republicans on community action boards was about more than just patronage possibilities. Their tactics held cross-class appeal: the state Republicans' blatantly racially motivated efforts to minimize African American control over antipoverty funds brought them the support of the rural whites who would form the majority of Republican supporters in Mississippi.[28]

The state Republican Party's responses to the war on poverty, then, reflected a two-pronged approach. These approaches reflected the ideological divisions within the party as well as the desperate need of the party to gain money and influence wherever possible. At the grassroots, the response of conservative Mississippians to the war on poverty did not incorporate this pragmatism. Rather, grassroots conservatives used the war on poverty as a target around which opponents of liberalism, racial integration, and big government could unite. These conservatives were instrumental in developing a race-neutral opposition to antipoverty programs. Their opposition to the war on poverty targeted Mississippi Democrats, linking them to the liberalism of the national party. Women's groups played an important role in fostering conservative ideology and building the burgeoning base of support for the state Republican Party, and they were also instrumental in forging race-neutral opposition to the war on poverty. In doing so, they were aiming to establish Republicans as the "true conservative" party. In Forrest County in 1966, for example, the local chapter of the Federation of Republican Women held a potluck party featuring "true conservative" James Moye speaking about LBJ and the Great Society. In an ironic flyer advertising the event, the Republican women of Forrest County invited "poor pulverized patriots" to help fight the war on poverty by voting Republican and defeating President Johnson.[29]

They utilized language that contained no reference to race but which couched antipoverty programs as un-American—against God, freedom, and independence. Such rhetoric was essential to the slow but steady growth of the state Republican Party. By linking their conservatism to patriotism and religion, Republicans at the grassroots were attempting to undermine

YOU ARE INVITED

TO A

POVERTY POTLUCK PARTY

For
Poor Pulverized Patriots
Y.W.C.A. October 20 7 P.M.

We can't qualify for the Great Society's Anti-Poverty Program, so please bring your own covered dish. We do promise to furnish fun along with cokes, coffee, and a true Conservative speaker, James Moye, who will tell you what he thinks of L.B.J. and the Great Society. Be prepared with questions. He knows the answers.

You may bring your God-Fearing, freedom loving, Independent minded friends too, plus nickels, dimes, and quarters. We might have to pass the hat.

Wear last year's clothes. We can't afford new ones either.

Forrest County Republican Women

Co-Chairmen

Cola Emmons   2-3396
Grace Hamilton   2-4332

PLEASE PHONE IF YOU CAN'T
COME

HELP DEFEAT L.B.J.
VOTE REPUBLICAN

Fig. 6.1. "Help Fight the War on Poverty" flyer, ca.1965/6, Box F-6, Folder MRP-OF 1965/66 Forrest County, Series VI, Mississippi Republican Party Records, Mitchell Memorial Library, Special Collections, Mississippi State University, Starkville.

Mississippi Democrats by framing such programs as un-American. The language of un-Americanism was a powerful tool for conservatives, particularly—though not always—when labeling their opponents as communist. Based on identity and status politics, those classed as un-American were those who failed to meet the criteria for membership in what historian Alex Goodall describes as "the mythic community from which the modern nation is assumed to have been founded—usually defined in racial, ethnic, and gendered terms." In Orange County, California, for example, accusations of un-Americanism were used by conservatives in their struggles to defend their morality. Those advocating sex education in public schools were, in the words of one conservative mother, "immoral, atheistic, and un-American elements whose aims are to destroy us." As in

Orange County, the defense against un-Americanism in Forrest County was linked closely to religion. Such language also drew on a long segregationist tradition that celebrated a "true Americanism" that "opposed government intervention, programs, and entitlements." Articulated by white supremacist and New South supporter Henry Grady in the 1890s, such language had been revitalized by massive resisters in the 1950s.[30]

Much of the work to develop a distinctive Republican conservatism in Mississippi was carried out by women. As Lisa McGirr, Michelle M. Nickerson, Elizabeth Gillespie McRae, and Catherine E. Rymph have illustrated, this is a common feature of modern conservatism. White women in California "put themselves forward as representatives of local interests who battled bureaucrats for the sake of family, community, and God." White southern conservative women, building segregationist networks, had already begun to expose "early fault lines" in the Solid South, partly through opposition to the New Deal. For many middle-class white segregationist women in Mississippi, the "protection of their homes, nation, and Christianity" meant voting for Eisenhower in 1952. Political activist Florence Ogden Sillers, for example, founded Bolivar County Women for Eisenhower. While their efforts did not deliver Mississippi to Eisenhower, he did have majorities in some of the state's Black Belt districts. Such grassroots political activism continued, and as the war on poverty arrived, the fight against federal social welfare programs once again became central to their efforts.[31]

White women had long been defenders of white supremacy through their roles in shaping welfare and public education policy. In the 1960s conservative women were drawn into the fight against the war on poverty not because of concerns of their children attending integrated Head Start centers—these women were mostly middle class, not poor. Instead, they took up the fight against the war on poverty because of their concerns about what the "immoral" and "communist" nature of antipoverty programs would do to their communities. Maye Donaldson, for example, was president of the Yalobusha-Calhoun Republican Women's Club. She was, she informed Clarke Reed, "working daily with all my strength to promote our party." Donaldson knew the election of Richard Nixon gave Mississippi Republicans another opportunity on which they must capitalize by repairing the damage the liberal Democratic administrations had caused. "We want to clean up Washington," she told Reed, "but . . . with the postal problems and Negroes running Head Start and all there [sic] 'give away' agencies we'll never do it!"[32]

She despaired over the "immoral conduct" that "prevails in our local Head Start." "One Negro," Donaldson continued, "has 7 children, on welfare and works here in the center. She's not married and will have the 8th child soon." Repairing the damage wrought by liberal Democrats on families and morality would have to begin in local communities, Maye Donaldson knew, because there was little assistance coming from senators or the president. Donaldson was angry over Senator Eastland's seeming acceptance of Head Start ("whose side is he on, anyway?") and at President Nixon's willingness to "court Big Jim." "We must," she told Reed "giv[e] these good Head Start jobs to white Republicans." Little progress was made in 1969, however. Donaldson wrote to Reed again five months later in considerable agitation. "I don't like what is happening right here in our state," she opined. "These militant negroes and tricky whites are taking over. They are communists." Donaldson told Reed that a "good Republican" working in a nearby Head Start program had told her that, in collusion with local NAACP leaders, "OEO and Head Start workers all took Friday from work and used OEO office time money, paper and machines to run off militant copies to be used in the 'Black Sunday' demonstration." Donaldson went to that march where, she told Reed, she witnessed the "mobs, heard the 'freedom chants.'" While the march was going on, Donaldson used the opportunity to "sneak in" to the office and gather evidence, which she also sent to Reed.[33]

Donaldson was using the familiar language of massive resistance and racialized opposition to welfare, combining it with conservative fears of an overweening federal government, the threat of communism, and the spread of immorality. She was drawing on familiar accusations too. Claims that OEO resources had been used to promote civil rights activism and riots were leveled against antipoverty programs in Newark and Detroit among other places in the wake of the July 1967 riots. Such allegations had persisted, despite the findings of the Kerner Commission praising many antipoverty workers for helping to ease tensions. Maye Donaldson was urging party officials to eradicate the program. She ended her letter to Reed, "I almost detest this left wing group." Clarke Reed was sympathetic but pragmatic. He was, of course, happy to use these links to grassroots activists and powerful rhetoric to attract white conservative voters. He assured Donaldson that he would pass the material along and secure an investigation. However, Reed also had an eye to the value of Republican influence in these programs. Donaldson's local antipoverty program, Central Mississippi, Inc., for example, operated a Head Start program, an emergency food and medical program, a homemakers' aide program, and Project FIND. Influence in such an antipoverty program was a valuable prospect. Central Mississippi, Inc., covered six counties, with federal funding levels of $1.8 million in 1967, $2.1 million in 1968, and $2.3 million by 1969.[34]

The state Republican Party was drawing considerable strength from the growing networks of women's groups. In addition to support from the grassroots, though, the party needed help from the national level if they were to have any hope of challenging the powerful state Democrats. With Nixon's election, opportunities for the state Republican Party to undermine the Democrats became even more frequent. While not achieving widespread electoral success on Nixon's coattails in 1968, Reed and Wilkins were determined to capitalize on the opportunities provided by having a Republican White House. State Republicans were not happy with Nixon's failure to demolish the OEO immediately. However, connections with Republican officials were valuable and could be used to undermine African American–operated antipoverty programs and thus enhance the state Republicans' credibility with white Mississippians. Reed quickly sought to establish relationships with members of the regional offices of OEO and the Department of Health, Education, and Welfare (HEW). Reed hoped to form an "open channel" for communication on potentially mutually beneficial situations. Nixon's decision to move the administration of Head Start from OEO to the established department of HEW in 1969 proved useful for Reed's ambitions, particularly when the new Office of Child Development within HEW took control of Head Start in 1970.[35]

Clarke Reed cultivated a relationship with both OEO director Donald Rumsfeld and Cary Hall, HEW's southeast regional director. Reed and Wilkins used these connections to assist Republican mayors, politicians, and supporters to extend white control over the defunded Child Development Group remnants. In Yazoo City, for example, Republican mayor Jeppie Barbour (one of only four Republican mayors in the state in 1969) received Reed's help in gaining OEO's support for the segregationist activities of the local community action program, Yazoo Community Action.[36] In Sunflower County the machinations of Wilkins and the regional Office of Child Development staff destroyed the independence of the Associated Communities of Sunflower County, a defunded Child Development Group remnant. Wilkins's involvement ensured the African American program was placed under the control of the white establishment program, Sunflower County Progress. In both of these segregated Delta counties the role of the Mississippi Republican Party proved decisive in reestablishing white control over burgeoning African American economic advancement—control which undermined African American involvement in antipoverty programs. Pragmatists such as Clarke Reed had been flexible on the question of whether the party should appeal to black voters. However, the growing strength of the party's ultraconservatives combined with many white conservatives' commitment to undermining black control of antipoverty programs meant that increasingly the state Republican Party was bolstering white control of the war on poverty. It was a move that was proving politically beneficial for the nascent party.

At the same time, changes wrought by the Nixon White House and Rumsfeld's OEO were providing new opportunities for whites in their fight against the war on poverty. Under the control of Rumsfeld, OEO's lackluster record in addressing the systematic discrimination evident in many Mississippi antipoverty programs worsened. Prior to 1969 OEO's record of addressing the many violations of regulations on the involvement of poor people in antipoverty programs was weak. This weakness resulted largely from administrative failings of OEO staff at the regional and national levels. However, under the Nixon administration, the failure of OEO staff to address such violations became one facet of a covert and systematic attack on antipoverty programs at the grassroots. Historians, including Annelise Orleck, have suggested that Nixon's actions and attitude toward OEO during his first administration were at worst a case of benign neglect. However, Nixon's unwillingness to dismantle the OEO during his first term was a pragmatic decision based on his reluctance to risk political capital with direct attacks on the war on poverty. Indeed, Rumsfeld accepted his appointment as director of OEO on the condition the agency would not be dismantled from underneath him. The actions of both Nixon and Rumsfeld quietly undermined antipoverty programs at the local level, subverting the intent of the drafters of the Economic Opportunity Act.[37]

One of the most significant facets of the war on poverty and central to the concept of community action was the intent of community action programs to redistribute power from city halls to the poor—or at least, to nonprofit organizations representing the poor. Community action was already unpopular for undermining local political control over federal funds when riots swept across America's cities in the summer of 1967. The riots provided politicians with the perfect opportunity to blame the "maximum feasible participation" requirement for fomenting unrest. Despite the findings of the Kerner Commission, this view persisted. Under pressure from local mayors and their constituents, both Democratic and Republican politicians pushed amendments to the Economic Opportunity Act that would curb and control the participation of the poor and extend the influence of city halls in antipoverty programs. The 1967 amendments to the Economic Opportunity Act included such curbs on community action. Most notably, the Green Amendment, introduced by Oregon's Democratic congresswoman Edith Green. The Green Amendment required community action boards to be designated by local elected officials, thus increasing the power of the political establishment over antipoverty programs.[38]

The amendment not only increased the power of local politicians in the running of antipoverty programs. It also undermined the role of the poor representatives sitting on the boards of community action programs. The original Economic Opportunity Act of 1964 had required that one-third of the members of the board of a community action program be democratically elected members of the target area. In other words, one third of the board must be representatives of the poor community the program served, there to give the community a say in the running of their program. While the Green Amendment did not alter that requirement, it did include specific requirements that undermined the voice of these poor representatives. The amendment included changes to the structure of the boards, including changing the requirements on the length of time each representative could serve and the quorum requirements. Most significantly, the amendment dictated that, in addition to the poor representatives, the boards must consist of one-third public officials, with the remaining third representatives of the community, including representatives of business, labor, minority, and religious organizations. The changes, instigated in large part at the behest of infuriated city mayors, were designed to facilitate local governments in taking control of community action programs. In Mississippi they resulted in the increased influence of the white establishment on antipoverty programs. In STAR, for example, two-thirds of the board had been democratically elected poor representatives before the amendment. The amendment thus significantly reduced the voice of the poor in the running of the program. As a result, antipoverty programs became more vulnerable to incorporation into the traditional power structure and its ingrained patterns of racial discrimination.[39]

STAR had been exempt from implementation of the Green Amendment in 1967 because the amendment referred to community action agencies, rather than single-purpose programs like STAR. However, reorganizing STAR's board in accordance with the Green Amendment was made a special condition of the program's funding in October 1970. The requirement caused huge controversy, provoking a strong reaction and engendering a great deal of confusion at the local and state levels. The executive committee of STAR's board put on record its rejection of any reorganization of its board in line with the amendment, which threatened not only the presence of poor representatives, but also that of several powerful whites. Implementing Green required the resignation of several of the powerful white board members, as they had served on the board for longer terms than allowed under the amendment's restrictions. For civil rights activists, though, the implementation of Green was not simply about individual resignations but a shift in power. Owen Brooks, STAR's board secretary, objected to the amendment because it would undermine the voice of the poor representatives, while increasing the control of the political establishment over the program.[40]

It was not only STAR that was attempting to prevent this quashing of the voice of the poor in community action programs. By 1970 there was a "regional pattern" identified by poverty warriors "which seems to be developing within the OEO to restructure independent programs such as STAR and force them to conform to Green Amendment restrictions." While the Green Amendment had been passed in 1967, it was only sporadically implemented in 1967 and 1968. Under Nixon and Rumsfeld, however, the amendment was used to systematically strip the poor of their say in the running of antipoverty programs. For poverty warriors, such as Owen Brooks, implementing the Green Amendment was more significant than simply altering board composition and tightening quorum requirements. It destroyed the opportunity for the development of black leadership and set the stage for a "second post-reconstruction regression into dependency," and it closed the last avenue for African Americans to give meaning to their political rights as the outside support for civil rights and for southern blacks diminished.[41]

The Nixon administration was facilitating a tightening of establishment control over community action programs in order to meet what Rumsfeld referred to as a "difficult organizational problem." Rumsfeld was already planning to "separate" community action programs in line with the "revised goals of OEO" and implementing "stricter management regulations." He also asked regional offices for a "net 15% cut on a selective basis" on community action programs. Other changes in OEO under Rumsfeld—from the significant staff changes and administrative and procedural shifts to changes in the poverty threshold—included a simplification of the Green Amendment to make it easier for mayors across the country to take control of the local antipoverty programs and change the focus of the program.

Rumsfeld thus facilitated the demise of the voice and role of the poor in the war on poverty. These changes were also useful in currying favor with local politicians who hoped the Republican administration would address the "socialism" of the War on Poverty.[42]

In 1971 state party chair Clarke Reed sent out to Mississippi Republicans a memo from OEO director Frank Carlucci, in which Carlucci delineated efforts by the Nixon administration to implement the often ignored Green Amendment to "give public officials and responsible citizens a strong hand in governing OEO funded program." Reed urged Republican leaders in Mississippi to convince "responsible citizens" to serve on poverty program boards in order for the Green Amendment to have a "beneficial effect." Race was never mentioned in discussions of the Green Amendment by Rumsfeld's OEO, Nixon's White House, or even the Mississippi Republican Party. However, the language used, such as the emphasis on the importance of "responsible citizens"—an echo of the "local responsible people" that Governor Paul Johnson and Senator Stennis had appealed to five years earlier—clearly indicates the racial dimension to these changes that was always present but never explicitly articulated. Their language emphasized the responsibilities of the "citizen" who was able and expected to vote, and to vote Republican.[43]

There were many dimensions of the politicization of the war on poverty. It by no means originated under the Nixon administration. Indeed, the creation of Mississippi Action for Progress was an exercise in establishing a biracial basis for the Democratic Party in the state, later replicated in the Loyalist Democrats. On a smaller scale the biracial cooperation forged on the boards of antipoverty programs across the state were likewise the forerunners of later political alliances. They "cut across class lines of black and affluent whites," reflecting the coalition that would in the 1970s support the moderate governorships of William Waller and Cliff Finch. Some Republicans had participated in forging fragile, integrated ties in antipoverty programs, such as Carmichael's involvement with Lauderdale Economic Action Program. However, as the ultraconservative Republicans began to drown out the voices of moderates, "racially nuanced targets . . . and welfare" were increasingly recognized as being "central to the Republican appeal." Their fight against the war on poverty was an important step toward the eventual success of these ultraconservatives in capturing the Mississippi Republican Party "as they tapped into the rage of whites, specializing in 'demonizing and scapegoating the powerless.'" As Dan T. Carter has described, by the time the conservative revolution reached high tide in the 1980s, "it was no accident that the groups singled out for relentless abuse and condemnation were welfare mothers and aliens, groups that are both powerless and, by virtue of color and nationality, outsiders."[44]

Southwest Mississippi Opportunity became a target for political opposition to perceived Great Society excesses and a way to "demonize" the powerless. Southwest Mississippi Opportunity was an establishment-sanctioned program under the control of the white power structure. It had thus enjoyed the support of Democratic Congressman Charles Griffin and Senator Stennis since its inception. So when local Republican Richard Watson sought to prevent the renewal of SMO's grant because of "personal grudges" the stage was set for a partisan battle. According to board member Steve Reed, Richard Watson was a "Jackleg attorney" and "big Republican." Watson wanted to halt program funding, Steve Reed claimed, in order to gain personal glory. Alarmed at the potential damage Richard Watson could inflict on the program, Steve Reed turned to the program's Democratic supporters for assistance, including Senator Stennis. Stennis told Reed he was "glad to express his strong interest in SMO." The resulting partisan battle left Southwest Mississippi Opportunity stuck in limbo for six months without secured funds. State Republicans supported Richard Watson's attempts to prevent its refunding. Democratic politicians meanwhile, including Stennis and Congressman Griffin, sought to protect the program's funds. Ultimately, Watson's efforts proved futile and SMO's grant remained unchanged. But Republicans' efforts were not wholly unsuccessful. His attacks on SMO brought Watson and the state Republicans valuable media exposure.[45]

The attack by Richard Watson on Southwest Mississippi Opportunity had also signaled the program's vulnerability. It was controversial with the local white community, due to its African American delegate Head Start program, which descended from the high-profile and much maligned Child Development Group. Thus a targeted attack on SMO was a valuable opportunity for any Republican looking to link local Democrats with overweening government intervention, to invoke the threat of black power and communism, and to appeal directly to grassroots conservatives. For Republican candidate Dr. Ray Lee it was an opportunity too good to miss. During the 1970 election campaign SMO's delegate Head Start agency, the Child Development Council, was targeted by Ray Lee. A rising star of the Mississippi Republican Party and president of the Liberty Chamber of Commerce, Lee was running for Congress in Mississippi's third district. Lee's decision to target the Child Development Council was astute. While Richard Watson's earlier attacks had been directed at the establishment-sanctioned

Southwest Mississippi Opportunity, Lee's target—the Child Development Council—was a former Child Development Group program operated by and largely for African Americans. Thus while Southwest Mississippi Opportunity may have enjoyed the support of Democratic politicians, the Child Development Council would not have such protection.[46]

The Child Development Council was in 1970 still operating semi-independently under a delegate arrangement with the white-establishment program, SMO. However, the Child Development Council remained the target of suspicion and was vulnerable to criticism. At the time of Lee's public attack, the agency was operating without funds because an administrative error had halted their funding. Staff members were struggling to keep Head Start centers open on a voluntary basis. At the same time Southwest Mississippi Opportunity was still trying to undermine the agency in the hope that the operation of Head Start could be forced under their complete control. Lee's public allegations could not have come at a worse time for the program. In the course of SMO's attempts to undermine its delegate agency, its director, Kathleen O'Fallon, had called on a range of state mechanisms of white segregationists. By late 1969 SMO's board had escalated its attack from the state to the federal level. The board of SMO made a series of spurious claims alleging widespread corruption in the Child Development Council, resulting in an FBI investigation. Although the FBI found insufficient evidence to prove the board's allegations, the investigation did uncover evidence of poor administration and recordkeeping. This evidence prompted OEO to conduct its investigation, resulting in the severe funding delays.[47]

In an open letter to Don Rumsfeld, Lee made public accusations against the Child Development Council. There was, Lee claimed, widespread misconduct and corruption in the delegate agency. Lee made eight claims, including, for example, that all black SMO employees were required to be members of the NAACP. He claimed that they "taught their students Black Power" and that they "used OEO resources to support NAACP boycotts." Though patently false, these claims found favor with local whites. Lee played upon fears of Black Power and boycott activity to boost his political profile and prospects. He alleged the Child Development Council was "teaching black power, militancy, and outright rebellion against the American system in its schools." Its employees, he claimed, were "arrested for advocating all out violence" and "organizing militant activities." He combined the vague but threatening specter of Black Power with the immediate economic threat of boycott activity, labeling both as "un-American." These alleged threats hit a chord with the local press and local people. Lee's accusations, designed to resurrect white fears of federally funded Black Power, drew on the language of massive resistance.[48]

While there was no evidence to back up his claims, Lee's publicity stunt provoked an outburst of public opposition to the antipoverty program. Writing to their politicians, local people were appalled that taxpayers' money was, according to Lee, funding such a program and potentially even supporting boycott activities. Lee's claims appealed to the white residents of southwest Mississippi, many of whom remained members or supporters of the numerous violent white supremacist organizations operating in the area. Combining the rhetoric of massive resistance with attacks on antipoverty programs was an astute tactic. This rhetoric also drew on the language of conservatism that was emerging in Mississippi, drawing in part on massive resistance, but also emphasizing the rights of individuals, an opposition to federally funded welfare programs, and the position that such programs were un-American. The language and tactics utilized by Lee did indeed provoke the anger of many local whites. Despite this renewed public opposition to the Child Development Council, however, Lee failed to secure the agency's demise or win the election. Such tactics were increasingly potent but not enough in 1969 to overcome decades of Democratic political dominance.[49]

Republicans' attempts to gain political advantage by maligning antipoverty programs combined the tactics of the earlier massive resistance with the language deployed by grassroots conservatives. These attempts were not always successful, as in the case of Ray Lee. However, these tactics reflected a stage in the development of the Mississippi Republican Party and its relationship with the growing conservatism. As ultraconservative Republicans dominated the state party, it abandoned any attempts to appeal to black voters and focused more on utilizing the tactics honed in the years of opposition to the war on poverty. The state party also benefitted, to a certain extent, from the opportunities to extend white establishment control over antipoverty programs offered by the actions of the Nixon administration and Rumsfeld's OEO. Perhaps most significant is the nature of the response to grassroots white women's groups to the war on poverty. These women were instrumental in articulating the language of conservatism that drew on race-neutral rhetoric promoting individual rights, a religious fervor that decried antipoverty efforts as un-patriotic and immoral, and an intense antipathy to federally funded welfare programs. In Mississippi, as in states such as California and across the Sunbelt, the grassroots organizing efforts of these women also played an important role in the conservative capture of the Republican Party.

The nature of the relationship between grassroots conservatives and the state Republican Party as they fought in and against war on poverty exposes a distinctive strand of the emerging national conservatism. In Mississippi the fight against the war on poverty provided common ground for rural Black Belt whites and middle-class suburban whites. In this common fight, white conservatives were seeking to assert their authority over their local community to control the pace and nature of black advancement and crucially reshape the function of the war on poverty by minimizing the voice of the poor. The fight against the war on poverty exposes critical connections between the evolving white resistance and Mississippi's conservatism. There were transformative shifts in post–civil rights Mississippi not limited to desegregation. Mississippi fundamentally altered its politics, economy, and society after 1965. Changes resulting from redistricting; the shift in economic and political power away from the Black Belt; the altered demography of the state, especially through the exodus of African Americans; the growing power of evangelism; the landscape of public and private education systems; and black political successes were integral to this transformation and woven into the rise of the new conservatism.

The fight against the war on poverty exposes but one aspect of this fundamental transformation. It is an important aspect, however. In the fight against the war on poverty, white Mississippians developed a conservatism that had national resonance and drew on racial and class divisions that were not purely products of the Sunbelt suburbs. Conservatives fighting against the war on poverty entangled African Americans and welfare and constructed as communist, un-American, and a violation of the ostensibly meritocratic basis of the American dream. They ensured that when future Republican politicians such as Ronald Reagan and Mississippi Governor Kirk Fordice blew the dog-whistle, white Mississippians knew exactly what they were hearing. It was a language of their own.[50]

- Chapter Seven -

STAR, THE AFL-CIO, AND THE DIOCESE OF NATCHEZ-JACKSON

As the 1960s drew to a close, the Nixon administration—and Don Rumsfeld's OEO—continued to undermine the war on poverty. At the grassroots, the fight against the war on poverty also raged on. However, STAR, the statewide job-training and adult education program, was thriving. By 1970 STAR had developed a strong and stable organizational structure. Eighteen regional centers spread across the state, from the Delta to the Gulf Coast—in Holly Springs, Clarksdale, Mound Bayou, Greenwood, Greenville, Yazoo City, Carthage, Canton, Philadelphia, Meridian, Natchez, Kiln, Pass Christian-DeLisle, Biloxi, Dedeaux, Pascagoula, and Gulfport. With strong numbers of black employees (55 percent of STAR staff were African American) the program had also secured an impressive number of white enrollees. For an integrated antipoverty program operating in Mississippi's fraught racial climate, this level of integration was remarkable. Particularly in contrast to the uproar that resulted from the court-ordered integration of Mississippi's public schools in the 1969/1970 school year.[1]

In the fifteen years following the Supreme Court's ruling in *Brown v. Board of Education*, the violence, delays, and the freedom of choice maneuvers meant that "many black Mississippians despaired of efforts to integrate the schools" by the late 1960s. Although little assistance had come from the federal government to implement school desegregation, African American parents continued to fight for change. As activists turned back to legal challenges after 1965, white segregationists and black parents once again fought in the courts. Supreme Court rulings in *Griffin v. School Board* (1964) and *Green v. County School Board of New Kent County* (1968) struck down attempts to implement a "freedom of choice" system, signaling that the time for "all deliberate speed" was over. HEW desegregation plans were finally drawn up for thirty Mississippi school districts in July 1969. The plans were set to be implemented at the start of the 1969/1970 school year. However, both HEW and the Justice Department requested a delay, arguing that the plans would result in confusion. Segregationist federal judge William Harold Cox granted the delay, but parents of black children in Mississippi immediately appealed his ruling. The case, *Alexander v. Holmes County*, was decided by the Supreme Court justices on October 29, 1969. The Supreme Court vacated Judge Cox's delay, ruling that "continued operation of racially segregated schools under the standard of 'all deliberate speed' is no longer constitutionally permissible," thus Mississippi's school districts "must immediately terminate dual school systems based on race."[2]

HEW's plans were implemented in January 1970 prompting renewed opposition to school desegregation. Massive resistance had evolved since the response to *Brown*. By 1970 the protection of white supremacy was based on practical segregation and the deployment of "strategic accommodations" to racial change. The integration in Head Start, for example, was built on an acceptance by some mostly middle-class Mississippians that racial change could not be avoided, but its pace and nature could be controlled. At the same time, many white segregationists had been honing an ostensibly colorblind language of opposition to Head Start, deriding it as communist, immoral, and un-American. The massive resistance to school integration in 1970 reflected these strands of segregationism and conservatism. A very few moderate white parents left their children in public schools, where they witnessed the rapid transformation of their schools from all-white to nearly all-black. The vast majority of white parents, however, removed their children into a host of newly created, segregated Christian academies. This rejection of integrated public schooling was enabled by the legal maneuvering that segregationists had been undertaking for years. Mississippi's attorney general Joe Patterson, for example, had been involved in legal battles since 1966 to secure tax-exempt status and tuition support for white segregation academies. Out of legal options in Mississippi, Senator Stennis instead turned his attention out-of-state, hoping to stir northern opposition to school desegregation.[3]

The nature of the white segregationist response to desegregation in 1970 illustrates the strength and complexity of massive resistance. Far from a top-down, elite-led backlash that lasted a decade, massive resistance was driven primarily by grassroots segregationists. By 1970 the segregationists had honed their massive resistance, drawing on a colorblind conservative language of rights and individualism. The connection between massive resistance and conservatism was by no means limited to the rural Deep South, but was clear in the urban and suburban areas of Mississippi and of the Sunbelt states. In the rural Black Belt as well as the Sunbelt suburbs, the maintenance of white supremacy was a significant facet of the new conservatism and

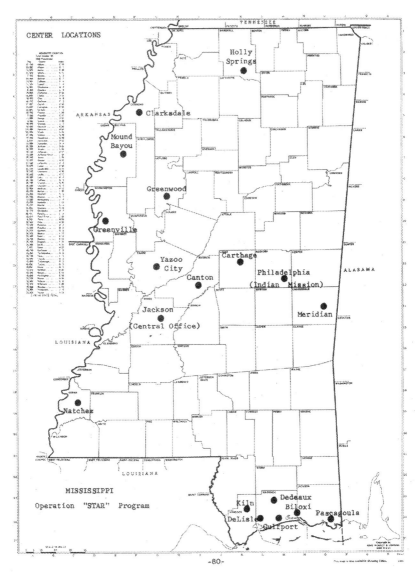

Fig. 7.1. "Operation 'STAR,'" May 1965, 82, Box 3, Folder 4, Michael Miller Civil Rights Collection, McCain Library and Archives, University of Southern Mississippi, Special Collections, Hattiesburg, http://digilib.usm.edu/cdm/ref/collection/manu/id/3907. Courtesy Archives of the Catholic Diocese of Jackson.

was most frequently expressed through class-based as well as overtly racialized language. Indeed, the class dimensions of massive resistance and conservatism align most clearly when viewed through opposition to the war on poverty.[4]

Middle-class whites were more willing to make concessions on the issue of integrating antipoverty programs because their children would not be directly affected. At the same time, seats on these program boards offered opportunities for middle-class whites to wield their economic and political power. It was these middle-class whites who utilized the war against the war on poverty to build a conservative language based on individual rights and opposition to social welfare and black advancement. Poor whites most often rejected integrated Head Start programs, sometimes violently, unwilling to send their children to integrated classes. In doing so, they aligned with the rights-based language opposing social welfare programs. Many poor whites were, however, willing to take advantage of adult-education and job training programs. Lacking the perceived threat to their children, such programs offered economic opportunities that poor whites could not afford to overlook. White Mississippians' responses to the war on poverty thus illustrate the complexity of Deep South conservatism. The acceptance of programs such as STAR by poor whites also shows that practical segregation was not limited to political elites.

STAR provided its enrollees with valuable skills from basic literacy to job-specific training and development. It was, however, still merely a "stopgap," according to one *Delta Democrat Times* journalist. While staff members remained optimistic about the program's potential, the war on poverty's struggles in Washington meant that STAR's funding was renewed in 1968, but at a reduced level. Reduced funding meant the dismissal of many of STAR's administrative staff and the suspension of operations at some of its centers. Despite this setback, the program developed a strong record of tackling African American illiteracy and maintained integrated staff and centers. In large part the successes of STAR and the acceptance of the program from the white establishment was the role of the two organizations integral to the operation of STAR: the Catholic Diocese and the state AFL-CIO. Only the Catholic Church had the institutional framework and will to operate an integrated antipoverty program in mid-1960s Mississippi.[5]

However, the association between STAR and the Catholic Church was controversial. For many of the Catholic clergy working in STAR, antipoverty efforts were central to their faith. For Msgr. Roland Winel, a Catholic priest and STAR's executive director, to do anything less would have been to "abandon [their] mission." However, relatively few Mississippi Catholics agreed with his stance. According to Winel, the "lack of sympathy for the poor that is shown by others who have made their own way" was compounded in Mississippi because of race. Individual activism remained muted by the demands of segregationist parishioners, who responded angrily to diocesan involvement in STAR. For STAR the support of the Diocese of Natchez-Jackson and the endorsement of Bishop Brunini provided useful connections and a powerful, respected front for the program. For example, Brunini's brother's law firm provided free legal services for STAR until the legal demands of the program became too great. The bishop's connections were not always advantageous to STAR, though. Brunini's ties to the white establishment also served to entrench white control of the program. The Brunini family's close friendship with Senator Stennis ensured that a mutual "respect" was transmuted into Stennis's support for STAR. Beneath the exchange of pleasantries in correspondence between Stennis and Brunini, however, their association provided a means of indirect assurance for Stennis that STAR remained under white control. Both Senator Stennis and Senator Eastland relied upon this kind of patronage politics. Here an old family connection was serving to ensure Stennis could keep an inside view of the racial power play at work in STAR's board and centers.[6]

Nonetheless, according to Father Nathaniel, Brunini's "courageous leadership" had won him new respect from black Mississippians. Still at work in St. Francis Mission, Father Nathaniel reported to Brunini in 1971 that due to STAR Brunini's "stature with them [black people] has grown tremendously." Such praise was reflected in the Catholic press outside of the tense racial atmosphere of Mississippi. Catholic support of STAR was seen as heralding the future of Mississippi and Catholic activism. One journalist for Catholic newspaper *Divine Word Messenger*, having visited some of the program's eighteen centers, reported that Mississippi's future "is built upon such programs as . . . STAR." Bishop Brunini's endorsement of STAR thus gave the program vital cache with powerful white Mississippians. However, internally, Brunini's sponsorship proved problematic. Two major roles within STAR—that of executive director and director of education—were held by diocesan staff. Msgr. Roland Winel proved less than successful as executive director. His failings prompted the board to request his resignation, blaming the "turmoil and bickering" in the central office on Winel's failures of administrative management and supervision.[7]

The tenure of Catholic nun Sister Donatilla as education director, meanwhile, was even more problematic. It was marked not only by her patronizing attitude toward African American enrollees but also by failures to perform her duties. Sister Donatilla "failed to relate to a totally racially integrated situation" with black employees. STAR's enrollees complained of multiple instances of unkind, unfair, and unjust treatment under her supervision. She caused confusion at local centers by spreading misinformation and providing false information regarding programs and personnel. Charles Horwitz, a white Delta Ministry worker, witnessed Donatilla's actions and their effects firsthand. He felt that Sister Donatilla "lack[ed] sensitivity" in dealing with poor black enrollees. She did not, he felt, have the "attitudes and perspectives necessary for a statewide education director of a program serving predominately black, low-income people." Horwitz believed her to have "sincere concern for her trainees passing the GED tests." But "her paternalism [is] very insulting." Complaints of this paternalism have, Horwitz noted, "come from trainees and teachers and STAR staff across the state." Sister Donatilla's actions ensured that STAR, instead of empowering black Mississippians, reified the narrative of benevolent white paternalism in the face of black inferiority.[8]

Sister Donatilla was also party to the efforts of some board and staff members to secure the resignation or dismissal of African American Richard Polk, the program's manpower director. Richard Polk's tenure with STAR was marked by notable success in the program's activities under his department. Indeed, OEO had tried twice to recruit Polk and regarded him as the "main reason for the success of STAR training and job development efforts." But Sister Donatilla, together with powerful board members, leveled public charges against Polk. They questioned his competence and integrity and mounted a determined character assassination that resulted in his dismissal from STAR. According to Polk, Sister Donatilla used her status as a nun as a shield to deflect the accusations of racial discrimination. Writing to Msgr. Winel in 1970, Polk described how she cultivated her "inviolability." "Ensconced in her 'Habit,'" Polk claimed, "she uses its connotation of inviolability to distort the truth." Despite the evidence of many enrollees and staff, both white and African American, of Donatilla's racism and destructive influence in the program, her role within STAR was secure.[9]

Her position was secured in large part due to her "inviolability." Also significant was the support she received from the board and Bishop Brunini. Assured of her position then, Sister Donatilla undercut Polk and the staff in his department by perpetuating "subtle underminings [sic] that frustrate, bedevil, and beset." Msgr. Winel likewise received the support of Bishop Brunini. The shortcomings of Winel and Donatilla (stemming partly, in

Donatilla's case, from her openly racist attitude) speak to the lack of professionalism of the Catholic staff in STAR, a shortcoming that was enabled by the peculiarities of the sponsor-program relationship and the support of Bishop Brunini. In addition to this failure, Brunini resolutely stayed out of any dispute he saw as "being among black men." This inaction, according to Polk, led to the bishop being "totally insensitive to the hardships being created on the STAR personnel and trainees." More than just insensitivity, Brunini's inaction under the façade of racial justice served to prop up a situation in which there was "no crevice in the most remote section of personnel practices and supervision that provided for a Negro to function programmatically and maintain any resemblance of dignity," Polk believed. The diplomacy that was central to Brunini's role as bishop was ill suited to the demanding and controversial situations that arose in the administration of STAR. These problems, similar to antipoverty programs across the state, were intensified by the state's racial landscape.[10]

The support of the diocese brought STAR the dedication of the Catholic members of the board and staff and generous in-kind contributions. Indeed, the diocese provided the impetus and apparatus that enabled the program's creation. Many of the Catholic staff in the program—including Father Broussard, Father Nathaniel, and Marge Baroni—played significant roles in its successes. However, the vital flaws in the diocesan involvement also played a significant role in the perpetuation of racial discrimination. These flaws contributed to the increasing disillusionment of staff and enrollees. Bishop Brunini's unwillingness to become involved in controversial racial issues prevented him from acting at important moments when his voice may have had an impact on the direction of the program. The Catholic hierarchy was willing to support moderate, indirect civil rights activities earlier in the decade. Now that the color lines were beginning to blur, however, Bishop Brunini and the diocese retreated to the safety of inaction. The relationship between the diocese and STAR thus ultimately served to perpetuate the racial discrimination endemic in the program. It also undermined the support the Mississippi Catholic Church had shown for moderate civil rights activists earlier in the 1960s.[11]

The Catholic Church was not the only powerful backer of STAR. State AFL-CIO chair Claude Ramsay was central to STAR's operation. Labor was inherently a part of the war on poverty. Unionists had a formative impact on the war on poverty at both the national level and the grassroots. OEO's first deputy director was Jack T. Conway, the executive director of the industrial union department in AFL-CIO. Labor activists such as

Conway played a role in drafting the 1964 Economic Opportunity Act and in shaping the early months of the OEO. Conway recalled that he used the skills and experience he had gained in the labor movement to shape community action. A big part of community action, Conway believed, was the "facilitation of African American participation in the South." Labor unionists also played an important role in shaping community action at the grassroots. Membership on community action boards was, according to a 1965 AFL-CIO pamphlet, "essential both to the poor and to the union membership." Union activism and community action could interact in mutually beneficial, if controversial, ways.[12]

By the time of STAR's creation, labor unionism was becoming a feature of Mississippi's freedom movement. Racial violence, economic oppression, and the mechanization of cotton had spurred a northward migration of African Americans since the 1940s. By 1965 black cotton workers suffered debilitating working and living conditions and pay of thirty cents per hour. In January 1965, building on the legacy of Freedom Summer, black workers in the Delta developed a union to challenge the power of plantation owners and demand a wage increase. The Mississippi Freedom Labor Union, with 1,350 members from six counties, organized a series of strikes. In March, beginning in Shaw—a small Delta town on the county line of Bolivar and Sunflower—workers went on strike demanding hourly pay of $1.25. Plantation owners responded by evicting strikers from their homes. In response, activists occupied a vacant air force base in Greenville, demanding food, jobs, and a specific appeal to OEO to fund Head Start programs in the Delta. Their action brought national attention to the plight of African Americans in the Delta. Martin Luther King Jr., for example, sent a telegram to President Johnson, asking for aid for those whom the federal government had "callously disregard[ed]." The sit-in brought promise of renewed federal aid from both the OEO and Department of Agriculture, even as strikers were evicted from the base on February 1, 1966. The strikes, however, did little to bolster black economic power or to convince white plantation owners to raise the pay of sharecroppers.[13]

STAR's creation was a seemingly opportune moment to combine the efforts of civil rights activists and labor unions. Instead, STAR became the site of renewed conflict between the two groups. Rather than bringing new energy to black union activism, the cooperation between labor activists and labor-training programs actually served to preserve the racial status quo. This is in part because labor unions remained segregated into the 1960s across much of the South. Nationally, the AFL-CIO made efforts to

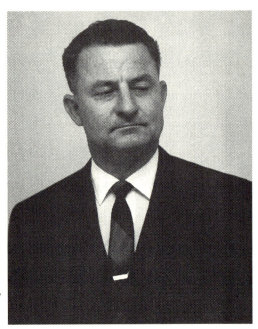

Fig. 7.2. Claude Ramsay, Mississippi AFL-CIO President, 1965, Folder 10, Labor Photographs, Mississippi State AFL-CIO Records, Southern Labor Archives, Special Collections and Archives, Georgia State University, Atlanta, http://digitalcollections.library.gsu.edu/cdm/ref/collection/labor/id/4187.

remain apart from civil rights activities such as the March on Washington. In Mississippi, state AFL-CIO president Claude Ramsay was not publicly active in the movement until 1964. While Ramsay cultivated friendships with civil rights activists in the early 1960s, particularly Medgar Evers, he kept such relationships private. "We often talked about what had to be done in this state," Ramsay later recalled of his friendship with Evers, "and that we had to develop a political alliance between organized labor and the black people primarily to turn things around." The opportunity to "turn things around" came after the passage of the Voting Rights Act, when the AFL-CIO appropriated fifty thousand dollars to spend on voter registration in five southern states. Mississippi, Ramsay recalled, "was one of them . . . they gave me five thousand dollars to spend on voter registration here in Mississippi."[14]

Such support meant that Ramsay was able to openly support civil rights activism with the backing of the national AFL-CIO, and it laid the groundwork for his later involvement in STAR. But Ramsay's advocacy for racial enfranchisement was by no means simple. His public support for civil rights came at a time when such support threatened his job, the strength of the AFL-CIO in Mississippi, and his life. Union activists who advocated integration were targets of Klan threats and violence. In November 1964, for example, a gang of masked men kidnapped and beat Otis Matthews before pouring corrosive liquid onto his wounds. Otis Matthews was the financial secretary of the local AFL-CIO International Woodworkers of America and was attacked because the union had approved a federal order "giving Negroes equal treatment at the Masonite plant in Laurel." Claude Ramsay also came under fire: the Klan sent him threatening messages, including a postcard from the "grand drag-on" warning Ramsay to "quit messin [sic] around in other people's buziness [sic]." A former Klansman later admitted he had been assigned to kill Ramsay.[15]

Ramsay's support for civil rights in the face of such threats was in part reflective of a moral or at least pragmatic dedication to achieving black enfranchisement and integration. His actions won him admiration from civil rights activists and politicians. In the 1980s, for example, he received awards for his advocacy of civil rights. Ramsay had a "natural inclination to treat all people alike." However, there was more than just a moral dimension to Ramsay's support for civil rights. Ramsay was determined to overhaul the Mississippi Democratic Party. He spent much of the late 1960s pursuing this goal, at times in collaboration with NAACP and the Freedom Democrats. Ramsay's political activism made him a person of concern in the eyes of the state Sovereignty Commission. Erle Johnston was concerned about the link between Ramsay and black activists in 1967. Ramsay was, Johnston claimed, gathering blacks together to register in order to "make a grasp for political power." Ramsay was also motivated by his belief that in order to make advances for labor rights, race relations in Mississippi much be addressed. Ramsay felt, he later recalled, that the "race question" had held back the state AFL-CIO for years. When Ramsay began supporting voter registration, the local unions dominated by White Citizens' Councils disaffiliated from the Mississippi AFL-CIO. Even the "predominantly Negro" labor unions remained unaffiliated with it, Ramsay recalled. Racial divisions thus undermined the lukewarm support for labor activism evident in the state. Beyond the labor activism, Ramsay felt that a preoccupation with race had also "harmed Mississippi." This preoccupation had, Ramsay believed, "prevented the state from sorting out its true problems."[16]

These "true" problems were ignorance and historic legislation against labor, Ramsay stated in a 1967 speech. These two factors more than any other were, for Ramsay, holding back Mississippi's economic development—and the development of the state AFL-CIO. Ramsay's support for civil rights activism was thus part of his role, dictated by necessity if he was to do his job as a union leader. But Ramsay thought that addressing the issues that held back Mississippi's economy—and which were less racially charged—was of primary importance. Prevalent among these issues was, Ramsay believed, adult education. This belief in the importance of adult education resulted in Ramsay's close association with STAR. He served as a member of the board's executive committee from the program's inception. In 1965 he told a reporter that STAR was "probably one of the best [antipoverty programs] to come out of OEO." He emphasized the significance of the support the program had from "all segments of the community." He pointed to the diverse membership of the board: from the head of the Jackson Chamber of Commerce to poor representatives to Ramsay himself. Ramsay also spoke eloquently in defense of STAR and the importance of adult education before the Senate hearings in Jackson in April 1967. In 1968 he received OEO's rural service award.[17]

However, by 1970 Ramsay had become a central actor in the STAR board's white "dominating clique." As part of this clique, Ramsay perpetuated the executive staff's racially discriminatory actions. He manipulated board regulations to ensure his continued presence within the executive committee. For example, in order to pursue his agenda more effectively, Ramsay sought election to the poor area committee of the Edwards STAR center. Ramsay was successful, thus doubling his voting power. But the Edwards committee went to considerable effort to remove Ramsay from its board because he never attended a committee meeting. Nonetheless, Ramsay's maneuvering secured two AFL-CIO votes on the board, both of whom supported the practices that buttressed civil rights compliance violations and blatant racial discrimination in hiring and promotion practices. Ramsay also participated in character assassinations of STAR's black manpower director, Richard Polk. He accused Polk of contributing money to the "political machine" of Charles Evers. The national AFL-CIO—through Ramsay at times—had also contributed to Charles Evers's civil rights work in the mid-1960s. But by the late 1960s, Ramsay's opinion of Evers had declined as, according to Ramsay, "he started playing all kinds of political games." Ramsay believed that Evers had in fact kept a lot of the money that he and many others donated to support activism in Fayette. Evers was "well respected at one time," Ramsay recalled, "before he got money hungry." Ramsay's disapproval of Evers extended to Polk, not just because of Polk's support for Evers. Ramsay labeled Polk a "black militant." Polk responded scathingly that "to them [board president Cornelius Turner and Ramsay] a militant is anyone who says no to oppression or oppressive and intimidating tactics of the governor." Polk's comments reflect the shift in the definition of a "radical." By the late 1960s any African Americans or whites unwilling to ensure that STAR remained solely an adult education program were depicted as radical.[18]

Far from seeking genuine equality among the races through STAR there was a return to the paternalism characteristic of southern race relations under the cover of OEO-mandated integration. White domination was institutionalized by the executive committee, which was empowered to act for the board in between the board's quarterly meetings. Thus, just one or two members of the clique made the majority of the important decisions regarding program operation. This clique sought to shape STAR into a program in line with Governor John Bell Williams's wishes: a "nice program educating the colored folk." White board members utilized threats and intimidation to keep white STAR staff in line. They renewed tactics reminiscent of the earlier white segregationists in a manner that maintained their intimidatory value but stopped short of outright violence. They embraced racially discriminatory hiring, firing, and pay practices and wielded STAR's power to suppress black activism.[19]

Ramsay's involvement with STAR was in line with his belief in the importance of education, manpower training, and the AFL-CIO. He was determined to secure increased support for, and influence of, the AFL-CIO in Mississippi politics. His decision to embrace a coalition with the controlling clique of STAR's board can be best understood in this light. The changing racial realities had resulted in the reluctant acceptance by the white establishment of integration in antipoverty programs. This acceptance was conditional, based on securing white control of the federal funds. It was thus through participation in this reluctant biracialism that Ramsay could forge associations and influence policy. Involvement with this clique provided Ramsay—as it did the Catholic diocese to a lesser extent—the opportunity to be an "insider." Both the Catholic Church and the labor union in Mississippi had the onus of being classed as "outsiders." This status had united them loosely with civil rights activists but had prevented Ramsay from making inroads in the state. Thus, the opportunity STAR represented was one Ramsay valued. Whatever pragmatic or moral considerations drove his support of civil rights, both his racial moderation and involvement with STAR proved detrimental to black advancement. Ramsay's "moderation" had a damaging impact on the efforts of the Mississippi Freedom Labor Union in their 1965 strike. Likewise, Ramsay's role within STAR reveals the limitations of that pragmatic commitment to black advancement in the late 1960s.[20]

Ramsay's actions in STAR then were for him not a betrayal of the civil rights organizations he had supported in earlier phases of the movement. "We did a lot of good," Ramsay recalled. "I really feel that that program, where we were able to get blacks and whites together in a schoolroom—you know, we are talking about uneducated whites and blacks now, not just the uneducated black. We had both white and black in the Catholic schoolrooms. That program perhaps did as much or more than anything that I know in terms of breaking down racial barriers." His involvement in STAR reflected his belief in the value of education and its potential to produce integration. This was, for Ramsay, the best way to secure his goal of securing AFL-CIO's political power and future.[21]

Just as the Head Start program in Mississippi was more than simply a preschool program, STAR was more than merely a labor-training program. It was created to train and educate the vast poor segment of workers on which Mississippi's former economic strength had rested, the same people who had been denied access to education and job training. STAR could thus alter the very culture of the state. It had the potential to disrupt every aspect of life, from the rigid racial and economic structure of the state to the daily realities of family life. In preparing poor Mississippians for urban industrial jobs, STAR transformed the nature of the relationship between the poor and white landowners. It undermined a relationship that had defined rural life in the Delta for decades. For OEO this was a distinct advantage of the program. Shriver pointed to STAR's effective effort to tie literacy training to job training, home improvement, and informed consumer practices that had a tangible impact on students' lives. However, for many white Mississippians—and, ultimately, for the state AFL-CIO and the diocese—this was deeply concerning. STAR posed a threat to the established racial structure and had the potential to provide African Americans with the economic stability that would render their newly acquired political rights meaningful.[22]

Such a threat impelled the STAR board and its ruling clique—including supposed racial moderates such as Ramsay—to limit black empowerment through the program. Civil rights activists across the state complained to STAR, to OEO, and to civil rights organizations such as the NAACP, but the regional OEO was never particularly responsive to such complaints and their resources were stretched to breaking point. It was not until 1969 that OEO's civil rights division finally got around to investigating racial discrimination in one of STAR's affiliated training program, the Delta Concentrated Employment Program. Inspectors found that widespread discrimination "adversely affects the STAR program and the community action agencies in the Delta counties." At the same time, Mississippi's conservative press began offering praise of the program. According to one *Clarion Ledger* reporter, STAR "has been especially successful." This praise was a clear indication of the failure of the program to achieve racial change.[23]

It was the state NAACP who finally took action to address the discrimination that had infected STAR. They had, by 1970, received over four hundred complaints regarding racial discrimination within the program. In response the state NAACP organized a hearing in December 1970 to investigate these allegations. The hearing was headed by Alex Waites, the state NAACP field representative. He called the complainants and STAR board and staff members before a panel including Aaron Henry, OEO consultant Patricia Derian, and Community Education Extension director David Rice, and Mississippi's only black legislator, Representative Robert Clark. The hearing revealed the horrific abuses of power and authority that were being perpetuated through the program.[24]

The middle-class members of the board came under particular criticism at the NAACP hearing. African American manpower director Richard Polk used the labels "pseudoliberal" and "ultraconservative" to describe members of the controlling clique of STAR's board. For Polk the pseudoliberals were establishment whites such as AFL-CIO state chair Claude Ramsay and Catholic priest Msgr. McGuff. The ostensible commitment of these pseudoliberals to biracial cooperation masked a determination to use their involvement with STAR to preserve their racial, class, and gender privileges, Polk believed. Board chair Cornelius Turner was, for Polk, the archetypal "ultraconservative" African American. Turner was from the established middle class, what the *Clarion Ledger* referred to as the "Negro ruling class." Turner was unwilling or unable to jeopardize his relationship with establishment whites—and thus his livelihood—by pursuing an agenda they opposed.[25]

Polk utilized these labels in order to pursue his objective of undermining the board's controlling clique. Thus while evocative, these labels lack sufficient nuance to describe or explain the complex and contradictory motivations of the board members. As in Mississippi Action for Progress, the integration evidence within STAR was a significant step forward for race relations in the state. The experience of integration, and of both races working together on an ostensibly equal footing, was a new experience for all the board members. Polk, as with many African Americans in the late-1960s, was expressing his frustration that these early, tentative steps toward progress soon halted. The interracial cooperation soon meant the suppression of black activism. As journalist Christopher Jencks noted, the "moderation" of many of the black community action board members was "manifested by their invariable habit of agreeing with whatever their white counterparts said." For some of those Polk labeled "ultraconservative" blacks, this capitulation represented their only choice. Whatever their undoubtedly multifaceted and complex motivations, the result was the suppression of black activism and the advancement of the economic interests of the middle class.[26]

The December 1970 NAACP hearing into STAR uncovered the breadth and consistency of the racial discrimination within the program. The panel's findings included "substantial noncompliance" by STAR's board since 1965 "with the OEO mandated goal of effective participation of the poor in the decision-making process of STAR." They also found that "participation by the full board in the decision-making process has been thwarted from the program's inception by the actions of the President of the board, with the support of a small group of board members." Other findings included "substantial and unauthorized interference" by some board members in staff functions and "widespread unlawful or unfair employment practices," including "widespread racial discrimination in initial hirings, salaries, and advancement."

The panel made a number of recommendations to address these issues. They proposed that OEO withdraw the 1970/1971 grant requirement to restructure the board, to allow genuine participation of the poor in the decision-making process. The panel also recommended the immediate resignation of the president of STAR's board and that of "other board members whose past actions have been detrimental to the best interest of STAR." Other proposals included review of the board's duties and investigations into hiring practices and into the circumstances surrounding the dismissal of employees such as Richard Polk. Such changes, the panel hoped, would "resolve many of the internal difficulties" in STAR and enable it to fulfill its "potential to be an unusually effective program." But the board, led by Cornelius Turner and Claude Ramsay, rejected the panel's findings and recommendations. Turner claimed that the NAACP had allowed itself to be used by "scurrilous individuals led by Richard Polk." The NAACP was, according to the board, just perpetuating the "untrue and unfounded" accusations against Turner, the Catholic diocese, the bishop, and the state AFL-CIO. Turner made one final attempt to dismiss what he termed the "troublemakers" in STAR's equal opportunities office. But in the wake of the hearing, Turner's authority was diminished, and the dismissals were soon overturned by the program's grievance committee. Turner resigned the following month.[27]

His resignation did not mark the end of discrimination that was being perpetrated within—and through—the program, though. The rejection of the NAACP findings and recommendations heralded the continuation of the entrenched patterns of racial discrimination that endured until STAR's demise. Gerald Davis, who replaced Msgr. Winel as executive director, perpetuated the culture of discrimination and racism within STAR. Davis's actions prompted Aaron Henry, who had sat on the NAACP panel, to threaten public demonstrations against Davis and STAR. The uproar contributed to Davis's dismissal only six weeks after his appointment as executive director. But the hearing and the public opposition to Davis's actions raised the profile of STAR. The program had been largely immune to opposition from the white establishment and of little interest to the Sovereignty Commission. In the wake of the hearing, however, the white establishment took a renewed interest in the program. The state economic opportunity office, the governor's office and the commission all agreed to "monitor STAR carefully" in the wake of the hearing.[28]

The state economic opportunity office took particular interest in STAR after 1970. The agency was set up under Governor Paul Johnson and instructed to get community action funds in the hands of the white establishment. It was integral to the drive to ensure that federal antipoverty funds were controlled by "local responsible people." Over the years of the late-1960s, the office had "grown into a deep-seeded [sic] front of segregation." The state economic opportunity office itself remained a segregated workplace into the 1970s. The head of the office, Lee Sutton, monitored all communication, according to a report by one of her staff. She only allowed white staff members to enter her office. Far from supporting the aims of the war on poverty, the state economic opportunity office was more like an outcropping of the Sovereignty Commission. One of Lee Sutton's employees, Clovis Williams, had been an investigator with the Sovereignty Commission before moving to the state economic opportunity office. Unsurprisingly, Williams maintained a close and rewarding relationship with W. Webb Burke, Erle Johnston's successor as Sovereignty Commission director. Williams used this connection to gain access to commission reports monitoring black antipoverty workers, including STAR staff, such as the program's new executive director Al Rhodes and board member Owen Brooks. From the initial acceptance of STAR in 1966, the white establishment had, by 1971, adopted the same tactics to undermine STAR that they used to control and contain Mississippi Action for Progress.[29]

The NAACP hearing was merely one of a series of problems facing STAR by 1970. A delay in submitting their refunding application had delayed their funding. Governor John Bell Williams's refusal to sign STAR's grant package compounded the problem. Worse was to come, however. On August 2, 1971, OEO's southeast regional director, Roy Batchelor, informed the board of his tentative decision not to refund STAR. Batchelor's decision was based on a number of alleged failures. Prominent among those was the board's inability to provide stable direction, meet minimum standards of administration, and ensure adequate recordkeeping. Batchelor was also responding to concerns that the program was not producing the most meaningful benefits to the poor. For Batchelor, though, the most serious problem was the allegation that STAR provided overwhelmingly for black women.[30]

Far from disproportionately aiding black women, STAR perpetuated the discrimination they faced. Sarah Johnson, a black woman who worked in a number of Mississippi antipoverty programs including STAR, recalled facing gender and racial discrimination from her boss. Johnson was initially employed at STAR as a recruiter secretary. "Shortly after I was hired," Johnson recalled,

> *the young lady who was the executive [secretary] . . . left and my boss began to look for another executive secretary. He wanted a male and, of course, all of the males who were looking for jobs—white males specifically—wanted too much salary, so he wasn't able to hire them. At that time I felt I was being denied an opportunity to move up because he was looking for somebody over me, plus I was the person there doing the job. So after all his looking—about four months—he didn't find anybody, [so] I was promoted from recruiter secretary to executive secretary.*[31]

Richard Polk reported similar instances of racially and discriminatory hiring practices. Mary Coleman, for example, was a black woman with an honors degree in business administration. Coleman applied for a post within STAR, but received no communication from the fiscal office. The position was later filled, Polk noted "without any notice being sent to Miss Coleman that the position had been filled. When she enquired of the status of her application, she was told that the position had since been filled and that it was filled with the best applicant." When Polk was informed of this, he reviewed Mary Coleman's application and that of the successful candidate—who was white and male. Polk found that the successful candidate had "only a junior college level education from several institutions and is in no way comparable to Miss Coleman."[32]

STAR also failed to address the gender and race discrimination faced by its trainees once they had completed their GED certificate. "Very few STAR trainees," Charles Horwitz reported to executive director Msgr. Winel, "have been placed in jobs . . . any jobs. We realize that few jobs are available for black women in this state but we feel that STAR should make more diligent efforts in opening up jobs traditionally reserved for men." STAR should, Horwitz reported, on behalf of the STAR's Hinds County poor area committee, file lawsuits against employers who discriminate against women or black people. But STAR, Horwitz concluded, has failed to file any such lawsuits.[33]

Batchelor's accusations—especially allegations that STAR provided overwhelmingly for black women—reflect the growing conservatism of OEO staff. Rumsfeld had replaced Democratic appointees with his own selections, including Ray Batchelor. Batchelor's allegations fed back into the racial and gender discrimination that had undermined the war on poverty from the outset. Under Rumsfeld, this discrimination was validated at the national and regional levels. The effect was amplified by the decentralization Rumsfeld was implementing. This change in atmosphere at OEO was the result of Nixon's covert attempts to subvert the intent of the Economic Opportunity Act and quietly dismantle the OEO. Emanating from OEO regional offices, this racialized and gendered opposition resonated with the conservative depictions of the mythical welfare queen. STAR did indeed involve a disproportionate number of African American women. But this was not a failure of the program. Rather, it was a reflection of the population STAR served. Many working-age black men had migrated from the poorest areas of Mississippi. Thus the remaining black population was disproportionately female, who struggled under the combined weight of poverty and racial and gender discrimination.[34]

Bishop Brunini, executive committee chair Alix Sanders, and other board members reacted angrily to Batchelor's allegations. They sent Batchelor a detailed letter that refuted the allegations point by point, at times very convincingly. They saw Bachelor's decision as a personal attack on the integrity of board members, program staff, and the diocese, and they went on the offensive in order to protect STAR funding—and their reputations. Brunini and Sanders called on the connections that STAR and the diocese had cultivated with the white establishment. Brunini urged Senators Stennis and Eastland to pressure OEO to reconsider their decision. Alix Sanders, meanwhile, wrote to Congressman Carl Perkins and other public officials requesting their support. The local establishment also rallied behind STAR. Mayor Davis urged Stennis to intervene in support of STAR at least to get a "full and impartial hearing," as well as appealing directly to the president.[35]

The support STAR received from the white establishment was reflective of the goodwill the program had generated in the state. Even Senator Stennis urged OEO to give STAR a hearing, although he made it clear that his support was due to his friendship with the bishop's brother, attorney Ed Brunini. Whatever the motivation, this pressure from Stennis and other powerful STAR supporters gained the program a reprieve. The regional OEO office granted STAR a hearing, taking place in Atlanta on August 31, 1971. Attorney Hamah King would hear from a number of STAR staff, board members, and enrollees, and then decide the program's fate. Those giving evidence included Bishop Brunini, executive director Al Krumlauf, board members Father Broussard and the Delta Ministry's Owen Brooks, and program staff including Leola Williams.[36]

STAR staff, testifying at the hearing, spoke eloquently in support of the program despite its many problems. There were not only protective of a program that was, according to one member of staff, "an agent for change." They were also suspicious of the motives of the decision to defund the program. Father Bernard Law, Vicar General of the Diocese of Natchez-Jackson, called the allegations "weak" and the facts in support of them "sloppy and sparse." There was, Father Law said, "a disturbing question that keeps arising in my own mind, and it's what lies behind these allegations, because certainly something must as they themselves are so manifestly weak . . . is it a determination, possibly, to do away with programs such as STAR? Is this a general policy decision that people who are responsible for bureaucratic administrative have no control over but are forced to put into effect?"

King was in no position to either confirm or deny Law's suspicions, but his findings spoke for themselves. The hearing revealed ongoing problems with STAR's administration, board, and equal opportunity compliance. However, King also found that OEO inspectors had failed to take into account the positive steps the new board was taking. Perhaps more significantly, King reassessed STAR's relationship with poor black women. He did not consider the high proportion of black women as the result of bias, nor did he see it as detrimental to the program. Rather King believed the high number of black female enrollees was one of the program's significant achievements.[37]

Based on King's findings, Batchelor reversed his tentative decision and refunded STAR from October 1971 at its previous funding rate of $2.2 million. This was a significant moment for STAR. It stood firm against the early attempts of OEO and the Nixon administration to slowly chip away at the war on poverty. Aside from securing STAR's refunding, the hearing proved beneficial to the program in another way. Frank discussion of STAR's shortcomings provided a turning point for the program. STAR had a patchy record of adhering to OEO's grant conditions and implementing the required administrative procedures. The program remained noncompliant with numerous equal opportunity regulations in late 1971. After the refunding crisis, though, STAR's board began to make some headway in addressing these issues.[38]

Improvements were made in program administration and poor participation. STAR did not become a vehicle for community action. African Americans and whites seen by the board as "militant" activists were still excluded. Even before the improvement was made, however, the basis on which Batchelor decided to defund STAR was not sound. His decision was reflective of the increasing conservatism of the OEO under the Nixon administration. STAR, as the *Delta Democrat Times* reported, had been caught in a "game of bureaucratic chess with the poor the obvious losers" that was being played by the Nixon administration. At the same time, the racial and gender discrimination omnipresent in the war on poverty was being used to propagate a gendered and racially charged image of social welfare.[39]

Despite the improvements made within STAR, it could not withstand the change in philosophy at OEO. When in late 1972 Governor William Waller attempted to veto STAR's grant, the program's demise seemed inevitable. Nixon's slow unraveling of OEO was speeding up. From decentralization he moved onto plans for regionalization. Combined with decreasing OEO appropriations, Nixon's dismantling of the war on poverty had already sealed STAR's fate. This time the only negotiations that took place between the STAR board and OEO were to decide the length and conditions placed on STAR's phase out grant. The program was given six months to spin off its functions and create a manpower programming structure that could be operated through Mississippi's community action programs. STAR was an early casualty of the decreased funding of the war on poverty, but many antipoverty programs in Mississippi and the nation soon followed.[40]

- Chapter Eight -

THE DEMISE OF THE WAR ON POVERTY

It was not only STAR that suffered under the severe cuts to war on poverty funding under Nixon and Rumsfeld. Funding cuts and delays to approve grants affected many of the state's antipoverty programs, fostering insecurity for staff and the program's poor participants. These funding cuts came at the instigation of both the president and Congress. However, the change in the impetus of OEO and the usage of these funds was the result of Nixon's decisions. Nixon played an important role in securing and fine-tuning the legislative victories of the civil rights movement. His decision-making on civil rights operated at a complex moment and was molded by a combination of political expediency, practicality, and principle. These considerations also affected his actions with regard to the war on poverty. Nixon may well have wanted to dissolve OEO in 1969 had Republicans been in control of Congress. But the Great Society, despite its shortcomings, encapsulated the aspirational ideology of postwar America. Nixon was aware of the "limitations of attacking the Great Society without having anything to put in its place."[1]

That did not stop him from undermining the war on poverty, though. One of the most significant ways Nixon changed the impetus of the war on poverty was through decentralization. The strategy of decentralization was apparent from the outset of his presidency. While the impact of this decentralization was felt increasingly during Nixon's second term, the strategy was put in place soon after Nixon took office in 1969. "I believe greater and more uniform decentralization of federal agencies is essential," Nixon wrote to his cabinet in March 1969. This decentralization was, Nixon emphasized, "urgent and important." "Every step in each process," he reminded his cabinet, "should be examined with a view toward elimination if at all possible." Nixon was positioning OEO for eventual elimination but was constrained by the political and ideological context.[2]

Nonetheless, Nixon's strategy had a significant impact on the war on poverty. By June 1971 Michigan's Democratic congressman William D. Ford told a national meeting of community action program directors that the war on poverty was "floundering." This was because, Ford claimed, of "decisions made in the Executive Office of Management and Budget to provide too little money and to disperse too widely the authority for planning and carrying out the battle." It was not just the funding cuts that were worrying supporters of the war on poverty, but also the shift in emphasis away from community action, a shift of intent exemplified by the maneuvering of programs out of OEO and into established government departments. Also troubling was the subsequent power given to the regional offices of these departments, which would prove advantageous to the white establishment in Mississippi.[3]

This regionalism was particularly damaging to Head Start. While HEW was reviled by white Mississippi as the author of school desegregation, the regional department was another matter. The regional Office of Child Development had proven far more receptive to the demands of Mississippi's white politicians in its administration of Head Start. Mississippi's nascent Republican Party was eager to take advantage of this trend. Party officials had utilized their connections with Don Rumsfeld and Dick Cheney in OEO to good effect and were eager to do the same with the regional Office of Child Development. In the Deep South the perception of Head Start as a black program with undesirable, radical connotations had remained, embodied by the Child Development Group. Mississippi's Republicans were thus well aware of the political mileage to be gained by exploiting this perception. Chair Clarke Reed and executive secretary W. T. Wilkins assisted white community action agencies in getting black grassroots Head Start programs under their control. They utilized their connections in order to capitalize politically on their efforts. In collaboration with officials in the regional Office of Child Development, Mississippi Republicans systematically undermined black Head Start programs. The collaboration was beneficial to both the Republicans and the regional office.[4]

Barbara Whitaker, the assistant regional director of the Office of Child Development, had a number of "undesirable" Head Start programs in her sights. The Head Start programs she targeted were independent from the establishment-controlled community action programs and were run by African Americans. In Jackson, for example, Barbara Whitaker attempted to bring the Head Start program under the control of Community Services Association, but was unsuccessful. Whitaker also sought to undermine the independence of two African American Head Start programs in the Delta, in Sunflower County and in Bolivar County. With the aid of Reed and Wilkins, Whitaker was successful in stripping Sunflower County's African American

Head Start program of its independence and ensuring its incorporation into the white-establishment program.[5]

The damaging effects of this regionalism were not limited to Head Start, however. This trend had an impact on antipoverty efforts across the state and, indeed, across the nation. The move was particularly concerning in Mississippi. In February 1971 the executive director of Jackson's community action agency informed his board of this worrying "shift of community action to special revenue sharing or other resources available at the community level." President Nixon wanted to implement Special Revenue Sharing in order to return responsibilities and resources to states and localities as part of his "New Federalism." This was a particularly destructive maneuver for Mississippi's programs. New Federalism would be even more detrimental to community and minority participation in antipoverty programs than the existing level of regionalization.[6]

Worse was to come in 1972. HEW's decision that year to equalize funding between the states had severe consequences in Mississippi. Due to historic inequities in the distribution of funds across Region IV, Mississippi had received the major share of funds each year since 1965. Region IV (previously designated Region III) contained the states of Alabama, Florida, Georgia, Kentucky, Mississippi, North Carolina, South Carolina, and Tennessee. By fiscal year 1970 Mississippi received 43 percent of the full year's Head Start funds allocated to Region IV and 41 percent in fiscal year 1971. In a bid to correct this inequity, HEW collected data on the number poor of children eligible for Head Start by state and allocated funds accordingly. Florida had the highest number of eligible children (89,900) and South Carolina the lowest (26,940), with Mississippi coming fifth with 58,370 eligible children. This new allocation policy resulted in substantial cuts in funds for Head Start in Mississippi in fiscal year 1972. These funding cuts did not mean local Head Start centers could reduce the number of children they served, however. The regional Office of Child Development frequently required programs with reduced funding to continue providing the same level of service for the same number of children. As a result, Head Start centers were consolidated by moving classes from local communities and into bigger, centralized locations. This move had the potential to destroy the community nature of the Head Start program. Perhaps even more detrimentally, this meant fewer opportunities for parent participation, which was one of the most significant aspects of the program.[7]

After Nixon's 1972 reelection, his plans to dismantle OEO accelerated. Nixon was determined to terminate OEO after years of slowly eroding its power through decentralization. The president had been vetoing OEO funding sent to him by Congress since 1971. In his 1974 budget message, delivered on January 29, 1973, he did not request any funds for OEO and withheld millions of dollars of congressionally allocated funding from the agency. That month he appointed of Howard J. Phillips as director of OEO to be both "human bomb and walking target." Through Phillips, Nixon demanded the resignation of senior OEO staff members, replacing them with right-wing Young Americans for Freedom and Committee to Reelect the President staff. Phillips was the "point man in the Administration's budget cutting exercise," bearing the brunt of the attacks from Great Society liberals and the media after his appearances before Congress in March 1973.[8]

Despite Nixon's deliberate omission in the budget and Phillips's attempts to dismantle OEO, funding for OEO received bipartisan support. Many Democratic politicians pushed for the war on poverty's survival, still supporting its aim and recognizing its achievements. Some conservative Democratic and Republican politicians, meanwhile, recognized that a sense of entitlement among the poor had developed after a decade of federal funding. They feared potentially violent consequences should the programs cease. Historian Gareth Davies blamed this sense of entitlement for the failure of the war on poverty. Here, however, it prompted Congress to provide OEO with a brief stay of execution.[9]

The attempts of Nixon—and Phillips—to dismantle OEO and end the war on poverty were halted by Judge William B. Jones in April 1973. Judge Jones ruled Phillips's appointment invalid and ordered his actions be overturned. Few war on poverty scholars address the impact of Phillips at any length, perhaps because his tenure was short lived and his actions overturned. Phillips's role in the dismantling is more often mentioned in studies of conservatism. As Sara Diamond and Chip Berlet have noted, for example, Nixon's decision to appoint Phillips was in part a response to conservative pressure. Phillips's belief that OEO was a "wasteful funding conduit" for "'radical' leftist recipients" was a popular opinion among conservative opponents of the war on poverty. But Phillips's actions, even if they were quickly overturned, had significant consequences for many war on poverty programs. His beliefs about the war on poverty reflected the philosophy of a number of Nixon appointees to the agency who were present before Phillips's high-profile appointment and stayed after his dramatic departure. For many antipoverty programs in Mississippi—and across the country—the damage that had been done during the funding delays caused by Phillips was irreversible.[10]

In Jackson, Phillips delayed the community action program's $208,900 grant and defunded its Legal Services program. Phillips's actions resulted in one hundred employees going without pay, prompting the program's board of directors to appeal directly to Nixon. They begged for "intervention in this bureaucratic chaos to give immediate financial relief to this agency and its dedicated outreach workers." Ultimately, it was a combination of Mississippi Republican Representative Thad Cochran and the "old guard" Mississippi Democrat Senator Stennis that salvaged the program rather than Nixon. Legal Services was one of the most controversial elements of the war on poverty. Created in 1965 Legal Services was developed in large part due to the efforts of lawyers Edgar Cahn and Jean Cahn, who both worked in OEO and who believed legal aid for the poor should be part of the war on poverty. The program had a tumultuous history, as its lawyers took on high-profile cases that often produced major social reforms. At the same time, these victories "aroused the enmity of the program's political and ideological opponents," according to Robert F. Clark. The program was initially administered as part of community action programs, but director Earl Johnson Jr. soon began lobbying for greater independence. Despite the controversies it created, the 1967 Economic Opportunity Amendments designated Legal Services an independent program.[11]

Despite this independence, the program remained highly controversial. It was especially reviled by southern politicians and conservatives who viewed it as "government sponsored radicalism." Legal services' flagship program was California Rural Legal Assistance, which quickly ran into a series of high-profile battles with Republican governor Ronald Reagan. These battles weakened the Legal Services program, both in California and nationally. After Nixon's election, the program suffered from successive crises under OEO director Don Rumsfeld, who sought to bring it under tighter control.[12] In Mississippi, Legal Services programs suffered from the same coordinated attacks. Opposition came from the state Republican Party, powerful Democratic senators, the governor, and the white community. These were similar opponents to those community action programs faced across the state and the Deep South. Placing these local struggles against Legal Services into context illustrates the way in which the long massive resistance contributed to a national conservative discourse articulated by southern conservatives—both the old guard Democrat Party and the developing state Republican Party. Genuine concerns over wasted federal funds were expressed in ostensibly race-neutral language. Such language masked the true purpose of opposition to Legal Services programs: to neutralize this potential threat to white establishment.

The threat the white establishment perceived from Legal Services was threefold. First, there was concern that providing federal funding for lawyers would enable poor people to challenge the discriminatory activities of local, state, and federal programs. Second, the white establishment was concerned that federal funds would likewise enable lawyers to fight cases which sought to remove racial barriers to employment, education, housing, and other economic and social rights. Third, many white Mississippians were concerned Legal Services could support the legal challenges mounted by civil rights activists. This was particularly concerning in the wake of the civil rights legislation and even more so into the late 1960s and early 1970s. During these years activists were increasingly returning to legal challenges, but they lacked the necessary funds for such litigation—funds that could be provided by the federal government through Legal Services.[13]

On its creation, a range of prominent organizations endorsed OEO's Legal Services program, including National Defenders Association and Negro American Bar Association. These groups saw it as welcome support for the continuation of the legal profession's effort to provide legal services for all. While the American Bar Association was initially somewhat reluctant to throw its support behind the program, its cooperation was secured by the promise of strong influence on the program's board of directors. Thus, the legal establishment was heavily involved in the creation and development of the program. This provided Legal Services program with the kind of heavyweight backers that many new OEO programs lacked. Their support ensured Legal Services was "among the most respected products of the war on poverty." But the Bar Association's influence ultimately minimized the institutional changes and legal reforms achieved by the program.[14]

Nevertheless, the program spread rapidly across the country. In its first year, the program made grants of over $27 million in forty-three states and opened over five hundred new law offices serving the poor. Based on this early success, Harry McPherson noted in 1996 that it had "been one of the most useful poverty programs." However, Legal Services soon became problematic on a number of fronts. It quickly became target of intense criticism from southern conservatives in particular, who opposed wasteful spending and the loss of local control. The program compounded its troubles and alienated some of its supporters by creating difficulties for other war on poverty programs. Across the country, including the well-publicized cases in California, federally funded lawyers brought suits against antipoverty programs. While this was often necessary—especially given the level of discrimination evident in antipoverty programs in Mississippi alone— it did not win Legal Services many fans in the establishment. Internally, there was trouble too. The actions of Legal Services staff created additional complications for successive presidents and OEO directors.[15]

When Nixon came into office, Legal Services was an obvious target for the kind of "housecleaning" he employed in Head Start and Job Corps. However, Legal Services was something of a "sacred cow" of congressional liberals and retained powerful supporters in the legal establishment. And Nixon and some of his aides (with the notable exception of Howard Phillips) did believe the program had some value. While Legal Services remained a target of southern conservatives, the program survived into the 1970s. Although Nixon vetoed the OEO legislative package in December 1971, his target was not Legal Services but a proposed new multibillion-dollar child development program. So instead of abolishing the program—which Congress would not let him get away with—or bringing it under tighter control as he had with other OEO programs, Nixon choose regionalization. This was an ideal solution for Nixon. Regionalization was "a favorite southern device for blocking unwanted reforms." It would hand power over the funding and administration of Legal Services to OEO regional offices and silence conservative critics.[16]

Mississippi's Clarke Reed was one of many southern Republicans who endorsed regionalization. Opposition to Legal Services was a useful opportunity for the nascent party, who were seeking to "out-conservative" the powerful Mississippi Democratic politicians. Opposing Legal Services was a means of distinguishing themselves from Eastland and Stennis, and their failure to control OEO. Reed's opposition to Legal Services, like that of his fellow southern conservatives, was rooted in genuine concerns about the misuse of federal funds. Ultimately, however, Reed was driven by the desire to wrest control of Legal Services funds from "radicals." The main concern was that these "radicals" in OEO's Legal Services office would authorize the use of funds in Mississippi to pursue social reform. Reed, therefore, was a vocal supporter of the proposed regionalization of Legal Services. OEO's newly appointed Republican southeastern director Ray Batchelor was also behind the idea. Rumsfeld agreed. He had been warned by his predecessor of the dangerous propensity of the Legal Services staff to attempt to gain advantage for their program at the expense of OEO. As director, Rumsfeld found that Legal Services had constituted "five percent of [his] budget and fifty per-cent of [his] headaches." He sacked Legal Services director Terry Lenzner and his deputy, Mississippi-born African American Frank N. Jones, in November 1970 because they were "either unwilling or unable" to carry out his policies. Rumsfeld sought to portray Lenzner as a "wild-eyed radical," an accusation Lenzner publically challenged, claiming he had simply tried to provide lawyers to help poor people.[17]

One of Rumsfeld's first acts as OEO director was to establish an internal security unit charged with "sniffing out 'revolutionaries' who might be funneling government funds to 'subversives.'" Such language was echoed by southern conservatives who drew on the white segregationists' clarion call of states' rights and the tactics of earlier massive resistance in their opposition to alleged "radicals" at the local and national levels. In concert with Nixon's electioneering and Rumsfeld's dictatorial leadership, Reed and his colleagues almost succeeded in ensuring local control over the Legal Services program. This control would have resulted in the domination of local programs by segregated state bar organizations across the South. Even the conservative Senate Appropriations Committee opposed the regionalization plan as it would be "stripping [Legal Services] of the political independence it needs if it is to retain its vitality." Damaging leaks of the proposed plans for regionalization put a halt to the plan. When a letter from Clarke Reed urging Rumsfeld to implement regionalization was accidentally leaked to the press, it became a politically inexpedient proposition for Nixon and Rumsfeld to pursue.[18]

Legal services was thus saved from the regionalization. But for southern conservatives such as Reed this national campaign was merely one of many fronts in an ongoing battle. Reed was determined to wrest control of local Legal Services programs from black and white radicals who were using federal funds to pursue class actions and achieve lasting social change. Conservatives combined the mechanisms of earlier massive resistance with race-neutral language, which drew on white southerners' genuine fears over the misuse of federal funds. In 1969, for example, Mississippi's (segregated) state bar association launched an attack on the state's earliest and largest Legal Services program, North Mississippi Rural Legal Services. Their opposition was couched in this colorblind language. The bar claimed the program was "socialism in its purest form," used for "crusading and political objectives rather than serving the poor." The bar asserted, in the best tradition of white segregationists' willful self-delusions, that they would "in reality, furnish Legal Services to the poor regardless of race, creed, or color." This was an ironic claim, from a segregated bar whose members had spent most of the last few years fighting against desegregation cases. The language of opposition was an attempt to mask the true motivation of the bar: to neutralize the threat to the white establishment posed by Rural Legal Services' focus on class action litigation for its mostly black clientele.[19]

Into this highly contested landscape, Community Legal Services submitted its funding application to OEO in April 1969 seeking to operate a Legal Services program through Community Services Association. And from the moment of submitting that application, CLS faced opposition from a cross-section of white Mississippi. Some CSA board members attempted to distance themselves from the proposed program. White board member Joe Jack Hurst, for example, wrote to Governor Williams to assure him that CLS did not have the support of Community Services Association. Hurst used ostensibly colorblind language which drew on fears of civil rights activism threatening law and order, claiming that funding the program would "encourage the influx of outside radical elements" that would "harass and cause trouble for public officials and our law enforcement agencies." Most vocal in their opposition was the Hinds County Bar Association. Its president, Cary E. Bufkin, wrote a long and detailed list of the association's objections to the proposed program in a letter to CSA's executive director E. L. Lipscomb. Community Legal Services had, Bufkin claimed, failed to adhere to the rules and regulations of the Mississippi State Bar. Their application, he continued, provided a "largely general and ill-defined" proposal which was "an indictment of the entire system of government . . . more intent on remaking it in your own image" than providing Legal Services to the poor. Most significantly, Bufkin claimed CLS equated civil rights and poverty.[20]

Bufkin's intent was to portray Community Legal Services as a radical organization staffed by civil rights activists who were intent on overthrowing the government. His association sent OEO a proposal for their own Legal Services program in Hinds County, to operate in place of the proposed CLS. Bufkin's accusations are familiar. The Sovereignty Commission made similar accusations against the state's antipoverty programs, from the Child Development Group onwards. As with many commission claims, the majority of Bufkin's complaints were hyperbolic or simply untrue. The Hinds County Bar Association was utilizing all the weapons at its disposal to prevent the funding of Community Legal Services. At the state level, the Mississippi Bar Association was working equally hard to create and enforce a framework within which it could contain and constrain the OEO-funded Legal Services programs. While these organizations utilized tactics redolent of the Sovereignty Commission in opposing CLS, mechanisms of massive resistance were being employed from other sources.[21]

State Republicans were particularly active in their opposition. Reed and party executive W. T. Wilkins were not only concerned that CLS would fund civil rights cases. They were equally worried that CLS could be used to stir up political support for the Democratic Party among newly enfranchised blacks. The Republicans' campaign also had other political dimensions. Reed was determined that the state party gain the credit for getting rid of Legal Services programs. Perhaps even more significantly, Reed was concerned about the negative political consequences should he fail to stop CLS. There was no longer a liberal Democrat running OEO to blame for such programs. Now, the Republicans would bear the responsibility for allowing such a program into the state. The state Republican Party was growing slowly, so it was essential that they capitalized on having a Republican president (for whom the majority of white Mississippi had voted).[22]

Reed and Wilkins had carefully cultivated a relationship with Dick Cheney, Rumsfeld's executive assistant. But the leaking of the letter from Reed to Rumsfeld caused considerable political fallout and undermined that connection. In the wake of this, Reed's complaints regarding CLS appeared to hold little weight with Rumsfeld. Community Legal Services was funded in 1970 over the opposition of Reed and Governor John Bell Williams, while the application of the Hinds County Bar Association was rejected. Reed publicly condemned OEO's decision to fund CLS over the Hinds County Bar's program as "an exercise of poor and irresponsible judgment destined to aid political activists more than the poor." It represented, Reed asserted, "a callous insensitivity to the needs of the poor on the part of the OEO." Community Legal Services was, Reed maintained, "politically motivated and reads like the membership list for radical Young Democrats."[23]

The Hinds County Bar Association echoed Reed, claiming the group was "supported by the ultra-liberal Young Democrats ... the radical revolutionary groups, and militant civil rights groups." "Obviously," Bufkin stated, "the best interest of the poor people, both black and white, in Jackson and Hinds County will be served by the program proposed by the Bar Association," which, they claimed would "receive the cooperation and support of the vast majority of both black and white citizens of this county." Bufkin's claims that the program would receive black support were as unlikely as his accusations against CLS. However unlikely his claims, Bufkin's overblown rhetoric and inflammatory language cast Community Legal Services as radical, amplifying the fears of the white establishment and local white community.[24]

For the controlling white board members of Community Services Association, the funding of CLS was outrageous. Their disbelief was echoed in local press reports. One *Clarion Ledger* reporter noted, with horrified incredulity, that in Community Legal Services, "one federally funded agency sues another federally funded agency on behalf of people who benefit from both." Many board members were quick to distance themselves from CLS, despite it having been funded through Community Services Association. While the Community Legal Services program did manage to operate despite the intense opposition to its creation, that opposition did not die down. Governor Williams vetoed CLS funding in 1970 and 1971, although the OEO director overruled both vetoes. Each year after its initial application, the Hinds County Bar Association sent an application to OEO for a Legal Services program. As with their first, each subsequent application was turned down. However, by 1973 there was a new governor, William Waller—and a new OEO director, Howard Phillips. This time the governor's veto of CLS was successful.[25]

Howard Phillips, who publicly expressed "great delight in his assigned demolition task" of OEO, paid special attention to Legal Services. Phillips all but invited governors to veto Legal Services grants. He approved the proposal of the Hinds County Bar Association, and redirected Community Legal Services to this new program. Waller's veto—the culmination of years of white establishment and community opposition to Community Legal Services spearheaded by the Hinds County Bar Association—had finally coincided with the overt efforts of Nixon to dismantle OEO. But that was not the end for CLS. Community Legal Services' funding was restored—along with a number of other programs across the country—when a federal judge ruled that Phillips had acted beyond his legal authority because Nixon had not submitted his name to the Senate for confirmation.[26]

Local struggles against Mississippi's Legal Services programs stand at the confluence of the evolving white resistance and new conservatism. A developing, colorblind discourse was deployed by the Mississippi Republican Party, drawing on tropes of earlier massive resistance. The tactics of white opposition flowed seamlessly into themes of emerging national conservatism. They were a central part of the opposition of successive OEO directors against Legal Services at the national and local levels. This diverse and potent opposition meant Community Legal Services faced an arduous struggle during the first five years of its existence. This opposition produced a program hardened by battle, and the program eventually secured several powerful supporters.

White establishment antipoverty programs undermined the majority of African American delegate agencies across the state. However, Community Legal Services beat this trend. In 1976 Community Legal Services absorbed the establishment program, Hinds County Bar Association Legal Services. The ability of the program to withstand this barrage of opposition from a cross-section of white Mississippi and OEO resulted partially from the resilience and commitment of its staff. More significant, however, was the support of the national Legal Services program—national backing that had been entirely lacking for the majority of Mississippi's community action programs.[27]

While national support proved instrumental to the survival of Community Legal Services, it was national developments that contributed to the demise of its parent agency, Community Services Association. Continual funding insecurity amplified problems with CSA's administration, staff, and board. The program continued its operations into the 1970s, though its capacity to operate an effective program was severely hampered by continued divisions within the board. At best, Community Services Association survived as a service-oriented operation that served both the black and white population of Hinds County, although often on a de facto segregated basis. The board's incompetence resulted in a lack of proper planning and program development. Meanwhile the well-meaning but ineffectual leadership of executive director E. L. Lipscomb did little to assert control over program operation or personnel. Lipscomb was repeatedly accused of being an "Uncle Tom," particularly during his initial role as CSA's deputy director. During his five-and-a-half-year tenure as executive director, he provided "unusually unimaginative" leadership, according to member of the poor community. At a public meeting about the program, Lipscomb's failures to engage the poor community and to move the program out of white control were decried. A 1970 report by CSA's program committee concluded that, as executive director, Lipscomb did not make his voice heard in preventing ongoing injustices. Nor did he have the influence and independence necessary to force the power structure to negotiate. Nonetheless, Lipscomb continued in his post for three more years, before his resignation in June 1973.[28]

It was Lipscomb's ineffectual leadership, however, that allowed him to remain in post for such a long time. His tenure as executive director was a considerable length of time, particularly in the context of the short lifespan of many community action program directors. The fact that Lipscomb was an African American makes his achievement even more remarkable. On his resignation in June 1973 Lipscomb was replaced by his white deputy Joe Hemingway. Unlike Lipscomb, Hemingway attempted to exert authority over the disruptive staff and inept board. A liberal by Mississippi standards, Joe Hemingway had been a member of the Young Democrats and was a strong leader. Nonetheless, he was unable to overcome the divisions within the board and staff that sprung from racial, class, and ideological divides.[29]

There was a mass resignation of board members in 1973, prompted in part by the requirements of the Green Amendment. This mass resignation went some way to dissolve the two factions: the interracial middle-class coalition and the so-called "Horwitz faction." In theory, OEO's board requirements ensured a cross-section of the local community was represented. In reality, the board of Community Services Association failed to find the unity of purpose needed to make use of the disparate skills and knowledge each group brought to the board. In line with the amendment, board membership was drawn from three segments of the local community, most often referred to as groups A, B, and C. Group A members—mostly business leaders and politicians—had administrative ability and experience in abundance, though they lacked knowledge of the "dynamics of poverty" and too often demonstrated a damaging lack of understanding of the needs of the poor. Group B members included representatives of local organizations and were thus drawn from groups "likely to be socially conscious and administratively knowledgeable," but they still lacked perspective in balancing ideals with organizational priorities. Group C were the poor participants—elected representatives of the "target area" who had little administrative experience and were given no training by CSA, meaning that their "potentially valuable firsthand knowledge" was not utilized.

In Community Services Association, as in other Mississippi community action programs, race and class divisions undermined the program. These divisions frustrated any attempts at board unity as many powerful white businessmen exerted their control over the board, often through pressuring target area representatives to comply with their wishes to reduce community engagement and focus on service provision. Community representatives on the board included civil rights activists and community leaders in CSA's early years. But by the mid-1970s many of these activist members who had fought for community action had resigned or been pushed from the board. And as with the majority of antipoverty programs, CSA's board lacked women. So while the two factions of the board were fighting over the distribution of money and the level of integration, there was little to no awareness of the specific needs of poor women. The voice of poor blacks was stifled; the voice of poor women, meanwhile, was simply not present.

By late 1973 the infighting that had characterized the Community Services Association board of the late 1960s had ceased, replaced with apathy. White board members such as Catchings still placed the blame with so-called "activist" board members. Catchings continued to employ the by-now tired rhetoric of massive resistance to label board members such as African

American A. B. Evans "rabble rousers" who encouraged the "disruptive and subversive elements" among the staff. In the wake of the unpopular House Committee on Un-American Activities investigation into the Ku Klux Klan, appealing to anticommunism had become a less successful trope of white opposition to black advancement in the late 1960s. The Cold War détente of the early 1970s robbed such language of the last of its potency.

Indeed, the fact Evans was the target of accusations of militancy speaks to the lack of true radicalism. Evans was the target area representative who had so disappointed the poor community by consistently voting with the dominating faction of the board. He had opposed the earlier activism of Don Jackson (Kenyatta), for example, and voted against board measures that would assist the poor people he was meant to represent. More indication of the board's conservatism came from Catchings's other complaints. It was not merely Evans who was disrupting the program with what he called "rabble rous[ing]." Catchings identified community involvement—what he euphemistically referred to as the "decentralization of authority"—as one of the major contributing factors to the program's deficiencies. It was an ironic accusation: the very purpose of community action agencies was to involve the community in the program's operation. Yet here, that involvement was blamed for the failure of the program with the claim that it had led to the erosion of "respect for authority," a euphemism for white control.[30]

CSA's slow demise was caused by a number of interrelated factors. After Lipscomb's remarkably long tenure, the program had a series of short-lived executive directors with poor or at least unsuccessful administrative and leadership abilities. After only three months in post, Hemingway was followed by Ben Bradley and then Emma D. Sanders, neither of whom lasted for more than a year. Worse still was the uncertain future that faced all antipoverty programs. Howard Phillips's appointment signaled to all that war on poverty funding would not last much longer. Such uncertainty crippled long-term planning and made program development impossible. CSA struggled with other problems too. Internally, a lack of unity among staff and board members weakened the program, while difficulties also arose from the pervasive climate of hostility in which the program operated.[31]

In April 1975 Sanders was fired by the board for a multitude of administrative failings, most serious of which was her failure to spend half of CSA's yearly grant. The opposition the program faced from a cross-section of white Hinds County combined with the control asserted over the program by the interracial middle-class coalition had brought the program to the brink of collapse. The white establishment, long hostile to the program, had been encroaching on CSA's independence since 1974. That year, the Hinds County Board of Supervisors had become the sponsor of Community Services Association—functionally it controlled the program's funds. This board took the opportunity presented by Sanders's mismanagement and sacking to bring CSA under its complete control.[32]

Those who had previously provided the program with support, albeit of a limited nature, now used the program's vulnerability as an opportunity to attack. The state economic opportunity office—a "deep-seeded [sic] front of segregation"—had "a field day with threats and innuendoes, rumors and grandstand plays," an assistant informed the mayor of Jackson. Mayor Russell C. Davis had a close relationship with the program since its inception. But the program was so weakened and ineffectual by 1975 that he ignored the repeated appeals for assistance from the staff and board. Instead, he chose to stand back and "let it die." Davis then stepped in to take over the administration of federal funds, without any obligation to the current CSA staff. Governor Waller, meanwhile, saw an opportunity to end the program altogether and vetoed its $152,988 grant.[33]

In an exhaustive explanation of his veto, Waller alleged there were over twenty instances of administrative, leadership, board, and program failures. Despite OEO's willingness to give the board and staff more time to address the shortcomings, Waller concluded that the program was working to the detriment of the poor. The board of supervisors had been waiting for this chance. The board refused to extend its sponsorship of Community Services Association unless they could appoint a majority of the CSA board in order to stop "radicals from radical organizations" from dominating the public sector section of the board membership.[34]

When no response was forthcoming, the board of supervisors created its own community action program, the Hinds County Human Resource Agency, in November 1975. The board of supervisors selected two-thirds of the new program's board—five members were drawn from the board of supervisors and five appointed by the board from private organizations and interest groups. The remaining five members were target area representatives. Thus, this takeover by the white establishment ended board divisions once and for all by removing the slight moderating influence achieved by the civil rights activists on CSA's board. Under Hinds County Human Resources Agency, the board of supervisors secured the complete exclusion of the poor representatives from decision-making.[35]

OEO suffered a long, slow demise. Due to Nixon's actions, OEO was left with only the most controversial programs. By 1974 only community action programs and economic development remained within OEO, with the rest delegated or transferred to other departments. The war on poverty did survive both the covert and overt attacks from Nixon, although it was fundamentally altered by both delegation and regionalization. But his presidency had devastating consequences at the local level. It allowed white Mississippians who had been attacking undesirable antipoverty programs to finally seize control. Nixon's actions enabled establishment control over community action boards, clearing the way for the exclusion of any persons who wanted to ensure community engagement or activism. It removed the (albeit limited) protection OEO had provided to those attempting to engage and involvement the poor. His administration decreased funding levels and increased funding insecurity. Most damagingly, Nixon's legacy of regionalization increased the control of the local establishment over the disbursement and usage of federal funds, thus undermining poor black involvement in local programs and strengthening white control over community action programs.[36]

EPILOGUE

The Headstart, Economic Opportunity, and Community Partnership Act was the first bill signed into law under Gerald Ford's administration on January 4, 1975. The act brought an end to the Office of Economic Opportunity, but it ensured the survival of the war on poverty through a new agency, the Community Services Administration. Despite Nixon's efforts to dismantle the war on poverty and the damaging efforts of regionalism, Watergate had drained both his attention and political capital in the final years of his presidency. The war on poverty survived, although it was fundamentally altered in form and scale. Its survival was due in part to its powerful supporters. The constraints on Nixon's attempts to destroy antipoverty efforts were also an important factor. More significantly, its survival was the product of the liberalism of the 1960s. The federal government retreated from the peak of its 1960s activism, but it never returned to pre–Great Society (or indeed, pre–New Deal) levels. While liberalism declined, it had already secured the acceptance of an expanded welfare state into the 1970s.[1]

In Mississippi the economic, political, and social transformation continued unabated in the 1970s. Changes to the state's demographics, electoral districts, culture, economy, politics, rural, urban and suburban spaces, and the numbers of black voters altered Mississippi beyond recognition. The evolution of massive resistance also continued. Private, Christian academies flourished ensuring the public school system remained segregated—transitioning rapidly from all-white to almost entirely African American. Voter dilution efforts persisted, even as the numbers of registered African American voters soared. Politicians were forced to accept the new political and racial realities, even formerly hardline segregationist Democrats, such as Congressman Jamie Whitten and Senator Stennis. But the cultural, political, and economic power of whiteness was sustained.[2]

Mississippi Democrats overcame internal divisions with the unification of the Regular and Loyalist factions in 1976 but were never able to regain their previously unassailable power. The Mississippi Republican Party also resolved its internal divisions, with ultraconservatives winning dominance and gradually replacing Democratic incumbents. When Ronald Reagan visited Neshoba County's state fair on the campaign trail in August 1980, he announced his belief in the primacy of states' rights. Speaking only a few miles from the place where civil rights activists Chaney, Schwerner, and Goodman had been murdered by Klansmen, Reagan told Mississippians that "there are problems like [welfare], education, and others that should be turned back to the states and the local communities with the tax sources to fund them. I believe in states' rights and people doing as much as they can for themselves." White Mississippians had finally found a home for their segregationism, fiscal conservatism, and opposition to social welfare in the party of Reagan.[3]

Once elected, President Reagan immediately closed down OEO's successor agency, the Community Services Administration. Reagan had been an early foot soldier in the fight against the war on poverty. As president, he no longer needed to fight against the war on poverty. Instead, Reagan fought a war on welfare. In his 1988 State of the Union address he announced, "Some years ago, the federal government declared war on poverty, and poverty won." Reagan's quip that "poverty won"—which was met with laughter from the assembled representatives—was the culmination of over twenty years of conservative attacks on the war on poverty. Reagan was echoing a critique of the war on poverty that by 1988 had become familiar. Antipoverty programs, Reagan proclaimed, "only made poverty harder to escape. Federal welfare programs have created a massive social problem. With the best of intentions, government created a poverty trap that wreaks havoc on the very support system the poor need most to lift themselves out of poverty: the family. Dependency has become the one enduring heirloom."[4]

Since running for governor of California, Reagan had been the "standard bearer for the conservative critique of the war on poverty." Reagan embodied the conservatism of many white Mississippians. As Joseph Crespino has noted, Reagan's positions on a range of issues from welfare to busing and taxes "lined up remarkably well with those of the Citizens' Council." Indeed, Reagan's references on the campaign trail to the Cadillac-driving "welfare queen"—whose race was never mentioned, but never in question—embodied the gender, racial, and class hostilities that had been honed in the fight against the war on poverty in Mississippi. This powerful imagery was not the work of Reagan and his political advisors. Reagan drew on a grassroots hostility that had been developed first by a network of grassroots conservatives and quickly capitalized on by state and local politicians and the media. Reagan drew on this artful forging of "racial hostility with conservative economic policy," successfully tapping into the fear and hostility that whites not just in Mississippi but across America had been expressing toward African Americans, poverty warriors, and welfare recipients for years. This coded racial opposition to social welfare also helped propel into office Kirk Fordice, who in 1992 became the first Republican governor of Mississippi in over a century.[5]

Mississippi's war on poverty and its war against the war on poverty illustrate the ways in which antipoverty programs became both a force for black empowerment and a mechanism of massive resistance. One reason for the distinctiveness of Mississippi's war on poverty is the strength of Mississippi's network of civil rights activists. Grassroots activists converged with "outsiders" who stayed after Freedom Summer, leaving African Americans primed to take immediate advantage of the opportunities presented by the war on poverty. Mississippi's earliest, formative experiences of the war on poverty were forged by black activists through the Child Development Group. CDGM had such potent consequences because African Americans, drawing on the dynamism of Mississippi's movement, were the first to unleash the potential of the war on poverty to promote black empowerment and give meaning to African Americans' newly won political and civil rights. White Mississippi was then playing catch-up—not only to take advantage of the war on poverty but also to stifle this new form of black activism.

This dynamic shaped the white response to the war on poverty, a fight which changed over time and in response to the intensely local economic, political, and racial variations. The mechanisms utilized by Senator Stennis and Governor Johnson in their opposition to the Child Development Group in 1965 were far removed from the Klan violence unleashed on white antipoverty workers in 1967. Different again were the methods of white Jacksonians and the segregationists of southwest Mississippi, as they participated in biracial antipoverty programs in order to shore up white supremacy. White opposition to the war on poverty was in part enabled by the administrative failings of OEO, which resulted in a near-total failure to address racial discrimination. Perhaps more instrumental in the fight against the war on poverty was the colorblind language used by white segregationists that encouraged "local responsible people" to join the boards of antipoverty programs. Middle-class whites were encouraged to take up new ways to exercise their economic power over blacks, just as antipoverty programs were providing African Americans with new opportunities for economic empowerment. The distinctiveness of Mississippi's war on poverty is thus a result of the power, endurance, and flexibility of white segregationism.

Massive resistance in Mississippi—and across the nation—was far more than a decade-long backlash. Far from ending in 1965, white resistance to black advancement began a new phase that year with the arrival of the war on poverty in Mississippi. This phase encompassed practical segregationism as many whites accepted integrated antipoverty programs. It also saw a wave of white extremist violence directed at antipoverty warriors. It involved politicians, lawyers, Klansmen, businessmen, and women in both the domestic and professional sphere. This post-1965 phase of massive resistance incorporated some of the methods and mechanisms of earlier phases of resistance, such as accusations of communism and "outside agitators." It drew on the power of the state Sovereignty Commission. This evolving resistance fed into an emerging national conservatism. Conservative opponents of the war on poverty articulated a new language of opposition that combined conceptions of Americanism, streams of antiwelfare ideology, and notions of individual rights and privilege. In opposing the war on poverty, white Mississippians thus linked the evolving massive resistance seamlessly with the emerging national conservatism.

Recent scholarship on the rise of the New Right has focused on the conservative transformation of the Sunbelt suburbs. Historians, such as Kevin M. Kruse, Matthew D. Lassiter, Sean P. Cunningham, Darren Dochuk, and Lisa McGirr, have explored this transformation, stressing its relationship with the maintenance of white supremacy, the individualism of the suburban middle-class, evangelical Christianity, and suburban women's groups. The white response to the war on poverty reveals a conservatism that drew from poor rural whites of the Black Belt and suburban middle-class whites. Both suburbanites and rural whites articulated a language of opposition that drew on notions of rights and individualism, employing colorblind language in their opposition to antipoverty programs. Class and gender shaped white Mississippians responses to the war on poverty, signifying a complexity to Mississippi's contributions to the emerging national conservatism that has too often been overlooked.[6]

In the 1960s Mississippi was a formative space for an important facet of this national conservatism. Opposition to the war on poverty provided a crucible in which racial hostility, conservative fiscal policy, and opposition to social welfare was forged into an ostensibly colorblind rhetoric that advocated individual rights and privileges. White supremacy had always constructed at the grassroots in terms of individual power, be it economic, gendered, or political. This language of individual rights was central to the preservation of Jim Crow. Opposing the war on poverty provided an outlet for this language to be expressed in a way that preserved white power and targeted liberalism and federal intervention. This was not a backlash—grassroots white conservatives were carrying on the work of their parents and grandparents in reshaping and transmitting white supremacy for each new generation. From the 1930s the race-neutral language opposing social welfare and black advancement became increasingly intertwined. By the 1960s this language forged by white conservative Mississippians was shaping national streams of segregationism and conservatism.

Women played significant roles both in the war on poverty and the fight against the war on poverty. Beginning with the Child Development Group, the war on poverty in Mississippi provided a vital source of work and income for African American women. This income was beyond the control of white segregationists and thus secure, even if women chose to register to vote or participate in civil rights activism, and far exceeded the money black women could earn in most other roles available to them. These women, along with the many mothers who volunteered their time, were the lifeblood of the Child Development Group. Working as teachers, teaching assistants, and cooks, roles mostly linked to women's domestic experiences as mothers, cleaners or cooks, they achieved empowerment that went beyond the money they earned, important though that was. For many black women, the professionalization of maternalism through the Child Development Group was transformative. The income, experience, and empowerment opened doors: to new forms of political activism, to career opportunities, and to the opportunity to reshape their local communities.

The war on poverty also provided new opportunities for white women. Unlike black mothers working in Head Start, the white women working in the war on poverty were mostly middle-class and worked in administrative roles. These roles—including Pat Derian's as OEO consultant, Marjorie Baroni as antipoverty program founder, Kathleen O'Fallon as program director, and Sister Donatilla as education director—offered white women empowerment of a different nature. These women took up roles in positions of power that were mostly off limits to women in 1960s Mississippi outside of the war on poverty. Though these positions were still within the traditionally female sphere of teaching and welfare, the war on poverty enabled the professionalization of women's roles in these fields. This professionalization enabled women to move beyond roles linked to their maternalism and administer programs, direct men, and control budgets in the millions of dollars.

While such roles were mostly limited to white women, one notable exception was Helen Bass Williams, the African American executive director of Mississippi Action for Progress. Williams's role embodied black empowerment through the war on poverty, both for herself, a middle-class black woman directing a multimillion-dollar nonprofit organization, and for the hundreds of poor black parents she empowered through MAP. The white response to Williams's role—from a Christian, moderate business leader and a hardline segregationist—is the pinnacle of the white fight against the war on poverty. Erle Johnston's quiet manipulation of MAP's board illustrates the flexibility and above all the endurance of white power. Accommodating the moderation of white business leaders did not signal the end of massive resistance. Rather this response to the war on poverty was the evolution of massive resistance to a more subtle, nuanced, and lasting manifestation of white supremacy.

Women were equally important in the war against the war on poverty. At the grassroots, conservative women such as Maye Donaldson articulated an opposition to the war on poverty that drew on patriotism and fears of welfare as promoting immorality. Conservative women used their opposition to the war on poverty as a rallying point for true conservatives, aligning conservatism with true Americanism. This grassroots opposition provided national template for a race-neutral opposition to social welfare. Women like Donaldson forged networks of segregationists that fed into national networks of conservatives. White women were also instrumental in using antipoverty programs to defend and bolster white supremacy. Kathleen O'Fallon, executive director of Southwest Mississippi Opportunity, for example, shaped her antipoverty program into a mechanism to preserve white power and marginalize black control over Head Start. Sister Donatilla, education director in STAR, meanwhile used the power of her position to reshape white power in another way. By treating African American adults in the literacy program with a paternalistic attitude, Sister Donatilla undermined the purpose of STAR and reinforced traditional patterns of race relations.[7]

Men were the driving force behind the more violent form of opposition to the war on poverty. Tracing this opposition exposes the ongoing influence and violence of the Klan into the late 1960s. The wave of white supremacist violence against white antipoverty workers in 1967 illustrates the endurance of white extremist ideology. While the eras of white violence clothed and hooded in Klan robes makes this violence more visible, the violence lasted beyond the demise of these groups. The driving force of this white violence— from Reconstruction, throughout Jim Crow, into the civil rights era, and beyond—was the economic status of whites. The violent white response and the mass rejection of antipoverty programs by poor whites despite their desperate need for them was a result of the economic anxieties of white Mississippians, particularly white men. Increasing levels of white on black violence during times of economic hardship was a long-established pattern. As Klan literature attacking the socialist programs of the "Black Republic" signifies, these economic anxieties shaped white supremacy during the war on poverty.[8]

White Mississippi's responses to the war on poverty were thus shaped by class. Middle-class whites, who had no need of the services provided by antipoverty programs, were often willing to sit on program boards in order to control the nature of black advancement and participation. Middle-class whites thus showed a limited acceptance of integration in order to reshape white supremacy by regaining control of the economic opportunities offered by the war on poverty. Poor whites, on the other hand, were unwilling to participate in integrated antipoverty programs not because it put them in close proximity to African Americans, but because participation would put poor white and poor blacks on an equal footing. Poor whites were, in the vast majority, willing to forgo the economic opportunities of the war on poverty rather than threaten their white supremacy. Instead, many poor whites turned to violent extremism in order to bolster and reinforce their threatened racial privileges. These class divisions in turn shaped the development of Deep South conservatism. For poor, rural whites, class was not subsumed under race—far from it. The language of individual rights and meritocracy was no less important to whites in the Black Belt. Class shaped the experience of whiteness for the rural poor perhaps more profoundly than it did for middle-class suburbanites.

Intraracial class divisions also played a central role in establishing white control over Mississippi's community action programs. Antipoverty programs across Mississippi, and across the country, not only exposed but also magnified African American class divisions. These class divisions predated the war on poverty and, indeed, predated the creation of civil rights organizations. War on poverty programs intensified these divisions, breaking open the fault lines that had become clear in the civil rights activism of the late 1950s and early 1960s. Mississippi Action for Progress drew on the middle-class African American men who were willing to accept the Atlantic City compromise, while the Child Development Group was run by former SNCC activists—mostly women—who knew what it was to be poor. In Jackson, Community Services Association deepened the class and generational divisions evident in the Jackson movement of the early 1960s. Community action programs entrenched class differences by positioning middle-class African Americans on program boards while stifling the voice of poor blacks. Most often this process was facilitated by whites who were willing to sit on integrated boards with the perceived "moderate" African Americans.

Activists such as Muhammad Kenyatta opposed this form of accommodation through the war on poverty. Kenyatta expressed a particular form of Black Power that proliferated in Mississippi in the late 1960s. Publications such as the Hinds County Freedom Democratic Party newsletter reprinted familiar calls for Black Power alongside descriptions of how to make a Molotov cocktail. More enduring, however, was the black empowerment espoused by Kenyatta in his role as Neighborhood Youth Corps counselor. For Kenyatta, Black Power went beyond armed resistance to white violence. Perhaps even more important was economic empowerment—the power that came from access to quality education and job opportunities. This was the form of black empowerment that the Child Development Group achieved, the NYC of Jackson's Community Services Association strove for, and that Helen Bass Williams attempted to promote through MAP.[9]

Fault lines in the war on poverty were also caused by its myriad organizational shortcomings. The relationship between STAR and its sponsor, the Diocese of Natchez-Jackson, exposes the conflicts engendered by the connection between religious organizations and the war on poverty. Studies of the activism of the Catholic Church in the wake of Vatican II have pointed to its commitment to social justice and (relatively) early support for the civil rights movement. The Diocese of Natchez-Jackson was indeed more supportive of black activists than most other religious groups in Mississippi, in both the work of individual activists of the laity and clergy and the Church as an institution. However, STAR's relationship with the diocese complicates this narrative of a progressive commitment to social justice. Activist laity and clergy, such as Marjorie Baroni and Father Nathaniel Machesky, played significant roles in shaping their local antipoverty programs. The diocesan role in STAR, while significant in enabling the creation and function of the program, did little to empower poor African Americans. The actions of a number of clergy were instrumental in entrenching established patterns of white power through STAR and in removing any antipoverty warriors—black or white—who attempted to move STAR beyond a service-oriented program to one that fostered genuine community participation.

Mississippi's war on poverty was shaped in large part by the highly politicized responses. In fighting against the Child Development Group, white Mississippi brought to bear the weight of its political establishment spearheaded by Senator Stennis. Mississippi Action for Progress was created to replace CDGM by providing the white establishment with an "acceptable" Head Start program. Its creation, shaped by President Johnson aide Harry McPherson, provided a template for the reconstruction of the state Democratic Party on an integrated basis. MAP was a testing ground for the political alliances that would come to fruition in the creation of the Loyalist Democrats. The Democratic Party members were not the only ones playing politics with the war on poverty. For the nascent state Republican Party the war on poverty provided two important opportunities. First, board membership for party members meant useful patronage opportunities, which were thin on the ground. Second, for ultraconservative Republicans, opposition to the war on poverty became a way to illustrate their difference from Mississippi Democrats. The fight against the war on poverty also served a useful political purpose for grassroots conservatives who used their opposition to welfare and the overweening federal government to shape the state Republican Party in their image.

Drawing links between national political events and local developments is often tenuous. However, the design of community action programs meant that national policy changes often had immediate consequences in local communities. After Nixon's election Rumsfeld's OEO worked to quietly undermine the war on poverty by pulling back from community action and moving control of antipoverty programs to the regional level. These actions had a potent effect in Mississippi, where regional control of grant decisions worked in favor of the white establishment. While Rumsfeld's and Nixon's actions were detrimental to the war on poverty as a whole, it was the programs run by and for African Americans that suffered earliest and most. Through both regionalism and the systematic implementation of the Green Amendment, the OEO stifled community action and silenced the voice of the poor. Nixon's election also provided new opportunities for Mississippi Republicans. They utilized their connections to the administration to gain political credit by opposing the independence or continuation of black-controlled antipoverty programs. State Republicans cultivated relationships with OEO and HEW and, particularly, with the regional offices of OEO and HEW's Office of Child Development, winning white support by undercutting African American programs.

Today, Mississippi's poverty rates remain the highest in the nation. In 2017, out of a population of 2.9 million people, just over 602,000 people were living in poverty, a poverty rate of 20.8 percent. Poverty remains racially skewed: 32 percent of African Americans living in Mississippi are poor, while 13.2

percent of whites in Mississippi are poor. Despite the poverty that remains in the state, parts of the war on poverty have survived. The Community Services Administration, which Reagan closed in 1981, was replaced with Community Services Block Grants. The Legal Services Corporation was created in 1974 and continues to provide vital legal aid to the poor. Community action programs survived massive funding cuts and the hostile political and ideological climate. In fact, over one thousand community action programs are still in operation today across the nation.[10]

In Mississippi, twenty community action agencies are currently in operation. Mississippi Action for Progress has just celebrated its fiftieth anniversary. MAP runs sixty-one Head Start centers for over 6000 children, and employs more than 1200 people. One of the successors of the Child Development Group—Friends of the Children of Mississippi—operates a range of services, including Head Start and Early Head Start programs in fifteen counties. Legal Services programs still in operation include North Mississippi Rural Legal Services and the statewide Mississippi Legal Services. Hinds County Human Resource Agency—the successor of Community Services Association, run by the white establishment—is still providing services to the poor communities of the state capital. Southwest Mississippi Opportunity is likewise still in operation, and the program now serves Walthall County in addition to Pike, Amite, and Wilkinson Counties. It provides a home energy assistance program, family daycare services, and a food supplement program. There has been little in the way of a resurgence of public and political desire for the federal government to address poverty. But as the survival of these antipoverty efforts in Mississippi illustrate, community action has a power and momentum of its own.[11]

NOTES

INTRODUCTION

1. "The Leader" flyer, n.d., Box 1, Folder Harassment, Hodding Carter III Papers, Mitchell Memorial Library, Special Collections, Mississippi State University, Starkville (hereafter cited as Carter Papers).

2. Homer Hill interview with Bennie S. Gooden, March 15, 1994, University of Southern Mississippi, Center for Oral History and Cultural Heritage (hereafter cited as COHCH), http://digilib.usm.edu/cdm/ref/collection/coh/id/16083; Charles C. Bolton, "The Last Stand of Massive Resistance: Mississippi Public School Integration, 1970," *Journal of Mississippi History* 61, no. 4, (1999), 329–50.

3. James W. Silver, *Mississippi: The Closed Society* (New York: Harcourt, Brace & World, 1964); Don Williams interview with Right Reverend Duncan Montgomery Gray Jr., April 16, 1999, COHCH, http://digilib.usm.edu/cdm/ref/collection/coh/id/15577.

4. Joseph Crespino, *In Search of Another Country: Mississippi and the Conservative Counterrevolution* (Princeton, NJ: Princeton University Press, 2007); Kevin M. Kruse, *White Flight: Atlanta and the Making of Modern Conservatism* (Princeton, NJ: Princeton University Press, 2005); Matthew D. Lassiter, *The Silent Majority: Suburban Politics in the Sunbelt South* (Princeton, NJ: Princeton University Press, 2006); Michelle M. Nickerson, *Mothers of Conservatism: Women and the Postwar Right* (Princeton, NJ: Princeton University Press, 2012); Lisa McGirr, *Suburban Warriors: The Origins of the New American Right* (Princeton, NJ: Princeton University Press, 2001); Darren Dochuk, *From Bible Belt to Sunbelt: Plain-Folk Religion, Grassroots Politics, and the Rise of Evangelical Conservatism* (London: W. W. Norton, 2012); Sean P. Cunningham, *American Politics in the Postwar Sunbelt: Conservative Growth in a Battleground Region* (Cambridge: Cambridge University Press, 2014).

5. Susan Y. Ashmore, *Carry It On: The War on Poverty and the Civil Rights Movement in Alabama, 1964–1972* (Athens: University of Georgia Press, 2008), 15; Robert Bauman, "The Black Power and Chicano Movements in the Poverty Wars in Los Angeles," *Journal of Urban History* 33, no. 2 (2007): 281; James W. Loewen, *The Mississippi Chinese: Between Black and White* (Cambridge, MA: Harvard University Press, 1971), 154–84; Robert Seto Quan, with Julian B. Roebuck, *Lotus among the Magnolias: The Mississippi Chinese* (Jackson: University Press of Mississippi, 1982), 3, 146–54; Unita Blackwell, with JoAnne Prichard Morris, *Barefootin': Life Lessons from the Road to Freedom* (New York: Crown Publishers, 2006), 22–23; Daniel M. Cobb, "The War on Poverty in Mississippi and Oklahoma: Beyond

Black and White," in *The War on Poverty: A New Grassroots History, 1964–1980*, ed. Annelise Orleck and Lisa Gayle Hazirjian (Athens: University of Georgia Press, 2011), 392–95; William S. Clayson, *Freedom Is Not Enough: The War on Poverty and the Civil Rights Movement in Texas* (Austin: University of Texas Press, 2010), 100–120.

6. Crespino, *In Search of Another Country*, 1; John Dittmer, *Local People: The Struggle for Civil Rights in Mississippi* (Urbana: University of Illinois Press, 1994), 273; Jack Bell, *Mr. Conservative: Barry Goldwater* (New York: Doubleday, 1962).

7. "Persons by Poverty Status in 1959, 1969, 1979, 1989 by State," US Census Bureau, http://www.census.gov/hhes/www/poverty/data/census/1960/index.html; "Shriver Announces New Yardstick to Determine the Standard of Poverty," *New York Times*, May 3, 1965, 24; "Summary: Federal Social Economic Programs, State Program Summary FY1967," Box 158, Office Files of Fred Panzer, Lyndon Baines Johnson Presidential Library, Austin, Texas (hereafter cited as LBJL). Adopted by the OEO in 1966, the poverty threshold was based on family size, the gender of the head of the house and the area (farm or nonfarm). The threshold ranged from $1,138 per annum for a single woman living in a farm area to $5,335 for a male-headed family of seven in a nonfarm area.

8. Blackwell, *Barefootin'*, 17–18.

9. Neil R. McMillen, *Dark Journey: Black Mississippians in the Age of Jim Crow* (Urbana: University of Illinois Press, 1990), 113; Joe White interview with John M. Perkins, April 23, 2003, COHCH, http://digilib.usm.edu/cdm/ref/collection/coh/id/16504.

10. Joe White interview with John M. Perkins, COHCH.

11. Terry Buffington interview with Minnie McFarland Weeks, March 2007, COHCH, http://digilib.usm.edu/cdm/ref/collection/coh/id/15984.

12. Blackwell, *Barefootin'*, 27–28.

13. Charles M. Payne, *I've Got the Light of Freedom: The Organizing Tradition and the Mississippi Freedom Struggle* (Berkeley: University of California Press, 1995), 15; Dittmer, *Local People*, 19, 31. The 1944 Supreme Court ruling in *Smith vs. Allwright* outlawing the white primary was a significant factor in driving this early campaign; Minion K. C. Morrison, *Aaron Henry of Mississippi: Inside Agitator* (Fayetteville: University of Arkansas Press, 2015), xvi; Neil R. McMillen, "Fighting for What We Didn't Have: How Mississippi's Black Veterans Remember World War II," in *Remaking Dixie: The Impact of World War II on the American South*, ed. McMillen (Jackson: University Press of Mississippi, 1997), 95.

14. Payne, *I've Got the Light of Freedom*, 31.

15. Michael Vinson Williams, *Medgar Evers: Mississippi Martyr* (Fayetteville: University of Arkansas Press, 2011), 60; Myrlie Evers, with William Peters, *For Us, the Living* (Garden City, NY: Doubleday, 1967; reprinted, Jackson: University Press of Mississippi, 1996), 85; Morrison, *Aaron Henry of Mississippi*, 31.

16. Payne, *I've Got the Light of Freedom*, 25–27; Anne Moody, *Coming of Age in Mississippi* (New York: Dell, 1968), 126.

17. Françoise N. Hamlin, "Collision and Collusion: Local Activism, Local Agency, and Flexible Alliances," in *The Civil Rights Movement in Mississippi*, ed. Ted Ownby (Jackson: University Press of Mississippi, 2013), 40.

18. James P. Marshall, *Student Activism and Civil Rights in Mississippi: Protest Politics and the Struggle for Racial Justice, 1960–1965* (Baton Rouge: Louisiana State University Press, 2013), 5; Annie Romaine interview with Fannie Lou Hamer, 1966, Freedom Summer Digital Collection, Wisconsin Historical Society, Madison, Wisconsin (hereafter cited as FSDC), http://content.wisconsinhistory.org/cdm/ref/collection/p15932coll2/id/13742.

19. Payne, *I've Got the Light of Freedom*; Dittmer, *Local People*; Françoise N. Hamlin, *Crossroads at Clarksdale: The Black Freedom Struggle in the Mississippi Delta after World War II* (Chapel Hill: University of North Carolina Press, 2012); Emilye Crosby, *A Little Taste of Freedom: The Black Freedom Struggle in Claiborne County, Mississippi* (Chapel Hill: University of North Carolina Press, 2005); J. Todd Moye, *Let the People Decide: Black Freedom and White Resistance Movements in Sunflower County, Mississippi, 1945–1986* (Chapel Hill: University of North Carolina Press, 2004); Williams, *Medgar Evers*; Morrison, *Aaron Henry of Mississippi*; Chana Kai Lee, *For Freedom's Sake: The Life of Fannie Lou Hamer* (Urbana: University of Illinois Press, 1999); James F. Findlay Jr., *Church People in the Struggle: The National Council of Churches and the Black Freedom Movement, 1950–1970* (New York: Oxford University Press, 1997); Mark Newman, *Divine Agitators: The Delta Ministry and Civil Rights in Mississippi* (Athens: University of Georgia Press, 2004); Charles Marsh, *God's Long Summer: Stories of Faith and Civil Rights* (Princeton, NJ: Princeton University Press, 1997); Carolyn Renée Dupont, *Mississippi Praying: Southern White Evangelicals and the Civil Rights Movement, 1945–1975* (New York: New York University Press, 2015); Joseph T. Reiff, *Born of Conviction: White Methodists and Mississippi's Closed Society* (Oxford: Oxford University Press, 2016); Carter Dalton Lyon, *Sanctuaries of Segregation: The Story of the Jackson Church Visit Campaign* (Jackson: University Press of Mississippi, 2017). David Cunningham, *Klansville, U.S.A.: The Rise and Fall of the Civil Rights–Era Ku Klux Klan* (Oxford: Oxford University Press, 2013); Robert E. Luckett Jr. *Joe T. Patterson and the White South's Dilemma: Evolving Resistance to Black Advancement* (Jackson: University Press of Mississippi, 2017); Debbie Z. Harwell, *Wednesdays in Mississippi: Proper Ladies Working for Radical Change, Freedom Summer 1964* (Jackson: University Press of Mississippi, 2014); Akinyele Omowale Umoja, *We Will Shoot Back: Armed Resistance in the Mississippi Freedom Movement* (New York: New York University Press, 2014); Lance Hill, *The Deacons for Defense: Armed Resistance and the Civil Rights Movement* (Chapel Hill: University of North Carolina Press, 2004); Charles E. Cobb Jr., *This Nonviolent Stuff'll Get You Killed: How Guns Made the Civil Rights Movement Possible* (Durham, NC: Duke University Press, 2016).

20. Marshall, *Student Activism and Civil Rights in Mississippi*, 46, 57; John Lewis and Archie E. Allen, "Black Voter Registration Efforts in the South," *Notre Dame Law Review* 48, no. 1 (1972): 112.

21. Paul B. Johnson quoted in John W. Bowers, Donovan J. Ochs, Richard J. Jensen, and David P. Schulz, *The Rhetoric of Agitation and Control: Third Edition* (Long Grove: Waveland Press, 2010), 98; Douglas McAdam, *Freedom Summer* (Oxford: Oxford University Press, 1990), 27–28; Bruce Watson, *Freedom Summer: The Savage Season of 1964 That Made Mississippi Burn and Made America a Democracy* (London: Penguin, 2010), 129; Jon N. Hale, *Freedom Schools: Student Activists in the Mississippi Civil Rights Movement* (New York: Columbia University Press, 2016); Blackwell, *Barefootin'*, 158; Joseph Brenner, Robert Coles,

Alan Mermann, Milton J. E. Senn, Cyril Walwyn, and Raymond Wheeler, "Special Report: Hungry Children," n.d., Southern Regional Council, *Civil Rights Movement Veterans*, http://www.crmvet.org/docs/src_hungry_children.pdf; Ellen B. Meacham, *Delta Epiphany: Robert F. Kennedy in Mississippi* (Jackson: University Press of Mississippi, 2018), tells the story of Kennedy's visit to the Delta in 1967 and the Senate hearings that took place in Jackson.

22. Mike Garvey interview with JC Fairley, January 31, 1977, COHCH, http://digilib.usm.edu/cdm/ref/collection/coh/id/15720.

23. Mike Garvey interview with Rev. Sammie Rash, March 30, 1977, COHCH http://digilib.usm.edu/cdm/ref/collection/coh/id/15387; Crosby, *A Little Taste of Freedom*, 29.

24. Moye, *Let the People Decide*, 31, 36; Blackwell, *Barefootin'*, 16; Mike Garvey interview with Rev. Sammie Rash; Clyde Woods, *Development Arrested: Race, Power, and the Blues in the Mississippi Delta* (London: Verso, 1998), 15; James C. Cobb, *The Most Southern Place on Earth: The Mississippi Delta and the Roots of Regional Identity* (New York: Oxford University Press, 1992), 253; Sharon D. Wright Austin, *The Transformation of Plantation Politics: Black Politics, Concentrated Poverty and Social Capital in the Mississippi Delta* (Albany: State University of New York Press, 2006).

25. Blackwell, *Barefootin'*, 32.

26. Jason Sokol, *There Goes My Everything: White Southerners in the Age of Civil Rights, 1945–1975* (New York: Vintage Books, 2007), 25.

27. Moody, *Coming of Age*, 113.

28. Terry Buffington interview with Minnie McFarland Weeks; Joe White interview with John M. Perkins.

29. Crosby, *A Little Taste of Freedom*, 8.

30. Mike Garvey interview with JC Fairley.

31. Crosby, *A Little Taste of Freedom*, 33–35; McMillen, *Dark Journey*, 28; Payne, *I've Got the Light of Freedom*, 20; Dittmer, *Local People*, 22.

32. "Conservative" to John C. Stennis, September 7, 1965, Series 1, Box 4, Folder 7, John C. Stennis Papers, Congressional and Political Research Center, Mississippi State University (hereafter cited as Stennis Papers).

33. F. M. Tatum to John C. Stennis and William Colmer, May 26, 1967, Series 25, Box 15, Folder 22, Stennis Papers; R. P. Turner Jr. to John C. Stennis, February 20, 1967, Series 11, Box 35, Folder 2, Stennis Papers; Polly Greenberg, *The Devil Has Slippery Shoes: A Biased Biography of the Child Development Group of Mississippi (CDGM), A Story of Maximum Feasible Poor Parent Participation*, rev. ed. (Washington, DC: Youth Policy Institute, 1990), 35.

34. Allen J. Matusow, *The Unraveling of America: A History of Liberalism in the 1960s*, new ed. (Athens: University of Georgia Press, 2009), 255; Crystal R. Sanders, *A Chance for Change: Head Start and Mississippi's Black Freedom Struggle* (Chapel Hill: University of North Carolina Press, 2016); Ashmore, *Carry It On*; Clayson, *Freedom Is Not Enough*; Robert R. Korstad and James L. Leloudis, *To Right These Wrongs: The North Carolina Fund and the Battle to End Poverty and Inequality in 1960s America* (Chapel Hill: University of North Carolina Press, 2010); Robert Bauman, *Race and the War on Poverty: From Watts to East L.A.* (Norman: University of Oklahoma Press, 2008); Thomas J. Kiffmeyer, *Reformers to*

Radicals: The Appalachian Volunteers and the War on Poverty (Lexington: University Press of Kentucky, 2008).

35. Michael Woodsworth, *Battle for Bed-Stuy: The Long War on Poverty in New York* (Cambridge, MA: Harvard University Press, 2016), 11; Kent B. Germany, *New Orleans after the Promises: Poverty, Citizenship, and the Search for the Great Society* (Athens: University of Georgia Press, 2007); Guian A. McKee, *The Problem of Jobs: Liberalism, Race, and Deindustrialization in Philadelphia* (Chicago: University of Chicago Press, 2008); Matusow, *The Unraveling of America*, 260–65; Martin Meeker, "The Queerly Disadvantaged and the Making of San Francisco's War on Poverty, 1964–1967," *Pacific Historical Review* 81, no. 1 (2012): 59; Telephone Conversation between Lyndon B. Johnson and Richard Daley, December 24, 1965, WH6512-04-9329, Recordings and Transcripts of Conversations and Meetings, http://whitehousetapes.net/transcript/johnson/wh6512-04-9329.

36. Numan V. Bartley, *The Rise of Massive Resistance: Race and Politics in the South during the 1950s*, 2nd ed. (Baton Rouge: Louisiana State University Press, 1999), 26, 32, 189–90, 277; Neil R. McMillen, *The Citizens' Council: Organized Resistance to the Second Reconstruction, 1954–1964*, 2nd ed. (Urbana: University of Illinois Press, 1994), 360–62; James W. Ely Jr., *The Crisis of Conservative Virginia: The Byrd Organization and the Politics of Massive Resistance* (Knoxville: University of Tennessee Press, 1976); Robbins L. Gates, *The Making of Massive Resistance: Virginia's Politics of Public School Desegregation, 1954–1956* (Chapel Hill: University of North Carolina Press, 1964); Francis M. Wilhoit, *The Politics of Massive Resistance* (New York: George Braziller, 1973), 227–28.

37. Charles Eagles, "Toward New Histories of the Civil Rights Era," *Journal of Southern History* 66, no. 4 (2000): 842. Exceptions include Elizabeth Jacoway and David R. Colburn, eds., *Southern Businessmen and Desegregation*, (Baton Rouge: Louisiana State University Press, 1982); Jeff Roche, *Restructured Resistance: The Sibley Commission and the Politics of Desegregation in Georgia* (Athens: University of Georgia Press, 1998); Dan T. Carter, *The Politics of Rage: George Wallace, the Origins of the New Conservatism, and the Transformation of American Politics*, 2nd ed. (Baton Rouge: Louisiana State University, 2000); David L. Chappell, *Inside Agitators: White Southerners in the Civil Rights Movement* (London: Johns Hopkins University Press, 1994); Jacquelyn Dowd Hall, "The Long Civil Rights Movement and the Political Uses of the Past," *Journal of American History* 91, no. 4 (2005): 1233–63; Elizabeth Gillespie McRae, *Mothers of Massive Resistance: White Women and the Politics of White Supremacy* (Oxford: Oxford University Press, 2018), 4; Sokol, *There Goes My Everything*; Glenn Feldman, ed., *Before Brown: Civil Rights and White Backlash in the Modern South* (Tuscaloosa: University of Alabama Press, 2004); Jason Morgan Ward, *Defending White Democracy: The Making of a Segregationist Movement and the Remaking of Racial Politics, 1936–1965* (Chapel Hill: University of North Carolina, 2014); Arnold R. Hirsch, "Massive Resistance in the Urban North: Trumbull Park, Chicago, 1953–1966," *Journal of American History* 82, no. 2 (1995): 522–50; Nickerson, *Mothers of Conservatism*, xx.

38. Kruse, *White Flight*; Crespino, *In Search of Another Country*, 276, 271; Chris Danielson, *After Freedom Summer: How Race Realigned Mississippi Politics, 1965–1986* (Gainesville: University Press of Florida, 2011); Frank R. Parker, *Black Votes Count: Political Empowerment*

in Mississippi after 1965 (Chapel Hill: University of North Carolina Press, 1990), 34–77; Luckett, *Joe T. Patterson and the White South's Dilemma*.

39. Payne, *I've Got the Light of Freedom*, 155.

40. Silver, *Mississippi: The Closed Society*; James C. Cobb, *The Most Southern Place on Earth*; Danielson, *After Freedom Summer*, 2.

CHAPTER ONE: FROM CIVIL RIGHTS TO ECONOMIC EMPOWERMENT

1. Lyndon B. Johnson, "Annual Message to the Congress on the State of the Union," January 8, 1964, in Gerhard Peters and John T. Woolley, *Papers of the President*, http://www.presidency.ucsb.edu/ws/index.php?pid=26787; Scott Stossel, *Sarge: The Life and Times of Sargent Shriver* (Washington, DC: Smithsonian Books, 2004), 346–53; Lyndon B. Johnson, "The President's News Conference," February 1, 1964, in Peters and Woolley, *Papers of the President*, http://www.presidency.ucsb.edu/ws/?pid=26055.

2. Noel A. Cazenave, *Impossible Democracy: The Unlikely Success of the War on Poverty Community Action Programs* (Albany: State University of New York Press, 2007), 30; Sanford Kravitz and Ferne K. Kolodner, "Community Action: Where Has It Been? Where Will It Go?" *Annals of the American Academy of Political and Social Science* 385 (September 1969): 30–40; William W. Moss interview with D. Patrick Moynihan, May 3, 1972, John F. Kennedy Oral History Program, John F. Kennedy Library, https://www.jfklibrary.org/Asset-Viewer/Archives/JFKOH-DPM-01.aspx.

3. Ashmore, *Carry It On*, 28; Guian A. McKee, "'This Government Is With Us': Lyndon Johnson and the Grassroots War on Poverty," in *The War on Poverty*, ed. Orleck and Hazirjian, 33.

4. Recording of Telephone Conversation between Lyndon B. Johnson and Olin Teague, August 5, 1964, 2:56 pm, Citation #4728, Recordings and Transcripts of Conversations and Meetings, LBJL; Lyndon B. Johnson, "Remarks upon signing the Economic Opportunity Act," August 20, 1964, in Peters and Woolley, *Papers of the President*, http://www.presidency.ucsb.edu/ws/?pid=26452.

5. James T. Patterson, *America's Struggle against Poverty in the Twentieth Century* (Harvard: Harvard University Press, 2000), 139–40; Saul D. Alinsky, "The War on Poverty—Political Pornography," *Journal of Social Issues* 21, no. 1 (1965): 41–47.

6. Economic Opportunity Act, 1964; Robert D. Plotnick and Felicity Skidmore, *Progress against Poverty: A Review of the 1964–1974 Decade* (New York: Academic Press, 1975), 4–5; Jill Quadagno, *The Color of Welfare: How Racism Undermined the War on Poverty* (Oxford: Oxford University Press, 1994), 30–31; William M. Epstein, *Democracy without Decency: Good Citizenship and the War on Poverty* (Philadelphia: Pennsylvania State University Press, 2010), 59.

7. Ashmore, *Carry It On*, 29; Alice O'Connor, *Poverty Knowledge: Social Science, Social Policy, and the Poor in Twentieth-Century US History* (Princeton, NJ: Princeton University Press, 2001), 163–70. Jack T. Conway quoted in Michael Gillette (ed.), *Launching the War on Poverty: An Oral History*, 2nd ed. (New York: Oxford University Press, 2010), 236.

8. Ashmore, *Carry It On*, 281; Korstad and Leloudis, *To Right These Wrongs*, 4; Clayson, *Freedom Is Not Enough*; Bauman, *Race and the War on Poverty*; Kiffmeyer, *Reformers to Radicals*, 214.

9. Literature on the development and operation of Head Start is vast. For an introduction see Kay Mills, *Something Better for My Children: The History and People of Head Start* (New York: Dutton, 1998), 58–75; or Maris A. Vinovskis, *The Birth of Head Start: Preschool Education Policies in the Kennedy and Johnson Administrations* (Chicago: University of Chicago Press, 2008).

10. "Proposal for a Full Year Head Start Program of CDGM," ca. 1966, Box 14, Folder Poverty (1966) [2 of 2], Office Files of Harry McPherson, LBJL; John Dittmer interview with Rosie Head, March 13, 2013, Tchula, Mississippi, Civil Rights History Project, American Folklife Center, Library of Congress, https://www.loc.gov/item/afc2010039_crhp0074/; Child Development Group of Mississippi pamphlet, ca. 1966, Box 3, Folder 4, Michael J. Miller Civil Rights Collection, McCain Library and Archives Special Collections, University of Southern Mississippi, Hattiesburg (hereafter cited as Miller Collection); Dittmer, *Local People*, 364.

11. Amy Jordan, "Fighting for the Child Development Group of Mississippi: Poor People, Local Politics, and the Complicated Legacy of Head Start," in *The War on Poverty*, ed. Orleck and Hazirjian, 280.

12. Child Development Group of Mississippi pamphlet; Dittmer, *Local People*, 369–70.

13. Stossel, *Sarge*, 428; Thomas G. Abernethy to Gladys McDearmon, August 17, 1965, Box 161, Folder OEO 1965–6, Thomas G. Abernethy Collection, Archives and Special Collections, University of Mississippi, Oxford; Dittmer, *Local People*, 370–71, 377.

14. "Johnson Backs Biracial Group for Mississippi Head Start," *Times Picayune*, October 11, 1966, Subgroup 3, Series 13, Box 76, Folder 1A, Owen Cooper Papers, Mississippi Department of Archives and History, Jackson (hereafter cited as Cooper Papers); Paul B. Johnson to Lyndon B. Johnson, February 23, 1966, Box 46, Folder WE9-1 10/21/65–6/3/66 GEN, WHCF GEN WE9-1 11/22/63–11/2/66, LBJL; Silver, *Mississippi: The Closed Society*, 44; "Stand Tall with Paul" pamphlet, ca. 1963, Box 2, Folder 6, Miller Collection; Erle Johnston, "Attitudes in Mississippi," December 1967, Box 8, Folder 26, Erle Johnston Papers, McCain Library and Archives Special Collections, University of Southern Mississippi, Hattiesburg, http://digilib.usm.edu/cdm/ref/collection/manu/id/8442.

15. Sanders, *A Chance for Change*, 127; Jeff Woods, *Black Struggle, Red Scare: Segregation and Anti-Communism in the South, 1948–1968* (Baton Rouge: Louisiana State University Press, 2004), 96–97; Silver, *Mississippi: The Closed Society*, 8.

16. Jon N. Hale, "The Struggle Begins Early: Head Start and the Mississippi Freedom Movement," *History of Education Quarterly* 52, no. 4 (2012): 510; e.g., Tom Scarborough, Report, September 15, 1965, SCR ID # 6-45-1-91-1-1-1, Series 2515: Mississippi State Sovereignty Commission Records, 1994–2006, Mississippi Department of Archives and History, Jackson (hereafter cited as MSSC Records), http://mdah.state.ms.us/arrec/digital_archives/sovcom/result.php?image=images/png/cd06/046379.png&otherstuff=6|45|1|91|1|1|1|45696|#; Erle Johnston to Herman Glazier, September 7, 1965, SCR ID # 6-45-1-92-1-1-1, MSSC Records, http://mdah.state.ms.us/arrec/digital_archives/sovcom/result.php?image=images/png/

cd06/046380.png&otherstuff=6|45|1|92|1|1|1|45700|#; Greenberg, *The Devil Has Slippery Shoes*, 223–29; Erle Johnston, Memo to File, May 29, 1967, SCR ID # 6-45-5-25-2-1-1, MSSC Records, http://mdah.state.ms.us/arrec/digital_archives/sovcom/result.php?image=/data/sov_commission/images/png/cd06/047421.png&otherstuff=6|45|5|25|1|1|1|46731|.

17. Victor Riesel, "Red Influence Seen in Unrest," *Commercial Appeal*, July 30, 1967; Bob Howie, "Poverty Hanky Panky," *Jackson Daily News*, ca. August 1965.

18. J. Lee Annis Jr., *Big Jim Eastland: The Godfather of Mississippi* (Jackson: University Press of Mississippi, 2016), 210; "More Bad Apple Money," Unknown Newspaper, March 5, 1966, Box 20, Folder RS Southeast Region, Papers of Bernard L. Boutin, LBJL; *Delta Ministry Newsletter* 2, no. 2 (October 1965), http://www.crmvet.org/docs/6510_dm_newsletter.pdf; Rowland Evans and Robert Novak, "Radicals Fighting to Keep State Poverty War Control," *Clarion Ledger*, January 30, 1967.

19. Bartley, *The Rise of Massive Resistance*, 32, 81; Congressional Record: Economic Opportunity Amendments of 1966, September 29, 1966, 21–37, Lucile Montgomery Papers, FSDC, http://content.wisconsinhistory.org/cdm/ref/collection/p15932coll2/id/35597.

20. Wesley G. Phelps, *A People's War on Poverty: Urban Politics and Grassroots Activists in Houston* (Athens: University of Georgia Press, 2014), 134; Ashmore, *Carry It On*, 191.

21. Walter Heller to Lyndon B. Johnson, December 21, 1965, Box 98, Folder WE9, Confidential File: WE/MC, LBJL; Phillip S. Hughes to Joseph Califano, August 6, 1966, Box 165, Folder LE/WE9 EX, WHCF EX LE/WE7, LBJL; J. A. Loftus, "$20,000 Donated to Poverty Unit," *New York Times*, December 11, 1966.

22. Phillip S. Hughes to Sargent Shriver, March 23, 1966, Box 14, Folder FI, Papers of Bernard L. Boutin, LBJL; "Summary: Federal Social Economic Programs Summary FY1967," Box 158, Office Files of Fred Panzer, LBJL.

23. "Say It Isn't So, Sargent Shriver," *New York Times*, October 19, 1966; G. H. Jack Woodard to the Editor, *New York Times*, October 31, 1966; Stossel, *Sarge*, 462–64.

24. Rebecca S. New and Moncreiff Cochran, eds., *Early Childhood Education: An International Encyclopedia, Volume 1* (Westport: Praeger, 2007), 124; Greenberg, *The Devil Has Slippery Shoes*, 303. The story of CDGM's creation and fight for survival is remarkable. Beyond Greenberg, see Chloe Gibbs, Jens Ludwig, and Douglas Miller, "Head Start Origins and Impact," in *Legacies of the War on Poverty*, ed. Martha J. Bailey and Sheldon Danziger (New York: Russell Sage Foundation, 2013), 39–65; Edward Zigler and Sally J. Styfco *The Hidden History of Head Start* (New York: Oxford University Press, 2010), 55–86; and most recently Sanders, *A Chance for Change*.

25. "CDGM Histories," September 1966, Box 3, Folder 4, Miller Collection; Crystal R. Sanders, "More Than Cookies and Crayons: Head Start and African American Empowerment in Mississippi, 1965–1968," *Journal of American History* 100, no. 4 (2015): 586–609.

26. John C. Stennis to Clyde Smith, October 19, 1967, Series 25, Box 7, Folder 51, Stennis Papers.

27. Tom P. Brady, "Review of *Black Monday*," October 28, 1954, Box 3, Folder 21, William D. McCain Pamphlet Collection, Special Collections, University Libraries, University of Southern Mississippi, Hattiesburg; "Southern Manifesto on Integration," March

12, 1956, *Congressional Record: 84th Congress Second Session*, vol. 102, part 4 (Washington, DC: Governmental Printing Office, 1956).

28. Douglas A. Blackmon, *Slavery by Another Name: The Re-Enslavement of Black Americans from the Civil War to World War II* (New York: Doubleday, 2008); Jason Morgan Ward, *Defending White Democracy*, 2; Timothy J. Minchin and John A. Salmond, *After the Dream: Black and White Southerners since 1965*, (Lexington: University Press of Kentucky, 2011), 2.

29. Jesse N. Curtis, "Remembering Racial Progress, Forgetting White Resistance," *History & Memory* 29, no. 1 (2017): 134–60; Thomas J. Sugrue has illustrated the "defensive localism" in *The Origins of the Urban Crisis: Race and Inequality in Postwar Detroit* (Princeton, NJ: Princeton University Press, 2005), 210; "OEO Status of Programs as of 1 January 1966: Mississippi," Box 565, Folder OEO, Office Files of Fred Panzer, LBJL; David C. Colby, "Black Power, White Resistance, and Public Policy: Political Power and Poverty Program Grants in Mississippi," *Journal of Politics* 47, no. 2 (1985): 579–95.

30. P. J. Cotter, and W. J. Miller, "Report on Review of OEO Programs in Mississippi," December 5, 1967, Office of Economic Opportunity, Vertical Files, Mississippi State University, Mitchell Memorial Library, Special Collections, Starkville; (hereafter cited as OEO Vertical Files), Homer Hill interview with Bennie S. Gooden, 15 March 1994, COHCH http://digilib.usm.edu/cdm/ref/collection/coh/id/16083.

31. "About FCM, Inc.," Friends of the Children of Mississippi, 2013, http://www.friendsofchildren.org/about-us/.

32. Grant Announcement, December 17, 1968, Series 5, Box 45, Folder OEO, Charles H. Griffin Collection, Congressional and Political Research Center, Mississippi State University, Starkville; 1960 Census, *US Census Bureau*, http://www.census.gov/hhes/www/poverty/data/census/1960/index.html; Community Profile of Amite, Wilkinson, and Pike Counties, Box 49, OEO Information Center 1966, Office Files of Fred Panzer, LBJL. The high African American populations (54 percent in Amite and 70 percent in Wilkinson) meant that African Americans, who were always disproportionately affected by poverty, were numerically the largest poor group.

33. Community Profile of Pike County, Box 49, OEO Information Center 1966, Office Files of Fred Panzer, LBJL; Dittmer, *Local People*, 112–30, 306; Payne, *I've Got the Light of Freedom*, 113; Newman, *Divine Agitators*, 68–83; Crespino, *In Search of Another Country*, 124; *United States v. Wood*, 295 F.2d 772 (5th Cir. 1961), cert. denied, 369 U.S. 850 (1962).

34. Cazenave, *Impossible Democracy*, 1.

35. CAP Application: "III: Characteristics of Applicant Agency," September 9, 1969, Box 7, Folder CAP Southwest Mississippi, Record Group 381, Records of the Community Services Administration Region IV, National Archives and Record Administration, Atlanta, Georgia (hereafter cited as RG381).

36. Mississippi Task Force Community Profiles and Recommendations, September 1966–January 1967: Amite, Pike, and Wilkinson, Box 1, Folder 14, Patricia Derian Papers, Mitchell Memorial Library, Special Collections, Mississippi State University, Starkville, (hereafter cited as Derian Papers); Payne, *I've Got the Light of Freedom*, 158. SNCC activist Harry Bowie recalled Bryant was "conservative." Harry Bowie interview, 2004, *Veterans of*

the Mississippi Civil Rights Movement, http://www.crmvet.org/audio/msoh/2004_bowie _harry.mp3; Roy L. Jones, "SMO Inc. Status Report," May 12, 1969, Box 6, Folder CAP Southwest Mississippi, RG381; Jimmy Dykes interview with Curtis C. Bryant, November 11, 1995, COHCH, http://digilib.usm.edu/cdm/ref/collection/coh/id/16249; Joseph Sinsheimer interview with C. C. Bryant, February 7, 1985, Joseph A. Sinsheimer Papers, Duke University, Durham, North Carolina, http://library.duke.edu/digitalcollections/media/jpg/sinsheimer-joseph/pdf/sinsio1004.pdf; and more recently One Person, One Vote: SNCC Legacy Project, Duke University, Durham, North Carolina, http://onevotesncc.org/map/mccomb-mississippi/. In 2014, Bryant's legacy was honored placement of a marker on the Mississippi Freedom Trail, seven years after his death.

37. Edwin Marger to Robert W. Saunders, "Civil Rights and Equal Opportunities Review of SMO," June 8, 1970, Box 13, Folder Mississippi: SMO, Education, RG381.

38. Leland E. Cole Jr., "Southwest Mississippi Opportunity, Inc.," October 20, 1966, SCR ID # 99-37-0-61-1-1-1, MSSC Records, http://www.mdah.ms.gov/arrec/digital_archives/sovcom/result.php?image=images/png/cd10/076691.png&otherstuff=99|37|0|61|1|1|1|75716|.

39. Leland E. Cole, "Pearl River Community Action Agency Inc.," 18 November 1966, SCR ID # 6-67-0-34-1-1-1, MSSC Records, http://mdah.state.ms.us/arrec/digital_archives/sovcom/result.php?image=/data/sov_commission/images/png/cd07/050229.png&otherstuff=6|67|0|34|1|1|1|49510|; Leland E. Cole, "Southwest Mississippi Opportunity, Inc.," October 20, 1966, SCR ID # 99-37-0-61-1-1-1, MSSC Records, http://mdah.state.ms.us/arrec/digital_archives/sovcom/result.php?image=images/png/cd10/076691.png&otherstuff=99|37|0|61|1|1|1|75716|#.

40. Erle Johnston, "Memo to File," October 18, 1966, SCR ID # 6-67-0-2-1-1-1, MSSC Records, http://mdah.state.ms.us/arrec/digital_archives/sovcom/result.php?image=/data/sov_commission/images/png/cd07/050102.png&otherstuff=6|67|0|2|1|1|1|49385|; Erle Johnston, "Memo to File," October 13, 1966, SCR ID # 6-67-0-9-1-1-1, MSSC Records, http://mdah.state.ms.us/arrec/digital_archives/sovcom/result.php?image=/data/sov_commission/images/png/cd07/050113.png&otherstuff=6|67|0|9|1|1|1|49396|; Erle Johnston, *Mississippi's Defiant Years, 1953–1973: An Interpretive Documentary with Personal Experiences* (Forrest: Lake Harbor Publishers, 1990), 292; Harry Bowie interview; Leland E. Cole, "Southwest Mississippi Opportunity, Inc," October 24, 1966. SCR ID # 6-67-0-11-1-1-1, MSSC Records, http://www.mdah.ms.gov/arrec/digital_archives/sovcom/result.php?image=images/png/cd07/050117.png&otherstuff=6|67|0|11|1|1|1|49400|.

41. Erle Johnston, "Proposed Statement for Governor Johnson," October 30, 1966, SCR ID # 6-67-0-40-1-1-1, MSSC Records, https://www.mdah.ms.gov/arrec/digital_archives/sovcom/result.php?image=images/png/cd07/050244.png&otherstuff=6|67|0|40|1|1|1|49525|#; Paul B. Johnson to Sargent Shriver, November 15, 1966, Series 1, Box 4, Folder 15, Stennis Papers; "Woodville, Mississippi, and Wilkinson County," April 21, 1967, SCR ID # 2-110-0-64-1-1-1, MSSC Records, http://mdah.state.ms.us/arrec/digital_archives/sovcom/result.php?image=/data/sov_commission/images/png/cd05/037173.png&otherstuff=2|110|0|64|1|1|1|36588|; Leland E. Cole, "Rev. W. F. Summers," June 14, 1968, SCR ID # 1-116-0-13-1-1-1, MSSC Records,

http://mdah.state.ms.us/arrec/digital_archives/sovcom/result.php?image=/data/sov_commission/images/png/cd02/008793.png&otherstuff=1|116|0|13|1|1|1|8579|.

42. Aram Goudsouzian, *Down to the Crossroads: Civil Rights, Black Power, and the Meredith March against Fear* (New York: Farrar, Straus and Giroux, 2014), 113; Fannie Lou Hamer, "I'm Sick and Tired of Being Sick and Tired," December 20, 1964, Williams Institutional CME Church, Harlem, New York, *Civil Rights Movement Veterans*, http://www.crmvet.org/docs/flh64.htm.

CHAPTER TWO: MARJORIE BARONI, ADULT EDUCATION, AND THE MISSISSIPPI CATHOLIC CHURCH

1. "Setting the Record Straight," *Delta Ministry Newsletter* 2, no. 2 (October 1965), *Civil Rights Movement Veterans*, http://www.crmvet.org/docs/6510_dm_newsletter.pdf; "A Double Dose at OEO?" *Bolivar Commercial*, January 27, 1966, Box 20, Folder RS–Southeast Region, Papers of Bernard L. Boutin, LBJL; James M. Ward, "Well, Mt. Beulah Is Closed," *Jackson Daily News*, October 15, 1965.

2. Ann Waldron, *Hodding Carter: Reconstruction of a Racist* (New York: Workman Publishing, 1993); Ginger Rudeseal Carter, "Hodding Carter, Jr., and the *Delta Democrat-Times*," in *The Press and Race: Mississippi Journalists Confront the Movement*, ed. David R. Davies (Jackson: University Press of Mississippi, 2001), 276. Glenda Elizabeth Gilmore, *Gender and Jim Crow: Women and the Politics of White Supremacy in North Carolina, 1896–1920* (Chapel Hill: University of North Carolina Press, 1996); McRae, *Mothers of Massive Resistance*; Bolton, *The Hardest Deal of All: The Battle over School Integration in Mississippi, 1870–1980*. Jackson: University Press of Mississippi, 2005, 113; Harwell, *Wednesdays in Mississippi*, 3.

3. Annelise Orleck, *Storming Caesars Palace: How Black Mothers Fought Their Own War on Poverty* (Boston: Beacon Press, 2005); Nancy A. Naples, *Grassroots Warriors: Activist Mothering, Community Work, and the War on Poverty* (London: Routledge, 1998); Christina Greene, "Someday . . . the Colored and White Will Stand Together: The War on Poverty, Black Power Politics, and Southern Women's Interracial Alliances," in *The War on Poverty*, ed. Orleck and Hazirjian, 162; Laurie B. Green, "Saving Babies in Memphis," in *The War on Poverty*, ed. Orleck and Hazirjian, 133–58; Adina Black, "'Parent Power': Evelina López Antonetty, the United Bronx Parents, and the War on Poverty," in *The War on Poverty*, ed. Orleck and Hazirjian, 184–208. The impact of Head Start on women—particularly mothers—has been considerable in the decades the program has been in operation. E.g., Barbara J. Peters, *The Head Start Mother: Low-Income Mothers' Empowerment through Participation* (New York: Garland Publishing, 1998).

4. Robert Bauman, "Gender, Civil Rights Activism, and the War on Poverty in Los Angeles," in *The War on Poverty*, ed. Orleck and Hazirjian, 209–27; Edwin Marger to Robert W. Saunders, "Civil Rights and Equal Opportunities Review of SMO," June 8, 1970, Box 13, Folder Mississippi: SMO, Education, RG381; Matthew Reonas, "Served Up on a Silver Platter: Ross Barnett, the Tourism Industry, and Mississippi's Civil War Centennial," *Journal of Mississippi History* 72, no. 2 (2010): 136. In 1974, O'Fallon would make an unsuccessful

attempt to take Steve Reed's place on the Wilkinson County Board of Supervisors after his death. She came fourth in a race of nine candidates—in first place was a black constable, Bill Ferguson. "Ferguson, White in Runoff for Supervisor Post," *Woodville Republican*, January 18, 1974.

5. Charles Stuart Kennedy interview with Patricia Derian, March 12, 1999, Foreign Affairs Oral History Project, *The Association for Diplomatic Studies and Training*, https://adst.org/wp-content/uploads/2013/12/Derian-Patricia.19961.pdf.

6. Susan Sullivan, "Marjorie Baroni: Ordinary Southern Woman, Extraordinary Activist," October 4, 2000, Box 20, Folder 1, Marge Baroni Papers, J. D. Williams Library, Archives and Special Collections, University of Mississippi, Oxford, (hereafter cited as Baroni Papers); Patterson, *America's Struggle against Poverty*, 132.

7. Marjorie Baroni quoted in Sullivan, "Marjorie Baroni: Ordinary Southern Woman, Extraordinary Activist."

8. Danny Duncan Collum, *Black and Catholic in the Jim Crow South: The Stuff That Makes Community* (Mahwah, NJ: Paulist Press, 2006), 111, 85–87; Sullivan, "Marjorie Baroni: Ordinary Southern Woman, Extraordinary Activist"; "Outreach Session Held in Area," June 5, 1969, *Rhinelander Daily News*, Box 15, Folder 18, Baroni Papers.

9. Dorothy Day, "Fall Appeal," October 1965, *The Catholic Worker*, 2, https://www.catholicworker.org/dorothyday/articles/833.html; Dorothy Day, "On Pilgrimage," September 1964, *The Catholic Worker*, 2, 8, https://www.catholicworker.org/dorothyday/articles/818.html; Dorothy Day, "On Pilgrimage," October 1968, *The Catholic Worker*, 3, 5, 7, https://www.catholicworker.org/dorothyday/articles/889.html; Stossel, *Sarge*, 337, 674.

10. Amy L. Koehlinger, *The New Nuns: Racial Justice and Religious Reform in the 1960s* (Cambridge, MA: Harvard University Press, 2007), 58; Ashmore, *Carry It On*, 108. Other examples of white Catholic poverty activism: Tom Adam Davies, *Mainstreaming Black Power* (Oakland: University of California Press, 2017), 165; Lyle E. Schaller, *The Churches' War on Poverty* (New York: Abingdon Press, 1967), 11; Justin D. Poché, "Religion, Race, and Rights in Catholic Louisiana, 1938–1970" (PhD diss., University of Notre Dame, 2007), 280.

11. Dittmer, *Local People*, 10; Michael Newton, *The Ku Klux Klan in Mississippi: A History* (Jefferson, NC: McFarland & Company, 2010), 128; Mississippi White Caps, "Liberty is a boisterous sea. Timid men prefer the calm of despotism," n.d., SCR ID # 6-53-0-10-1-1-1, MSSC Records, http://www.mdah.ms.gov/arrec/digital_archives/sovcom/result.php?image=images/png/pages/135417.png&otherstuff=6|53|0|10|1|1|1|48191|#.

12. Susan Sullivan and Tim Murphy interview with Louis Baroni, February 7, 2000, Folder 3, Box 20, Baroni Papers; Collum, *Black and Catholic*, 103–4.

13. Collum, *Black and Catholic*, 104.

14. Susan Sullivan, "Marjorie Baroni: Ordinary Southern Woman, Extraordinary Activist"; Collum, *Black and Catholic*, 106; Roland T. Winel to Joseph B. Brunini, January 15, 1971, STAR, Inc., 1966–1973, File 15, Papers of Bishop Brunini, Archives of the Catholic Diocese of Jackson, Mississippi (hereafter cited as Brunini Papers).

15. "Operation 'STAR,'" May 1965, Box 3, Folder 4, Miller Collection, http://digilib.usm.edu/cdm/ref/collection/manu/id/3907.

16. Dupont, *Mississippi Praying*, 18.

17. "Operation 'STAR,'" May 1965; Collum, *Black and Catholic*, 1.

18. Collum, *Black and Catholic*, 2; Dupont, *Mississippi Praying*, 98; Payne, *I've Got the Light of Freedom*, 325; Mark Newman, "The Catholic Church in Mississippi and Desegregation, 1963–1973," *Journal of Mississippi History* 67, no. 4 (2005): 343; "Discrimination and the Christian Conscience: U.S. Bishops on Segregation," *Catholic Herald*, November 21, 1958, http://archive.catholicherald.co.uk/article/21st-november-1958/8/discrimination-and-the-christian-conscience; Michael V. Namorato, *The Catholic Church in Mississippi, 1911–1984: A History*, (Westport, CT: Greenwood Press, 1998), 63; Paul T. Murray, "Father Nathaniel and the Greenwood Movement," *Journal of Mississippi History* 72, no. 3 (2010), 284.

19. Collum, *Black and Catholic*, 86–88; Charles Marsh, *God's Long Summer*, 141; Randy J. Sparks, *Religion in Mississippi* (Jackson: University Press of Mississippi, 2001), 240.

20. Pope Paul VI, *Gaudium Et Spes*, December 7, 1965, Part II: Problems of particular urgency, Chapter III: Economic and Social Life, Section 1: Economic Development, Point 66, http://www.vatican.va/archive/hist_councils/ii_vatican_council/documents/vat-ii_cons_19651207_gaudium-et-spes_en.html; Collum, *Black and Catholic*, 86; James T. McGreevy, "Racial Justice and the People of God: The Second Vatican Council, the Civil Rights Movement, and American Catholics," *Religion and American Culture* 4, no. 2 (1994): 224–25; Findlay, *Church People*, 58; Andrew S. Moore, *The South's Tolerable Alien: Roman Catholics in Alabama and Georgia, 1945–1970* (Baton Rouge: Louisiana State University Press, 2007), 6; Newman, "The Catholic Church in Mississippi," 338–44; Sandra Yocum Mize, "North America," in *The Blackwell Companion to Catholicism*, ed. James J. Buckley, Frederick Christian Bauerschmidt, and Trent Poplum (Oxford: Blackwell Publishing, 2007), 202.

21. "Operation 'STAR,'" May 1965; Dupont, *Mississippi Praying*, 98; e.g., Nancy MacLean, *Behind the Mask of Chivalry: The Making of the Second Ku Klux Klan* (Oxford: Oxford University Press, 1994), 140; Gladys McDearmon to Thomas G. Abernethy, August 17, 1965, Box 181, Folder OEO STAR Inc., Thomas G. Abernethy Collection, J. D. Williams Library, Archives and Special Collections, University of Mississippi, Oxford; Moore, *South's Tolerable Alien*, 130.

22. L. B. Taylor to James O. Eastland, August 8, 1967, and attached cartoon "Go Out and Spread the Word!" *Unknown Paper*, ca. August 1967, File Series 3, Subseries 1, Box 45, Folder 1967 Civil Rights, James O. Eastland Collection, J. D. Williams Library, Archives and Special Collections, University of Mississippi, Oxford, (hereafter cited as Eastland Collection); Newton, *The Ku Klux Klan in Mississippi*, 147; Namorato, *The Catholic Church in Mississippi*, 169; e.g., see Paul T. Murray, "Father Nathaniel and the Greenwood Movement," 277–312.

23. Koehlinger, *The New Nuns*; Dittmer, *Local People*, 128–29; "Issue V of a Series," *A Delta Discussion*, n.d., Box 2132, Folder 1, Mississippi State AFL-CIO Records, Southern Labor Archives, Georgia State University, Atlanta (hereafter cited as MS AFL-CIO); Paul T. Murray, "Father Nathaniel and the Greenwood Movement," 286; "Operation 'STAR,'" May 1965; Susan Sheridan, "Father Nathaniel Machesky to Leave Greenwood," *Greenwood Commonwealth*, August 20, 1981, Folder Machesky, Nathaniel, Brunini Papers; W. B. Garrett, "Graham Says He's Been Converted on Poverty War," *Capital Baptist*, June 22, 1967.

24. William Henderson interview with Father Peter Oliver Quinn, November 2, 1999, COHCH, http://www.lib.usm.edu/legacy/spcol/coh/cohquinnp.html; Joseph B. Brunini

to Walter Maloney, May 7, 1968, Folder Greenwood—St. Francis File 15, Brunini Papers; Joseph Sinsheimer interview with Father Nathaniel Machesky, June 26, 1985, Box 1, Joseph A. Sinsheimer papers, Duke University, Durham, North Carolina, http://library.duke.edu/rubenstein/findingaids/sinsheimerjoseph/#aspace_ref412_b65.

25. Charles Bolton interview with Claude Ramsay, September 30, 1997, COHCH, http://www.lib.usm.edu/legacy/spcol/coh/cohclarko.html.

26. OEO Press Release, n.d., Series 25, Box 7, Folder 6, Stennis Papers; "STAR Progress Report 1," August 13–November 30, 1965, Box 2224, Folder 9, MS AFL-CIO; "Operation 'STAR,'" May 1965; James C. Cobb, *The Selling of the South: The Southern Crusade for Industrial Development, 1936–1980*, (Baton Rouge: Louisiana State University Press, 1982), 116.

27. *The Reveille*, January 20, 1966, Box 17, Folder MC Meetings, Conferences, Papers of Bernard L. Boutin, LBJL; James J. Hearn to Paul B. Johnson Jr., December 1, 1965, Box 119, Folder 7, Johnson Family Papers, McCain Library and Archives Special Collections, University of Southern Mississippi, Hattiesburg (hereafter cited as Johnson Family Papers).

28. Dennis J. Mitchell, *A New History of Mississippi* (Jackson: University Press of Mississippi, 2014), 341; Clayson, *Freedom Is Not Enough*, 37.

29. The governor's acceptance of STAR was reminiscent of the earlier paternalistic relationships between powerful white planters and blacks that resulted in "reciprocal accommodations" to protect white economic interests. William H. Chafe, *Civilities and Civil Rights: Greensboro, North Carolina, and the Black Struggle for Freedom* (Oxford: Oxford University Press, 1981), 38–41, 67–70; Jack M. Bloom, *Class, Race, and the Civil Rights Movement* (Bloomington: Indiana University Press, 1987), 4; Bernard Boutin, "Region III: Weekly Report," February 25, 1966, Box 20, Folder RS—Southeast Region, Papers of Bernard L. Boutin, LBJL.

30. Neil Rosenbaum to P. M. Busby, August 26, 1966, Series 1, Box 4, Folder 42, Stennis Papers.

31. "Readers Give Their Views On," *Delta Democrat Times*, April 9, 1967, Box 2225, Folder 3, MS AFL-CIO; F. J. McGill to Paul Busby, March 14, 1969, and William J. Anderson to Paul Busby, April 21, 1971, Series 1, Box 4, Folder 42, Stennis Papers.

32. Marion D. Gambrel to Paul Busby, June 25, 1970, and Rosa H. King to O'Neil Hudson, August 2, 1971, Series 1, Box 4, Folder 42, Stennis Papers; Paul T. Murray, "Father Nathaniel and the Greenwood Movement," 286.

33. Mayor J. J. Nosser to John Cameron, August 31, 1966, and Arlie C. Warren to Marjorie Baroni, September 2, 1966, Box 2224, Folder 12, MS AFL-CIO; Mayor Sam Coopwood to Shelby Power, September 7, 1966, C. Preston Holmes to Earl S. Lucas, September 10, 1966, W. J. Johnson Jr., to Jackson STAR director, September 13, 1966, Frank England Jr., to whom it may concern, September 15, 1966, Theodore Robinson to Edward Blasi, September 15, 1966, Box 2224, Folder 12, MS AFL-CIO.

34. "Statement Delivered by Claude Ramsay before the US Senate Subcommittee on Employment, Manpower, and Poverty in Jackson, Mississippi," April 10, 1967, Box 2225, Folder 3, MS AFL-CIO; Reiff, *Born of Conviction*, 203; Orley B. Caudill second interview with Claude Ramsay, April 30, 1981, COHCH, http://digilib.usm.edu/cdm/ref/collection/coh/id/9543; Rev. C. Osborne Moyer to Charles L. Young, September 15, 1966, Folder 17, Box

1, Series III, Gilbert E. Carmichael Papers, Mitchell Memorial Library, Special Collections, Mississippi State University, Starkville (hereafter cited as Carmichael Papers).

35. Martin Luther King Jr., "The Christian Way of Life in Human Relations," December 4, 1957, *The King Center*, http://www.thekingcenter.org/archive/document/christian-way-life-human-relations; Bishop Paul Moore Jr., "To a Total Ministry," in *Through the Long, Hot Summer* pamphlet, Hank Werner Papers, Box 2, Folder 6, FSDC, http://content.wisconsinhistory.org/cdm/ref/collection/p15932coll2/id/46312; "Delta Ministry Fact Sheet," January 1965, Congress of Racial Equality: Mississippi 4th Congressional District records, 1961–1966, FSDC, http://content.wisconsinhistory.org/cdm/ref/collection/p15932coll2/id/41199.

36. Findlay, *Church People*, 128, 122; Newman, *Divine Agitators*, 21.

37. "Delta Ministry at a Glance," ca. 1965, Box 3, Folder 1, Miller Collection, http://digilib.usm.edu/cdm/singleitem/collection/manu/id/97/rec/1; Newman, *Divine Agitators*, 40.

38. W. Knight "Shriver Interview: The Church and the Poverty War," *Home Missions*, June 1967, 6–11, Series I, Subgroup 1, Box 120, Folder 7, Papers of William M. Colmer, McCain Library and Archives Special Collections, University of Southern Mississippi, Hattiesburg.

39. E.g., Marc Dollinger, "The Other War: American Jews, Lyndon Johnson, and the Great Society," *American Jewish History* 89, no. 4 (2001): 444; Sargent Shriver to James O. Eastland, July 12, 1967, and attached clipping, W. B. Garrett, "Graham Says He's Been Converted on Poverty War," *Capital Baptist*, June 22, 1967, File Series 1, Subseries 17, Box 8, Folder OEO, Eastland Collection.

40. Sullivan, "Marjorie Baroni: Ordinary Southern Woman, Extraordinary Activist."

CHAPTER THREE: THE KU KLUX KLAN AND THE WAR ON POVERTY

1. David Cunningham, "Shades of Anti-Civil Rights Violence: Reconsidering the Ku Klux Klan in Mississippi," in *The Civil Rights Movement in Mississippi*, ed. Ownby, 182; "Government of Southern States to Change Completely," *Christian Conservative Communique* 1, no. 21 (August 10, 1965), Race Relations Collection, Box 3, Folder 3, J. D. Williams Library, Archives and Special Collections, University of Mississippi, Oxford (hereafter cited as Race Relations Collection).

2. Newton, *The Ku Klux Klan in Mississippi*, 4, 13, 19, 22, 56.

3. Laura Lipsey Bradley, "Protestant Churches and the Ku Klux Klan in Mississippi during the 1920s: Study of an Unsuccessful Courtship" (MA thesis, University of Mississippi, 1962), 24; David M. Chalmers, *Hooded Americanism: The History of the Ku Klux Klan* (Durham, NC: Duke University Press, 1987), 67; Newton, *The Ku Klux Klan in Mississippi*, 85; Gordon A. Martin Jr., *Count Them One by One: Black Mississippians Fighting for the Right to Vote* (Jackson: University Press of Mississippi, 2011), 226.

4. Chalmers, *Hooded Americanism*, 388; Orley B. Caudill interview with Edward L. McDaniel, 12 August 1977, COHCH, http://digilib.usm.edu/cdm/ref/collection/coh/id/16215; Newton, *The Ku Klux Klan in Mississippi*, 115.

5. Newton, *The Ku Klux Klan in Mississippi*, 129, 139; Arnold Forster and Benjamin R. Epstein, *Report on the Ku Klux Klan* (New York: Anti-Defamation League of B'nai B'rith, 1965), 7; David Cunningham, *Klansville*, 56; House Committee on Un-American Activities, "The Present-Day Ku Klux Klan Movement," Report, Ninetieth Congress, first session, part one (Washington, DC: US Government Printing Office, 1967), 69; Newton, *The Ku Klux Klan in Mississippi*, 126.

6. Moye, *Let the People Decide*, 25; David Cunningham, *Klansville*, 5, 8, 86; Hill, *Deacons for Defense*, 188.

7. SNCC press release, May 26, 1964, SCR ID # 2-61-1-99-1-1-1, MSSC Records, http://www.mdah.ms.gov/arrec/digital_archives/sovcom/result.php?image=images/png/cd03/023843.png&otherstuff=2|61|1|99|1|1|1|23365|#; "Burning of African American Churches in Mississippi and Perceptions of Race Relations," *Mississippi Advisory Committee to the US Commission on Civil Rights*, July 10–11, 1996, https://www.law.umaryland.edu/marshall/usccr/documents/cr12b873.pdf; "'Reorganization' of the KKK Revealed," *Vicksburg Evening Post*, November 1, 1966, Box 1, Folder 11, Ku Klux Klan Collection, J. D. Williams Library, Archives and Special Collections, University of Mississippi, Oxford (hereafter cited as KKK Collection).

8. Lynne Olson, *Freedom's Daughters: The Unsung Heroines of the Civil Rights Movement from 1830 to 1970* (New York: Simon and Schuster, 2001), 205; Mendy Samstein, "September 1964 Letter about McComb Bombing," September 21, 1964, Pamela P. Allen Papers, 1967–1974, *Wisconsin Historical Society*, Madison, Wisconsin, http://content.wisconsinhistory.org/cdm/ref/collection/p15932coll2/id/31898.

9. Mendy Samstein, "September 1964 Letter about McComb Bombing"; Mendy Samstein, "The Murder of a Community," *Student Voice* 5, no. 22 (September 23, 1964), Freedom Summer Digital History Collection, *Wisconsin Historical Society*, Madison, Wisconsin, http://cdm15932.contentdm.oclc.org/cdm/ref/collection/p15932coll2/id/50279; Dittmer, *Local People*, 308, 310–11.

10. Roy K. Moore to Governor Paul B. Johnson, March 31, 1966, Box 142, Folder 1, Johnson Family Papers; Silver, *Mississippi: The Closed Society*, 154; Drew Pearson, "Church Remains a Shambles, KKK is Powerful in McComb," *Clarion Ledger*, November 6, 1964; "The Ku Klux Klan—1965," in *Facts* 16, no. 3, May 1965, Box 1, Folder 10, KKK Collection.

11. "General Report," October 8, 1964, SCR ID # 2-36-2-38-4-1-1, MSSC Records, http://www.mdah.ms.gov/arrec/digital_archives/sovcom/result.php?image=images/png/cd01/006883.png&otherstuff=2|36|2|38|1|1|1|6709|#; Newton, *The Ku Klux Klan in Mississippi*, 140. For detail on the murders see Seth Cagin and Philip Dray's *We Are Not Afraid: The Story of Goodman, Schwerner, and Chaney and the Civil Rights Campaign for Mississippi*, new ed. (New York: Nation Books, 2006).

12. McRae, *Mothers of Massive Resistance*, 218; Jules Irving, "Notes on Visit to Jackson, Mississippi, 1964," Box 3, Folder 14, Miller Collection, http://digilib.usm.edu/cdm/ref/collection/manu/id/4488; Kathleen M. Blee, "Women in the 1920s' Ku Klux Klan Movement," *Feminist Studies* 17, no. 1 (1991): 58; David M. Chalmers, *Backfire: How the Ku Klux Klan Helped the Civil Rights Movement* (New York: Rowman & Littlefield, 2003), 89; David Cunningham, *Klansville*, 147–48; Dan T. Carter, *The Politics of Rage*, 140; Newton, *The Ku*

Klux Klan in Mississippi, 154. The Deacons for Defense used language that was a "clarion call to manhood," *Deacons for Defense*, 182.

13. Orley B. Caudill interview with William F. Dukes, January 23, 1973, COHCH, http://digilib.usm.edu/cdm/ref/collection/coh/id/1998; David Cunningham, *Klansville*, 147–48; Luckett, *Joe T. Patterson and the White South's Dilemma*, 47; Debra Spencer interview with Samuel H. Bowers Jr., October 24, 1983, Mississippi Department of Archives and History, Jackson, http://mdah.ms.gov/arrec/digital_archives/bowers/transcript.php; Moye, *Let the People Decide*, 70.

14. Stephanie Scull Millet interview with Franzetta Sanders, May 17, 2000, COHCH, http://digilib.usm.edu/cdm/ref/collection/coh/id/11046.

15. Witness testimony of Alvin Cobb, Transcript of the conversation held on May 9, at Baton Rouge, Louisiana, FBI Reports: Original Knights of the Ku Klux Klan, Part 5, 76, *FBI Vault*, https://vault.fbi.gov/The%20Ku%20Klux%20Klan%20%28KKK%29; United Klans of America, "Aren't You Grown-Ups Ashamed?" n.d., Folder 6, KKK Collection.

16. Mississippi Association for Constitutional Government, "Which Side?" n.d., Box 13, Folder 7, Baroni Papers; "A Delta Discussion," Issue IV of a Series, November 19, 1965, Box 3, Folder 2, Race Relations Collection; "A Delta Discussion," Issue V of a Series, n.d., Box 3, Folder 2, Race Relations Collection.

17. "Anti–Julian Bond Cartoon," April 4, 1967, Brownsville Klan Collection, *Crossroad to Freedom Digital Archive*, Rhodes College, http://www.crossroadstofreedom.org/info.pdf?pid=rds:855.

18. "Local," *Christian Conservative Communique* 1, no. 2 (March 17, 1965), Box 3, Folder 3, Race Relations Collection; "Government of Southern States to Change Completely," *Christian Conservative Communique* 1, no. 21 (August 10, 1965), Box 3, Folder 3, Race Relations Collection.

19. Newton, *The Ku Klux Klan in Mississippi*, 127–82; Chalmers, *Hooded Americanism*, 386–423; John Drabble, "FBI, COINTELPRO-WHITE HATE, and the Decline of the KKK Organizations in Mississippi, 1964–1971," *Journal of Mississippi History* 46, no. 4 (2004): 353–402; George Lewis, "'An Amorphous Code': The Ku Klux Klan and Un-Americanism, 1915-1965," *Journal of American Studies* 47, no. 4 (2013): 1–22; Luckett, *Joe T. Patterson and the White South's Dilemma*, 171.

20. "Race Violence Work of Klan, Flowers Says," *Birmingham News*, October 17, 1965, Box 1, Folder 11, KKK Collection; Orley B. Caudill interview with William F. Dukes, January 23, 1973, COHCH, http://digilib.usm.edu/cdm/ref/collection/coh/id/1998; A. Schardt, "A Mississippi Mayor Fights the Klan," *The Reporter*, January 27, 1966, Box 142, Folder 1, Johnson Family Papers.

21. Payne, *I've Got the Light of Freedom*, 398; "The Murder of Vernon Dahmer," *Civil Rights Movement Veterans*, http://www.crmvet.org/tim/timhis66.htm#1966dahmer; Orley B. Caudill interview with Ellie J. Dahmer, July 2, 1974, COHCH, http://digilib.usm.edu/cdm/ref/collection/coh/id/15828.

22. Orley B. Caudill interview with Ellie J. Dahmer; Orley B. Caudill interview with William F. Dukes.

23. J. Bonney, "Associated Press Investigation Shows Klan's Mississippi Empire Is Crumbling," *Meridian Star*, March 24, 1967, Box 1, Folder 11, KKK Collection. In the trial of Dahmer's murders, the court heard evidence that Bowers was unhappy the Forrest County KKK had not already acted. *Byrd vs. State* (1969), https://law.justia.com/cases/mississippi/supreme-court/1969/45559-0.html.

24. "Continued Investigation of the Boycott of White Merchants in Edwards, Mississippi and Buy-Ins Sponsored by the AWPR in This Town," October 27, 1966, SCR ID # 6-36-0-58-1-1-1, MSSC Records, http://mdah.state.ms.us/arrec/digital_archives/sovcom/result.php?image=/data/sov_commission/images/png/cd06/044457.png&otherstuff=6|36|0|58|1|1|1|43799|; Crespino, *In Search of Another Country*, 134; Newton, *The Ku Klux Klan in Mississippi*, 129; Virgil Downing, "Dynamite Bombings of Negro Homes in McComb, Mississippi," June 25, 1964, SCR ID # 2-36-2-14-2-1-1, MSSC Records, http://mdah.state.ms.us/arrec/digital_archives/sovcom/result.php?image=/data/sov_commission/images/png/cd01/006754.png&otherstuff=2|36|2|14|2|1|1|6586|.

25. Orley B. Caudill interview with Ellie J. Dahmer; "APWR Trying to Raise Money for Defense," *Clarion Ledger*, February 29, 1968; Dan T. Carter, *The Politics of Rage*, 11, 210, 276; Joseph E. Lowndes, *From the New Deal to the New Right: Race and the Southern Origins of Modern Conservatism* (New Haven, CT: Yale University Press, 2008), 143–45; John Pearce, "Ace Carter in Defense of APWR," *Clarion Ledger*, December 2, 1967; Dan T. Carter, "The Transformation of a Klansman," *New York Times*, October 4, 1991.

26. *The Citizen*, Special Educational Issue, 14, no. 4, (January 1970), Box 37, John C. Satterfield Collection, J. D. Williams Library, Archives and Special Collections, University of Mississippi, Oxford; Bolton, *The Hardest Deal of All*, 100.

27. "Jackson Police Department Intelligence Division Special Investigative Report," n.d., Box 44, Folder Ku Klux Klan, Russell C. Davis Papers, Mitchell Memorial Library, Special Collections, Mississippi State University, Starkville (hereafter cited as Davis Papers); David Cunningham, *Klansville*, 147; House Committee on Un-American Activities, "The Present-Day Ku Klux Klan Movement," 97.

28. Don Williams interview with Right Reverend Duncan Montgomery Gray Jr., April 16, 1999, COHCH, http://digilib.usm.edu/cdm/ref/collection/coh/id/15577; "Shriver Comes Across," *New Republic*, January 7, 1967, 10, Box 2, Loose Materials, Carter Papers.

29. Graham Lee Hales interview with Owen Cooper, 11 December 1972, COHCH, http://digilib.usm.edu/cdm/ref/collection/coh/id/1369; Charles E. Snodgrass to Chief A. D. Morgan, March 31, 1967, Box 149, Folder 1, Johnson Family Papers; Ashmore, *Carry It On*, 131; Kent B. Germany, "Poverty Wars in the Louisiana Delta: White Resistance, Black Power, and the Poorest Place in America," in *The War on Poverty*, ed. Orleck and Hazirjian, 231–55.

30. Milton Bryant, "Fact Sheet: Problems and Victories of Lincoln County MAP Head Start Program," November 29, 1967, Box 1, Folder Executive Session, Carter Papers.

31. Homer Hill interview with Honorable Harvey Ross, December 12, 1994, COHCH, http://digilib.usm.edu/cdm/ref/collection/coh/id/8957; Patricia Derian, Report, February 13, 1967, Box 1, Folder 5, Derian Papers; Patricia Derian, Derian Report re Violence, June 1, 1967, Box 1, Folder 6, Derian Papers; Findlay, *Church People*, 120, 166; John Doar, Justice re Violence in South, DeLoach (FBI) March 23, 1967, Weekly Situation and Status

240

NOTES

Report—Region III, February 7, 1967, Box 43, Folder Conference File: Washington, DC, Papers of Bertrand M. Harding, LBJL; Araminta Stone Johnston, *And One Was a Priest: The Life and Times of Duncan M. Gray Jr.* (Jackson: University Press of Mississippi, 2011), 227; "Threats Against Teachers Challenge Johnson's Plan," *Commercial Appeal*, July 10, 1966. The history of Mount Beulah is complex, but at the time it was used as a Head Start training center it was being rented by the Delta Ministry; Note to File, November 23, 1966, SCR ID # 6-45-4-33-1-1-1, MSSC Records, http://mdah.state.ms.us/arrec/digital_archives/sovcom/result.php?image=/data/sov_commission/images/png/cd06/047088.png&otherstuff=6|45|4|33|1|1|1|46399|.

32. T. B. Birdsong to Owen Cooper, February 20, 1967, SCR ID # 2-42-0-35-1-1-1, MSSC Records, http://mdah.state.ms.us/arrec/digital_archives/sovcom/result.php?image=/data/sov_commission/images/png/cd02/009170.png&otherstuff=2|42|0|35|1|1|1|8950|.

33. Owen Cooper to T. B. Birdsong, February 23, 1967, SCR ID # 2-42-0-35-2-1-1, MSSC Records, http://mdah.state.ms.us/arrec/digital_archives/sovcom/result.php?image=/data/sov_commission/images/png/cd02/009172.png&otherstuff=2|42|0|36|1|1|1|8952|; Erle Johnston to Mayor Frank P. Ellis, February 16, 1967, Box 2, Loose Materials, Carter Papers.

34. Rowland Evans and Robert Novak, "Extremists Aim Attacks at Moderates," *Pascagoula Paper*, March 6, 1967, Box 2, Loose Material, Carter Papers; memos between Bertrand Harding and Sargent Shriver, March 1967, Box 43, Folder Conference File: Washington, DC, John Doar, Justice re Violence in South, DeLoach (FBI) March 23, 1967, Papers of Bertrand M. Harding, LBJL.

35. Patricia Derian, P. Derian Report, May 10, 1967, Box 1, Folder 1, Derian Papers; Patricia Derian, P. Derian Report, June 21, 1967, Box 1, Folder 6, Derian Papers.

36. Patricia Derian, Derian Report re Assignment MAP, January 26, 1967, Box 1, Folder 4, Derian Papers; Weekly Situation and Status Report-Region III, February 7, 1967, Box 43, Folder Conference File: Washington, DC, John Doar, Justice re Violence in South, DeLoach (FBI) March 23, 1967, Papers of Bertrand M. Harding, LBJL.

37. Gail S. Murray, "White Privilege, Racial Justice: Women Activists in Memphis," in *Throwing Off the Cloak of Privilege: White Southern Women Activists in the Civil Rights Era* ed. Gail S. Murray (Gainesville: University Press of Florida, 2004), 222.

38. J. Todd Moye, "Discovering What's Already There: Mississippi Women and Civil Rights Movements," in *Mississippi Women: Their Histories, Their Lives, Volume 2*, ed. Elizabeth Anne Payne, Martha H. Swain, and Marjorie Julian Spruill (Athens: University of Georgia Press, 2010), 256–60; "The Leader" flyer, n.d., Box 1, Folder Harassment and Negative Attitudes, Carter Papers.

39. "The Leader" flyer, n.d., Box 1, Folder Harassment and Negative Attitudes, Carter Papers; "Issue V of a Series," *A Delta Discussion*, n.d., Box 2132, Folder 1, MS AFL-CIO.

40. Pat Derian to Bob Martin, William Holland, Hugh Saussy, August 6, 1967, Box 1, Folder 19, Derian Papers.

41. Harry McPherson to Lyndon B. Johnson, August 10, 1967, Box 30, Folder WE9 7/13/67–6/15/67 EX, WHCF EX WE9 7/13/67–11/21/67, LBJL; Bertrand M. Harding to Sargent Shriver, April 17, 1967, Box 43, Conference File: Washington, DC White House Meeting (Califano's Office), Papers of Bertrand M. Harding, LBJL; Joseph Califano to Lyndon B. Johnson,

October 14, 1967 and attached letter from Morrie Leibman to Lyndon B. Johnson, October 12, 1967, Presidential Task Force Subject File, Box 26, Folder National Advisory Council on Economic Opportunity, Office Files of James Gaither, LBJL.

42. "Report on Sunflower County Progress," 1968, Box 23, Folder Poverty (1968), Office Files of Harry McPherson, LBJL.

43. "Racial Climate Is Improving in Mississippi," *St. Louis Post-Dispatch*, March 8, 1967, Box 27, Folder HU2/ST24 2/15/66-EX, WHCF EX HU 2/ST 24 7/17/64–1/20/69, LBJL; FBI, "A Byte out of History: The Case of the 1966 KKK Firebombing," September 1, 2006, https://archives.fbi.gov/archives/news/stories/2006/january/kkk_dahmer010906.

44. Orley B. Caudill interview with William F. Dukes; Don Whitehead, *Attack on Terror: The FBI against the Ku Klux Klan in Mississippi* (New York: Funk & Wagnalls Co., 1970), 237; Martin, *Count Them One by One*, 232. Bowers was finally convicted for his role in Vernon Dahmner's murder in 1998 and sentenced to life in prison, while Edgar Ray Killen was convicted of the manslaughter of Chaney, Schwerner, and Goodman in 2005.

CHAPTER FOUR: BLACK EMPOWERMENT IN JACKSON

1. John R. Salter Jr., *Jackson, Mississippi: An American Chronicle of Struggle and Schism* (1979), new ed. (Lincoln: University of Nebraska Press, 2011, 76.6; Williams, *Medgar Evers*, 227; Lyon, *Sanctuaries of Segregation*, 26.

2. Dittmer, *Local People*, 35–36; Payne, *I've Got the Light of Freedom*, 23; Harriet Tanzman interview with James C. Coleman, April 12, 2000, COHCH, https://digitalcollections.usm.edu/uncategorized/deliverableUnit_0711df4f-ac94-45e2-a98d-2c80027445ab/.

3. Harriet Tanzman interview with James C. Coleman; Salter, *Jackson, Mississippi*, 122.3.

4. Dittmer, *Local People*, 97; "Don't! Don't Shop for Christmas!" The Jackson Movement: Information Bulletin, n.d., *Civil Rights Movement Veterans*, http://www.crmvet.org/docs/6312_jax_murder.pdf.

5. "Don't! Don't Shop for Christmas!" The Jackson Movement: Information Bulletin, n.d.; Salter, *Jackson, Mississippi*, 217.1.

6. Payne, *I've Got the Light of Freedom*, 286; Dittmer, *Local People*, 163–64; Williams, *Medgar Evers*, 259; Lyon, *Sanctuaries of Segregation*, 32.

7. Dupont, *Mississippi Praying*, 157–58; Williams, *Medgar Evers*, 253–54; Salter, *Jackson, Mississippi*, 455.5. See also M. J. O'Brien, *We Shall Not Be Moved: The Jackson Woolworth's Sit-In and the Movement It Inspired* (Jackson: University Press of Mississippi, 2014).

8. Salter, *Jackson, Mississippi*, 532.4, 563; Williams, *Medgar Evers*, 254; *City of Jackson vs. John R. Salter Jr., et. al.*, (1963); Officers of the North Jackson Youth Council to Out-of-state friends, "Situation in Jackson—mass action ahead," May 20, 1963, *Civil Rights Movement Veterans*, http://www.crmvet.org/docs/630519_naacp_jackson.pdf.

9. Payne, *I've Got the Light of Freedom*, 47, 51–53, 175; Orlando Bagwell interview with Myrlie Evers, November 27, 1985, *Eyes on the Prize: America's Civil Rights Years*, Henry Hampton Collection, Film and Media Archive, Washington University Libraries, http://digital.wustl.edu/e/eop/eopweb/eve0015.0753.036myrlieevers.html; Williams, *Medgar Evers*, 286–87, 290.

10. O'Brien, *We Shall Not Be Moved*, 204; Williams, *Medgar Evers*, 290, 306; Salter, *Jackson, Mississippi*, 648.2; Jim Dann, *Challenging the Mississippi Fire Bombers: Memories of Mississippi, 1964-65* (Quebec: Baraka Books, 2013), 39; Dupont, *Mississippi Praying*, 159. The role of the Sovereignty Commission was reported by *Clarion Ledger* journalist Jerry Mitchell in 1991, creating public outrage. District attorney Bobby DeLaughter began inquiries that prompted a new investigation. Beckwith was tried for a third time and, on February 5, 1994, was convicted of the murder of Medgar Evers.

11. Payne, *I've Got the Light of Freedom*, 286; Raymond Arsenault, *Freedom Riders: 1961 and the Struggle for Racial Justice* (Oxford: Oxford University Press, 2006), 370-71; McAdam, *Freedom Summer*, 27-28; "Official Report of On-Site Findings: CSA, Jackson, Mississippi, May 27-29, 1969."

12. SNCC WATS Report: Chronology of Events, June 14-20, 1965, *Civil Rights Movement Veterans*, http://www.crmvet.org/docs/wats/wats65_jun15-ju130.pdf; Ira Grupper, "The Fairgrounds Motel," *Civil Rights Movement Veterans*, http://www.crmvet.org/nars/jax65.htm; Hardy Frye, "Everyone Was a Leader," March 27, 2010, Speech at the 50th anniversary of the student-led sit-ins of 1960, *Civil Rights Movement Veterans*, http://www.crmvet.org/nars/stor/s_hardy.htm; Rev. Ian McCrae, Rev. W. Raymond Barry and John M. Pratt, "Statement Presented to Congressional Briefing," June 22, 1965, *Civil Rights Movement Veterans*, http://www.crmvet.org/docs/6506_jackson_ncc.pdf.

13. Dittmer, *Local People*, 234; Salter, *Jackson, Mississippi*, 732; Payne, *I've Got the Light of Freedom*, 229.

14. Tom B. Scott Jr., to Frank K. Sloan, June 28, 1967; "Official Report of On-Site Findings: CSA, Jackson, Mississippi," May 27-29, 1969, Box 3, Folder CSA, Jackson, Mississippi, RG381; "Report," July 25, 1966, SCR ID # 6-45-3-79-1-1-1, MSSC records, http://www.mdah.ms.gov/arrec/digital_archives/sovcom/result.php?image=images/png/pages/135394.png&otherstuff=6|45|3|79|1|1|1|46315|#.

15. The Citizens Co-ordinating Committee of Jackson, "Citizens of Jackson, Wake up!" June 1965, *Civil Rights Movement Veterans*, http://www.crmvet.org/docs/6506_jax_flyer.pdf.

16. Campbell Gibson and Kay Jung, "Historical Census Statistics on Population Totals by Race, 1790 to 1990, and by Hispanic Origin, 1970 to 1990, for the United States, Regions, Divisions, and States," Population Division, US Census Bureau, Working Paper Series No. 56, (2002), http://www.census.gov/population/www/documentation/twps0056/twps0056.html.

17. This racial composition reflects the statewide composition in 1960: 57.7 percent white, 42 percent black, 0.1 percent Asian and 0.1 percent American Indian. "OEO Information Center: Community Profile," Mississippi Volume I of VI, Hinds County, Box 49, Office Files of Fred Panzer, LBJL.

18. Dr Beittel had been targeted by Johnston's earlier massive resistance campaigns, see Yasuhiro Katagiri, *The Mississippi State Sovereignty Commission: Civil Rights and States' Rights*, (Jackson: University Press of Mississippi, 2001), 152-57; Ted Seaver and Nancy Levin, "How to Perpetuate the Racist Power Structure in Mississippi using Federal Funds ... or the Atlanta Regional OEO in Action," June 14, 1966, 9, Box 25, Folder CAP, Mississippi Council

on Human Relations Records 1960–1980, Mississippi Department of Archives and History, Jackson (hereafter cited as MCHR Records).

19. Crespino, *In Search of Another Country*, 93; Crosby, *A Little Taste of Freedom*, 234; Seaver and Levin, "How to Perpetuate," 1–2.

20. Mississippi Task Force Community Profiles and Recommendations, September 1966–January 1967: Hinds County, Box 1, Folder 14, Derian Papers.; "Narrative Description of the CSA," 1966, Box 2, Folder 5, Bryan R. Dunlap Papers, 1964–1972, FSDC, http://cdm15932 .contentdm.oclc.org/cdm/ref/collection/p15932coll2/id/696.

21. Seaver and Levin, "How to Perpetuate," 11, 14.

22. Edwin Marger, "Evaluation Report: CSA," May 30, 1969, Box 3, Folder CSA, Jackson, Mississippi, RG381.

23. Claire Parkinson, Paul Hackel, and Sonya Hackel moderated by Michael Sherman, "The Vermont in Mississippi Project: A Panel Discussion," January 16, 2007, Vermont in Mississippi: The Center for Research on Vermont, the Vermont Historical Society, and Burlington College, https://www.youtube.com/watch?v=sjrs4xhbbBg; Tiyi M. Morris, *Womanpower Unlimited and the Black Freedom Struggle in Mississippi* (Athens: University of Georgia Press, 2015), 79.

24. Seaver and Levin, "How to Perpetuate."

25. Hinds County Community Council to Frank K. Sloan, n.d., Box 25, Folder CAP, MCHR Records. The Council made these accusations in a letter to Sloan: James Mays, Richard Anderson, and Aaron Evans on behalf of the Hinds County Community Council to the CSA Board of Directors, n.d., Box 4, Folder 42, Charles Horwitz Papers, Mississippi Department of Archives and History, Jackson (hereafter cited as Horwitz Papers).

26. Greenberg, *The Devil Has Slippery Shoes*, 30; Henry Hampton interview with Marian Wright Edelman, December 21, 1988, *Eyes on the Prize: America's Civil Rights Years*, Henry Hampton Collection, Film and Media Archive, Washington University Libraries, http:// digital.wustl.edu/e/eii/eiiweb/ede5427.0676.044marianwrightedelman.html.

27. Larry Tye, *Bobby Kennedy: The Making of a Liberal Icon* (New York: Random House 2016), 349; "Robert Kennedy," John F. Kennedy Presidential Library, http://www.jfklibrary .org/JFK/The-Kennedy-Family/Robert-F-Kennedy.aspx.

28. Payne, *I've Got the Light of Freedom*, 344; "Are They Deliberately Starving Negroes in Mississippi?" August 1967, Folder 8, Box 1, Series I, Carmichael Papers.

29. Investigator Hopkins to Erle Johnston Jr., June 29, 1967, SCR ID # 2-55-12-51-1-1-1, MSSC Records, http://www.mdah.ms.gov/arrec/digital_archives/sovcom/result.php?image =images/png/cd03/021349.png&otherstuff=2|55|12|51|1|1|1|20888|#.

30. Irving Adler, "VIM State President Describes His Visit to Jackson, Miss," *Vermont Tribune*, August 5, 1965; Erle Johnston, Memo to File, August 28, 1967, SCR ID # 6-65- 0-15-1-1-1, MSSC Records, http://mdah.state.ms.us/arrec/digital_archives/sovcom/result .php?image=/data/sov_commission/images/png/cd07/049842.png&otherstuff=6|65|0| 15|1|1|1|49127|; Telephoned Report, August 29, 1967, SCR ID # 1-125-0-17-1-1-1, MSSC Records, http://mdah.state.ms.us/arrec/digital_archives/sovcom/result.php?image=/data/sov_com mission/images/png/cd02/009024.png&otherstuff=1|125|0|17|1|1|1|8809|; Erle Johnston, Memo to File, August 23, 1966, SCR ID # 2-55-12-14-1-1-1, MSSC Records, http://mdah

.state.ms.us/arrec/digital_archives/sovcom/result.php?image=images/png/cd03/021272. png&otherstuff=2|55|12|14|1|1|1|20811|#; Erle Johnston, Memo to File, August 28, 1967, SCR ID # 6-65-0-15-1-1-1, MSSC Records, http://mdah.state.ms.us/arrec/digital_archives/sov com/result.php?image=images/png/cd07/049842.png&otherstuff=6|65|0|15|1|1|1|49127|#; Dan T. Carter, *The Politics of Rage*, 201. "Burr heads" was a common segregationist derogatory term for African Americans—as Carter notes it was most prominently used by George Wallace.

31. Erle Johnston, "Editorial: M.I.V. vs. V.I.M.," *Scott County Times*, February 23, 1966, SCR ID # 2-156-0-35-1-1-1, MSSC Records, http://mdah.state.ms.us/arrec/digital_archives/ sovcom/result.php?image=/data/sov_commission/images/png/cd07/048405.png&otherst uff=2|156|0|35|1|1|1|47705|; Ted Seaver, 'Here are some of the things poor people can do and are doing around the state', n.d., SCR ID # 2-156-0-20-4-1-1, MSSC Records, http://mdah .state.ms.us/arrec/digital_archives/sovcom/result.php?image=/data/sov_commission/im ages/png/cd07/048351.png&otherstuff=2|156|0|20|4|1|1|47652|; Ted Seaver, "Evans Votes Against Poor People," *Hinds County Freedom Democratic Party News* 1, no. 11 (March 25, 1967), SCR ID # 6-65-0-4-1-1-1, MSSC Records, http://mdah.state.ms.us/arrec/digital_ar chives/sovcom/result.php?image=/data/sov_commission/images/png/cd07/049825.png&o therstuff=6|65|0|4|1|1|1|49110|; SCR ID # 2-72-3-30-1-1-1.

32. Erle Johnston, "Attitudes in Mississippi," December 1967, 2, Box 8, Folder 26, Erle E. Johnston Papers, University of Southern Mississippi, Hattiesburg, http://digilib.usm.edu/ cdm/ref/collection/manu/id/8442.

33. Tom B. Scott Jr. to Frank K. Sloan, June 28, 1967; "Official Report of On-Site Findings: CSA, Jackson, Mississippi," May 27–29, 1969, Box 3, Folder CSA, Jackson, Mississippi, RG381; "Report," July 25, 1966, SCR ID # 6-45-3-79-1-1-1, MSSC records, http://www.mdah .ms.gov/arrec/digital_archives/sovcom/result.php?image=images/png/pages/135394.png& otherstuff=6|45|3|79|1|1|1|46315|#.

34. "Neighborhood Youth Corps: An Economic Opportunity Program," June 1966, *Department of Labor*, https://archive.org/details/ERIC_ED027350; Examination of the war on poverty: hearings before the Subcommittee on Employment, Manpower, and Poverty of the Committee on Labor and Public Welfare, United States Senate, Ninetieth Congress, first session (Washington, DC: US Government Printing Office, 1967), 2436–44; "The Neighborhood Youth Corps: Three Years of Success," 1968, *Department of Labor*, 15, https:// archive.org/stream/ERIC_ED026423. Mississippi received $15.2 million for NYC from January 1965 to July 1967 to support 24,500 "enrollment opportunities."

35. Palmer R. Anderson, "Jobs Corps and Neighborhood Youth Corps: A Critical Review," *Humboldt Journal of Social Relations* 1, no. 1 (1973): 13; Gerald G. Somers and Ernst W. Stromsdorfer, "A Cost-Effectiveness Analysis of In-School and Summer Neighborhood Youth Corps: A Nationwide Evaluation," *Journal of Human Resources* 7, no. 4 (1972): 446–59; Michael E. Borus, John P. Brennan, and Sidney Rosen, "A Benefit-Cost Analysis of the Neighborhood Youth Corps: The Out-of-School Program in Indiana," *Journal of Human Resources* 5, no. 2 (1970): 139–59; Examination of the war on poverty: hearings before the Subcommittee, 2436–44; Regis H. Walther and Margaret L. Magnusson, *A Retrospective Study of the Effectiveness of Out-of-School Neighborhood Youth Corps Programs in Four*

Urban Sites, (Washington, DC: George Washington University, 1967), 39; Darrell Duane Spoon, "Role Perception of Neighborhood Youth Corps Trainees and their Supervisors" (MA thesis, Kansas State University, 1969), 40.

36. "The Purpose of Neighborhood Youth Corps," February 2, 1970, Box 2260, Folder CSA Programs Descriptives, Records of the Governor's Office: Series 1001, Community Development Files, 1966–1975, Mississippi Department of Archives and History, Jackson (hereafter cited as Community Development Files); Don Jackson, "NYC—A Broken Promise? A Preliminary Examination of Community Services Association's Neighborhood Youth Corps with Some Immediate Recommendations Submitted by Don Jackson, June 1967," Box 25, Folder CAP, MCHR Records.

37. Jackson, "NYC—A Broken Promise?" June 1967, Box 25, Folder CAP, MCHR Records.

38. Carol Hinds to Fred Alexander, September 13, 1968, Box 3, Folder 38, Horwitz Papers; Telephoned Report of August 29, 1967, SCR ID # 1-125-0-17-1-1-1, MSSC Records, http://mdah.state.ms.us/arrec/digital_archives/sovcom/result.php?image=images/png/cd02/009024.png&otherstuff=1|125|0|17|1|1|1|8809|#; Don Jackson to the CSA Board, Colonel H. F. Frank and Stephen Canon, August 21, 1967, Box 25, Folder CAP, MCHR Records.

39. Release by the *Ad Hoc* Committee of Black Youth in Hinds County, ca. August 1967, SCR ID # 2-160-0-8-1-1-1, MSSC Records, http://mdah.state.ms.us/arrec/digital_archives/sovcom/result.php?image=/data/sov_commission/images/png/cd07/051449.png&otherstuff=2|160|0|8|1|1|1|50722|.

40. Release by the *Ad Hoc* Committee of Black Youth in Hinds County.

41. Release by the *Ad Hoc* Committee of Black Youth in Hinds County; Don Jackson to the CSA Board, Colonel H. F. Frank and Stephen Canon, August 21, 1967, Box 25, Folder CAP, MCHR Records; Orleck, *Storming Caesar's Palace*, 243.

42. Don Jackson to the CSA Board, Colonel H. F. Frank and Stephen Canon, August 21, 1967.

43. Erle Johnston, Memo to File, December 4, 1967, SCR ID # 2-156-0-69-1-1-1, MSSC Records, http://www.mdah.ms.gov/arrec/digital_archives/sovcom/result.php?image=images/png/cd07/048530.png&otherstuff=2|156|0|69|1|1|1|47830|#; Don Jackson to the CSA Board, Colonel H. F. Frank and Stephen Canon, August 21, 1967; "Charges Dropped Against Negro Sit In Group," *Jackson Daily News*, August 24, 1967.

44. "Donald Wilson Jackson, AKA Muhammad Kenyatta," SCR ID # 1-120-0-5-1-1-1, MSSC Records, http://www.mdah.ms.gov/arrec/digital_archives/sovcom/result.php?image=images/png/cd02/008895.png&otherstuff=1|120|0|5|1|1|1|8681|; Don Jackson, "New Politics," *Mississippi Newsletter*, September 22, 1967, SCR ID # 2-163-0-8-1-1-1, MSSC Records, http://www.mdah.ms.gov/arrec/digital_archives/sovcom/result.php?image=images/png/cd07/051649.png&otherstuff=2|163|0|8|1|1|1|50919|#.

45. Don Jackson, "Open Letter," *Hinds County FDP News* 1, no. 35 (September 8, 1967), SCR ID # 1-121-0-3-2-1-1, MSSC Records, http://www.mdah.ms.gov/arrec/digital_archives/sovcom/result.php?image=images/png/cd02/008909.png&otherstuff=1|121|0|3|2|1|1|8695|#; John Hunter Bear interview, July 2005, *Civil Rights Movement Veterans*, http://www.crmvet.org/nars/hunteri.htm.

46. Untitled Report, January 30, 1969, SCR ID # 6-65-0-28-1-1-1, MSSC Records, http://www.mdah.ms.gov/arrec/digital_archives/sovcom/result.php?image=images/png/cd07/049879.png&otherstuff=6|65|0|28|1|1|1|49164|#; Erle Johnston Jr., "Memorandum to File," March 1, 1968, SCR ID # 6-45-6-40-1-1-1, MSSC Records, http://www.mdah.ms.gov/arrec/digital_archives/sovcom/result.php?image=images/png/cd07/047776.png&otherstuff=6|45|6|40|1|1|1|47083|#; Untitled Report, February 13, 1969, SCR ID # 6-65-0-29-1-1-1, MSSC Records, http://www.mdah.ms.gov/arrec/digital_archives/sovcom/result.php?image=images/png/cd07/049880.png&otherstuff=6|65|0|29|1|1|1|49165|#; Jessica Gordon Nembhard, *Collective Courage: A History of African American Cooperative Economic Thought and Practice* (University Park: Pennsylvania State University Press, 2014), 197; Report, March 7, 1969, SCR ID # 6-65-0-31-1-1-1, MSSC Records, http://www.mdah.ms.gov/arrec/digital_archives/sovcom/result.php?image=images/png/cd07/049882.png&otherstuff=6|65|0|31|1|1|1|49167|#; Michel Marriott, "Muhammad Kenyatta, 47, Dies; Professor and Civil Rights Leader," *New York Times*, January 6, 1992.

47. J. Barry Vaughn, *Bishops, Bourbons, and Big Mules: A History of the Episcopal Church in Alabama* (Tuscaloosa: University of Alabama Press, 2013), 170; Muhammad Kenyatta, "Community Organizing, Client Involvement, and Poverty Law," *Monthly Review* (October 1983): 18–27.

CHAPTER FIVE: HELEN BASS WILLIAMS AND MISSISSIPPI ACTION FOR PROGRESS

1. Orleck, "Introduction," 18–22; for example, Bauman "Gender, Civil Rights Activism, and the War on Poverty in Los Angeles," in *The War on Poverty*, ed. Orleck and Hazirjian, 209–27.

2. James C. Cobb, *The Most Southern Place on Earth*, 272; Sanders, *A Chance for Change*, 170; Recordings and Transcripts of Conversations and Meetings, Lyndon B. Johnson and Roy Wilkins, 5 January 1964, Tape WH6601.03, Citation #9429, LBJL.

3. Winson Hudson and Constance Curry, *Mississippi Harmony: Memoirs of a Freedom Fighter* (New York: Palgrave Macmillan, 2002), 76; Payne, *I've Got the Light of Freedom*, 321; "Considerations underlying the development of the MFDP," 1964, Ella Baker Papers, FSDC, http://content.wisconsinhistory.org/cdm/ref/collection/p15932coll2/id/18105; Fannie Lou Hamer, "Testimony Before the Credentials Committee," August 22, 1964, *American Public Media*, http://americanradioworks.publicradio.org/features/sayitplain/flhamer.html; Walter Mondale, *The Good Fight: A Life in Liberal Politics* (New York: Simon and Schuster, 2010), 23.

4. Mondale, *The Good Fight*, 22–26; Jere Nash and Andy Taggart, *Mississippi Politics: The Struggle for Power, 1976–2008*, 2nd ed. (Jackson: University Press of Mississippi, 2009), 26; Aaron Henry, with Constance Curry, *Aaron Henry: The Fire Ever Burning* (Jackson: University Press of Mississippi, 2000), 186–97; Clayborne Carson, *In Struggle: SNCC and the Black Awakening of the 1960s*, new ed. (Cambridge, Harvard University Press, 1995), 126.

5. Morrison, *Aaron Henry of Mississippi*, 135; Interview with Robert Moses, May 19, 1986, *Eyes on the Prize: America's Civil Rights Years*, Henry Hampton Collection, Film and Media Archive, Washington University Libraries, http://digital.wustl.edu/e/eop/eopweb/mos0015.0875.073robertmoses.html; Fannie Lou Hamer, "I'm Sick and Tired of Being Sick and Tired," December 20, 1964, *Civil Rights Movement Veterans*, http://www.crmvet.org/

docs/flh64.htm; Kai Lee, *For Freedom's Sake*, 43; Payne, *I've Got the Light of Freedom*, 321–22; Wesley Hogan, "Grassroots Organizing in Mississippi That Changed National Politics," in *The Civil Rights Movement in Mississippi*, ed. Ownby, 7; John Lewis, with Michael D'Orso, *Walking with the Wind: A Memoir of the Movement* (New York: Simon and Schuster, 2015), 292. Kay Mills, *This Little Light of Mine: The Life of Fannie Lou Hamer* (New York: Dutton, 1993), 105–33.

6. Henry, *Aaron Henry*, 197–98; Carson, *In Struggle*, 127; Moye, *Let the People Decide*, 140; John Lewis, *Walking with the Wind*, 292; Eric R. Burner, *And Gently He Shall Lead Them: Robert Parris Moses and Civil Rights in Mississippi* (New York: New York University Press, 1995), 193.

7. Nash and Taggart, *Mississippi Politics*, 26; Mills, *This Little Light of Mine*, 131; Lyndon Johnson and Douglas Wynn, August 25, 1964, Conversation WH6408-38-5209, in *Lyndon B. Johnson: Civil Rights, Vietnam, and the War on Poverty*, ed. David G. Coleman, Kent B. Germany, Guian A. McKee, and Marc J. Selverstone (Charlottesville: University of Virginia Press, 2014), http://prde.upress.virginia.edu/conversations/4002896; Lyndon Johnson, Edward Clark, and Douglas Wynn, November 7, 1964, Conversation WH6411-12-6283-6284, in *Lyndon B. Johnson*, ed. Coleman, Germany, McKee, and Selverstone, http://prde.upress. virginia.edu/conversations/4005044/.

8. Lyndon Johnson and Jack Valenti, August 31, 1964, Conversation WH6408-43-5286, in *Lyndon B. Johnson*, ed. Coleman, Germany, McKee, and Selverstone, http://prde.upress. virginia.edu/conversations/4002901; Lyndon Johnson and Nicholas Katzenbach, August 31, 1964, Conversation WH6408-43-5294, in *Lyndon B. Johnson*, ed. Coleman, Germany, McKee, and Selverstone, http://prde.upress.virginia.edu/conversations/4002892; Lyndon Johnson and Roy Wilkins, November 12, 1964, Conversation WH6411-19-6348, in *Lyndon B. Johnson*, ed. Coleman, Germany, McKee, and Selverstone, http://prde.upress.virginia.edu/ conversations/4005052/.

9. Douglas Wynn to Harry McPherson, April 2, 1966, Folder Poverty (1966) [2 of 2], Box 14, Office Files of Harry McPherson, LBJL; Crespino, *In Search of Another Country*, 209–10; Greenberg, *The Devil Has Slippery Shoes*, 790; "Cooper Named Head of MAP Program," *Baptist Record*, October 27, 1966, Folder 1A, Box 76, Series 13, Subgroup 3, Cooper Papers; Payne, *I've Got the Light of Freedom*, 343; Newman, *Divine Agitators*, 37; James C. Cobb, *The Most Southern Place*, 272; Dittmer, *Local People*, 378; Morrison, *Aaron Henry of Mississippi*, 157–66. Six white and six African American board members were joined by six target area representatives. A number of the MAP board members were central in creating the Loyalist Democrats, who embodied this integrated but middle-class restructuring of the Mississippi Democratic Party. The Loyalist Democrats were seated at the 1968 convention over the Regular Democrats, led by Hodding Carter III, Aaron Henry, Charles Evers, and Patricia Derian. Nash and Taggart, *Mississippi Politics*, 30.

10. Mississippi Freedom Democrat Party, "Why Are We Here?" October 8, 1966, SCR ID #6-45-4-4-1-1-1, MSSC Records, http://mdah.state.ms.us/arrec/digital_archives/sovcom /result.php?image=/data/sov_commission/images/png/cd06/047013.png&otherstu ff=6|45|4|4|1|1|1|46325|; Dittmer, *Local People*, 378; Anne and Howard Romaine interview with Fannie Lou Hamer, 1966, *Anne Romaine Interviews*, FSDC, http://content.wisconsin

history.org/cdm/ref/collection/p15932co112/id/14003; Marvin Hoffman and John Mudd, "The New Plantation," *The Nation*, October 24, 1966, 411–15, and "Flyer 3," ca. October 1966, Box 2, Loose Materials, Carter Papers; Orley B. Caudill second interview with Claude Ramsay, April 30, 1981, COHCH, http://digilib.usm.edu/cdm/ref/collection/coh/id/9543.

11. Patricia Derian, P. Derian Report, January 26, 1967, Box 1, Folder 4, Derian Papers; J. Biggers, "Civil Rights Agitators Block Delta MAP Election," *Clarion Ledger*, January 24, 1967; S. Criss, "Militant Groups Delay Action for Leflore Poverty Program," *Commercial Appeal*, January 24, 1967; Morrison, *Aaron Henry of Mississippi*, 164; David C. Carter, *The Music Has Gone out of the Movement: Civil Rights and the Johnson Administration, 1965–1968* (Chapel Hill: University of North Carolina, 2009), 125–26.

12. Thomas J. Ward Jr., *Out in the Rural: A Mississippi Health Center and Its War on Poverty* (Oxford: Oxford University Press, 2017), xii; Daniel M. Cobb, "The War on Poverty in Mississippi and Oklahoma," in *The War on Poverty*, ed. Orleck and Hazirjian, 299.

13. "Shriver Comes Across," *New Republic*, January 7, 1967, 10, Box 2, Loose Materials, Carter Papers; Charles Bolton interview with Peter H. Stewart, August 20, 1997, COHCH, http://digilib.usm.edu/cdm/ref/collection/coh/id/16365; Betsy Nash interview with Pat Derian, December 17, 1991, John C. Stennis Oral History Project, Mississippi State University, Starkville, http://cdm16631.contentdm.oclc.org/cdm/ref/collection/jcs1/id/882.

14. John Ott to Walter Smith, May 17, 1967, Box 1, Loose Materials, Carter Papers.

15. E.g., Orleck, *Storming Caesar's Palace*; Premilla Nadasen, *Welfare Warriors: The Welfare Rights Movement in the United States* (New York: Routledge, 2005); Tiyi M. Morris illustrates the importance of black women in the Mississippi movement in *Womanpower Unlimited*.

16. "Henry Sees Racial Advance in New Antipoverty Group," *Commercial Appeal*, October 2, 1966; The twenty-five MAP counties: Hancock, Pearl River, Perry, Greene, Wayne, Clarke, Lauderdale, Scott, Neshoba, Lincoln, Franklin, Claiborne, Warren, Yazoo, Humphreys, Leflore, Yalobusha, Calhoun, Chickasaw, Union, Tippah, Itawamba, Prentiss, Tishomingo, and Alcorn.

17. Stan J. Hale, *Williamson County, Illinois, Sesquicentennial History* (Paducah, KY: Turner, 1993), 304; Mary O'Hara, "'Let It Fly': The Legacy of Helen Bass Williams" (PhD diss., Southern Illinois University, 2004); "Note," January 9, 1968, SCR ID #6-45-6-13-1-1-1, MSSC Records, http://mdah.state.ms.us/arrec/digital_archives/sovcom/result.php?image=/data/sov_commission/images/png/cd06/047709.png&otherstuff=6|45|6|13|1|1|1|47018|. Typical of the inaccuracies in the reports of Commission investigators Tom Scarborough and Leland Cole, it took them six months to establish, incorrectly, that Williams was from South Carolina. O'Hara, "'Let It Fly,'" 200; Jack E. Harper to Owen Cooper, June 26, 1967, Subgroup 3, Series 13, Box 76, Folder 5b, Cooper Papers.

18. Sanders, *A Chance for Change*, 85; Greenberg, *The Devil Has Slippery Shoes*, 181–91; O'Hara, "'Let It Fly,'" 175.

19. Orley B. Caudill interview with Erle Johnston, July 30, 1980, COHCH, http://digilib.usm.edu/cdm/ref/collection/coh/id/3986; Johnston, *Mississippi's Defiant Years*, 292.

20. Johnston, *Mississippi's Defiant Years*, 298; Kenneth Dean to Owen Cooper, August 28, 1967, Folder 8, Box 78, Series 13, Subgroup 3, Cooper Papers; Memo to File, June 16, 1967, SCR ID #6-45-5-35-1-1-1, MSSC Records, http://mdah.state.ms.us/arrec/digital_archives/

sovcom/result.php?image=/data/sov_commission/images/png/cd06/047438.png&otherst uff=6|45|5|35|1|1|1|46748|.

21. Kenneth Dean to Owen Cooper, August 28, 1967, Folder 8, Box 78, Series 13, Subgroup 3, Cooper Papers.

22. Memo to File, June 16, 1967, SCR ID #6-45-5-35-1-1-1, MSSC Records, http://mdah.state.ms.us/arrec/digital_archives/sovcom/result.php?image=/data/sov_commission/images/png/cd06/047438.png&otherstuff=6|45|5|35|1|1|1|46748|.

23. Memo to File, October 5, 1967, SCR ID #99-48-0-489-1-1-1, MSSC Records, http://mdah.state.ms.us/arrec/digital_archives/sovcom/result.php?image=/data/sov_commission/images/png/cd10/081217.png&otherstuff=99|48|0|489|1|1|1|80181|; Memo to File, October 2, 1967 SCR ID #99-48-0-488-1-1-1, MSSC Records.

24. Crosby, *A Little Taste of Freedom*, 207; Betsy Nash interview with Ken Dean, June 9, 1992, John C. Stennis Oral History Project, Mississippi State University, Starkville, http://cdm16631.contentdm.oclc.org/cdm/ref/collection/jcs1/id/881.

25. Crespino, *In Search of Another Country*, 143; J. Nash interview with Hodding Carter III, n.d., Nash and Taggart Collection, J. D. Williams Library Archives and Special Collections, University of Mississippi, Oxford.

26. Graham Lee Hales interview with Owen Cooper, December 11, 1972, COHCH, http://digilib.usm.edu/cdm/ref/collection/coh/id/1369.

27. Mississippi Industrial and Special Services, Inc., Charter, December 1967, Folder 10, Box 74, Series 12, Subgroup 2, Cooper Papers.

28. J. Nelson, "Mississippians Set Up Biracial Poverty Panel: Business Leaders Say They Are Tired of State's War with Federal Government," *Unknown Paper*, n.d.; Folder 10, Box 74, Series 12, Subgroup 2, Cooper Papers; Betsy Nash interview with Pat Derian, December 17, 1991, John C. Stennis Oral History Project, Mississippi State University, Starkville, http://cdm16631.contentdm.oclc.org/cdm/ref/collection/jcs1/id/882; Memo to File, October 17, 1967, SCR ID #99-48-0-484-1-1-1, MSSC Records, http://mdah.state.ms.us/arrec/digital_archives/sovcom/result.php?image=/data/sov_commission/images/png/cd10/081212.png&otherstuff=99|48|0|484|1|1|1|80176|; John Dean to Owen Cooper, January 29, 1968, Folder 8b, Box 76, Series 13, Subgroup 3, Cooper Papers.

29. Ashmore, *Carry It On*, 255; Clayson, *Freedom Is Not Enough*, 103; Michael K. Honey, *Going Down Jericho Road: The Memphis Strike, Martin Luther King's Last Campaign* (London: W. W. Norton, 2007), 11; Lee J. Alston and Joseph P. Ferrie, *Southern Paternalism and the American Welfare State: Economics, Politics, and Institutions in the South, 1865–1965* (Cambridge: Cambridge University Press, 1999), 140–41; Bruce Nicholas to MAP Board, January 26, 1968, SCR ID #6-45-6-58-1-1-1, MSSC Records, http://mdah.state.ms.us/arrec/digital_archives/sovcom/result.php?image=/data/sov_commission/images/png/cd07/047820.png&otherstuff=6|45|6|58|1|1|1|47125|.

30. Bruce Nicholas to MAP Board, January 26, 1968; Erle Johnston, Note to file, February 27, 1968, Folder 62, Box 4, Series 39, Stennis Papers; Memo to File, January 30, 1968, SCR ID #6-45-5-76-4-1-1, MSSC Records, http://mdah.state.ms.us/arrec/digital_archives/sovcom/result.php?image=/data/sov_commission/images/png/cd06/047554.png&otherstuff=6|45|5|76|2|1|1|46864|.

31. Memo to File, January 30, 1968, SCR ID #6-45-5-76-4-1-1, MSSC Records, http://mdah.state.ms.us/arrec/digital_archives/sovcom/result.php?image=/data/sov_commission/images/png/cd06/047554.png&otherstuff=6|45|5|76|2|1|1|46864|; "Two Charged in Greenwood Gun Incident," *Jackson Daily News*, March 5, 1965; Report on James Travis, November 15, 1967, Folder 62, Series 39, Box 4, Stennis Papers; David Highbaugh to Whom It May Concern, January 24, 1968, Folder 1b, Box 78, Series 13, Subgroup 3, Cooper Papers.

32. Owen Cooper to Helen Bass Williams, September 26, 1968, Folder 9a, Box 76, Series 13, Subgroup 3, Cooper Papers. DeCell later distanced himself from the commission, sponsoring legislation to abolish it in the 1970s because he felt it had "outlived its usefulness." Never "very effective," DeCell later claimed, but he believed it did serve a "useful purpose in being a focal point of fact gathering, information gathering, that sort of thing." Orley B. Caudill interview with Herman DeCell, June 9, 1977, COHCH, http://digilib.usm.edu/cdm/ref/collection/coh/id/1773; "Evidence (or Indication) of Race and Black Power Tactics Used by Mrs. Helen Bass Williams," n.d., Folder 62, Box 4, Series 39, Stennis Papers.

33. "Evidence (or Indication) of Race and Black Power Tactics Used by Mrs. Helen Bass Williams"; John D'Emilio and Estelle B. Freedman, *Intimate Matters: A History of Sexuality in America*, 2nd ed. (Chicago: University of Chicago Press, 1997), xvi.

34. O'Hara, "'Let It Fly,'" 192–93.

35. O'Hara, "'Let It Fly,'" 188–90.

36. Erle Johnston, Memo to File, January 30, 1968, SCR ID #99-48-0-182-1-1-1, MSSC Records, http://www.mdah.ms.gov/arrec/digital_archives/sovcom/result.php?image=images/png/cd10/080440.png&otherstuff=99|48|0|182|1|1|1|79407|#; Erle Johnston to Herman Glazier, January 23, 1968, and Erle Johnston to Governor John Bell Williams, January 22, 1968, Folder 62, Box 4, Series 39, Stennis Papers; Erle Johnston, Memo to File, February 27, 1968, SCR ID #99-48-0-188-1-1-1, MSSC Records, http://www.mdah.ms.gov/arrec/digital_archives/sovcom/result.php?image=images/png/cd10/080450.png&otherstuff=99|48|0|188|1|1|1|79417|#. Segregationist John Bell Williams had been a Democrat congressman since 1946, though he supported Strom Thurmond in 1948 and Barry Goldwater in 1964. His support for Goldwater meant he was stripped of his House seniority, but "had become a hero in Mississippi." Williams ran for governor in 1968, defeating moderates and future governors William Winter and Bill Waller in the primary, and Republican Rubel Phillips in the general election. Nash and Taggart, *Mississippi Politics*, 48.

37. Owen Cooper to board of directors, June 20, 1968, Box 1, Folder Hodding Carter III, Carter Papers; Helen Bass Williams to MAP Staff, September 3, 1968, SCR ID #6-45-6-67-1-1-1, MSSC Records, http://mdah.state.ms.us/arrec/digital_archives/sovcom/result.php?image=/data/sov_commission/images/png/cd07/047847.png&otherstuff=6|45|6|67|1|1|1|47152|; Johnston, Memo to File, August 27, 1968, SCR ID #99-48-0-491-1-1-1, MSSC Records, http://www.mdah.ms.gov/arrec/digital_archives/sovcom/result.php?image=images/png/cd10/081219.png&otherstuff=99|48|0|491|1|1|1|80183|#. Erle Johnston continued his intervention in MAP, claiming in a note to file on August 27 that "Aaron Henry was responsible for appointing Mrs. Helen Bass Williams as director" and that the Commission had "orally, through certain circles" suggested to OEO in Washington that Dr. Jacob Reddix would be a good replacement for Williams, though "no mention was made, however, that the suggestion originated with the Sovereignty Commission."

38. F. Bridges, "Civil Rights Leader Made Difference in Country and at Purdue," *Exponent*, February 16, 2009, http://www.purdueexponent.org/features/article_8ede15e0-2c09-56a5-b51c-38cdadc67f4e.html; Erle Johnston, Memo to File, March 5, 1968, SCR ID # 99-48-0-190-1-1-1, MSSC Records, http://www.mdah.ms.gov/arrec/digital_archives/sovcom/result.php?image=images/png/cd10/080452.png&otherstuff=99|48|0|190|1|1|1|79419|#.

39. "Purdue's Schleman Award Goes to Prof. Helen Bass Williams," *Indianapolis Recorder*, April 19, 1976, 14. Williams was also posthumously awarded Purdue's Title IX Distinguished Service Award.

40. Jacoway and Colburn, eds., *Southern Businessmen and Desegregation*.

CHAPTER SIX: MISSISSIPPI REPUBLICANS AND THE POLITICS OF POVERTY

1. Wilbur J. Cohen to Jim Jones, April 30, 1968, Folder WE9-1 6/16/67–5/31/68 EX, Box 45, WHCF GEN WE9 4/1/68–1/20/69 and EX WE9-1 11/22/63–1/20/69, LBJL; Richard M. Nixon, "Address Accepting the Presidential Nomination at the Republican National Convention in Miami Beach, Florida," August 8, 1968, in Peters and Woolley, *Papers of the President*, http://www.presidency.ucsb.edu/ws/?pid=25968; Robert Perrin, "Sic Transition Gloria OEO," 1970, Folder Published and Unpublished Articles 1970–1973, Box 1, Personal Papers of Robert Perrin, LBJL.

2. P. Pittman, "Mississippi Poverty Activities Tip-Off to OEO Downgrading," *Daily Journal (Tupelo)*, October 8, 1969, OEO, Vertical Files; Joan Hoff-Wilson, ed., *Papers of the Nixon White House, Part 7: President's Personal Files, 1969–1974* (Frederick, MD: University Publications of America, 1992), 7-173-0043; Press Release from US Department of Labor, April 11, 1969, Box 62, Folder Office Files: Job Corps Closures, Papers of Bertrand M. Harding, LBJL.

3. Lee Rainwater and William L. Yancey, *The Moynihan Report and the Politics of Controversy: A Trans-action Social Science and Public Policy Report* (Cambridge, MA: MIT Press, 1967); Daniel P. Moynihan, *Maximum Feasible Misunderstanding: Community Action in the War on Poverty*, (New York: Free Press, 1970); Nathan Glazer, *The Limits of Social Policy*, (Cambridge, MA: Harvard University Press, 1988), 5; Kenneth O'Reilly, *Nixon's Piano: Presidents and Racial Politics from Washington to Clinton* (New York: Free Press, 1995), 291, quotes journalist Chuck Stone calling Moynihan the "apostle of 'benign neglect' for blacks."

4. Andrew Cockburn, *Rumsfeld: An American Disaster* (London: Verso Books, 2007), 16; Korstad and Leloudis, *To Right These Wrongs*, 338; H. R. Haldeman to Mr. Moynihan, Mr. Flanigan, and Secretary Finch, February 17, 1969, Box 1, Folder EX FG6-7 OEO Begin-6/25/69, WHCF FG6-7 OEO, Richard M. Nixon Presidential Library, Yorba Linda, California (hereafter cited as Nixon Library).

5. Joan Hoff-Wilson, ed., *Papers of the Nixon White House, Part 5: H. R. Haldeman, Notes of White House Meetings, 1969–1973* (Frederick, MD: University Publications of America, 1992), 5-2-18; Perrin, "Sic Transition Gloria"; Robert J. Golten to Bertrand M. Harding, April 11, 1969, Box 62, Folder Office Files: Job Corps Closures, Papers of Bertrand M. Harding, LBJL.

6. Joan Hoff, *Nixon Reconsidered* (New York: Basic Books, 1994), 62; Hoff-Wilson, *Papers of the Nixon White House Part 5*, 5-1-93; Daniel P. Moynihan, "Memorandum for the Record,"

February 18, 1969, Box 1, Folder EX FG6-7 OEO Begin- 6/25/69, WHCF FG6-7 OEO, Nixon Library.

7. Richard M. Nixon "Memorandum to all cabinet members," February 19, 1969, Box 1, Folder EX FG6-7 OEO Begin- 6/25/69, WHCF FG6-7 OEO, Nixon Library.

8. John Ehrlichman to Pat Moynihan, Jim Keogh, Dr. Burns, and Chuck Stuart, March 18, 1969, Box 1, Folder EX FG6-7 OEO Begin- 6/25/69, WHCF FG6-7 OEO, Nixon Library.

9. Geoffrey Kabaservice, *Rule and Ruin: The Downfall of Moderation and the Destruction of the Republican Party, From Eisenhower to the Tea Party* (Oxford: Oxford University Press, 2012), 192–93; Lee Huebner to James Keogh, March 25, 1969, Box 1, Folder EX FG6-7 OEO Begin- 6/25/69, WHCF FG6-7 OEO, Nixon Library; Arthur F. Burns to Richard M. Nixon, March 21, 1969, Box 1, Folder EX FG6-7 OEO Begin- 6/25/69, WHCF FG6-7 OEO, Nixon Library.

10. For example, see Phelps, *A People's War on Poverty*, 150–60; O'Reilly, *Nixon's Piano*, 299; Hoff-Wilson, *Nixon White House Part 5*, 5-1-93, 6A-10-44.

11. Kevin P. Phillips, *The Emerging Republican Majority* (New York: Arlington House, 1969); Kim Phillips-Fein, "Conservatism: A State of the Field," *Journal of American History* 98, no. 3 (2011): 726.

12. Joseph Crespino, "Mississippi as Metaphor: Civil Rights, the South, and the Nation in the Historical Imagination," in *The Myth of Southern Exceptionalism*, ed. Joseph Crespino and Matthew D. Lassiter, (New York: Oxford University Press, 2010) 107–8; Lowndes, *From the New Deal to the New Right*, 5; Donald T. Critchlow, *The Conservative Ascendancy: How the GOP Right Made Political History* (Cambridge, MA: Harvard University Press, 2007), 77–78.

13. Crespino, "Mississippi as Metaphor," 107; Lassiter, *Silent Majority*, 3; Sean P. Cunningham, *American Politics in the Postwar Sunbelt*, 153; Kruse, *White Flight*.

14. Jonathan M. Schoenwald, *A Time for Choosing: The Rise of Modern American Conservatism* (Oxford: Oxford University Press, 2001), 10; Kim Phillips-Fein, *Invisible Hands: The Making of the Conservative Movement from the New Deal to Reagan* (London: W. W. Norton, 2009), xii; McGirr, *Suburban Warriors*; Nickerson, *Mothers of Conservatism*; Dochuk, *From Bible Belt to Sunbelt*; Steven P. Miller, *Billy Graham and the Rise of the Republican South* (Philadelphia: University of Pennsylvania Press, 2009); Michelle M. Nickerson, and Darren Dochuk, "Introduction," in *Sunbelt Rising: The Politics of Space, Place, and Region*, ed. Nickerson and Dochuk (Philadelphia: University of Pennsylvania Press, 2011), 19; Joseph Crespino, "Strom Thurmond's Sunbelt: Rethinking Regional Politics and the Rise of the Right" in *Sunbelt Rising*, ed. Nickerson and Dochuk, 58–81; Sean P. Cunningham, *American Politics in the Postwar Sunbelt*, 53.

15. Lassiter, *Silent Majority*, 227; Kruse, *White Flight*, 6.

16. McGirr, *Suburban Warriors*, 12.

17. Crespino, *In Search of Another Country*, 7, 12, 276–77; Danielson, *After Freedom Summer*, 5.

18. Crespino, *In Search of Another Country*, 8, 271; Silver, *Mississippi: The Closed Society*; James C. Cobb, *The Most Southern Place on Earth*; Hall, "The Long Civil Rights Movement and the Political Uses of the Past," 1238; Erle Black and Merle Black, *The Rise of Southern Republicans* (Cambridge, MA: Harvard University Press, 2002), 119, 136; Kruse, *White Flight*,

7; George Lewis, *Massive Resistance: The White Response to the Civil Rights Movement* (London: Hodder Arnold, 2006), 187.

19. Kruse, *White Flight*, 14; e.g., see Jason Morgan Ward, *Defending White Democracy*; Crespino, *In Search of Another Country*, 4; Danielson, *After Freedom Summer*, 3; Luckett, *Joe T. Patterson and the White South's Dilemma*.

20. Lassiter, *Silent Majority*, 1.

21. Critchlow, *The Conservative Ascendancy*, 4–5; Numan V. Bartley and Hugh Davis Graham, *Southern Politics and the Second Reconstruction* (Baltimore: Johns Hopkins University Press, 1975), 86, 95.

22. Schoenwald, *A Time for Choosing*, 164; Bartley and Graham, *Southern Politics*, 82; Danielson, *After Freedom Summer*, 36; Crespino, *In Search of Another Country*, 86–87.

23. Charles Noble, "From Neoconservative to New Right: American Conservatives and the Welfare State," in *Confronting the New Conservatism: The Rise of the Right in America*, ed. Michael J. Thompson (New York: New York University Press, 2007), 111; Clayson, *Freedom Is Not Enough*, 24; Michael Kazin, *The Populist Persuasion: An American History*. Rev. ed. (London: Cornell University Press, 1998), 246; Sean P. Cunningham, *American Politics in the Postwar Sunbelt*, 118.

24. Unsigned handwritten note, ca. October 1965, Series VI, Box F-6, Folder MRP-OF 1965/66 Coahoma County, Mississippi Republican Party Records, Mitchell Memorial Library, Special Collections, Mississippi State University, Starkville (hereafter cited as MRP Records).

25. Community Profile of Lauderdale County, Box 49, OEO Information Center 1966, Office Files of Fred Panzer, LBJL; Donald Paul Williams interview with Charles Lemuel Young Sr., November 14, 1998, Civil Rights Documentation Project, Tougaloo College, Jackson, http://www.usm.edu/crdp/html/transcripts/young_charles-i.shtml.

26. John Perkins, "Proposed By-Laws Weighed for Head Start Program," *Meridian Star*, August 31, 1966; Handwritten note "LEAP," January 31, 1973, Series 1, Box 4, Folder 30, Office Files of Fred Panzer, LBJL.

27. Senate Resolution 56: to commend Representative Young, Regular Session, March 29, 2006, Mississippi Legislature, http://billstatus.ls.state.ms.us/documents/2006/pdf/SR/SR0056IN.pdf; Henry Damon to Don Rumsfeld, 14 August 1970, Series I, Box 1, Folder 22 General Political 1970, Carmichael Papers; Georgia E. Frye, "AES Ltd. Celebrates 50 years," *Franklin County Times*, June 16, 2003. Damon began with a 1960 attempt to become mayor of Meridian, and he continued to be active in the Republican Party into the 1990s. Hugh Lassiter, Composite Evaluation Report of LEAP, Inc., July 1, 1970, Box 19, Mississippi: LEAP, FG381; Henry Eugene Damon to Don Rumsfeld, August 14, 1970, Series VII, Box G-5, Folder PATA/FA OEO 1970, MRP Records.

28. Unsigned handwritten note, ca. October 1965, Series VI, Box F-6, Folder MRP-OF 1965/66 Coahoma County, MRP Records.

29. Henry Damon to Don Rumsfeld, August 14, 1970, Series I, Box 1, Folder 22, Carmichael Papers.

30. "Help Fight the War on Poverty" flyer, ca. 1965–66, Series VI, Box F-6, Folder MRP-OF 1965/66 Forrest County, MRP Records; Alex Goodall, "Two Concepts of Un-Americanism,"

Journal of American Studies 47, no. 4 (2013): 925; McGirr, *Suburban Warriors*, 180; McRae, *Mothers of Massive Resistance*, 155.

31. McGirr, *Suburban Warriors*; Catherine E. Rymph, *Republican Women: Feminism and Conservatism from Suffrage through the Rise of the New Right* (Chapel Hill: University of North Carolina Press, 2006); Nickerson, *Mothers of Conservatism*, xiii; McRae, *Mothers of Massive Resistance*, 75, 158–59.

32. Maye Donaldson to Clarke Reed, September 20, 1969, Series VII, Box G-4, Folder PATA/FA OEO (March–August) 1969–1970, MRP Records.

33. Maye Donaldson to Clarke Reed, February 1970, Series VII, Box G-4, Folder PATA/FA OEO (March–August) 1969–1970, MRP Records.

34. *Report of the National Advisory Commission on Civil Disorders* (New York: US Government Printing Office, 1968), 62; Report of unexpended federal funds, August 28, 1968, John Jones McCall to Bob Williamson, November 14, 1968, and Statement of CAP grant, February 2, 1968, Box 1, CAP—Central Mississippi, Inc., RG381.

35. Nash and Taggart, *Mississippi Politics*, 26; Korstad and Leloudis, *To Right These Wrongs*, 347–49; Press release: "Reorganization of the Office of Economic Opportunity," August 11, 1969, Series VII, Box G-5, Folder PATA/FA OEO March–August 1969, MRP Records; Crespino, *In Search of Another Country*, 222–26; W. T. Wilkins to Roy Batchelor, May 14, 1970, Series VII, Box G-5, Folder PATA/FA OEO 1970, MRP Records.

36. Clarke Reed to Don Rumsfeld, April 28, 1969, and Mayor Jeppie Barbour to Clarke Reed, July 8, 1969, Series VII, Box G-4, Folder PATA/FA OEO (March–August) 1969–1970, MRP Records.

37. Orleck, "Conclusion," in *The War on Poverty*, ed. Orleck and Hazirjian, 438–39; Perrin, "Sic Transition Gloria": Donald Rumsfeld to John D. Ehrlichman, "Actions Taken at OEO—May 26 to July 7, 1969," ca. July 1969, The Rumsfeld Papers, http://library.rumsfeld.com/doclib/sp/583/To%20John%20Ehrlichman%20re%20Actions%20Taken%20at%20OEO%20-%20May%2026%20to%20July%207%201969.pdf.

38. *Report of the National Advisory Commission on Civil Disorders*, 62.

39. William Bozman to OEO Regional Directors, "Draft Implementation of the Green Amendment," January 9, 1968, Folder Response to 1967 Legislation, Box 18, Papers of Alfred H. Corbett, LBJL; Joseph B. Brunini to STAR Board of Directors, January 12, 1971, Folder 165, Box 8, Derian Papers; Mark I. Gelfand, Robert Lester, and Martin Paul Schipper, eds., *The War on Poverty, 1964–1968, Part 1* (Frederick, MD: University Publications of America, 1986), Reel 13, fr.0778–0779.

40. Roland T. Winel to Cornelius Turner, October 21, 1970, Folder 2, Box 2227, MS AFL-CIO; Statement of Owen Brooks before the NAACP Hearing, December 7, 1970, Folder STAR Controversy, Box 37, MCHR Records.

41. Roland T. Winel to Cornelius Turner, October 21, 1970; Carol M. Khosrovi to John C. Stennis, May 13, 1970, Folder 25, Box 4, Series 1, Stennis Papers.

42. "OEO Instruction: Revised OEO Income Poverty Guidelines," January 30, 1970, Folder 6, Box 2226, MS AFL-CIO; Donald Rumsfeld to John D. Ehrlichman, "Actions Taken at OEO—May 26 to July 7, 1969," ca. July 1969, *The Rumsfeld Papers*, http://library.rumsfeld.com/doclib/sp/583/To%20John%20Ehrlichman%20re%20Actions%20Taken%20at%20OEO%20-%20May%2026%20to%20July%207%201969.pdf.

43. Clarke Reed to Key Leaders, Internal Republican Party Memo, March 24, 1971, and attached article by Frank Carlucci, February 12, 1971, Folder PATA/FA OEO 1971, Box G-5, Series VII, MRP Records.

44. Anthony J. Badger, *New Deal / New South: An Anthony J. Badger Reader* (Fayetteville: University of Arkansas Press, 2007), 170, 174–75; Danielson, *After Freedom Summer*, 84; Dan T. Carter, *The Politics of Rage*, 474.

45. Steve Reed to John C. Stennis, July 26, 1969, Folder 23, Box 4, Series 1, Stennis Papers; John C. Stennis to Steve Reed, August 14, 1969, Folder 23, Box 4, Series 1, Stennis Papers; Charles Dunagin, "Area's Anti-Poverty Agency Is Under Fire," *McComb Enterprise-Journal*, n.d., Box 6, Folder CAP-Southwest Mississippi, RG381.

46. "Dr. Ray Lee in House Race," *Eagle: The Official Publication of the Mississippi Republican Party* 8, no. 1 (January 1970).

47. "Poverty Program helping boycott activities in SW Mississippi," *Meridian Star*, ca. December 1969, File Series 3, Subseries 4, Box 38, Folder: Mississippi OEO, Eastland Collection.

48. Ray Lee to Don Rumsfeld, November 5, 1969, Series VII, Box G-5, Folder PATA/FA OEO Regional Organization, 1969, MRP Records; "Poverty Program helping boycott activities in SW Mississippi," *Meridian Star*, ca. December 1969.

49. For example, Bryan Johnson to Senator James O. Eastland, ca. November 1969, File Series 3, Subseries 4, Box 38, Folder: Mississippi OEO, Eastland Collection.

50. Quadagno, *The Color of Welfare*, 190.

CHAPTER SEVEN: STAR, THE AFL-CIO, AND THE DIOCESE OF NATCHEZ-JACKSON

1. C. L. Stahler to Bishop Joseph B. Brunini, November 26, 1968, Folder STAR, Inc., 1966–1973, File 15, Brunini Papers; "STAR is back in operation in Greenwood," *Clarion Ledger*, February 2, 1968.

2. Bolton, *The Hardest Deal of All*, 164; Luckett, *Joe T. Patterson and the White South's Dilemma*, 199–200; *Alexander vs. Holmes County Board of Education*, (1969).

3. Teena Freeman Horn, "The Experiment: The 1970–1971 Academic Year and Other Pre-Murrah Experiences," in *Lines Were Drawn: Remembering Court-Ordered Integration at a Mississippi High School*, ed. Teena F. Horn, Alan Huffman, and John Griffin Jones (Jackson: University Press of Mississippi, 2016), 111–33; Crespino, *In Search of Another Country*, 4, 186–90, 240–48; Luckett, *Joe T. Patterson and the White South's Dilemma*, 187–88; *Coffey vs. State Educational Finance Commission* (1969).

4. McRae, *Mothers of Massive Resistance*, 10.

5. J. Carr, "STAR Hits the Widening Gap Caused by High Unemployment," *Delta Democrat Times*, April 9, 1967; Namorato, *The Catholic Church in Mississippi*, 85; Quadagno, *The Color of Welfare*, 42.

6. Older Americans in Rural Areas: Hearings before the Special Committee on Aging, United State Senate, 91st Congress, 1st Session, Part 5: Greenwood, Mississippi, October 9, 1969, http://www.aging.senate.gov/imo/media/doc/publications/1091969.pdf; John Hamner to General McDonnell, August 23, 1971, Folder 42, Box 4, Series 1, Stennis Papers; Joseph B.

Brunini to John C. Stennis, May 25, 1967, and John C. Stennis to Joseph B. Brunini, June 20, 1967, Folder 18, Box 4, Series 1, Stennis Papers.

7. Nathaniel Machesky to Joseph B. Brunini, August 23, 1971, Folder STAR, Inc., 1966–1973, File 15, Brunini Papers; W. J. Kelley, "Mississippi's STAR program," *Divine Word Messenger*, July–August 1967, Box 2225, Folder 6, MS AFL-CIO; Cornelius Turner to Roland T. Winel, August 5, 1970, Folder 9, Box 2226, MS AFL-CIO. Stennis and Ed Brunini attended law school together.

8. Richard Polk testimony, transcript of the NAACP Hearing into STAR, 19; "Addenda number two to CAP pre-review checklist from Hinds county LAC from Charles Horwitz: Chairman, Hinds LAC," n.d., Folder 166, Box 8, Derian Papers.

9. Richard Polk testimony, transcript of the NAACP Hearing into STAR, 19.

10. Joseph B. Brunini to Elliott Strum, January 5, 1971, Folder STAR, Inc., 1966–1973, File 15, Brunini Papers; Father George Broussard testimony, 49, and Richard Polk testimony, 34, Transcript of the NAACP Hearing into STAR, December 7, 1970; Richard Polk to Roland T. Winel, November 17, 1970, Box 8, Folder 165, Derian Papers.

11. Joseph B. Brunini to Aaron Henry, December 4, 1970, Folder STAR, Inc., 1966–1973 File 15, Brunini Papers.

12. Michael Gillette interview I with Jack T. Conway, August 13, 1980, Oral History Interviews, LBJL; Ashmore, *Carry It On*, 68; "Labor's Role in the War on Poverty . . . an AFL-CIO Guide," ca. 1965, Box 4, Folder 12, Papers of Victoria Gray Adams, McCain Library and Archives Special Collections, University of Southern Mississippi, Hattiesburg. Michael Honey in *Going Down Jericho Road* described the entrance of maximum feasible participation into Memphis's tense environment, 231–32.

13. James C. Cobb, *The Most Southern Place on Earth*, 269–71; Dittmer, *Local People*, 364–66; "Mississippi Freedom Labor Union," n.d., Folder 2, Box 4, Miller Collection, https://digitalcollections.usm.edu/uncategorized/digitalFile_0a251b12-5c93-46ae-82a6-4cdc5cc6a544/; Mississippi Freedom Labor Union Pledge, ca. 1965, *Civil Rights Movement Veterans*, http://www.crmvet.org/docs/flu_pledge.pdf.

14. Resume of Jessie Epps, February 18, 1967, Folder 7, Box 2132, MS AFL-CIO; Betsy Nash interview with Ken Dean, June 9, 1992, John C. Stennis Oral History Project, Mississippi State University, Starkville, http://cdm16631.contentdm.oclc.org/cdm/ref/collection/jcs1/id/881; "2 Florida Poverty Programs Blasted for Union Activity," *Miami Herald*, May 29, 1967, Folder 5a, Box 76, Cooper Papers; Joseph Califano to Lyndon B. Johnson, October 12, 1968, and attached by Victor Riesel, "Inside Labor: Bayonets on the Streets?," September 27, 1968, Folder WE9 [1 of 2], Confidential File WE/MC, Box 98, LBJL; Jill Quadagno, "Social Movements and State Transformation: Labor Unions and Racial Conflict in the War on Poverty," *American Sociological Review* 57, no. 5 (1992): 616; Orley B. Caudill second interview with Claude Ramsay, April 30, 1981, COHCH, http://digilib.usm.edu/cdm/ref/collection/coh/id/9543.

15. "The Ku Klux Klan—1965," in *Facts*, 16, No. 3, May 1965, Box 1, Folder 10, KKK Collection; Anonymous postcard to Claude Ramsay, n.d., Box 2132, Folder 1, MS AFL-CIO; Alan Draper, *Conflict of Interests: Organized Labor and the Civil Rights Movement in the South, 1954–1968* (Ithaca, NY: ILR Press, 1994), 141, 146.

16. Draper, *Conflict of Interests*, 3; Orley B. Caudill, "Abstract" from his interviews with Claude Ramsay, May 7, 1981, COHCH, http://digilib.usm.edu/cdm/ref/collection/coh/id/9543; Restricted Sovereignty Commission Report, April 4, 1967, Folder 2, Box 149, Johnson Family Papers; Orley B. Caudill second interview with Claude Ramsay, April 30, 1981.

17. Claude Ramsay to Ransom P. Jones III, January 15, 1968, Folder 2, Box 2225, MS AFL-CIO; "One Third of Population Is Illiterate, Is Statement," *Times-Picayune*, January 29, 1967; "Union Urges Compulsory Education," *Clarion Ledger*, June 22, 1967.

18. Charles H. Walters to Claude Ramsay, October 25, 1965, and Claude Ramsay to Charles H. Walters, October 28, 1965, Box 2132, Folder 1, MS AFL-CIO; Owen Brooks statement, transcript of the NAACP hearing into STAR, December 7, 1970, Box 37, Folder STAR Controversy, MCHR Records; Orley B. Caudill second interview with Claude Ramsay, April 30, 1981; John Crockett to Claude Ramsay, October 19, 1970, Box 2227, Folder 2, MS AFL-CIO; Polk to Winel, November 17, 1970.

19. Don Miller statement, transcript of the NAACP hearing into STAR, December 7, 1970; Jane D. Sample statement, 115–16, 121, transcript of the NAACP hearing into STAR, December 7, 1970.

20. Draper, *Conflict of Interests*, 122–60; Mark Newman, "The Mississippi Freedom Labor Union," in *Poverty and Progress in the US South since 1920*, ed. Suzanne W. Jones and Mark Newman (Amsterdam: VU University Press, 2006), 140.

21. Orley B. Caudill second interview with Claude Ramsay, April 30, 1981.

22. J. Carr, "STAR Hits the Widening Gap Caused by High Unemployment," *Delta Democrat Times*, April 9, 1967; Judy Carlile to W. T. Bush, September 23, 1966, Folder 12, Box 2224, MS AFL-CIO.

23. "STAR Program Receives $2 Million in Refunds," *Clarion Ledger*, December 18, 1970, Box 37, Folder STAR Controversy, MCHR Records.

24. Transcript of the NAACP Hearing into STAR, 2. Community Education Extension was the successor organization to the Child Development Group of Mississippi; Transcript of the NAACP Hearing into STAR; Polk to Winel, November 17, 1970.

25. Polk to Winel, November 17, 1970.

26. Polk to Winel, November 17, 1970; Dittmer, *Local People*, 376; "STAR Program Receives $2 Million in Refunds," *Clarion Ledger*, December 18, 1970.

27. "Findings and Recommendations of NAACP Public Hearing Panel on STAR Inc.," December 9, 1970, Box 8, Folder 165, Derian Papers; Cornelius Turner statement, December 14, 1970, STAR, Inc., Correspondence February 20, 1969–May 1, 1973, Brunini Papers; Gerald F. Davis to Jane D. Sample, Geraldine Kelly, and Robert Coleman, January 26, 1971; Resolution of the STAR Executive Committee, December 19, 1970, Box 2227, Folder 3, MS AFL-CIO.

28. Cornelius Turner to STAR Board, February 25, 1971, Folder STAR, Inc., 1966–1973, File 15, Brunini Papers; Aaron Henry to Gerald F. Davis, February 17, 1971, Folder STAR, Inc., 1966-1973, File 15, Brunini Papers.

29. W. Webb Burke to Clovis Williams, March 4, 1971, SCR ID #1-117-0-12-1-1-1, MSSC Records, http://mdah.state.ms.us/arrec/digital_archives/sovcom/result.php?image=/data/sov_commission/images/png/cd02/008820.png&otherstuff=1|117|0|12|1|1|1|8606|; SCR ID # 2-157-2-59-1-1-1; Alfred H. Rhodes, Jr., to Msgr. Bernard Law, July 6, 1972, STAR, Inc.,

Correspondence February 20, 1969–May 1, 1973, Brunini Papers; Alfred H. Rhodes, Jr., to Lee G. Sutton, May 22, 1972, STAR, Inc., Correspondence February 20, 1969–May 1, 1973, Brunini Papers; W. Webb Burke to Herman Glazier, "Addendum to April 21, 1970 Memorandum," April 21, 1970, SCR ID # 2-46-0-102-2-1-1, MSSC Records, http://mdah.state.ms.us/arrec/digital_archives/sovcom/result.php?image=/data/sov_commission/images/png/cd02/011263.png&otherstuff=2|46|0|102|2|1|1|11030|.

30. Roland T. Winel to Bruce Fausner, January 14, 1970, Box 7, Folder CAP–STAR Inc., RG381; Joseph B. Brunini to Roy Batchelor, 11 August 1971, Folder 42, Box 4, Series 1, Stennis Papers.

31. Thomas J. Healy interview with Sarah H. Johnson, September 10, 1978, COHCH, http://digilib.usm.edu/cdm/ref/collection/coh/id/15356.

32. Richard Polk statement, transcript of NAACP hearing into STAR, December 7, 1970, Folder 166, Box 8, Derian Papers.

33. "Addenda number two to CAP pre-review checklist from Hinds county LAC from Charles Horwitz: Chairman, Hinds LAC," n.d., Folder 166, Box 8, Derian Papers.

34. "Transcript of the Proceedings Hearing Before the Honorable Hamah King, Hearing Examiner: Non-Refunding Hearing in the Matter of STAR, Inc.," August 31, 1971, Folder 167, Box 8, Derian Papers.

35. Joseph B. Brunini to Roy Batchelor, August 11, 1971, Russell C. Davis to John C. Stennis, August 13, 1971, Joseph B. Brunini to John C. Stennis, August 16, 1971, Series 1, Box 4, Folder 42, Stennis Papers; Joseph B. Brunini to James O. Eastland, August 16, 1971, Folder Mississippi OEO, Box 38, Subseries 4, File Series 3, Eastland Collection; Michael B. Smith to Russell C. Davis, September 3, 1971, WHCF, FG6-7 OEO, Box 2, Folder EX FG6-7 OEO 6/29/71–3/20/72, Nixon Library.

36. John C. Stennis to Joseph B. Brunini, August 18, 1971, Folder STAR, Inc., 1966–1973, File 15, Brunini Papers; John Hamner to General McDonnell, August 23, 1971, Folder 42, Box 4, Series 1, Stennis Papers; "Transcript of the Proceedings Hearing Before the Honorable Hamah King," August 31, 1971.

37. "Transcript of the Proceedings Hearing Before the Honorable Hamah King," August 31, 1971.

38. "Decision on STAR Changed by OEO," *Unknown Paper*, (n.d.), Folder STAR, Inc., 1966–1973, File 15, Brunini Papers.

39. "OEO Ponders STAR Cut Off," *Delta Democrat Times*, September 1, 1971, Folder STAR Controversy, Box 37, MCHR Records.

40. B. Kovach, "Judge Halts Move to Disband OEO," *New York Times*, April 12, 1973, 1, 19; William "Sonny" Walker to Donna Myhre, September 21, 1972, Folder Mississippi OEO, Box 38, Subseries 4, File Series 3, Eastland Collection; Donna Myhre to William Sonny Walker, April 10, 1973, STAR, Inc., Correspondence February 20, 1969–May 1, 1973, Brunini Papers.

CHAPTER EIGHT: THE DEMISE OF THE WAR ON POVERTY

1. E.g., Ashmore, *Carry It On*, 278–79; Dean J. Kotlowski, *Nixon's Civil Rights: Politics, Principle, and Policy* (Cambridge, MA: Harvard University Press, 2001), 6; Clayson, *Freedom*

Is Not Enough, 141; Kevin L. Yuill, *Richard Nixon and the Rise of Affirmative Action: The Pursuit of Racial Equality in an Era of Limits* (Lanham, MD: Rowman and Littlefield), 105.

2. Richard M. Nixon to Clifford Hardin, Maurice H. Stans, Robert H. Finch, George W. Romney, George P. Schultz, John A. Volpe, John N. Mitchell, Bertrand Harding, Hilary J. Sandoval Jr., and Nils Boe, March 27, 1969, Box 1, Folder EX FG6-7 OEO Begin- 6/25/69, WHCF FG6-7 OEO, Nixon Library.

3. Speech of William D. Ford at the National CAP Directors Meeting in Chicago, June 10, 1971, Box 2261, Folder General Correspondence 1971, Community Development Files.

4. Barbara Whitaker to Dean Miller, March 11, 1970, and attached Evaluation Report of Hinds County Project Head Start by John Mouton and Weston Hare, Folder 53, Box 3, Horwitz Papers.

5. William T. Wilkins to Clarke Reed, February 10, 1971, and attached letter from Barbara Whitaker to Jimmy Herron, Series VII, Box G-4, Folder PAT DHEW—Head Start Programs, MRP Records; Emma Folwell, "The Legacy of the Child Development Group: White Opposition to Head Start in Mississippi, 1965–1972," *Journal of Mississippi History* 76, no. 1 (2014): 43–68.

6. Daniel M. Cobb, "The War on Poverty in Mississippi and Oklahoma," 401–2; Minutes of CSA Board of Directors Meeting, February 22, 1971, Folder Correspondence, Box 2259, Community Development Files.

7. William Sonny Walker to community action board chairmen, January 29, 1973, and attached "Summary of Provisions for OEO Programs in the President's FY1974 Budget," STAR, Inc., Correspondence, February 20, 1969–May 1, 1973, Brunini Papers; Barbara Whitaker to Marvin Hogan, October 29, 1971, Folder HEW Correspondence 1971, Box 2261, Community Development Files; Benjamin H. Bradley to Providers of Head Start Facilities, n.d., Folder Head Start Correspondence 1971, Box 2261, Community Development Files.

8. Alfred H. Rhodes Jr. to Lee G. Sutton, May 22, 1972, STAR, Inc., Correspondence February 20, 1969–May 1, 1973, Brunini Papers; O'Reilly, *Nixon's Piano*, 313–15; Patrick J. Buchanan recommending Nixon telephones Howard Phillips, March 1, 1973, Box 2, Folder EX FG6-7 OEO 1/1/73–4/30/73, WHCF FG6-7 OEO, Nixon Library; Tom Dowling, "Howie at the Helm: A Scuttling Lesson," *Evening Star*, March 1, 1973.

9. Korstad and Leloudis, *To Right these Wrongs*, 348; Gareth Davies, *From Opportunity to Entitlement: The Transformation and Decline of Great Society Liberalism* (Lawrence: University Press of Kansas, 1996), 235.

10. Sara Diamond, *Roads to Dominion: Right-Wing Movements and Political Power in the United States* (New York: Guilford Press, 1995), 116; Chip Berlet, "The New Political Right in the United States: Reaction, Rollback, and Resentment," in *Confronting the New Conservatism: The Rise of the Right in America*, ed. Michael J. Thompson (New York: New York University Press, 2007), 82.

11. R. Reed, "Mississippi Antipoverty Group Urges Nixon to Release Funds," *New York Times*, May 3, 1973; Joe Hemingway to Howard A. Bount, June 29, 1973, Box 2264, Folder South-Eastern Association of Community Action Agencies, Community Development Files; Leighton Sattler to John C. Stennis, January 9, 1974, Folder 32, Box 4, Series 1, Stennis Papers; Edgar S. Cahn and Jean C. Cahn, "The War on Poverty: A Civilian Perspective," *Yale Law Review* 73, no. 8 (July 1964): 1317–52; Robert F. Clark, *The War on Poverty: History*,

Selected Programs, and Ongoing Impact (Lanham, MD: University Press of America, 2002), 177; Earl Johnson Jr. wrote about his experience of Legal Services in *Justice and Reform: The Formative Years of the American Legal Services Program*, 2nd ed. (New Brunswick: Transaction Books, 1978).

12. Crespino, *In Search of Another Country*, 225; Kris Shepard, *Rationing Justice: Poverty Lawyers and Poor People in the Deep South* (Baton Rouge: Louisiana State University Press, 2007), 63–64; Governor Reagan vetoed the program a number of times, only to have the veto overridden by Shriver: "Governor Reagan Q&A," n.d., Folder Research File, Health and Welfare, OEO—Calif. Rural Legal Assistance, 1/2, Box GO 185, Governor's Office Files, Gubernatorial Papers 1966–1975, Ronald Reagan Presidential Library, Simi Valley, California; Richard M. Pious, "Advocates for the Poor: Legal Services in the War on Poverty" (PhD diss., Columbia University, 1976), 180–260.

13. Samuel F. Yette, "Draft Guideline on Civil Rights Cases," December 15, 1966, Folder Office of Civil Rights, Box 60, Papers of Bertrand M. Harding, LBJL; Hoff, *Nixon Reconsidered*, 62–63; Danielson, *After Freedom Summer*, 3.

14. Clark, *War on Poverty*, 179; Gillette, *Launching the War on Poverty*, 282; Shepard, *Rationing Justice*, 70.

15. Harry McPherson to Marvin Watson, September 28, 1966, Box 28, Folder WE9 9/1/66–10/14/66 EX, WHCF, EX WE 9 9/1/66–3/23/67, LBJL; First Annual Report of the Legal Services Program of the OEO to the American Bar Association at Annual Convention, Montreal, August 1966, Box 41, Folder JL7 Lawyers-Legal Aid EX, WHCF, GEN JL6 12/6/67–1/20/69, LBJL.

16. Hoff, *Nixon Reconsidered*, 61; Johnson, *Justice and Reform*, xiv–xvii; J. Anderson, "OEO Lawyers under Pressure," *Washington Post*, November 1, 1970.

17. Unsigned handwritten note, ca. October 1965, Series VI, Box F-6, Folder MRP-OF 1965/66 Coahoma County, MRP Records; Roy Batchelor to W. T. Wilkins, May 29, 1970, Series VII, Box G-5, Folder PATA/FA OEO Rural Legal Services (April–August), MRP Records; J. Anderson, "OEO Lawyers under Pressure"; Bertrand Harding to Don Rumsfeld, May 6, 1969, Box 41, Folder Reading File 3, March 1969–June 1969 OEO BMH [Book 19], Papers of Bertrand M. Harding, LBJL; Johnson, *Justice and Reform*, xii.

18. Cockburn, *Rumsfeld*, 17–19; "Fired Executive Says OEO Is Run by 'Southern Bigots,'" *Unknown Paper*, November 22, 1970, Box 5, Folder OEO, MCHR Records; J. Anderson, "OEO Lawyers under Pressure"; Crespino, *In Search of Another Country*, 225–26.

19. Clarke Reed to Donald Rumsfeld, October 22, 1969, and Clarke Reed to Dick Cheney, and attached report by the Mississippi State Bar, March 20, 1970, Series VII, Box G-5, Folder PATA/FA OEO—Rural Legal Services (April–August), MRP Records; Michael de L. Landon, *The Honor and Dignity of the Profession: A History of the Mississippi State Bar, 1906–1976* (Jackson: University Press of Mississippi, 1979), 161.

20. Joe Jack Hurst to John Bell Williams, February 16, 1971, Box 26, Mayoral Files, CSA 1968–1970, Davis Papers; Cary E. Bufkin to E. L. Lipscomb, June 9, 1969, Folder Hinds County, MS, Box 19, Subseries 4, File Series 3, Eastland Collection.

21. Cary E. Bufkin to E. L. Lipscomb, June 9, 1969.

22. W. T. Wilkins to Dick Cheney, July 9, 1970, Series VII, Box G-5, Folder PATA/FA OEO 1970, MRP Records.

23. W. T. Wilkins to Dick Cheney, July 9, 1970.

24. Cary E. Bufkin to E. L. Lipscomb, June 9, 1969, Folder Hinds County, MS, Box 19, Subseries 4, File Series 3, Eastland Collection; Press Release, February 26, 1971, and B. B. McClendon Jr. to William E. Timmons, February 23, 1971, Series VII, Box G-5, Folder PATA/FA OEO—Legal Services News, 1971, MRP Records.

25. J. Culbertson, "Free Lawyers for Poor Is Expanding Its Practice," *Clarion Ledger*, n.d., Folder Legal Services Correspondence, 1969–1971, Box 2262, Community Development Files; Hoff, *Nixon Reconsidered*, 61.

26. "Antipoverty Chief Looking Forward to OEO Shutdown," *Unknown Paper*, February 2, 1973, Box 26, Mayoral Files, CSA 1973, Davis Papers; B. Kovach, "Judge Halts Move to Disband OEO," *New York Times*, April 12, 1973, 1, 19; Shepard, *Rationing Justice*, 80.

27. Shepard, *Rationing Justice*, 81.

28. Sonny Walker to Russell C. Davis, February 8, 1973, Box 26, Mayoral Files, CSA 1973, Davis Papers; Draft Conclusions of CSA Public meetings, July and August 1970, Box 2260, Folder CSA Charter 1970/1971, Community Development Files.

29. Philip M. Catchings Jr. to Russell C. Davis, April 10, 1973, and Joe Hemingway to CSA Board of Directors, June 28, 1973, Box 26, Mayoral Files, CSA 1973, Davis Papers; Commission Report, Chicago, Illinois, August 25–31, 1968, SCR ID # 9-31-8-61-1-1-1, MSSC Records, http://mdah.state.ms.us/arrec/digital_archives/sovcom/result.php?image=/data/sov_commission/images/png/cd08/064865.png&otherstuff=9|31|8|61|1|1|1|64027|.

30. Philip M. Catchings Jr. to Mayor Russell C. Davis, April 10, 1973, Box 26, Mayoral Files, CSA 1973, Davis Papers.

31. Joseph Hemingway to Russell C. Davis, September 11, 1973, Box 26, Mayoral Files, CSA 1973, Davis Papers. Hemingway resigned having "reached the point of frustration with the board of directors that refuses to meet its obligations."

32. Rev. J. L. Brown to Emma Sanders, April 29, 1975, Box 26, Mayoral Files, CSA 1973, Davis Papers.

33. Alfred H. Rhodes Jr. to Msgr. Bernard Law, July 6, 1972, STAR, Inc., Correspondence February 20, 1969–May 1, 1973, Brunini Papers.

34. Albert J. Price to Mayor Russell C. Davis, February 14, 1975, and handwritten notes on a letter from John Crockett to Russell C. Davis, ca. July 1975, Box 26, Mayoral Files, CSA 1974–1975, Davis Papers.

35. William Waller to William Sonny Walker, June 5, 1975, Box 26, Mayoral Files, CSA 1974–1975, Davis Papers; J. Oglethorpe, "Hinds County May 'Hitch Up' with Poverty Program," *Jackson Daily News*, July 18, 1975.

36. Paul L. Kesaris, ed., *Papers of the Republican, Party Part II*, (Frederick, MD: University Publications of America, 1986), Reel 12, 0129; B. Kovach, "Judge Halts Move to Disband OEO," *New York Times*, April 12, 1973.

EPILOGUE

1. Gerald R. Ford, "Statement on Signing the Headstart, Economic Opportunity, and Community Partnership Act of 1974," January 4, 1975, in Peters and Woolley, *Papers of the President*, http://www.presidency.ucsb.edu/ws/?pid=4761.

2. Crespino, *In Search of Another Country*, 268.

3. Nash and Taggart, *Mississippi Politics*, 120.

4. Ronald W. Reagan, "Address Before a Joint Session of Congress on the State of the Union," January 25, 1988, in Peters and Woolley, *Papers of the President*, http://www.presidency.ucsb.edu/ws/?pid=36035.

5. Crespino, *In Search of Another Country*, 271; Orleck, "Conclusion," 446; Quadagno, *The Color of Welfare*, 196; Kathleen Hall Jamieson describes the power of the "visual cues" in Fordice's ads on "workfare not welfare," featuring a black mother holding her baby. *Dirty Politics: Deception, Distraction, and Democracy* (Oxford: Oxford University Press, 1993), 94.

6. Kruse, *White Flight*; Lassiter, *Silent Majority*; Sean P. Cunningham, *American Politics in the Postwar Sunbelt*; Dochuck, *From Bible Belt to Sunbelt*; McGirr, *Suburban Warriors*.

7. "Help Fight the War on Poverty" flyer, ca. 1965–66, Series VI, Box F-6, Folder MRP-OF 1965/66 Forrest County, MRP Records.

8. "Government of Southern States to Change Completely," *Christian Conservative Communique* 1, no. 21 (August 10, 1965), Race Relations Collection.

9. Tom Adam Davies describes the "mainstreaming of Black Power" through antipoverty programs, *Mainstreaming Black Power*, 3.

10. "Mississippi: Quick Facts," US Census Bureau, https://www.census.gov/quickfacts/ms; "Who We Are," Legal Services Corporation, http://www.lsc.gov/about-lsc/who-we-are; Greenberg, *The Devil Has Slippery Shoes*, 791.

11. "Resources," Mississippi Department of Human Services, 2016, http://www.mdhs.state.ms.us/community-services/resources/; Mississippi Action for Progress, Inc., 2016, http://www.mapheadstart.org/; "Friends of the Children of Mississippi History," 2011, http://www.friendsofchildren.org/documents/FCM-History-Brochure.pdf; "Who We Are," MS Legal Services 2016, http://www.mslegalservices.org/who-we-are; North Mississippi Rural Legal Services 2013, http://www.nmrls.com/; Hinds County Human Resources Agency 2016, http://hchra.org; Southwest Mississippi Opportunity, Inc. http://www.swmocaa.org/.

BIBLIOGRAPHY

PRIMARY SOURCES

Abernethy, Thomas G. Thomas G. Abernethy Collection. Archives and Special Collections, University of Mississippi, Oxford.

Boehm, Ralph H., ed. *Congress of Racial Equality Papers, Part 2: Southern Regional Office, 1959–1966*. Frederick, MD: University Publications of America, 1983.

Boehm, Ralph H., J. H. Bracey Jr., and A. Meier, eds. *Papers of the NAACP, Part 28: Special Subject Files, 1966–1970. Series A, Africa—Poor People's Campaign*. Frederick, MD: University Publications of America, 1996.

Boehm, Ralph H., J. H. Bracey Jr., and A. Meier, eds. *Papers of the NAACP, Part 20: White Resistance and Reprisals, 1956–1965*. Frederick, MD: University Publications of America, 1996.

Boutin, Bernard L. Papers of Bernard L. Boutin. Lyndon Baines Johnson Presidential Library, Austin, Texas.

Brenner, Joseph, Robert Coles, Alan Mermann, Milton J. E. Senn, Cyril Walwyn, and Raymond Wheeler. "Special Report: Hungry Children," n.d. Southern Regional Council, *Civil Rights Movement Veterans*. http://www.crmvet.org/docs/src_hungry_children.pdf.

Brunini, Joseph. Papers of Bishop Brunini. Archives of the Catholic Diocese of Jackson, Mississippi.

Campbell, Will D. Will D. Campbell Papers. McCain Library and Archives, Special Collections, University of Southern Mississippi, Hattiesburg.

Carmichael, Gilbert E. Gilbert E. Carmichael Papers. Mitchell Memorial Library, Special Collections, Mississippi State University, Starkville.

Carter, Hodding. Hodding Carter III Papers. Mitchell Memorial Library, Special Collections, Mississippi State University, Starkville.

Center for Oral History and Cultural Heritage. University of Southern Mississippi, Hattiesburg.

Civil Rights Documentation Project. Tougaloo College, Jackson, Mississippi.

Civil Rights History Project. American Folklife Center, Library of Congress.

Civil Rights Oral Histories. Charles W. Capps Jr. Archives and Museum, Delta State University, Cleveland, Mississippi.

Community Services Administration Records, Region IV, Record Group 381. National Archives and Record Administration, Atlanta, Georgia.

Cooper, Owen. Owen Cooper Papers. Mississippi Department of Archives and History, Jackson.
Corbett, Alfred H. Papers of Alfred H. Corbett. Lyndon Baines Johnson Presidential Library, Austin, Texas.
Council of Federated Organizations. COFO Records, Freedom Summer Digital Collection, Wisconsin Historical Society, Madison, Wisconsin.
Davis, Russell C. Russell C. Davis Papers. Mitchell Memorial Library, Special Collections, Mississippi State University, Starkville.
Department of Labor. "Neighborhood Youth Corps: An Economic Opportunity Program," June 1966. https://archive.org/details/ERIC_ED027350.
Department of Labor. "The Neighborhood Youth Corps: Three Years of Success," 1968. https://archive.org/stream/ERIC_ED026423.
Derian, Patricia. Patricia Derian Papers. Mitchell Memorial Library, Special Collections, Mississippi State University, Starkville.
Dunlap, Bryan R. Bryan R. Dunlap Papers: 1964–1972. Wisconsin Historical Society, Madison, Wisconsin.
Eastland, James O. James O. Eastland Collection. Archives and Special Collections, University of Mississippi, Oxford.
Economic Opportunity Act, 1964.
Examination of the War on Poverty: Hearings before the Subcommittee on Employment, Manpower, and Poverty of the Committee on Labor and Public Welfare, United States Senate, Ninetieth Congress, first session. Washington, DC: US Government Printing Office, 1967.
Gaither, James. Office Files of James Gaither. Lyndon Baines Johnson Presidential Library, Austin, Texas.
Gelfand, Mark I., Robert Lester, and Martin Paul Schipper, eds. *The War on Poverty, 1964–1968, Part 1: White House Central Files*. Frederick, MD: University Publications of America, 1986.
Governor's Office Records: Series 1001, Community Development Files, 1966–1975. Mississippi Department of Archives and History, Jackson.
Hoff-Wilson, Joan, ed. *Papers of the Nixon White House, Part 5: H. R. Haldeman, Notes of White House Meetings, 1969–1973*. Frederick, MD: University Publications of America, 1992.
Hoff-Wilson, Joan, ed. *Papers of the Nixon White House, Part 6A: The President's Office Files*. Frederick, MD: University Publications of America, 1992.
Hoff-Wilson, Joan, ed. *Papers of the Nixon White House, Part 7: President's Personal Files, 1969–1974*. Frederick, MD: University Publications of America, 1992.
Horwitz, Charles. Charles Horwitz Papers. Mississippi Department of Archives and History, Jackson.
House Committee on Un-American Activities. "The Present-Day Ku Klux Klan Movement." Report, Ninetieth Congress, first session, part one. Washington, DC: US Government Printing Office, 1967.
John C. Stennis Oral History Project, Mississippi State University, Starkville
Johnson, Lyndon B. Confidential File. Lyndon Baines Johnson Presidential Library, Austin, Texas.

Johnson, Lyndon B. Oral History Interviews. Lyndon Baines Johnson Presidential Library, Austin, Texas.

Johnson, Lyndon B. Presidential Papers. White House Central Files. Lyndon Baines Johnson Presidential Library, Austin, Texas.

Johnson, Lyndon B. Recordings and Transcripts of Conversations and Meetings. Lyndon Baines Johnson Presidential Library, Austin, Texas.

Johnson, Paul B. Paul B. Johnson Family Papers, McCain Library and Archives Special Collections, University of Southern Mississippi, Hattiesburg.

Kennedy, John F. Oral History Program. John F. Kennedy Presidential Library, Boston, Massachusetts.

Kesaris, Paul L., ed. *Papers of the Republican Party, Part II: Reports and Memoranda of the Research Division of the Headquarters of the Republican National Committee, 1938–1980.* Frederick, MD: University Publications of America, 1986.

Ku Klux Klan Collection. J. D. Williams Library, Archives and Special Collections, University of Mississippi, Oxford.

Lawson, Steven F., ed. *Civil Rights during the Johnson Administration, 1963–1969, Part V: Records of the National Advisory Commission on Civil Disorders (Kerner Commission).* Frederick, MD: University Publications of America, 1987.

McPherson, Harry. Office Files of Harry McPherson. Lyndon Baines Johnson Presidential Library, Austin, Texas.

Miller, Michael J. Michael J. Miller Civil Rights Collection. McCain Library and Archives, Special Collections, University of Southern Mississippi, Hattiesburg.

Mississippi Council on Human Relations Records, 1960–1980. Mississippi Department of Archives and History, Jackson.

Mississippi Republican Party Records. Mitchell Memorial Library, Special Collections, Mississippi State University, Starkville.

Mississippi State AFL-CIO Records. Southern Labor Archives, Georgia State University, Atlanta.

Mississippi State Sovereignty Commission Records, 1994–2006, Series 2515. Mississippi Department of Archives and History, Jackson.

Montgomery, Lucile. Lucile Montgomery Papers. Freedom Summer Digital Collection, Wisconsin Historical Society, Madison, Wisconsin.

Nixon, Richard M. Presidential Papers. White House Central Files. Richard M. Nixon Presidential Library, Yorba Linda, California.

Office of Economic Opportunity. Vertical Files. Mitchell Memorial Library, Special Collections, Mississippi State University, Starkville.

One Person, One Vote: SNCC Legacy Project. Duke University, Durham, North Carolina.

Panzer, Fred. Office Files of Fred Panzer. Lyndon Baines Johnson Presidential Library, Austin, Texas.

Perrin, Robert. Personal Papers of Robert Perrin. Lyndon Baines Johnson Presidential Library, Austin, Texas.

Reagan, Ronald W. Governor's Office Files, Gubernatorial Papers 1966–1975. Ronald Reagan Presidential Library, Simi Valley, California.

Romaine, Anne. Anne Romaine Interviews, 1966–1967. Freedom Summer Digital Collection, Wisconsin Historical Society, Madison, Wisconsin.
Satterfield, John C. John C. Satterfield Collection. J. D. Williams Library, Archives and Special Collections, University of Mississippi, Oxford.
Sinsheimer, Joseph A. Joseph A. Sinsheimer Papers, Duke University, Durham, North Carolina.
Stennis, John C. John C. Stennis Papers. Congressional and Political Research Center, Mississippi State University, Starkville.
Veterans of the Mississippi Civil Rights Movement. http://www.crmvet.org/.

SECONDARY SOURCES

Alinsky, Saul D. "The War on Poverty—Political Pornography." *Journal of Social Issues* 21, no. 1 (1965): 41–47.
Alston, Lee J., and Joseph P. Ferrie. *Southern Paternalism and the American Welfare State: Economics, Politics, and Institutions in the South, 1865–1965*. Cambridge: Cambridge University Press, 1999.
Anderson, Karen S. "Massive Resistance, Violence, and Southern Social Relations: The Little Rock, Arkansas, School Integration Crisis, 1954–1960." In *Massive Resistance: Southern Opposition to the Second Reconstruction*, edited by Clive Webb, 203–20. Oxford: Oxford University Press, 2005.
Anderson, Palmer R. "Jobs Corps and Neighborhood Youth Corps: A Critical Review." *Humboldt Journal of Social Relations* 1, no. 1 (1973): 8–16.
Andrews, Kenneth T. *Freedom Is a Constant Struggle: The Mississippi Civil Rights Movement and Its Legacy*. Chicago: University of Chicago Press, 2004.
Andrews, Kenneth T. "Social Movements and Policy Implementation: The Mississippi Civil Rights Movement and the War on Poverty, 1965 to 1971." *American Sociological Review* 66, no. 1 (2001): 71–95.
Annis, J. Lee, Jr. *Big Jim Eastland: The Godfather of Mississippi*. Jackson: University Press of Mississippi, 2016.
Applebome, Peter. *Dixie Rising: How the South Is Shaping American Values, Politics, and Culture*. New York: Times Books, 1996.
Arsenault, Raymond. *Freedom Riders: 1961 and the Struggle for Racial Justice*. Oxford: Oxford University Press, 2006.
Asch, Chris Myers. *The Senator and the Sharecropper: The Freedom Struggles of James O. Eastland and Fannie Lou Hamer*. New York: New Press, 2008.
Ashmore, Susan Y. *Carry It On: The War on Poverty and the Civil Rights Movement in Alabama, 1964–1972*. Athens: University of Georgia Press, 2008.
Ashmore, Susan Y. "More Than a Head Start: The War on Poverty, Catholic Charities and Civil Rights in Mobile, Alabama, 1965–1970." In *The New Deal and Beyond: Social Welfare in the South since 1930*, edited by Elna C. Green, 196–238. Athens: University of Georgia Press, 2003.

Austin, Sharon D. Wright. *The Transformation of Plantation Politics: Black Politics, Concentrated Poverty, and Social Capital in the Mississippi Delta*. Albany: State University of New York Press, 2006.

Badger, Anthony J. *New Deal / New South: An Anthony J. Badger Reader*. Fayetteville: University of Arkansas Press, 2007.

Bailey, Martha J., and Sheldon Danziger. "Legacies of the War on Poverty." In *Legacies of the War on Poverty*, edited by Martha J. Bailey and Sheldon Danziger, 1–36. New York: Russell Sage Foundation, 2013.

Bartley, Numan V. *The Rise of Massive Resistance: Race and Politics in the South during the 1950s*. 2nd ed. Baton Rouge: Louisiana State University Press, 1999.

Bartley, Numan V., and Hugh Davis Graham. *Southern Politics and the Second Reconstruction*. Baltimore: Johns Hopkins University Press, 1975.

Bass, Jack, and Walter De Vries. *The Transformation of Southern Politics: Social Change and Political Consequence since 1945*. New York: Basic Books, 1976.

Bauman, Robert. "The Black Power and Chicano Movements in the Poverty Wars in Los Angeles." *Journal of Urban History* 33, no. 2 (2007): 277–95.

Bauman, Robert. "Gender, Civil Rights Activism, and the War on Poverty in Los Angeles." In *The War on Poverty: A New Grassroots History, 1964–1980*, edited by Annelise Orleck and Lisa Gayle Hazirjian, 209–27. Athens: University of Georgia Press, 2011.

Bauman, Robert. *Race and the War on Poverty: From Watts to East L.A.* Norman: University of Oklahoma Press, 2008.

Beck, Susan Abrams. "'Limits of Presidential Activism: Lyndon Johnson and the Implementation of the Community Action Program," *Presidential Studies Quarterly* 17, no. 3 (1987): 541–57.

Beito, David T., and Linda Royster Beito. *Black Maverick: T. R. M. Howard's Fight for Civil Rights and Economic Power*. Urbana: University of Illinois Press, 2009.

Belknap, Michal R. *Federal Law and Southern Order: Racial Violence and Constitutional Conflict in the Post-Brown South*. Athens: University of Georgia Press, 1987.

Bell, Jack. *Mr. Conservative: Barry Goldwater*. New York: Doubleday, 1962.

Berkowitz, Edward D. *America's Welfare State: From Roosevelt to Reagan*. London: Johns Hopkins University Press, 1991.

Berlet, Chip. "The New Political Right in the United States: Reaction, Rollback, and Resentment." In *Confronting the New Conservatism: The Rise of the Right in America*, edited by Michael J. Thompson, 71–106. New York: New York University Press, 2007.

Bjerre-Poulsen, Niels. *Right Face: Organizing the American Conservative Movement, 1945–1965*. Copenhagen: Museum Tusculanum, 2002.

Black, Adina. "'Parent Power': Evelina López Antonetty, the United Bronx Parents, and the War on Poverty." In *The War on Poverty: A New Grassroots History, 1964–1980*, edited by Annelise Orleck and Lisa Gayle Hazirjian, 184–208. Athens: University of Georgia Press, 2011.

Black, Erle, and Merle Black. *The Rise of Southern Republicans*. Cambridge, MA: Harvard University Press, 2002.

Blackmon, Douglas A. *Slavery by Another Name: The Re-Enslavement of Black Americans from the Civil War to World War II*. New York: Doubleday, 2008.

Blackwell, Unita, with JoAnne Prichard Morris. *Barefootin': Life Lessons from the Road to Freedom*, New York: Crown Publishers, 2006.

Blee, Kathleen M. "Women in the 1920s' Ku Klux Klan Movement." *Feminist Studies* 17, no. 1 (1991): 57–77.

Bloom, Jack M. *Class, Race, and the Civil Rights Movement*. Bloomington: Indiana University Press, 1987.

Bolton, Charles C. *The Hardest Deal of All: The Battle over School Integration in Mississippi, 1870–1980*. Jackson: University Press of Mississippi, 2005.

Bolton, Charles C. "The Last Stand of Massive Resistance: Mississippi Public School Integration, 1970." *Journal of Mississippi History* 61, no. 4 (1999): 329–50.

Bolton, Charles C. "William F. Winter and the Politics of Racial Moderation in Mississippi." *Journal of Mississippi History* 70, no. 4 (2008): 335–82.

Borus, Michael E., John P. Brennan, and Sidney Rosen. "A Benefit-Cost Analysis of the Neighborhood Youth Corps: The Out-of-School Program in Indiana." *Journal of Human Resources* 5, no. 2 (1970): 139–59.

Bowers, John W., Donovan J. Ochs, Richard J. Jensen, and David P. Schulz. *The Rhetoric of Agitation and Control*. 3rd ed. Long Grove: Waveland Press, 2010.

Bradley, Laura Lipsey. "Protestant Churches and the Ku Klux Klan in Mississippi during the 1920s: Study of an Unsuccessful Courtship." MA thesis, University of Mississippi, 1962.

Brauer, Carl M. "Kennedy, Johnson, and the War on Poverty," *Journal of American History* 69, no. 1 (1982): 98–119.

Brennan, Mary C. *Turning Right in the Sixties: The Conservative Capture of the GOP*. Chapel Hill: University of North Carolina Press, 1995.

Brinkley, Alan. "The Problem of American Conservatism." *American Historical Review* 99, no. 2 (1994): 409–29.

Brown, Sarah Hart. "Communism, Anticommunism, and Massive Resistance: The Civil Rights Congress in Southern Perspective." In *Before Brown: Civil Rights and White Backlash in the Modern South*, edited by Glenn Feldman, 170–97. Tuscaloosa: University of Alabama Press, 2004.

Burner, Eric R. *And Gently He Shall Lead Them: Robert Parris Moses and Civil Rights in Mississippi*. New York: New York University Press, 1995.

Cagin, Seth, and Philip Dray. *We Are Not Afraid: The Story of Goodman, Schwerner, and Chaney and the Civil Rights Campaign for Mississippi*. New ed. New York: Nation Books, 2006.

Cahn, Edgar S., and Jean C. Cahn. "The War on Poverty: A Civilian Perspective'" *Yale Law Review* 73, no. 8 (July 1964): 1317–52.

Califano, Joseph A., Jr. *The Triumph and Tragedy of Lyndon Johnson: The White House Years*. New York: Simon & Schuster, 1991.

Carson, Clayborne. *In Struggle: SNCC and the Black Awakening of the 1960s*. New ed. Cambridge, Harvard University Press, 1995.

Carter, Dan T. *From George Wallace to Newt Gingrich: Race in the Conservative Counterrevolution, 1963–1994*. Baton Rouge: Louisiana State University Press, 1996.

Carter, Dan T. *The Politics of Rage: George Wallace, the Origins of the New Conservatism, and the Transformation of American Politics*. 2nd ed. Baton Rouge: Louisiana State University Press, 2000.

Carter, Dan T. "Southern Conservatives: Race and Poverty, 1980–2006." In *Poverty and Progress in the US South since 1920*, edited by Suzanne W. Jones and Mark Newman, 189–202. Amsterdam: VU University Press, 2006.

Carter, David C. *The Music Has Gone Out of the Movement: Civil Rights and the Johnson Administration, 1965–1968*. Chapel Hill: University of North Carolina, 2009.

Carter, Ginger Rudeseal. "Hodding Carter, Jr., and the *Delta Democrat-Times*." In *The Press and Race: Mississippi Journalists Confront the Movement*, edited by David R. Davies, 265–93. Jackson: University Press of Mississippi, 2001.

Cazenave, Noel A. *Impossible Democracy: The Unlikely Success of the War on Poverty Community Action Programs*. Albany: State University of New York Press, 2007.

Chafe, William H. *Civilities and Civil Rights: Greensboro, North Carolina, and the Black Struggle for Freedom*. Oxford: Oxford University Press, 1981.

Chafe, William H., and Harvard Sitkoff, eds. *A History of Our Time: Readings on Postwar America*. 4th ed. Oxford: Oxford University Press, 1995.

Cha-Jua, Sundiata Keita, and Clarence Lang. "The 'Long Movement' as Vampire: Temporal and Spatial Fallacies in Recent Black Freedom Studies." *Journal of African American History* 92, no. 2 (2007): 265–88.

Chalmers, David M. *Hooded Americanism: The History of the Ku Klux Klan*. Durham, NC: Duke University Press, 1987.

Chalmers, David M. *Backfire: How the Ku Klux Klan Helped the Civil Rights Movement*. New York: Rowman & Littlefield, 2003.

Chappell, David L. *Inside Agitators: White Southerners in the Civil Rights Movement*. London: Johns Hopkins University Press, 1994.

Chappell, David L. *A Stone of Hope: Prophetic Religion and the Death of Jim Crow*. Chapel Hill: University of North Carolina Press, 2003.

Clark, Kenneth B., and Jeannette Hopkins. *A Relevant War against Poverty: A Study of Community Action Programs and Observable Social Change*. New York: Harper & Row, 1969.

Clark, Robert F. *The War on Poverty: History, Selected Programs, and Ongoing Impact*. Lanham, MD: University Press of America, 2002.

Clayson, William S. "'The Barrios and the Ghettos Have Organized!' Community Action, Political Acrimony, and the War on Poverty in San Antonio." *Journal of Urban History* 28, no. 2 (2002): 158–83.

Clayson, William S. *Freedom Is Not Enough: The War on Poverty and the Civil Rights Movement in Texas*. Austin: University of Texas Press, 2010.

Cobb, Charles E., Jr. *This Nonviolent Stuff'll Get You Killed: How Guns Made the Civil Rights Movement Possible*. Durham, NC: Duke University Press, 2016.

Cobb, Daniel M. "The War on Poverty in Mississippi and Oklahoma: Beyond Black and White." In *The War on Poverty: A New Grassroots History, 1964–1980*, edited by Annelise Orleck and Lisa Gayle Hazirjian, 387–410. Athens: University of Georgia Press, 2011.

Cobb, James C. *The Most Southern Place on Earth: The Mississippi Delta and the Roots of Regional Identity*. New York: Oxford University Press, 1992.

Cobb, James C. *The Selling of the South: The Southern Crusade for Industrial Development, 1936–1990*. Urbana: University of Illinois Press, 1993.

Cobb, James C. "Somebody Done Nailed Us on the Cross: Federal Farm and Welfare Policy and the Civil Rights Movement in the Mississippi Delta." *Journal of American History* 77, no. 3 (1990): 912–36.

Cockburn, Andrew. *Rumsfeld: An American Disaster*. London: Verso Books, 2007.

Colby, David C. "Black Power, White Resistance, and Public Policy: Political Power and Poverty Program Grants in Mississippi." *Journal of Politics* 47, no. 2 (1985): 579–95.

Coleman, David G., Kent B. Germany, Guian A. McKee, and Marc J. Selverstone, eds. *Lyndon B. Johnson: Civil Rights, Vietnam, and the War on Poverty*. Charlottesville: University of Virginia Press, 2014.

Collum, Danny Duncan. *Black and Catholic in the Jim Crow South: The Stuff That Makes Community*. Mahwah, NJ: Paulist Press, 2006.

Cowart, Andrew T. "Anti-Poverty Expenditures in the American States: A Comparative Analysis." *Midwest Journal of Political Science* 13, no. 2 (1969): 219–36.

Crespino, Joseph. *In Search of Another Country: Mississippi and the Conservative Counterrevolution*. Princeton, NJ: Princeton University Press, 2007.

Crespino, Joseph. "Mississippi as Metaphor: Civil Rights, the South, and the Nation in the Historical Imagination." In *The Myth of Southern Exceptionalism*, edited by Matthew D. Lassiter and Joseph Crespino, 99–120. New York: Oxford University Press, 2010.

Crespino, Joseph. "Strom Thurmond's Sunbelt: Rethinking Regional Politics and the Rise of the Right." In *Sunbelt Rising: The Politics of Space, Place, and Region*, edited by Michelle M. Nickerson and Darren Dochuk, 58–81. Philadelphia: University of Pennsylvania Press, 2011.

Critchlow, Donald T. *The Conservative Ascendancy: How the GOP Right Made Political History*. Cambridge, MA: Harvard University Press, 2007.

Critchlow, Donald T. *Phyllis Schlafly and Grassroots Conservatism: A Woman's Crusade*. Princeton, NJ: Princeton University Press, 2007.

Crosby, Emilye. *A Little Taste of Freedom: The Black Freedom Struggle in Claiborne County, Mississippi*. Chapel Hill: University of North Carolina Press, 2005.

Crosby, Emilye. "The Politics of Writing and Teaching Movement History." In *Civil Rights History from the Ground Up: Local Struggles, a National Movement*, edited by Emilye Crosby, 1–42. Athens: University of Georgia Press, 2011.

Cunningham, David. *Klansville, U.S.A.: The Rise and Fall of the Civil Rights-Era Ku Klux Klan*. Oxford: Oxford University Press, 2013.

Cunningham, David. "Shades of Anti-Civil Rights Violence: Reconsidering the Ku Klux Klan in Mississippi." In *The Civil Rights Movement in Mississippi*, edited by Ted Ownby, 180–203. Jackson: University Press of Mississippi, 2013.

Cunningham, Sean P. *American Politics in the Postwar Sunbelt: Conservative Growth in a Battleground Region*. Cambridge: Cambridge University Press, 2014.

Curry, Constance. *Silver Rights*. Chapel Hill: Algonquin Books, 1995.

Curtis, Jesse N. "Remembering Racial Progress, Forgetting White Resistance: The Death of Mississippi Senator John C. Stennis and the Consolidation of the Colorblind Consensus." *History & Memory* 29, no. 1 (2017): 134–60.

D'Emilio, John, and Estelle B. Freedman. *Intimate Matters: A History of Sexuality in America*. 2nd ed. Chicago: University of Chicago Press, 1997.

Dailey, Jane. "Sex, Segregation, and the Sacred after *Brown*." *Journal of American History* 91, no. 1 (2004): 119–44.

Dallek, Matthew. *The Right Moment: Ronald Reagan's First Victory and the Decisive Turning Point in Modern American Politics*. New York: Free Press, 2000.

Daniel, Pete. *Dispossession: Discrimination against African American Farmers in the Age of Civil Rights*. Chapel Hill: University of North Carolina Press, 2013.

Danielson, Chris. *After Freedom Summer: How Race Realigned Mississippi Politics, 1965–1986*. Gainesville: University Press of Florida, 2011.

Danielson, Chris. "'Lily White and Hard Right': The Mississippi Republican Party and Black Voting, 1965–1980." *Journal of Southern History* 75, no. 1 (2009): 82–118.

Dann, Jim. *Challenging the Mississippi Fire Bombers: Memories of Mississippi, 1964–65*. Quebec: Baraka Books, 2013.

Davies, Gareth. *From Opportunity to Entitlement: The Transformation and Decline of Great Society Liberalism*. Lawrence: University Press of Kansas, 1996.

Davies, Tom Adam. *Mainstreaming Black Power*. Oakland: University of California Press, 2017.

Davis, Jack E. *Race against Time: Culture and Separation in Natchez Since 1930*. Baton Rouge: Louisiana State University Press, 2001.

Dawson, Michael C. *Behind the Mule: Race and Class in African-American Politics*. Princeton, NJ: Princeton University Press, 1995.

De Jong, Greta. *A Different Day: African American Struggles for Justice in Rural Louisiana, 1900–1970*. Chapel Hill: University of North Carolina Press, 2002.

De Jong, Greta. *Invisible Enemy: The African American Freedom Struggle after 1965*. Chichester: Wiley-Blackwell, 2010.

De Jong, Greta. "Plantation Politics: The Tufts-Delta Health Center and Intraracial Class Conflict in Mississippi, 1965–1972." In *The War on Poverty: A New Grassroots History, 1964–1980*, edited by Annelise Orleck and Lisa Gayle Hazirjian, 256–79. Athens: University of Georgia Press, 2011.

Diamond, Sara. *Roads to Dominion: Right-Wing Movements and Political Power in the United States*. New York: Guilford Press, 1995.

Dionne, E. J., Jr. *Why Americans Hate Politics*. New York: Simon & Schuster, 1991.

Dittmer, John. *Local People: The Struggle for Civil Rights in Mississippi*. Urbana: University of Illinois Press, 1994.

Dochuk, Darren. *From Bible Belt to Sunbelt: Plain-Folk Religion, Grassroots Politics, and the Rise of Evangelical Conservatism*. London: W. W. Norton, 2012.

Dollinger, Marc. "The Other War: American Jews, Lyndon Johnson, and the Great Society." *American Jewish History* 89, no. 4 (2001): 437–61.

Donovan, John C. *The Politics of Poverty*. New York: Pegasus, 1967.

Drabble, John. "The FBI, COINTELPRO-WHITE HATE, and the Decline of the KKK Organizations in Mississippi, 1964–1971." *Journal of Mississippi History* 46, no. 4 (2004): 353–402.

Draper, Alan. "Class and Politics in the Mississippi Movement: An Analysis of the Mississippi Freedom Democratic Party Delegation." *Journal of Southern History* 82, no. 2 (2016): 269–304.

Draper, Alan. *Conflict of Interests: Organized Labor and the Civil Rights Movement in the South, 1954–1968*. Ithaca: ILR Press, 1994.

Dudziak, Mary L. *Cold War Civil Rights: Race and the Image of American Democracy*. Princeton, NJ: Princeton University Press, 2000.

Dupont, Carolyn Renée. *Mississippi Praying: Southern White Evangelicals and the Civil Rights Movement, 1945–1975*. New York: New York University Press, 2015.

Eagles, Charles, ed. *The Civil Rights Movement in America: Essays*. Jackson: University Press of Mississippi, 1986.

Eagles, Charles. "Toward New Histories of the Civil Rights Era." *Journal of Southern History* 66, no. 4 (2000): 815–48.

Edsall, Thomas Byrne, and Mary D. Edsall. *Chain Reaction: The Impact of Race, Rights, and Taxes on American Politics*. New York: Norton, 1991.

Egerton, John. *The Americanization of Dixie: The Southernization of America*. New York: Harper's Magazine Press, 1974.

Ely, James W., Jr. *The Crisis of Conservative Virginia: The Byrd Organization and the Politics of Massive Resistance*. Knoxville: University of Tennessee Press, 1976.

Epstein, William M. *Democracy without Decency: Good Citizenship and the War on Poverty*. Philadelphia: Pennsylvania State University Press, 2010.

Evers, Myrlie, with William Peters. *For Us, the Living*. Garden City, NY: Doubleday, 1967. Reprinted. Jackson: University Press of Mississippi, 1996.

Fairclough, Adam. "Historians and the Civil Rights Movement." *Journal of American History* 24, no. 3 (1990): 387–98.

Fairclough, Adam. *Race and Democracy: The Civil Rights Struggle in Louisiana, 1915–1972*. Athens: University of Georgia Press, 1995.

Feldman, Glenn, ed. *Before Brown: Civil Rights and White Backlash in the Modern South*. Tuscaloosa: University of Alabama Press, 2004.

Feldman, Glenn. "Ugly Roots: Race, Emotion, and the Rise of the Modern Republican Party in Alabama and the South." In *Before Brown: Civil Rights and White Backlash in the Modern South*, edited by Glenn Feldman: 268–310. Tuscaloosa: University of Alabama Press, 2004.

Findlay, James F., Jr. *Church People in the Struggle: The National Council of Churches and the Black Freedom Movement, 1950–1970*. New York: Oxford University Press, 1997.

Findlay, James F., Jr. "The Mainline Churches and Head Start in Mississippi: Religious Activism in the Sixties." *Church History* 64, no. 2 (1995): 237–50.

Fisher, Gordon M. "The Development of the Orshansky Poverty Thresholds and Their Subsequent History as the Official U.S. Poverty Measure." May 1992. Rev. September 1997. Accessed July 5, 2013. http://www.census.gov/hhes/povmeas/publications/orshansky.html.

Folwell, Emma. "The Legacy of the Child Development Group: White Opposition to Head Start in Mississippi, 1965–1972." *Journal of Mississippi History* 76, no. 1 (2014): 43–68.
Forster Arnold, and Benjamin R. Epstein. *Report on the Ku Klux Klan*. New York: Anti-Defamation League of B'nai B'rith, 1965.
Frederickson, Kari A. *The Dixiecrat Revolt and the End of the Solid South, 1932–1968*. Chapel Hill: University of North Carolina Press, 2001.
Friedman, Lawrence M. "The Social and Political Context of the War on Poverty: An Overview." In *A Decade of Federal Antipoverty Programs: Achievements, Failures, and Lessons*, edited by Robert H. Haveman, 21–47. New York: Academic Press, 1977.
Gaston Paul M., and Thomas T. Hammond. "Public School Desegregation: Charlottesville, Virginia, 1955–1962." Reproduced in *Congress of Racial Equality Papers, Part 2: Southern Regional Office, 1959–1966*, edited by Randolph Boehm. Reel 2, fr.0106. Frederick, MD: University Publications of America, 1983.
Gates, Robbins L. *The Making of Massive Resistance: Virginia's Politics of Public School Desegregation, 1954–1956*. Chapel Hill: University of North Carolina Press, 1964.
Gelfand, Mark I., Robert Lester, and Martin Paul Schipper, eds. *The War on Poverty, 1964–1968, Part 1: White House Central Files*. Frederick. MD: University Publications of America, 1986.
Germany, Kent B. *New Orleans after the Promises: Poverty, Citizenship, and the Search for the Great Society*. Athens: University of Georgia Press, 2007.
Germany, Kent B. "Poverty Wars in the Louisiana Delta: White Resistance, Black Power, and the Poorest Place in America." In *The War on Poverty: A New Grassroots History, 1964–1980*, edited by Annelise Orleck and Lisa Gayle Hazirjian, 231–55. Athens: University of Georgia Press, 2011.
Germany, Kent B. "'They Can Be Like Other People': Race, Poverty, and the Politics of Alienation in New Orleans's Early Great Society." In *The New Deal and Beyond: Social Welfare in the South since 1930*, edited by Elna C. Green, 163–95. Athens: University of Georgia Press, 2003.
Gerstle, Gary. "Race and the Myth of the Liberal Consensus." *Journal of American History* 82, no. 2 (1995): 579–86.
Gibbs, Chloe, Jens Ludwig, and Douglas L. Miller. "Head Start Origins and Impact." In *Legacies of the War on Poverty*, edited by Martha J. Bailey and Sheldon Danziger, 39–65. New York: Russell Sage Foundation, 2013.
Gilder, George F. *Wealth and Poverty*. London: Buchan & Enright, 1982.
Gillette, Michael, ed. *Launching the War on Poverty: An Oral History*. 2nd edition. New York: Oxford University Press, 2010.
Gilmore, Glenda Elizabeth. *Gender and Jim Crow: Women and the Politics of White Supremacy in North Carolina, 1896–1920*. Chapel Hill: University of North Carolina Press, 1996.
Glaser, James M. *Race, Campaign Politics, and the Realignment of the South*. New Haven, CT: Yale University Press, 1996.
Glazer, Nathan. "The Limits of Social Policy." *Commentary* 52, no. 3 (1971): 51–58.
Glazer, Nathan. *The Limits of Social Policy*. Cambridge, MA: Harvard University Press, 1988.
Goldberg, Robert Alan. *Barry Goldwater*. New Haven, CT: Yale University Press, 1995.

Goldstein, Alyosha. *Poverty in Common: The Politics of Community Action during the American Century*. Durham, NC: Duke University Press, 2012.

Goodall, Alex. "Two Concepts of Un-Americanism." *Journal of American Studies* 47, no. 4 (2013): 925–42.

Goudsouzian, Aram. *Down to the Crossroads: Civil Rights, Black Power, and the Meredith March against Fear*. New York: Farrar, Straus and Giroux, 2014.

Graham, Hugh Davis. *The Civil Rights Era: Origins and Developments of National Policy, 1960–1972*. Oxford: Oxford University Press, 1990.

Grantham, Dewey W. *The Life and Death of the Solid South: A Political History*. Lexington: University Press of Kentucky, 1988.

Green, Elna C. "Introduction." In *The New Deal and Beyond: Social Welfare in the South since 1930*, edited by Elna C. Green, vii–xix. Athens: University of Georgia Press, 2003.

Green, Laurie B. "Saving Babies in Memphis: The Politics of Race, Health, and Hunger during the War on Poverty." In *The War on Poverty: A New Grassroots History, 1964–1980*, edited by Annelise Orleck and Lisa Gayle Hazirjian, 133–58. Athens: University of Georgia Press, 2011.

Greenberg, Polly. *The Devil Has Slippery Shoes: A Biased Biography of the Child Development Group of Mississippi (CDGM), A Story of Maximum Feasible Poor Parent Participation*. Rev. ed. Washington, DC: Youth Policy Institute, 1990.

Greenberg, Polly, ed. *Head Start: With the Child Development Group of Mississippi*. New York: Folkway Records, 1967.

Greenberg, Polly. "Three Core Concepts of the War on Poverty: Their Origins and Significance in Head Start." In *The Head Start Debates*, edited by Edward Zigler and Sally J. Styfco, 61–84. Baltimore: Paul H. Brookes, 2004.

Greene, Christina. "'Someday . . . the Colored and White Will Stand Together': The War on Poverty, Black Power Politics, and Southern Women's Interracial Alliances." In *The War on Poverty: A New Grassroots History, 1964–1980*, edited by Annelise Orleck and Lisa Gayle Hazirjian, 159–83. Athens: University of Georgia Press, 2011.

Greenstone, J. David, and Paul E. Peterson. *Race and Authority in Urban Politics: Community Participation and the War on Poverty*. Chicago: University of Chicago Press, 1976.

Hale, Jon N. *Freedom Schools: Student Activists in the Mississippi Civil Rights Movement*. New York: Columbia University Press, 2016.

Hale, Jon N. "The Struggle Begins Early: Head Start and the Mississippi Freedom Movement." *History of Education Quarterly* 52, no. 4 (2012): 506–34.

Hale, Stan J. *Williamson County, Illinois, Sesquicentennial History*. Paducah, KY: Turner, 1993.

Hall, Jacquelyn Dowd. "The Long Civil Rights Movement and the Political Uses of the Past." *Journal of American History* 91, no. 4 (2005): 1233–63.

Hall, Simon. "Protest Movements in the 1970s: The Long 1960s." *Journal of Contemporary History* 43, no. 4 (2008): 655–72.

Hamilton, Dona Cooper, and Charles V. Hamilton. *The Dual Agenda: Race and Social Welfare Policies of Civil Rights Organizations*. New York: Columbia University Press, 1997.

Hamlin, Françoise N. "Collision and Collusion: Local Activism, Local Agency, and Flexible Alliances." In *The Civil Rights Movement in Mississippi*, edited by Ted Ownby, 35–58. Jackson: University Press of Mississippi, 2013.

Hamlin, Françoise N. *Crossroads at Clarksdale: The Black Freedom Struggle in the Mississippi Delta after World War II*. Chapel Hill: University of North Carolina Press, 2012.

Haney López, Ian. *Dog Whistle Politics: How Coded Racial Appeals Have Reinvented Racism and Wrecked the Middle Class*. New York: Oxford University Press, 2015.

Harrington, Michael. *The Other America: Poverty in the United States*. New York: Macmillan, 1962.

Harwell, Debbie Z. *Wednesdays in Mississippi: Proper Ladies Working for Radical Change, Freedom Summer 1964*. Jackson: University Press of Mississippi, 2014.

Hazirjian, Lisa Gayle. "Combating Need: Urban Conflict and the Transformations of the War on Poverty and the African American Freedom Struggle in Rocky Mount, North Carolina." *Journal of Urban History* 34, no. 4 (2008): 639–64.

Henry, Aaron, with Constance Curry. *Aaron Henry: The Fire Ever Burning*. Jackson: University Press of Mississippi, 2000.

Hill, Lance. *The Deacons for Defense: Armed Resistance and the Civil Rights Movement*. Chapel Hill: University of North Carolina Press, 2004.

Hirsch, Arnold R. *Making the Second Ghetto: Race and Housing in Chicago 1940–1960*. Cambridge: Cambridge University Press, 1983.

Hirsch, Arnold R. "Massive Resistance in the Urban North: Trumbull Park, Chicago, 1953–1966." *Journal of American History* 82, no. 2 (1995): 522–50.

Hirsch, Arnold R. "With or Without Jim Crow: Black Residential Segregation in the United States." In *Urban Policy in Twentieth-Century America*, edited by Arnold R. Hirsch and Raymond A. Mohl, 65–99. New Brunswick: Rutgers University Press, 1993.

Hodgson, Godfrey. *America in Our Time: From World War II to Nixon—What Happened and Why*. First Vintage Books ed. New York: Vintage Books, 1978.

Hodgson, Godfrey. *The World Turned Right Side Up: A History of the Conservative Ascendancy in America*. Boston: Houghton Mifflin, 1996.

Hoff, Joan. *Nixon Reconsidered*. New York: Basic Books, 1994.

Hogan, Wesley. "Grassroots Organizing in Mississippi That Changed National Politics." In *The Civil Rights Movement in Mississippi*, edited by Ted Ownby, 3–34. Jackson: University Press of Mississippi, 2013.

Honey, Michael K. *Going Down Jericho Road: The Memphis Strike, Martin Luther King's Last Campaign*. London: W. W. Norton, 2007.

Horn, Teena F., Alan Huffman, and John Griffin Jones, eds. *Lines Were Drawn: Remembering Court-Ordered Integration at a Mississippi High School*. Jackson: University Press of Mississippi, 2016.

Houck, Davis W., and David E. Dixon, eds. *Rhetoric, Religion, and the Civil Rights Movement, 1954–1965*. Waco, TX: Baylor University Press, 2006.

Hudson, Winson, and Constance Curry. *Mississippi Harmony: Memoirs of a Freedom Fighter*. New York: Palgrave Macmillan, 2002.

Jackson, Kenneth T. *Crabgrass Frontier: The Suburbanization of the United States*. Oxford: Oxford University Press, 1985.

Jackson, Thomas F. *From Civil Rights to Human Rights: Martin Luther King, Jr., and the Struggle for Economic Justice*. Philadelphia: University of Pennsylvania Press, 2007.

Jackson, Thomas F. "The State, the Movement, and the Urban Poor: The War on Poverty and Political Mobilization in the 1960s." In *The Underclass Debate: Views from History*, edited by Michael B. Katz, 403–39. Princeton, NJ: Princeton University Press, 1993.

Jacoway, Elizabeth. "An Introduction." In *Southern Businessmen and Desegregation*, edited by Elizabeth Jacoway and David R. Colburn, 1–14. Baton Rouge: Louisiana State University Press, 1982.

Jacoway, Elizabeth, and David R. Colburn, eds. *Southern Businessmen and Desegregation*. Baton Rouge: Louisiana State University Press, 1982.

Jamieson, Kathleen Hall. *Dirty Politics: Deception, Distraction, and Democracy*. Oxford: Oxford University Press, 1993.

Johnson, Earl, Jr. *Justice and Reform: The Formative Years of the American Legal Services Program*. 2nd ed. New Brunswick: Transaction Books, 1978.

Johnston, Araminta Stone. *And One Was a Priest: The Life and Times of Duncan M. Gray Jr.* Jackson: University Press of Mississippi, 2011.

Johnston, Erle. *Mississippi's Defiant Years, 1953–1973: An Interpretive Documentary with Personal Experiences*. Forrest: Lake Harbor Publishers, 1990.

Jordan, Amy. "Fighting for the Child Development Group of Mississippi: Poor People, Local Politics, and the Complicated Legacy of Head Start." In *The War on Poverty: A New Grassroots History, 1964–1980*, edited by Annelise Orleck and Lisa Gayle Hazirjian, 280–307. Athens: University of Georgia Press, 2011.

Kabaservice, Geoffrey. *Rule and Ruin: The Downfall of Moderation and the Destruction of the Republican Party, From Eisenhower to the Tea Party*. Oxford: Oxford University Press, 2012.

Katagiri, Yasuhiro. *The Mississippi State Sovereignty Commission: Civil Rights and States' Rights*. Jackson: University Press of Mississippi, 2001.

Katz, Michael B. *The Undeserving Poor: From the War on Poverty to the War on Welfare*. New York: Pantheon, 1989.

Katznelson, Ira. "Was the Great Society a Lost Opportunity?" In *The Rise and Fall of the New Deal Order, 1930–1980*, edited by Steve Fraser and Gary Gerstle, 185–211. Princeton, NJ: Princeton University Press, 1989.

Kaufman, Harold F., Kenneth P. Wilkinson, and L. W. Cole. *Poverty Programs and Social Mobility: Focus on Rural Populations of Lower Social Rank in Mississippi and the Lower South*. Starkville: Social Science Research Center, Mississippi State University, 1966.

Kazin, Michael. "The Grass-Roots Right: New Histories of U.S. Conservatism in the Twentieth Century." *American Historical Review* 97, no. 1 (1992): 136–55.

Kazin, Michael. *The Populist Persuasion: An American History*. Rev. ed. London: Cornell University Press, 1998.

Kesaris, Paul L., ed. *Papers of the Republican Party, Part II: Reports and Memoranda of the Research Division of the Headquarters of the Republican National Committee, 1938–1980*. Frederick, MD: University Publications of America, 1986.

Kiffmeyer, Thomas J. "From Self-Help to Sedition: The Appalachian Volunteers in Eastern Kentucky, 1964–1970." *Journal of Southern History* 64, no. 1 (1998): 65–94.

Kiffmeyer, Thomas J. *Reformers to Radicals: The Appalachian Volunteers and the War on Poverty*. Lexington: University Press of Kentucky, 2008.

King, Richard H. *Race, Culture, and the Intellectuals, 1940–1970.* Washington, DC: Woodrow Wilson Center Press; Baltimore: Johns Hopkins University Press, 2004.

Kirksey v. City of Jackson, Miss., 461 F. Supp. 1282 (S. D. Miss. 1978).

Klarman, Michael J. *From Jim Crow to Civil Rights: The Supreme Court and the Struggle for Racial Equality.* Oxford: Oxford University Press, 2004.

Klarman, Michael J. "How *Brown* Changed Race Relations: The Backlash Thesis." *Journal of American History* 81, no. 1 (1994): 81–118.

Kluger, Richard. *Simple Justice: The History of Brown v. Board of Education and Black America's Struggle for Equality.* Rev. and expanded ed. New York: Knopf, 2004.

Koehlinger, Amy L. *The New Nuns: Racial Justice and Religious Reform in the 1960s.* Cambridge, MA: Harvard University Press, 2007.

Korstad, Robert R., and James L. Leloudis. "Citizen-Soldiers: The North Carolina Volunteers and the South's War on Poverty." In *The New Deal and Beyond: Social Welfare in the South since 1930*, edited by Elna C. Green, 138–62. Athens: University of Georgia Press, 2003.

Korstad, Robert R., and James L. Leloudis. *To Right These Wrongs: The North Carolina Fund and the Battle to End Poverty and Inequality in 1960s America.* Chapel Hill: University of North Carolina Press, 2010.

Kotlowski, Dean J. *Nixon's Civil Rights: Politics, Principle, and Policy.* Cambridge, MA: Harvard University Press, 2001.

Kramer, Ralph M. *Participation of the Poor: Comparative Community Case Studies in the War on Poverty.* Englewood Cliffs, NJ: Prentice-Hall, 1969.

Kravitz, Sanford, and Ferne K. Kolodner. "Community Action: Where Has It Been? Where Will It Go?" *Annals of the American Academy of Political and Social Science* 385 (September 1969): 30–40.

Kristol, Irving. *Neoconservatism: The Autobiography of an Idea.* 2nd ed. Chicago: Elephant Paperbacks, 1999.

Kruse, Kevin M. *White Flight: Atlanta and the Making of Modern Conservatism.* Princeton, NJ: Princeton University Press, 2005.

Landon, Michael de L. *The Honor and Dignity of the Profession: A History of the Mississippi State Bar, 1906–1976.* Jackson: University Press of Mississippi, 1979.

Lassiter, Matthew D. "De Jure/De Facto Segregation: The Long Shadow of a National Myth." In *The Myth of Southern Exceptionalism*, edited by Matthew D. Lassiter and Joseph Crespino, 25–48. New York: Oxford University Press, 2010.

Lassiter, Matthew D. *The Silent Majority: Suburban Politics in the Sunbelt South.* Princeton, NJ: Princeton University Press, 2006.

Lawson, Steven F. *Civil Rights Crossroads: Nation, Community, and the Black Freedom Struggle.* New ed. Lexington: University Press of Kentucky, 2006.

Lawson, Steven F. "Freedom Then, Freedom Now: The Historiography of the Civil Rights Movement." *American Historical Review* 96, no. 2 (1991): 456–571.

Lee, Chana Kai. *For Freedom's Sake: The Life of Fannie Lou Hamer.* Urbana: University of Illinois Press, 1999.

Lemann, Nicholas. *The Promised Land: The Great Black Migration and How It Changed America.* New York: Knopf, 1991.

Levitan, Sar A. "The Community Action Program: A Strategy to Fight Poverty." *Annals of the American Academy of Political and Social Science* 385, no. 63 (1969): 63–75.
Levitan, Sar A., and Robert Taggart. *The Promise of Greatness*. London: Harvard University Press, 1976.
Lewis, George. "'An Amorphous Code': The Ku Klux Klan and Un-Americanism, 1915–1965." *Journal of American Studies* 47, no. 4 (2013): 1–22.
Lewis, George. *Massive Resistance: The White Response to the Civil Rights Movement*. London: Hodder Arnold, 2006.
Lewis, George. "Virginia's Northern Strategy: Southern Segregationists and the Route to National Conservatism." *Journal of Southern History* 72, no. 1 (2006): 111–46.
Lewis, George. *The White South and the Red Menace: Segregationists, Anticommunism, and Massive Resistance, 1945–1965*. Gainesville: University Press of Florida, 2004.
Lewis, John, and Archie E. Allen. "Black Voter Registration Efforts in the South." *Notre Dame Law Review* 48, no. 1 (1972): 105–32.
Lewis, John, with Michael D'Orso. *Walking with the Wind: A Memoir of the Movement*. New York: Simon and Schuster, 2015.
Ling, Peter J., and Sharon Monteith, eds. *Gender in the Civil Rights Movement*. London: Garland Publishing, 1999.
Locke, Mamie E. "Is This America? Fannie Lou Hamer and the Mississippi Freedom Democratic Party." In *Women in the Civil Rights Movement: Trailblazers and Torchbearers, 1941–1965*, edited by Vicki L. Crawford, Jacqueline Anne Rouse, and Barbara Woods, 27–37. New York: Carlson Publishing, 1990.
Loewen, James W. *The Mississippi Chinese: Between Black and White*. Cambridge, MA: Harvard University Press, 1971.
Lowndes, Joseph E. *From the New Deal to the New Right: Race and the Southern Origins of Modern Conservatism*. New Haven, CT: Yale University Press, 2008.
Lublin, David. *The Republican South: Democratization and Partisan Change*. Princeton, NJ: Princeton University Press, 2004.
Luckett, Robert E., Jr. *Joe T. Patterson and the White South's Dilemma: Evolving Resistance to Black Advancement*. Jackson: University Press of Mississippi, 2017.
Lyon, Carter Dalton. *Sanctuaries of Segregation: The Story of the Jackson Church Visit Campaign*. Jackson: University Press of Mississippi, 2017.
MacLean, Nancy. *Behind the Mask of Chivalry: The Making of the Second Ku Klux Klan*. Oxford: Oxford University Press, 1994.
Magnet, Myron. *The Dream and the Nightmare: The Sixties' Legacy to the Underclass*. 1st paperback ed. San Francisco: Encounter Books, 2000.
Marris, Peter, and Martin Rein. *Dilemmas of Social Reform: Poverty and Community Action in the United States*. 2nd ed. London: Routledge and Kegan Paul, 1972.
Marsh, Charles. *God's Long Summer: Stories of Faith and Civil Rights*. Princeton, NJ: Princeton University Press, 1997.
Marshall, F. Ray, and Lamond Godwin, *Cooperatives and Rural Poverty in the South*. Baltimore: Johns Hopkins Press, 1971.

Marshall, James P. *Student Activism and Civil Rights in Mississippi: Protest Politics and the Struggle for Racial Justice, 1960–1965*. Baton Rogue: Louisiana State University Press, 2013.

Martin, Gordon A., Jr. *Count Them One by One: Black Mississippians Fighting for the Right to Vote*. Jackson: University Press of Mississippi, 2011.

Matusow, Allen J. *The Unraveling of America: A History of Liberalism in the 1960s*. New ed. Athens: University of Georgia Press, 2009.

McAdam, Douglas. *Freedom Summer*. Oxford: Oxford University Press, 1990.

McGirr, Lisa. *Suburban Warriors: The Origins of the New American Right*. Princeton, NJ: Princeton University Press, 2001.

McGreevy, James T. "Racial Justice and the People of God: The Second Vatican Council, the Civil Rights Movement, and American Catholics." *Religion and American Culture* 4, no. 2 (1994): 221–54.

McKee, Guian A. *The Problem of Jobs: Liberalism, Race, and Deindustrialization in Philadelphia*. Chicago: University of Chicago Press, 2008.

McKee, Guian A. "'This Government Is With Us': Lyndon Johnson and the Grassroots War on Poverty." In *The War on Poverty: A New Grassroots History, 1964–1980*, edited by Annelise Orleck and Lisa Gayle Hazirjian, 31–62. Athens: University of Georgia Press, 2011.

McLaughlin, Malcolm. *The Long, Hot Summer of 1967: Urban Rebellion in America*. New York: Palgrave Macmillan, 2014.

McMillen, Neil R. *The Citizens' Council: Organized Resistance to the Second Reconstruction, 1954–1964*. 2nd ed. Urbana: University of Illinois Press, 1994.

McMillen, Neil R. *Dark Journey: Black Mississippians in the Age of Jim Crow*. Urbana: University of Illinois Press, 1990.

McMillen, Neil R. "Fighting for What We Didn't Have: How Mississippi's Black Veterans Remember World War II." In *Remaking Dixie: The Impact of World War II on the American South*, edited by Neil R. McMillen: 93–110. Jackson: University Press of Mississippi, 1997.

McRae, Elizabeth Gillespie. *Mothers of Massive Resistance: White Women and the Politics of White Supremacy*. Oxford: Oxford University Press, 2018.

McRae, Elizabeth Gillespie. "White Womanhood, White Supremacy and the Rise of Massive Resistance." In *Massive Resistance: Southern Opposition to the Second Reconstruction*, edited by Clive Webb, 181–202. Oxford: Oxford University Press, 2005.

Meacham, Ellen B. *Delta Epiphany: Robert F. Kennedy in Mississippi*. Jackson: University Press of Mississippi, 2018.

Mead, Lawrence M. *Beyond Entitlement: The Social Obligations of Citizenship*. New York: Free Press, 1986.

Meeker, Martin. "The Queerly Disadvantaged and the Making of San Francisco's War on Poverty, 1964–1967." *Pacific Historical Review* 81, no. 1 (2012): 21–59.

Miller, Steven P. *Billy Graham and the Rise of the Republican South*. Philadelphia: University of Pennsylvania Press, 2009.

Mills, Kay. *Something Better for My Children: The History and People of Head Start*. New York: Dutton, 1998.

Mills, Kay. *This Little Light of Mine: The Life of Fannie Lou Hamer*. New York: Dutton, 1993.

Minchin, Timothy J. *The Color of Work: The Struggle for Civil Rights in the Southern Paper Industry, 1945–1980*. Chapel Hill: University of North Carolina Press, 2001.

Minchin, Timothy J., and John A. Salmond. *After the Dream: Black and White Southerners since 1965*. Lexington: University Press of Kentucky, 2011.

Mitchell, Dennis J. *A New History of Mississippi*. Jackson: University Press of Mississippi, 2014.

Mize, Sandra Yocum. "North America." In *The Blackwell Companion to Catholicism*, edited by James J. Buckley, Frederick Christian Bauerschmidt, and Trent Poplum, 189–204. Oxford: Blackwell Publishing, 2007.

Mondale, Walter. *The Good Fight: A Life in Liberal Politics*. New York: Simon and Schuster, 2010.

Moody, Anne. *Coming of Age in Mississippi*, New York: Dell, 1968.

Moore, Andrew S. *The South's Tolerable Alien: Roman Catholics in Alabama and Georgia, 1945–1970*, Baton Rouge: Louisiana State University Press, 2007.

Morris, Tiyi M. *Womanpower Unlimited and the Black Freedom Struggle in Mississippi*. Athens: University of Georgia Press, 2015.

Morris, Willie. *Yazoo: Integration in a Deep-Southern Town*. New York: Harper's Magazine Press, 1971.

Morrison, Minion K. C. *Aaron Henry of Mississippi: Inside Agitator*. Fayetteville: University of Arkansas Press, 2015.

Moye, J. Todd. "Discovering What's Already There: Mississippi Women and Civil Rights Movements." In *Mississippi Women: Their Histories, Their Lives, Volume 2*, edited by Elizabeth Anne Payne, Martha H. Swain, and Marjorie Julian Spruill, 249–68. Athens: University of Georgia Press, 2010.

Moye, J. Todd. *Let the People Decide: Black Freedom and White Resistance Movements in Sunflower County, Mississippi, 1945–1986*. Chapel Hill: University of North Carolina Press, 2004.

Moynihan, Daniel P. *Maximum Feasible Misunderstanding: Community Action in the War on Poverty*. New York: Free Press, 1970.

Murray, Gail S. "White Privilege, Racial Justice: Women Activists in Memphis." In *Throwing Off the Cloak of Privilege: White Southern Women Activists in the Civil Rights Era*, edited by Gail S. Murray, 204–29. Gainesville: University Press of Florida, 2004.

Murray, Paul T. "Father Nathaniel and the Greenwood Movement." *Journal of Mississippi History* 72, no. 3 (2010): 277–311.

Nadasen, Premilla. *Welfare Warriors: The Welfare Rights Movement in the United States*. New York: Routledge, 2005.

Namorato, Michael V. *The Catholic Church in Mississippi, 1911–1984: A History*. Westport, CT: Greenwood Press, 1998.

Naples, Nancy A. *Grassroots Warriors: Activist Mothering, Community Work, and the War on Poverty*. London: Routledge, 1998.

Nash, Jere, and Andy Taggart. *Mississippi Politics: The Struggle for Power, 1976–2008*. 2nd ed. Jackson: University Press of Mississippi, 2009.

Nelson, H. Viscount, Jr. *Sharecropping, Ghetto, Slum: A History of Impoverished Blacks in Twentieth-Century America*. Xlibris: Bloomington, 2015.

Nembhard, Jessica Gordon. *Collective Courage: A History of African American Cooperative Economic Thought and Practice*. University Park: Pennsylvania State University Press, 2014.

Neubeck, Kenneth J., and Noel A. Cazenave. *Welfare Racism: Playing the Race Card against America's Poor*. New York: Routledge, 2001.
New, Rebecca S., and Moncreiff Cochran, eds. *Early Childhood Education: An International Encyclopedia, Volume 1*. Westport: Praeger, 2007.
Newman, Mark. "The Catholic Church in Mississippi and Desegregation, 1963–1973." *Journal of Mississippi History* 67, no. 4 (2005), 331–55.
Newman, Mark. *Divine Agitators: The Delta Ministry and Civil Rights in Mississippi*. Athens: University of Georgia Press, 2004.
Newman, Mark. "The Mississippi Freedom Labor Union." In *Poverty and Progress in the US South since 1920*, edited by Suzanne W. Jones and Mark Newman, 133–42. Amsterdam: VU University Press, 2006.
Newton, Michael. *The Ku Klux Klan in Mississippi: A History*. Jefferson, NC: McFarland & Company, 2010.
Nickerson, Michelle M. *Mothers of Conservatism: Women and the Postwar Right*. Princeton, NJ: Princeton University Press, 2012.
Nickerson, Michelle M., and Darren Dochuk. "Introduction." In *Sunbelt Rising: The Politics of Space, Place, and Region*, edited by Michelle M. Nickerson and Darren Dochuk, 1–30. Philadelphia: University of Pennsylvania Press, 2011.
Noble, Charles. "From Neoconservative to New Right: American Conservatives and the Welfare State." In *Confronting the New Conservatism: The Rise of the Right in America*, edited by Michael J. Thompson, 109–24. New York: New York University Press, 2007.
O'Brien, M. J. *We Shall Not Be Moved: The Jackson Woolworth's Sit-In and the Movement It Inspired*. Jackson: University Press of Mississippi, 2014.
O'Connor, Alice. *Poverty Knowledge: Social Science, Social Policy, and the Poor in Twentieth-Century US History*. Princeton, NJ: Princeton University Press, 2001.
O'Hara, Mary. "'Let It Fly': The Legacy of Helen Bass Williams." PhD diss., Southern Illinois University, 2004.
Olson, Lynne. *Freedom's Daughters: The Unsung Heroines of the Civil Rights Movement from 1830 to 1970*. New York: Simon and Schuster, 2001.
O'Reilly, Kenneth. *Nixon's Piano: Presidents and Racial Politics from Washington to Clinton*. New York: Free Press, 1995.
Orleck, Annelise. "Conclusion." In *The War on Poverty: A New Grassroots History, 1964–1980*, edited by Annelise Orleck and Lisa Gayle Hazirjian, 437–62. Athens: University of Georgia Press, 2011.
Orleck, Annelise. *Storming Caesars Palace: How Black Mothers Fought Their Own War on Poverty*. Boston: Beacon Press, 2005.
Parker, Frank R. *Black Votes Count: Political Empowerment in Mississippi after 1965*. University of North Carolina Press: Chapel Hill, 1990.
Patterson, James T. *America's Struggle against Poverty in the Twentieth Century*. Harvard: Harvard University Press, 2000.
Payne, Charles M. *I've Got the Light of Freedom: The Organizing Tradition and the Mississippi Freedom Struggle*. Berkeley: University of California Press, 1995.
Peters, Barbara J. *The Head Start Mother: Low-Income Mothers' Empowerment through Participation*. New York: Garland Publishing, 1998.

Peters, Gerhard, and John T. Woolley. *Papers of the President.* The American Presidency Project. http://www.presidency.ucsb.edu/.

Peterson, Paul E., and J. David Greenstone. "Racial Change and Citizen Participation: The Mobilization of Low-Income Communities through Community Action." In *A Decade of Federal Antipoverty Programs: Achievements, Failures, and Lessons*, edited by Robert H. Haveman, 241–78. New York: Academic Press, 1977.

Phelps, Wesley G. *A People's War on Poverty: Urban Politics and Grassroots Activists in Houston.* Athens: University of Georgia Press, 2014.

Phillips, Kevin P. *The Emerging Republican Majority.* New York: Arlington House, 1969.

Phillips-Fein, Kim. "Conservatism: A State of the Field." *Journal of American History* 98, No. 3 (2011): 723–43.

Phillips-Fein, Kim. *Invisible Hands: The Making of the Conservative Movement from the New Deal to Reagan.* London: W. W. Norton, 2009.

Pious, Richard M. "Advocates for the Poor: Legal Services in the War on Poverty." PhD diss., Columbia University, 1976.

Plotnick, Robert D., and Felicity Skidmore. *Progress against Poverty: A Review of the 1964–1974 Decade.* New York: Academic Press, 1975.

Poché, Justin D. "Religion, Race, and Rights in Catholic Louisiana, 1938–1970." PhD diss., University of Notre Dame, 2007.

Prichard, Jo G. *Making Things Grow: The Story of the Mississippi Chemical Corporation.* Jackson: University Press of Mississippi, 1998.

Quadagno, Jill. *The Color of Welfare: How Racism Undermined the War on Poverty.* Oxford: Oxford University Press, 1994.

Quadagno, Jill. "Social Movements and State Transformation: Labor Unions and Racial Conflict in the War on Poverty." *American Sociological Review* 57, no. 5 (1992), 616–34.

Quadagno, Jill, and Steve McDonald. "Racial Segregation in Southern Hospitals: How Medicare 'Broke the Back of Segregated Health Services.'" In *The New Deal and Beyond: Social Welfare in the South since 1930*, edited by Elna C. Green, 119–37. Athens: University of Georgia Press, 2003.

Quan, Robert Seto, with Julian B. Roebuck. *Lotus among the Magnolias: The Mississippi Chinese.* Jackson: University Press of Mississippi, 1982.

Rainwater, Lee, and William L. Yancey. *The Moynihan Report and the Politics of Controversy: A Trans-action Social Science and Public Policy Report.* Cambridge, MA: MIT Press, 1967.

Reiff, Joseph T. *Born of Conviction: White Methodists and Mississippi's Closed Society.* Oxford: Oxford University Press, 2016.

Reonas, Matthew. "Served Up on a Silver Platter: Ross Barnett, the Tourism Industry, and Mississippi's Civil War Centennial." *Journal of Mississippi History* 72, no. 2 (2010):123–61.

Report of the National Advisory Commission on Civil Disorders. New York: US Government Printing Office, 1968.

Rice, Leila M. "In the Trenches of the War on Poverty: The Local Implementation of the Community Action Program, 1964–1968." PhD diss., Vanderbilt University, 1997.

Rieder, Jonathan. "The Rise of the 'Silent Majority.'" In *The Rise and Fall of the New Deal Order, 1930–1980*, edited by Steve Fraser and Gary Gerstle, 243–68. Princeton, NJ: Princeton University Press, 1989.

Roche, Jeff. *Restructured Resistance: The Sibley Commission and the Politics of Desegregation in Georgia*. Athens: University of Georgia Press, 1998.

Rose, Harriett DeAnn. "Dallas, Poverty and Race: Community Action Programs in the War on Poverty." MA thesis, University of North Texas, 2008.

Rose, Marsha S. "Southern Feminism and Social Change: Sallie Bingham and the Kentucky Foundation for Women." In *The New Deal and Beyond: Social Welfare in the South since 1930*, edited by Elna C. Green, 239–58. Athens: University of Georgia Press, 2003.

Rymph, Catherine E. *Republican Women: Feminism and Conservatism from Suffrage through the Rise of the New Right*. Chapel Hill: University of North Carolina Press, 2006.

Salter, John R., Jr. *Jackson, Mississippi: An American Chronicle of Struggle and Schism*. 1979. New ed. Lincoln: University of Nebraska Press, 2011.

Sanders, Crystal R. *A Chance for Change: Head Start and Mississippi's Black Freedom Struggle*. Chapel Hill: University of North Carolina Press, 2016.

Sanders, Crystal R. "More Than Cookies and Crayons: Head Start and African American Empowerment in Mississippi, 1965–1968." *Journal of American History* 100, no. 4 (2015): 586–609.

Schaller, Lyle E. *The Churches' War on Poverty*. New York: Abingdon Press, 1967.

Schmitt, Edward R. *President of the Other America: Robert Kennedy and the Politics of Poverty*. Amherst: University of Massachusetts Press, 2011.

Schoenwald, Jonathan M. *A Time for Choosing: The Rise of Modern American Conservatism*. Oxford: Oxford University Press, 2001.

Shepard, Kris. *Rationing Justice: Poverty Lawyers and Poor People in the Deep South*. Baton Rouge: Louisiana State University Press, 2007.

Silver, James W. *Mississippi: The Closed Society*. New York: Harcourt, Brace & World, 1964.

Sokol, Jason. *There Goes My Everything: White Southerners in the Age of Civil Rights, 1945–1975*. New York: Vintage Books, 2007.

Somers Gerald G. and Ernst W. Stromsdorfer. "A Cost-Effectiveness Analysis of In-School and Summer Neighborhood Youth Corps: A Nationwide Evaluation," *Journal of Human Resources* 7, no. 4 (1972): 446–59.

Sparks, Randy J. *Religion in Mississippi*. Jackson: University Press of Mississippi, 2001.

Spoon, Darrell Duane. "Role Perception of Neighborhood Youth Corps Trainees and their Supervisors." MA thesis, Kansas State University, 1969.

Stossel, Scott. *Sarge: The Life and Times of Sargent Shriver*. Washington, DC: Smithsonian Books, 2004.

Sugrue, Thomas J. *The Origins of the Urban Crisis: Race and Inequality in Postwar Detroit*. Princeton, NJ: Princeton University Press, 2005.

Tye, Larry. *Bobby Kennedy: The Making of a Liberal Icon*. New York: Random House 2016.

Umoja, Akinyele Omowale. *We Will Shoot Back: Armed Resistance in the Mississippi Freedom Movement*. New York: New York University Press, 2014.

United States v. Wood, 295 F.2d 772 (5th Cir. 1961), cert. denied, 369 U.S. 850 (1962).

US Census Bureau. "Persons by Poverty Status in 1959, 1969, 1979, 1989 by State." Accessed July 30, 2013. http://www.census.gov/hhes/www/poverty/data/census/1960/index.html.

US Census Bureau. "Poverty Thresholds, 1966." Accessed July 5, 2013. http://www.census.gov/hhes/www/poverty/data/threshld/thresh66.html.

Vaughn, J. Barry. *Bishops, Bourbons, and Big Mules: A History of the Episcopal Church in Alabama*. Tuscaloosa: University of Alabama Press, 2013.

Vinovskis, Maris A. *The Birth of Head Start: Preschool Education Policies in the Kennedy and Johnson Administrations*. Chicago: University of Chicago Press, 2008.

Voting in Mississippi: A Report of the US Commission on Civil Rights (1965). https://www.law.umaryland.edu/marshall/usccr/documents/cr12v94.pdf.

Waldron, Ann. *Hodding Carter: Reconstruction of a Racist*. New York: Workman Publishing, 1993.

Walther Regis H., and Margaret L. Magnusson. *A Retrospective Study of the Effectiveness of Out-of-School Neighborhood Youth Corps Programs in Four Urban Sites*. Washington, DC: George Washington University, 1967.

Ward, Jason Morgan. *Defending White Democracy: The Making of a Segregationist Movement and the Remaking of Racial Politics, 1936–1965*. Chapel Hill: University of North Carolina, 2014.

Ward, Thomas J., Jr. *Out in the Rural: A Mississippi Health Center and Its War on Poverty*. New York: Oxford University Press, 2016.

Watson, Bruce. *Freedom Summer: The Savage Season of 1964 That Made Mississippi Burn and Made America a Democracy*. London: Penguin, 2010.

Webb, Clive. "Introduction." In *Massive Resistance: Southern Opposition to the Second Reconstruction*, edited by Clive Webb, 3–20. Oxford: Oxford University Press, 2005.

Whitehead, Don. *Attack on Terror: The FBI against the Ku Klux Klan in Mississippi*. New York: Funk & Wagnalls Co., 1970.

Wilhoit, Francis M. *The Politics of Massive Resistance*. New York: George Braziller, 1973.

Williams, Michael Vinson. *Medgar Evers: Mississippi Martyr*. Fayetteville: University of Arkansas Press, 2011.

Woods, Clyde. *Development Arrested: Race, Power and the Blues in the Mississippi Delta*. London: Verso, 1998.

Woods, Jeff. *Black Struggle, Red Scare: Segregation and Anti-Communism in the South, 1948–1968*. Baton Rouge: Louisiana State University Press, 2004.

Woodsworth, Michael. *Battle for Bed-Stuy: The Long War on Poverty in New York*. Cambridge, MA: Harvard University Press, 2016.

Wright, Gavin. "Economic Consequences of the Southern Protest Movement." In *New Directions in Civil Rights Studies*, edited by Armstead L. Robinson and Patricia Sullivan, 175–83. Charlottesville: University Press of Virginia, 1991.

Yuill, Kevin L. *Richard Nixon and the Rise of Affirmative Action: The Pursuit of Racial Equality in an Era of Limits*. Lanham, MD: Rowman and Littlefield.

Zigler, Edward, and Sally J. Styfco. *The Hidden History of Head Start*. New York: Oxford University Press, 2010.

INDEX

Abernethy, Thomas, 61
Adams County, 52–55, 67, 75–78. *See also* Adams Jefferson Improvement Corporation
Adams Jefferson Improvement Corporation, 53, 55, 70
AFL-CIO, 134, 179, 182–90
Agnew, Spiro, 150
Agriculture, Department of, 183
Alabama, 29, 30, 36–37, 56, 75, 78, 84, 87–88, 90, 93, 198
Alexander v. Holmes County (1969), 177
Alinsky, Saul, 28
Americans for the Preservation of the White Race, 76, 86–90, 143
Amite County, 42–43, 78, 85, 88, 221

Barber, Rims, 69
Barbour, Jeppie, 167
Barnett, Ross, 33, 137, 140
Baroni, Louis, 54, 57
Baroni, Marjorie (née Rushing), 52–60, 62, 67, 127, 216, 219
Batchelor, Roy, 191–95, 202
Beckwith, Byron De La, 104, 242n10
Beittel, A. D., 107–10
Berger, Fred, 131–32
Birdsong, Colonel T. B., 91–93
Birth of a Nation, 74
Black Belt, 154–58, 165, 175, 177, 215, 218
Black Panthers, 36, 124
Black Power, 4, 20, 36, 40, 47–48, 61, 67, 72, 82–83, 89, 96, 99, 107, 111, 120, 123–26
Blackwell, Unita, 7, 9, 11, 14–15, 32, 129

Bolivar County, 14, 48, 50, 67, 106, 134, 136, 165, 183, 197
Bond, Julian, 82–83
Boutin, Bernard, 65
Bowers, Samuel, 75, 80, 84–85, 98
Bowie, Rev. Harry, 47, 69
Boycotts, 62, 87, 101–4, 116, 125, 134, 173–74
Brady, Tom P., 39, 76, 80
Brooks, Owen, 170, 191, 194
Broussard, Father George, 182, 194
Brown v. Board of Education (1954), 3, 10, 20–21, 39–40, 76, 176–77
Brunini, Ed, 180, 194
Brunini, Bishop Joseph, 60, 180–82, 193–94
Bryant, C. C., 11, 44–45
Bryant, Milton, 90
Buchanan, John Hall, Jr., 36
Bucklew, William Henry, 85
Bufkin, Cary E., 204–5
Burke, W. Webb, 191
Burns, Arthur F., 153
Burns, Willie, 32
Busby, Paul, 66
Bush, George H. W., 159, 161

Cahn, Edgar, 200
Cahn, Jean, 200
California, 16, 21, 164–65, 174, 200–201, 213
California Rural Legal Assistance, 200
Canon, Stephen, 119
Carlucci, Frank, 171
Carmichael, Gil, 160–64, 171
Carmichael, Stokely, 48
Carr, Oscar, Jr., 132

Carter, Asa (Forrest Carter), 87–88
Carter, Hodding, II, 51
Carter, Hodding, III, 51, 66, 133, 143
Carter, William D., 91
Catchings, Philip M., Jr., 208–9
Catholic Church, 23–24, 54, 56, 58–64, 67–71. *See also* Baroni, Marjorie; Brunini, Bishop Joseph; Diocese of Natchez-Jackson; Donatilla, Sister; Machesky, Father Nathaniel; Strategic Training and Redevelopment
Central Mississippi, Inc., 166–67
Chaney, James, 13, 60, 79, 86, 97–98, 213
Cheney, Dick, 197, 205
Child Development Council (Southwest Mississippi), 45–47, 172–74
Child Development Group of Mississippi (CDGM), 23–24, 31–42, 46–47, 50, 52, 64, 67, 69, 72–73, 89, 96, 107, 114–16, 123, 127–29, 131–36, 138–41, 145, 147–48, 167, 172–73, 197, 204, 214, 216, 218–21
Christian Conservative Communique, 83
Civilian Conservation Corps, 28, 65
Civil Rights Act (1964), 3–4, 18, 28, 40, 65, 87–88, 105, 109
Clarion-Ledger, 35–36, 105, 188–89, 205
Clark, Edward, 131
Clark, Obie, 63
Clark, Robert, 189
Coahoma Opportunities, Inc., 91, 134
Cobb, Charles, 12, 130
Cochran, Thad, 200
COINTELPRO, 84, 124
Cole, Leland, 46–47, 145, 248n17
Coleman, James, 100–101
Coleman, J. P., 80
Coleman, Mary, 192–93
Color-blind rhetoric, 6, 22–23, 40, 61, 140–41, 154–60, 163–66, 174, 208–9, 215–16
Committee of Concern, 144
Committee to Re-Elect the President, 199
Communism (and anticommunism), 34–37, 39, 57, 61–62, 72, 74, 81, 83, 88, 116, 129, 156, 159, 164–66, 172, 175, 177, 209, 215
Community Action Program, 20, 27–30, 32, 36, 41, 48, 64–66, 99, 108, 115, 118, 150–53, 161–62, 167–70, 193, 197, 200, 207, 218–21. *See also* Maximum feasible participation
Community Legal Services, 204–7
Community Services Administration, 212–13
Community Services Association (CSA), 23, 110, 112–16, 118–24, 197, 204, 207–11
Congress of Racial Equality (CORE), 12, 68, 72, 101–2, 105
Conservatism, 4–6, 19–20, 22–25, 27–28, 30, 37, 65, 71, 154–68, 172, 174–79, 199–204, 206, 212–15
Conway, Jack T., 27, 182–83
Cooper, Owen, 68, 90–91, 93, 128, 132, 141–49. *See also* Committee for Concern; Mississippi Action for Progress
Coordinating Committee for Fundamental American Freedoms, 109
Council of Federated Organizations (COFO), 12, 31–32, 48, 68, 77–78, 105–6
Cox, W. Harold, 95, 102–3, 177

Dahmer, Betty, 86
Dahmer, Ellie, 85–87
Dahmer, Vernon, 11, 85–88
Daley, Richard, 20
Damon, Henry, 162
Danahy, Father William, 58
Dann, Jim, 107
Davis, Gerald, 191
Davis, Russell C., 193, 210
Day, Dorothy, 56
Dean, Ken, 141–43
DeCell, Herman, 146
Decentralization (regionalism; New Federalism), 152, 193–99, 209
Deloach, Cartha, 93
Delta Concentrated Employment Program, 188–89

Delta Democrat Times, 51, 66, 132–33, 179, 195
Delta Discussion, 82, 95
Delta Ministry, 43, 47, 51, 68–69, 115, 119, 132–33, 181, 194
Democratic National Convention (1964), 69, 129, 160
Democratic Party, 20, 73, 129, 150, 155, 159, 163, 165, 199–200, 205, 213, 220
Derian, Patricia (Pat), 52–53, 127, 134, 136, 144, 189, 216
Devine, Annie, 129
Dick, Arsene, 87
Dickson, N. A., 68
Diocese of Natchez-Jackson, 58–63, 67, 69–71, 178–82, 187–88, 190, 193–94, 219. *See also* Baroni, Marjorie; Brunini, Bishop Joseph; Catholic Church; Donatilla, Sister; Machesky, Father Nathaniel
Dixiecrat, 36
Doar, John, 93
Donaldson, Maye, 165–66, 217
Donatilla, Sister, 180–82, 217. *See also* Catholic Church; Strategic Training and Redevelopment
Dukes, William F., 80, 84
Duncan, Loyce, 46–47

Easterling, Rev. William, 121
Eastland, James O., 19, 35, 38, 61, 88, 94, 122, 131, 140, 166, 180, 193, 202
Economic Opportunity Act (1964), 18, 27–28, 32, 116, 168–69, 183, 193
Economic Opportunity Amendment (1967), 36, 200. *See also* Green, Edith
Edelman, Marian Wright, 114
Ehrlichman, John, 153
Ellis, Frank P., 93
Evans, A. B., 209
Evans, Rowland, 93
Evers, Charles, 57, 71, 141, 186
Evers, Medgar, 9–12, 40, 68, 99–100, 103–5, 111, 184
Evers, Myrlie, 99

Fairley, JC, 14, 17
Federation of Republican Women, 164–65
Finch, Cliff, 171
Finch, Robert, 152–53
Florida, 56, 198
Flowers, Richmond, 84
Ford, Gerald R., 212
Ford, William D., 196–97
Fordice, Kirk, 175
Frank, Colonel H. F., 112–15, 120–23
Freedom Summer, 12–13, 18, 23, 30–31, 44, 47–48, 51, 60, 62, 68, 76–79, 85, 105, 107, 110–11, 115, 128–29, 136, 143, 183, 214
Friends of the Children of Mississippi, 42, 221
Frye, Hardy, 105–6

Georgia, 37, 82, 198
Gerow, Bishop Richard O., 59–61. *See also* Catholic Church; Diocese of Natchez-Jackson
Goldwater, Barry, 6, 131, 159–60
Gooden, Bennie, 41
Goodman, Andrew, 13, 60, 79, 86, 97–98, 213
Grady, Henry, 165
Graham, Billy, 70
Gray, Rev. Duncan, 68, 89
Gray, Victoria, 129
Great Society, 4, 18, 26–30, 37, 64, 81–83, 153, 156, 159–60, 163, 172, 196, 199
Green, Edith (and the Green Amendment), 169–71, 208, 220
Greenberg, Polly, 38. *See also* Child Development Group of Mississippi
Green v. County School Board of New Kent County (1968), 176
Griffin, Charles, 172
Griffin v. School Board (1964), 176

Haldeman, H. R., 151–53
Hall, Cary, 167
Hamer, Fannie Lou, 11–12, 32, 48, 106, 129–34
Harding, Bertrand, 93

Harris, John, 107
HARYOU-ACT, 36
Head, Rosie, 31
Head Start, 3–4, 20, 23–24, 30–48, 52–53, 61, 64, 67, 72, 81, 88–98, 106–7, 127–28, 132–48, 150, 152–54, 165–67, 172–73, 177, 179, 183, 188, 197–98, 202, 216–17, 220–21. *See also* Child Development Group of Mississippi; Mississippi Action for Progress; Southwest Mississippi Child Development Council
Headstart, Economic Opportunity, and Community Partnership Act (1974), 212
Health, Education and Welfare, Department of (HEW), 152–54, 167, 176–77, 197–98, 220
Hearn, James J., 65
Heller, Walter, 37
Henry, Aaron, 9–10, 12, 106, 129–34, 189, 191
Highlander Folk School, 83
Hinds County Bar Association, 204–7
Hinds County Community Council, 112
Hinds County Freedom Democratic Party News, 107, 113, 115–16, 123–24, 219
Holladay, C. R., 131
Horwitz, Charles, 115–16, 120, 181, 192–93, 208. *See also* Community Services Association; Jackson, Don
House Committee on Un-American Activities, 34, 84, 89, 209
Howard, T. R. M., 9
Howie, Bob, 34–35
Huebner, Lee, 153
Humphrey, Hubert, 129, 150
Hurst, Joe Jack, 204

Inter-religious Committee Against Poverty, 56

Jackson, Don, 23, 99–100, 107–8, 116–26, 209. *See also* Kenyatta, Muhammad
Jackson, Wharlest, 57
Jackson Daily News, 34–35, 50, 105
Jackson Urban League, 119
Jason, Harold, 137

Jencks, Christopher, 189
Job Corps, 28, 152, 202
Johnson, Earl, Jr., 200
Johnson, Lyndon B., 6, 18, 26–30, 37, 40, 61, 70, 78, 83, 96, 131–33, 150–53, 163–64, 183, 220
Johnson, Paul, Jr., 13, 19–20, 33, 39–41, 47, 64–65, 93, 97, 109–10, 114, 128–29, 141, 171, 191, 214
Johnson, Sarah, 192
Johnston, Erle, Jr., 34, 46–47, 93, 115–16, 128, 139–43, 146–49, 185, 191, 217
Jones, Frank N., 202
Jones, William B., 199
Jordan, Kate, 62. *See also* Catholic Church; Machesky, Father Nathaniel

Katzenbach, Nicholas, 132
Kennedy, John F., 6, 26–27, 81, 104, 151
Kennedy, Robert F., 13, 113–14
Kentucky, 198
Kenyatta, Jomo, 124
Kenyatta, Muhammad, 23, 124–26. *See also* Community Services Association; Frank, Colonel H. F.; Jackson, Don; Neighborhood Youth Corps
Keogh, James, 153
Kerner Commission, 166–69
King, Rev. Ed, 129–30
King, Hamah, 194
King, Martin Luther, Jr., 60, 68, 74, 104, 130, 183
Krumlauf, Al, 194
Ku Klux Klan (KKK), 12–13, 23, 32, 40, 43–44, 57, 61–62, 67, 72–98, 101, 127, 132, 136, 143, 184–85, 209, 213–15, 217–18

Labor, Department of, 58, 61, 96, 117, 122, 152. *See also* Ramsay, Claude; Strategic Training and Redevelopment
Ladner, Dorie, 100, 104
Ladner, Joyce, 100
Lauderdale Economic Advancement Program, 63–64, 161–62, 171
Law, Father Bernard, 60, 194

Lawler, Ted, 148
Lee, Rev. Clay, 79
Lee, Ray, 172–74
Legal Services, 110, 180, 200–207, 221
Lenzner, Terry, 203–4
Levin, Nancy, 112, 115
Lewis, John, 105–6, 130–31
Lindsey, Rev. Merrill W., 133
Lipscomb, E. L., 116, 121–22, 204, 207–9
"Local responsible people," 39–42, 159, 171, 191, 214

Machesky, Father Nathaniel, 62, 67, 72, 219. *See also* Catholic Church
Marks, A., 46
Massive resistance, 3–6, 12, 20–23, 36, 39–41, 47, 59, 61–62, 79, 95, 138, 140, 146, 154, 158–59, 174, 177, 179, 200, 203–4, 206, 208, 212, 214–15, 217
Matthews, Otis, 184–85
Maximum feasible participation, 29, 32, 38, 44, 65, 151–52, 168
Mazique, Mamie, 55, 58
McDaniel, Edward L., 74, 80–81, 84
McGuff, Msgr., 189
McPherson, Harry, 96, 132–33, 201, 220
McRee, Rev. James, 133
Medgar Evers Community Guild, 111–12
Meredith, James, 33, 51, 65, 120
Michael Schwerner Fund, 119
Mississippi Action for Progress (MAP), 24, 42, 89–95, 127–49, 217
Mississippians for Public Education, 51, 53
Mississippi Association for Constitutional Government, 82
Mississippi Band of Choctaw Indians, 5, 134
Mississippi Council on Human Relations, 54, 142
Mississippi Freedom Democratic Party (MFDP), 13, 53, 69, 97, 105, 107, 111, 115, 129–33, 139, 160, 185
Mississippi Freedom Labor Union, 183, 187. *See also* Ramsay, Claude
Mississippi Industrial and Special Services, 143
Mississippi League of Women Voters, 112
Mississippi Program of the American Friends Service Committee, 110
Mississippi Republican Party, 5, 20, 23–24, 114, 150–75, 197, 200, 204–6, 212, 220
Mississippi State Sovereignty Commission, 11, 33–39, 46–47, 78, 87, 93–96, 101, 104, 109, 115–16, 122, 124, 128, 138–49, 185, 191, 204, 215. *See also* Cole, Leland; Johnston, Erle, Jr.; Sutton, Lee
Mississippi White Caps, 57, 76
Mondale, Walter, 129–30. *See also* Democratic National Convention (1964); Mississippi Freedom Democratic Party
Moody, Anne, 10–11, 16, 104
Moore, Amzie, 9–11, 106
Morrissey, Father, 54, 58
Moses, Bob, 11, 44, 77, 131
Mount Beulah, 33, 91
Moye, James, 163–64
Moynihan, Daniel Patrick, 27, 151–53
Mudd, John, 133–34. *See also* Child Development Group of Mississippi
Muhammad, Elijah, 124

NAACP, 9–13, 17, 31–32, 43–45, 48, 55, 69, 72, 77, 81, 83, 85, 87, 99–105, 109, 114, 130–31, 133, 166, 173, 185, 188–92
NAACP Youth Council, 100–105
National Advisory Council on Economic Opportunity, 96–97
National Black Economic Development Conference, 125. *See also* Kenyatta, Muhammad
National Council of Churches, 51, 68, 105–6
National Defenders Association, 201
National Sharecroppers Fund, 119
National Urban League, 110
Negro American Bar Association, 201
Neighborhood Youth Corps, 28, 44, 96, 110, 116–26, 219
New Deal, 8, 15, 22, 24, 27–28, 64–65, 81, 155, 159–60, 165
Nicholas, Bruce, 144

Nixon, Richard, 24, 150–55, 165–74, 176, 193–95, 196–200, 202–4, 206, 210–11, 212, 220
North Carolina, 20, 29–30, 76, 85, 106–7, 139, 198
North Mississippi Rural Legal Services, 203, 221
Nosser, John J., 67
Novak, Robert, 93

O'Fallon, Kathleen, 45–48, 52–53, 127, 173, 216–17. *See also* Southwest Mississippi Opportunity; Sturgeon, Maxie
Office of Child Development, 167, 197–98, 220
Office of Economic Opportunity (OEO), 19, 24, 28–31, 33–35, 37–42, 44–47, 50, 53, 58–59, 61, 63–65, 69–70, 92–93, 96–97, 107, 110, 112–13, 115, 122, 124, 128, 132, 134, 136, 139, 141, 144, 147, 150–54, 162, 166–68, 170–71, 173–74, 176, 181–83, 186–90, 192–208, 210–14, 216, 220
Orange County, California, 164–65
Original Knights of the KKK, 73, 75, 86
Ott, John, 91, 137
Outside agitators, accusations of, 13, 22–23, 34, 36, 47, 69, 82, 93, 106, 115, 122, 172, 204, 214–15

Patterson, Joe T., 22, 84, 177
Peace Corps, 26, 70
Perkins, Carl, 193
Perkins, Rev. John W., 7–8, 16
Phillips, Howard J., 199–200, 202, 206, 209
Phillips, Kevin, 154. *See also* Southern strategy; Sunbelt
Polk, Richard, 181–82, 186, 189–90, 192. *See also* Donatilla, Sister; Strategic Training and Redevelopment
Poole, Victor, 90
Price, Jack, 93–94
Prichard, Jo G., 144
Protestant work-ethic, 23, 63, 80, 159
Purdue University, 148–49

Quinn, Aylene, 77–78, 85
Quinn, Father Peter Oliver, 62–63

Ramsay, Claude, 67–68, 134, 182, 184–90
Rash, Rev. Sammie, 14, 17
Reagan, Ronald, 83, 154, 159, 175, 200, 213, 221
Reconstruction, 40, 71, 73–74, 134, 170, 217
Reed, Clarke, 162–63, 165–68, 171, 197, 202–5
Reed, Steve, 44–45, 51, 172, 233n4
Regionalism (New Federalism), 152, 193–99, 209
Regular Democrats, 53, 129–32, 160, 212, 247n9. *See also* Democratic National Convention (1964)
Republican Party, 6, 24, 37, 70, 131, 150–60, 162, 165–75, 196–200, 202, 205, 214, 220
Rhodes, Al, 191
Rice, David, 189
Ripon Society, 153
Rogers, Shelby, 109–10
Roessler, Gus, 91
Roosevelt, Franklin D., 8, 27, 81
Rumsfeld, Donald, 151, 162, 167–68, 170–71, 173, 176, 193, 196–97, 200, 202–3, 205, 220

Salter, John, 100, 102–4, 106, 124
Samstein, Mendy, 77–78
Sanders, Alix, 193–94
Sanders, Emma D., 209–10
Sanders, Franzetta, 81
Sanford, Ike, 142
Sanford, Terry, 29
Satterfield, John C., 109
Scarborough, Tom, 145
Schultz, George P., 152
Schutt, Jane, 91
Schwerner, Michael, 13, 60, 79, 86, 97–98, 119, 213
Seaver, Carol, 111
Seaver, Ted, 110–12, 115–16, 120–22
Second Vatican Council, 60–61, 219
Shell, Dan, 109–10
Shelton, Robert, 75

Shriver, Sargent, 19, 26–28, 33–35, 38, 41, 47, 56, 63–65, 70, 93, 128, 188
Siller, Florence Ogden, 165
Silver, James, 4, 79
Sloan, Frank K., 112–13
Smith, Hazel Brannon, 137
Smith, R. L. T., 108, 133
Smith, Walter, 137, 139, 141
South Bend, Indiana, 125
South Carolina, 139, 156, 198
Southern Christian Leadership Conference (SCLC), 12, 131
Southern Manifesto, 21, 33, 39–40
Southern Regional Council, 53
Southern strategy, 154–60
Southwest Mississippi Opportunity (SMO), 42–47, 51–53, 172–73
Stennis, John C., 19, 32–35, 38–41, 147, 171–72, 177, 180, 193–94, 200, 202, 212, 214, 220
Steptoe, E. W., 29
Stewart, Peter, 136
St. Francis Mission, 62–63, 180
Strategic Training and Redevelopment (STAR), 23–24, 54, 58–68, 70–71, 116, 118, 169–70, 176–96, 217, 219
Student Nonviolent Coordinating Committee (SNCC), 11–12, 31–32, 43–45, 48, 68–69, 72, 77, 82, 85, 93, 97, 101–2, 104–6, 130–31, 142, 146, 218
Sturgeon, Maxie, 44–45
Sugarman, Jules, 38
Sunbelt, 22–23, 155–60, 174–75, 177, 215
Sutton, Lee, 191
Swann, Jimmy, 88–89

Taylor, L. B., 61
Teague, Olin, 27
Tennessee, 37, 73, 95, 144, 198
Thomas, Art, 69
Thompson, Allen C., 13, 101–3, 105
Thompson, Donald, 108, 110
Thornhill, J. Emmett, 78
Toonen, Father Thomas, 56

Tougaloo College, 100–102, 104, 107–8, 123, 125, 139
Travis, James, 13
Tufts-Delta Health Center, 134
Turner, Cornelius, 186, 189–90

Uncle Tom, accusations of, 116, 121, 123, 133, 207
United Klans of America (UKA), 75, 81–84, 89

Valenti, Jack, 132
Vermont in Mississippi, Inc., 111, 116
Volunteers in Service to America (VISTA), 26, 70

Waites, Alex, 189
Walker, General, 120
Wallace, George, 36, 85, 87, 160
Waller, William, 171, 195, 206, 210
Warren Court, 21, 156
Watson, Richard, 172
Wednesdays in Mississippi, 12, 51
Weeks, Minnie McFarland, 8, 16
Welfare, 56, 63–64, 83, 118, 154, 159–61, 165–66, 171–72, 174–75, 179, 195, 213–14; rhetoric of welfare queen, 83, 154, 193, 213
Whitaker, Barbara, 197–98
White, Annie, 114
White Citizens' Councils, 10–11, 21–22, 24, 33–34, 39, 43, 52–53, 76, 80–81, 86–88, 90–91, 101, 104, 109, 112, 128, 137, 143, 185
Whitten, Jamie, 212
Wilkins, W. T., 159, 167, 197, 204–5. *See also* Mississippi Republican Party
Williams, Calvin, 14
Williams, Clovis, 91
Williams, Helen Bass, 24, 53, 127–49, 216, 219
Williams, John Bell, 148, 153, 187, 191, 205
Williams, Leola, 194
Wilson, Clifford, 87
Winel, Msgr. Roland T., 58, 179–81, 191–92
Wirtz, Willard, 96

Women in Community Service, 56
Wynn, Douglas, 131–32
Wynn, Leila, 131

Yalobusha-Calhoun Republican Women's
    Club, 165–66
Yarmolinsky, Adam, 27
Yazoo Community Action, Inc., 167. *See
    also* Barbour, Jeppie; DeCell, Herman
Yerger, Wirt, 159–60, 162
Young, Charles L., Sr., 161–62
Young Americans for Freedom, 199
Young Democrats, 132, 205, 207

ABOUT THE AUTHOR

Emma Folwell is a senior lecturer in history at Newman University, Birmingham. She studied at the University of Oxford and the University of Leicester, where she completed her PhD in 2014. Her research has been supported by grants from the Lyndon Baines Johnson Presidential Library, the British Association for American Studies, and the Royal Historical Society. In 2018/9, she received a Fulbright Award.

Printed in the United States
By Bookmasters